Gospel Light's
KidsTime

God's BiG Picture

Gospel Light

REPRODUCIBLE
Leader's Guide

HOW TO MAKE CLEAN COPIES FROM THIS BOOK

You may make copies of portions of this book with a clean conscience if

♦ you (or someone in your organization) are the original purchaser;

♦ you are using the copies you make for a noncommercial purpose (such as teaching or promoting your ministry) within your church or organization;

♦ you follow the instructions provided in this book.

However, it is ILLEGAL for you to make copies if

♦ you are using the material to promote, advertise or sell a product or service other than for ministry fund-raising;

♦ you are using the material in or on a product for sale; or

♦ you or your organization are not the original purchaser of this book.

By following these guidelines you help us keep our products affordable.

Thank you,
Gospel Light

Scripture quotations are taken from the *Holy Bible, New International Version®. NIV®.* Copyright © 1973, 1978, 1984 by International Bible Society. Used by permission of Zondervan Publishing House. All rights reserved.

Gospel Light

KidsTime Curriculum

Publisher
William T. Greig

Senior Consulting Publisher
Dr. Elmer L. Towns

Publisher, Research, Planning and Development
Billie Baptiste

Managing Editor
Lynnette Pennings, M.A.

Senior Consulting Editors
Dr. Gary S. Greig,
Wesley Haystead, M.S.Ed.

Senior Editor, Theological and Biblical Issues
Bayard Taylor, M.Div.

Editor
Sheryl Haystead

Editorial Team
Amanda Abbas, Mary Gross

Contributing Editors
David Arnold, Ivy Beckwith, Jay Bea Blair, Emmy Bonja, Debbie Cunningham, Coral Fife, Kevin Gordon, Linda Mattia, Karen McGraw, Patricia Moorhead, Willamae Myers, Vikki Randall, Melanie Ross, Craig Welsh, Mahlon Wilson

Designers
Curt Dawson, Carolyn Henderson

How to Use KidsTime

A few kids, one leader

If you teach alone, follow these simple steps to lead your class in a big picture look at God's Word.

1. Read *"God's Big Picture* Overview" on page 6 to get a clear view of what this course is all about.

2. Look at "Advice and Answers for Schedule Planning" on pages 7-10; choose the schedule that best fits your situation and decide which centers you will include.

3. Read the tip articles (pp. 11-21) for each center you will lead, taking note of the ways you can make each center an effective learning experience for the kids in your class.

Several kids, more than one teacher

If you teach with one or more other teachers, follow the above three steps and add one more!

Decide if each teacher will lead his or her class in all of the activities or if each teacher will lead only one activity for groups of students who rotate between the centers.

Lots of kids, several teachers, a director or coordinator

If you are the children's director or coordinator of *KidsTime*, follow the above steps and add two more!

1. Pay special attention to "Getting and Keeping the Very Best Staff" on pages 22-23. Remember to start recruiting early—several months before *KidsTime* begins.

2. Read "Questions and Answers for a Terrific Program" on pages 24-26 for tips on how to distribute and store curriculum, eye-catching decorating ideas and more!

Contents

How to Use *KidsTime* • 3
A step-by-step *KidsTime* introduction for teachers or leaders—
get a clear view of how to make the most of this course.

God's Big Picture

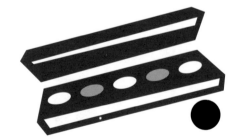

Music Resources

Song charts and lead sheets for all the music in this course • **447**

God's Big Picture Overview

God's Big Picture takes you and your students through a majestic gallery of the major characters and themes of God's Word! Its chronological approach will give your students an understanding of the Bible as a picture of God's plan and purposes.

Because children learn in diverse ways, *God's Big Picture* is filled with variety to appeal to kids' many learning styles. Every lesson includes a terrific kid-involving way to present the Bible story and an interesting object talk. Students may also participate in several learning centers involving active games, a palette of creative art activities that will help them express what they learn and a Worship Center with several options for student involvement (including a music video). Additionally, younger children are provided with a Bible story coloring page activity while older students get thought-provoking skits and meaty activities to develop Bible skills.

Because teachers are the heart of any teaching time, *God's Big Picture* is especially easy for teachers to use. Each team member can be given his or her own page for leading any given session's activity. Every activity also emphasizes that session's Big Picture Idea, so every team member understands the goal of the lesson. In addition, every lesson opens with a commentary taken from the notes of Dr. Henrietta Mears, well-known trainer of Sunday School teachers and founder of Gospel Light Publications.

The goal of this course is to generate excitement about the wonderful way God has revealed Himself to us. When you and your team members are full of eagerness and understanding of the lesson at hand, your students will be eager to learn and inspired by every lesson! As you pray and organize this course to meet the needs of your group, ask God for a sense of expectancy of what He wants to do during this time and for sensitivity to ways you can be part of what He desires to accomplish. This may be the most fun you've ever had in church!

Advice and Answers for Schedule Planning

Begin your planning for *KidsTime* by choosing a learning format. No matter when or where *KidsTime* takes place, there are two main format options—Self-Contained Groups and the Learning Center Plan. Read the following descriptions and select the format that fits your needs.

Self-Contained Groups

If you are confined to a single room or have a small class, Self-Contained Groups may be your best option. In this format, groups of seven or eight students are formed. Each group has a teacher who leads his or her group in the activities. (If the size of the group is larger, additional teachers or helpers are needed.)

The greatest benefit of Self-Contained Groups is that teachers are able to form meaningful relationships with the students since they remain together during the entire session. The biggest disadvantage is the difficulty in recruiting teachers who feel comfortable leading a variety of activities.

Self-Contained Groups are often the best option for small churches, house or cell churches, or Christian schools.

Learning Center Plan

The Learning Center Plan offers an exciting recruiting and schedule variation for *KidsTime*. In this plan, each teacher prepares and leads only one activity. Guides (adults, teenagers or even responsible fifth and sixth graders) lead groups of students to rotate between the centers. In other words, each teacher specializes in only one part of the lesson. Specialization simplifies teacher preparation and often improves teaching effectiveness. The Learning Center Plan also prevents inexperienced teachers from feeling overwhelmed. And teachers who don't enjoy leading games or who are apprehensive about telling Bible stories can leave those tasks to others more skilled in those areas.

The Learning Center Plan is often the best option for medium or large churches.

What do students do and who leads them?

Students are placed in small permanent groups (12 to 16 is the best size). Each group has at least one guide who leads the group to various centers. Each group, along with its guide(s), visits each center during each session. Another idea is to place eight students in each small group with one guide; then two small groups participate in a center at once.

What do teachers do?

Each teacher takes responsibility for one center, remaining at the center and instructing each group as it visits the center.

What are the centers?

One room or outside area is designated for each of the *KidsTime* learning centers. Post a large sign to identify each center. Give centers interesting names: The Gallery (for the Big Picture Story Center), The Studio (for the Art Center), The Action Station (for the Active Game Center) or The Praise Place (for the Worship Center). Start with the centers suggested in the following diagram:

Big Picture Story Center

Active Game Center

Worship Center

You may want to combine several groups together for one or more of the centers (for example, the Worship Center or the Big Picture Story Center). Other centers may be added (for example, Bible Verse Object Talk, Bible Story Coloring Center, Skit Center, Bible Skills Center).

How do I plan the time schedule?

Plan the activities in each center to last the same amount of time. The centers in *KidsTime* can be taught in any order. In a one-hour program, groups would remain in each center for 15 minutes. (Add 5 minutes to the first center each group attends to provide for a brief welcome time.) Allow 5 minutes for groups to move from center to center, following a pre-established route. With this schedule, groups would be able to participate in three centers. If you have more time for each session of the program, additional centers may be added or the time in each center may be lengthened (generally it is best to limit the time in each center to a maximum of 25 minutes in order to keep student interest high). Use this chart as an example of how to schedule groups:

Sample One-Hour Schedule

	11:00-11:20	11:25-11:40	11:45-12:00
Painters	Welcome and Big Picture Story Center	Worship Center	Active Game Center
Sculptors	Welcome and Active Game Center	Big Picture Story Center	Worship Center
Potters	Welcome and Worship Center	Active Game Center	Big Picture Story Center

How do I make the Learning Center Plan run smoothly?

♦ Predetermine the route each group will travel, including room and building entrances and exits. Ask guides to walk their routes in advance to become familiar with all locations.
♦ Establish a signal for notifying groups when it's time to move to the next center.
♦ Provide labeled tables or other areas where students may leave their projects and belongings during the session.
♦ Give each group a unique name. For example, name groups after famous painters: Picassos, Renoirs and Michaelangelos. Also consider using names such as Painters, Sculptors and Potters.
♦ Provide color-coded name tags to identify each group.

Schedule Options

The following schedules show the use of the Basic Plan for learning centers. You can adapt these sample schedules to the needs and interests of your church. Other centers can be added or substituted in order to meet the needs of younger or older students (see "Centers for Younger and Older Students" on p.10). In addition to the centers suggested in this course, many churches include centers such as service projects, recreational games (soccer, baseball, volleyball) and elective classes (cooking, woodworking).

When planning your *KidsTime* schedule, remember to include a variety of activities in an order that will meet the needs of children. For example, if students have been sitting in the adult worship service before coming to *KidsTime*, plan an active center at the beginning of *KidsTime*.

For help in staffing and recruiting, make a planning page to be completed on a weekly or monthly basis (see samples).

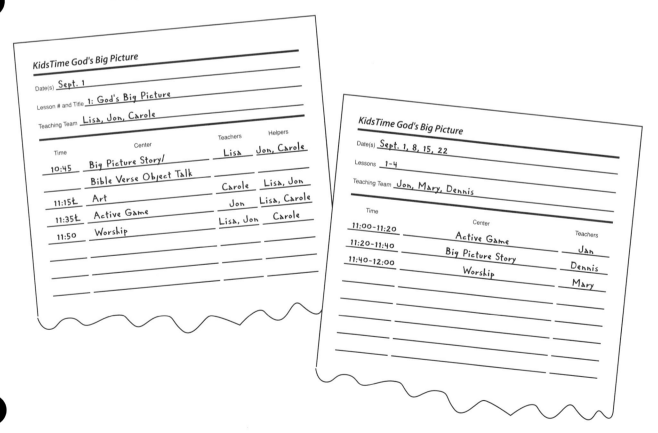

KidsTime God's Big Picture

Date(s) Sept. 1

Lesson # and Title 1: God's Big Picture

Teaching Team Lisa, Jon, Carole

Time	Center	Teachers	Helpers
10:45	Big Picture Story/ Bible Verse Object Talk	Lisa	Jon, Carole
11:15t	Art	Carole	Lisa, Jon
11:35t	Active Game	Jon	Lisa, Carole
11:50	Worship	Lisa, Jon	Carole

KidsTime God's Big Picture

Date(s) Sept. 1, 8, 15, 22

Lessons 1-4

Teaching Team Jon, Mary, Dennis

Time	Center	Teachers
11:00-11:20	Active Game	Jan
11:20-11:40	Big Picture Story	Dennis
11:40-12:00	Worship	Mary

Centers for Younger and Older Students

If you have primarily younger or older students in your program, consider offering the Bible Story Coloring Center (for students as young as kindergarten), Skit Center (for older students) or Bible Skills Center (for older students). Any of these centers can either be substituted for one of the Basic Plan centers or added to the Basic Plan.

If you would like to include preschoolers in *KidsTime*, here are some suggestions to follow:

♦ Provide a copy of the coloring page suggested in the Bible Coloring Pages Center for the youngest students to color during the Big Picture Story Center.

♦ Have preschoolers participate in the Art Center and the Worship Center.

♦ During the Active Game Center, either lead preschoolers in simple games such as Follow the Leader and Mother, May I? or allow students to play on playground equipment or with toys and puzzles indoors.

Basic Plan
(60-90 minutes)

Big Picture Story Center and Bible Verse Object Talk
15-30 minutes

Active Game Center
15-20 minutes

Art Center
15-20 minutes

Worship Center
15-20 minutes

Sunday Morning Option 1
(60-90 minutes)

Adult Worship Service
15-20 minutes

Active Game Center
15-20 minutes

Big Picture Story Center and Bible Verse Object Talk
15-30 minutes

Art Center
15-20 minutes

Sunday Morning Option 2
(60-90 minutes)

Big Picture Story Center and Bible Verse Object Talk
15-30 minutes

Active Game Center
15-20 minutes

Children's Choir
15-20 minutes

Art Center
15-20 minutes

Weekday Options
(75-90 minutes)

Active Game Center
15-20 minutes

Big Picture Story Center and Bible Verse Object Talk
15-20 minutes

Snack Time
15 minutes

Art Center
15-20 minutes

Worship Center
15 minutes

Big Picture Story Center

Maximize a student's understanding of God's big picture! Children will learn and understand Bible stories in a fresh way as they become personally involved in "drawing through" the stories. You'll find it easy to keep your students' interest!

Part 1: The *Big Picture Bible Time Line*

The grand opening for every Big Picture Story Center is the *God's Big Picture Bible Time Line.* The time line contains a full-color picture for each lesson's story.

   Post the time line at children's eye level, highlighting each lesson's story picture with the frame provided in the book. Display the entire time line if your room is large; if your room is small, post several pictures at a time or post the section of the Bible (Law, History, etc.) you are studying. By the end of the course, your time line will be a colorful reminder of God's big picture all around your room!

   If the time line must be taken down each week, glue the pictures in order to a roll of butcher paper. This paper can be rolled out each week, tacked to the wall and then rolled up for easy removal. Instead of using the frame, attach a new segment every two weeks.

   The time line can also attract interest if you use a real picture frame to highlight each picture. Use a colorful rope or heavy decorative braid to hang the frame from a wall molding. Slide the hanger to move the frame from picture to picture. (Thrift

shops and garage sales are an excellent source for used picture frames!) Another alternative for displaying the time line is to attach it to the walls of a hallway near your classroom to invite your students into God's big picture.

Part 2: Draw It!

You can do it! Even if you don't have an artistic bone in your body, the sketches that illustrate each story are designed to be user-friendly for easy drawing.

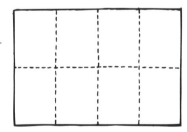

   Before telling the story, ask students to divide their drawing paper into eight (or more, if needed) sections either by drawing lines on their papers or by folding their papers in half three times.

   It's best to draw these sketches as you talk. However, if students have difficulty drawing along with you or if you have difficulty sketching while you talk, sketch before each paragraph and then encourage children to copy your sketch and to listen to find out what that sketch is about.

   A variety of drawing materials will work. Consider these options: butcher paper taped to wall, large pad on an easel, chalkboard, white board or overhead projector. Whatever option you choose, make sure that all students can clearly see your sketches. Varying the drawing materials from week to week will help to keep student interest high.

What drawing materials does the student need?

Provide a commercially produced sketch pad for each child or make individual sketch pads by stapling sheets of newsprint to poster board (see sketch). Students will enjoy personalizing their sketch-pad covers. Make sketchbooks for every 13-week quarter or one large sketchbook for the entire year.

If sketch pads are not possible, choose from these ideas: paper on clipboards (with extras for visitors), butcher paper taped to tabletops, sheets of paper taped to wall, sheets of paper that are collected weekly and compiled into a book (teacher makes copies of her drawings for absentees) or rolls of adding-machine tape (child draws every week to make a personal "big picture" mural).

What are some tips and alternatives to drawing the sketches?

♦ Another teacher or an older child can draw each sketch as you tell the story.

♦ You may lightly sketch the illustrations ahead of time and then copy over them with a felt marker during the Big Picture Story Center.

♦ Instead of drawing, simply tell the story. Remember to have a good "hook" to keep student interest—pictures, first-person storytellers, Bible-times costumes, skits, etc.

♦ Recruit older children to read or act out the skit provided in the Skit Center.

How can I help younger students draw?

♦ If your group is mainly younger students, reduce the number of sketches you make.

♦ Draw a bit more slowly.

♦ Lead students to complete their drawings before you tell each paragraph, encouraging children to listen to find out why they drew the sketch.

♦ Pair older students with younger ones.

♦ Remember that the point of sketching is not to produce great art; it's to involve children in remembering the Bible story. If a child seems to doodle, don't worry. What he or she is drawing will still aid the child's memory!

What are some options for older students?

♦ If your group is mainly older students, encourage them to expand and personalize their sketches.

♦ If the story is a familiar one, invite students to tell the story action as you draw sketches. Supplement story details as needed.

♦ Some students might enjoy making a dictionary of sketches to supplement the ones given in the lesson.

♦ Invite an older student to photocopy his or her page to send to an absentee.

Enrichment Tips

♦ If a child says "Wait! I'm not finished!" remind everyone that there will be time to copy sketches in greater detail when the story is over. Remind children, too, that their sketches are their own art. There is no wrong way to do them!

♦ Encourage children who finish early or seem bored to add more details to their sketches. **You might add more people to the crowd, Jana. I see Ron has added another tree.** As children personalize and expand their sketches, they will increase their enjoyment and understanding.

Bible Verse Object Talk

The Bible Verse Object Talk can be a highlight of each lesson, drawing children in and helping them apply the Bible verse to their lives. These object talks can be given as part of the Big Picture Story Center or as a separate center.

Getting the Most Out of an Object Talk

Preparation is the key to object talks! Read an object talk at least several days ahead of time to give ample time to gather the needed materials. You may find it helpful to practice some object talks before class.

Whenever possible, invite students to participate in the object talk. Ask a different student each week to read the Bible verse aloud (highlight the verse in your Bible and mark its location with a bookmark).

Occasionally describe situations in which knowing God's Word has helped you. Tell students how the Bible verse presented in the center has been important to you.

Using a Children's Sermon During Adult Worship

If the children in your church are in the adult service during the first part of the service, consider using the object talk as the basis for a weekly children's sermon. Introduce the idea of God's big picture to the adult audience by saying, **This year our children are getting the big picture of God's Word, the Bible, by studying all the way through the Bible in a year. Today they will be studying (the lesson title). Their Bible verse to memorize is (the Big Picture Verse and reference) and we will talk about (the life focus of the lesson).** Give the object talk, and then if possible, ask one or more of the Discussion Questions found at the bottom of the Bible Verse Object Talk page.

Active Game Center

The Active Game Center can be the perfect place for your students to let off steam, work out the wiggles and be open to guided discussion that relates the big picture of the day's lesson to students' lives.

Creating a Playing Area

Before leading a game, give yourself ample time to set up the game area. You may have little space in your classroom for a game area, so consider alternatives: outdoors, a gymnasium or a vacant area of the church from which sound will not carry to disturb other programs.

Once you have chosen the area, decide what (if any) adjustments need to be made:

- Will you need to move furniture?
- Will you need to mark boundaries? Use chalk or rope outdoors; yarn or masking tape indoors. (Remove masking tape from carpets after each session.)
- How much space will you need? Carefully review the game procedures to plan what amount and shape of space will be needed.

From time to time, take stock of your classroom area. Is it time to remove that large table or unused bookshelf? Should the chairs be rearranged or the rug put in a different place? Small changes in arrangement can result in more usable space!

Forming Groups or Teams

To keep students' interest high and to keep cliques from forming, use a variety of ways to determine teams or groups:

- Group teams by clothing color or other clothing features (wearing a sweater, wearing tennis shoes, etc.).
- Place equal numbers of two colors of paper squares in a bag. Students shake the bag and draw out a square to determine teams.
- Group teams by birthday month (for two teams, January through June and July through December); adjust as needed.
- Group teams by the alphabetical order of their first or last names.
- Group teams by telling them to stand on one foot: those standing on a right foot form one team; those standing on a left foot form the other team.

After playing a round or two of a game, announce that the person on each team who is wearing the most (red) should rotate to another team. Then play the game again. As you repeat this rotation process, vary the method of rotation so that students play with several different students each time.

Leading the Game

Explain rules clearly and simply. It's helpful to write out the rules to the game. Make sure you explain rules step by step.

When playing a game for the first time with your group, play it a few times just for practice.

Dealing with Competition

For younger children (and for some older ones) competition can make a game uncomfortable—especially for the losers. If your group is made up primarily of younger children, consider making a game more cooperative than competitive: give a special job (calling time, operating the CD player) to a child who is out; have the winning team serve a snack to the losing team; rotate players after every round.

Guiding Conversation

Guided conversation turns a game activity into discovery learning. Make use of the Discussion Questions provided in the curriculum all during game time. You might ask a game's winners to answer questions or to consult with each other and answer as a group. You might discuss three questions between the rounds of a game or ask a question at the beginning of the round, inviting answers at the end.

Bonus Games

Occasionally you may find that students lose interest in a game, you need a different game for a change of pace or you need a new game for the last few minutes of the Active Game Center. Lead children in such favorite games as Hide-and-Seek, Musical Chairs, Simon Says and Hot Potato. You may also choose from these game ideas:

Object Drop

Students sit in a circle with their hands cupped behind their backs. Choose one student to be "It." Give "It" a small object (eraser, block, chalk, sponge ball, etc.). "It" walks around circle and drops object into a student's cupped hands. Student with object chases "It" around the circle, trying to tag "It." Whether or not "It" is tagged, he or she sits down in circle. Student who was chasing "It" becomes new "It."

Paper-Plate Shoe Race

Form teams of four to six students. Teams line up in single-file lines on one side of the playing area. Place a chair across from each team at the opposite side of the playing area. Give the first student on each team two paper plates. Students stand on paper plates and, at your signal, begin sliding across the playing area, around chair and back to team, giving paper plates to next student in line. The next student repeats action. Teams sit down when all students on team have completed activity.

Popcorn Tag

Choose one volunteer to be "It." All students, including "It", can move only by hopping on both feet. "It" hops toward students to tag them. When "It" tags a student, the student joins hands with "It" and the two hop toward other students to tag them. Each student who is tagged joins hands with "It" and becomes an "It" as well. Play continues until there is only one untagged student left.

Quick Change

Students sit in a circle. Choose one volunteer to be "It." "It" stands in center of circle. Call out the names of any two students in circle. Students quickly try to change seats before "It" sits in one of their places. If students successfully change seats before "It" can sit, first student seated becomes new "It." If "It" took the seat of one of the players, that student becomes "It" for next round. Continue, calling different students' names each round. Add variation by assigning students names of Bible characters, animals, types of candy, etc. Students change seats when assigned names are called.

Art Center Tips

The Art Center is a place where children can become absorbed in a creative activity that opens their minds as you help them relate the big picture of the day's lesson to their lives. When students' hands are busy, they often talk freely!

Before You Begin

Preparation is the key to making an art experience a joyful, creative one. No one enjoys a long stretch of waiting for the right crayon. So make sure you have the following supplies on hand: newspaper (to protect surfaces), scissors, glue bottles and sticks, markers, crayons and chalk, tape, paint smocks (or men's old shirts) and butcher paper or newsprint end rolls (ask at your local newspaper office).

Before Every Activity

Before students arrive at your center, cover the work tables with newspaper, securing them with masking tape, if needed. Set out materials in an orderly fashion, making sure you have enough materials for the number of children who will visit the Art Center.

If table space is limited, set out materials on a nearby shelf or supply table. Encourage students to get materials from and return materials to the appropriate places.

As Children Create

Ask the questions listed at the bottom of each Art Center page to help children relate the big picture idea to their daily lives. As children create, they are relaxed and eager to talk. Guided discussion will take the activity beyond art to discovery of Bible truth.

Because the goal of this activity goes beyond an artistic product, take advantage of those moments when a child says "Look at my picture!" Instead of responding with "That's nice," focus on the child. Relate the child's work and interest to the big picture idea. Use "I see..." statements to affirm the value of the child's work while helping him or her see how his or her work relates to the big picture idea. **Billy, I see you used a lot of dark lines for the rain. God took care of Noah in that rain. And He cares for us, too.**

Avoid making value judgments ("That's nice" or "How pretty!"). First, any child who then doesn't hear such a positive judgment will be crushed! Second and most important, focusing on the visual appeal of the artwork will not help children better understand the lesson. How a child's work looks is far less important than the child's process of creating that work. Comment on colors, lines and ideas you see represented. **Suzi, I see you (glued many stars) on your project. Tell me about those stars.** As you invite children to tell you about their work, many opportunities will arise for you to ask the Discussion Questions printed at the bottom of the page or to make comments that will help children understand the Big Picture Idea. **Thank you for telling me about the stars, Suzi. Those stars make me think of how God cared for Paul in that big storm. God cares for us in scary times, too!**

Worship Center Tips

The Worship Center brings together all the other aspects of each center. It can be a fine small group time or can be an excellent large group time. Either way, the goal is to help children participate in meaningful worship. Prayer, saying or reading God's Word and lesson-related music activities are provided in the Worship Center, as well as a variety of options you can use to enrich the Worship Center or to involve older students.

A Time of Worship

What is worship for children? Adults sometimes see children's worship time as occupying kids with frenzied repetitions of "Father Abraham" or as simply teaching children to worship in the same way as adults. But children need informal worship opportunities at their own level of understanding. Worship experiences designed to meet children's needs help them respond in love and praise to their heavenly Father.

Worship is indeed a time to show reverence and respect for God, but it doesn't mean always sitting still and being quiet. The activities offered in the Worship Center involve children and help them interact with each other and with teachers in singing praise to God and hearing His Word.

A Place of Worship

Worship is also enhanced by setting apart a place especially for praising Him. Prayerfully consider the ages and abilities of the children in your group, the kind of worship experience appropriate for them and the time and space available.

Consider such ideas as displaying a contemporary picture of Jesus, spreading a rug on the floor upon which children sit and/or playing a song such as "Psalm 9:1,2,10" or "Psalm 86:8-10" (from *God's Big Picture* cassette/CD or music video) at the beginning of each Worship Center as an invitation to worship.

If taking an offering, singing a particular response or placing candles on an altarpiece are part of your church's adult worship, occasionally add those elements to the Worship Center as well. Give a simple explanation to help children understand why each of these acts is part of worship.

Keep in mind that the Worship Center is not a place for entertainment or observation; your goal is to see every child participate in a positive way that is in keeping with his or her development.

Leading Songs

The upbeat songs on the *God's Big Picture* cassette/CD and music video are designed to relate to the day's lesson or big picture focus. Singing the songs for several weeks in succession results in the songs' messages having a greater impact on the children.

Children may participate by singing, clapping, doing motions, playing rhythm instruments, helping to lead motions, holding up song charts, operating the overhead projector or adjusting the CD player. Older students may lead the group in the motions shown on the word chart or *God's Big Picture* music video. Help children understand that all these activities have one goal: to honor and praise God. Your loving example sets the tone—it is the strongest teaching about worship the children will receive.

Learning new songs can be difficult for some teachers. Listen to the song on the *God's Big Picture* cassette/CD or watch it on the music video. Then play the song again and sing along. Practice it several times (listen to it while driving in the car, while you cook, etc.).

To teach a new song to children, print the words on a large chart or use the song charts in this book to make a transparency to use with an overhead projector. Project the words on a place where they may be seen easily by all the children.

As you play the song, sing along with the song, inviting children to join in with you. It is usually a good idea to sing only one stanza and/or chorus the first time through. If you are using an overhead, cover the entire transparency with a blank sheet of paper. As you sing, move the paper to reveal words one line at a time.

Choosing Additional Songs

If your church chooses to lead students in additional worship songs, select songs with the same prayer and sensitivity with which you'd plan adult worship. Utilizing simple worship choruses and hymns from among your own church's favorites will prepare children for the transition to adult-level worship in a gradual, age-appropriate manner. In this way, children will become familiar with a body of songs used in adult worship.

Whatever songs you use, be sure to explain any words or concepts that are unfamiliar to children. If unfamiliar words are used, take the time to give a brief definition of the word. Use a children's Bible dictionary if needed. For example, **The word "holy" means to be chosen or set apart. When we sing that God is holy, it means that He is perfect and without sin.** If you cannot put the words or concepts of any song in terms a child can truly understand, recognize that the song is probably appropriate only for adult worship.

Big Picture Verse

The simple verse activity provided in the Worship Center encourages students to hear and/or say the Scripture in a creative way reflective of a more formal order of worship. While children may often memorize the verse as part of this activity, Bible memory is not the primary goal. Instead, the goal is simply the interactive reading or hearing of God's Word.

If the reading abilities of children and number of teachers permit, children may find and read the verse in Bibles as part of this activity.

Consider printing out each week's verse on a computer banner for easy reading.

Prayer Time

Prayer is an integral part of worship. Don't deny children this privilege because they seem unable to hold still with folded hands and bowed heads for long periods of time. Instead, involve children in prayer in ways that will help them understand that prayer is something they can do. Don't insist that students pray in a particular posture; keep prayer times short and make them times of high involvement. Remember that your prayers give the students in your class a model for prayer which they will follow. Keep your prayers brief and use simple words. Long sentences and long prayers make prayer seem boring and not something for a child.

Invite students to say sentence prayers; use a prayer journal to record requests and answers; list prayer requests on large paper and allow children to pray with eyes open so that they are able to read and recall requests.

Bible Coloring Center

The coloring pages from the *Bible Story Coloring Pages* provide an ideal activity for the youngest students in *KidsTime*. First and second graders (or even kindergartners) will enjoy the opportunity to color in their own style a picture of the lesson's Bible story (or occasionally a related story). It's easiest to copy at once, rather than on a weekly basis, all the pages needed. Store the pages in folders for easy use.

Color and Talk

While students are coloring, ask the suggested questions in the curriculum. Encourage student participation by introducing each question with a statement, **I'm looking for four students wearing red to answer this question.** Another way to attract the interest of students is to say, **Someone whose name begins with the letter *J* can answer this question.**

Reading the story on the back of the coloring page is another way to add learning to this coloring activity. If you read the story after students have completed coloring, stop occasionally during the story to invite several students to hold up their pages. For example, at the point in the story where you are describing Daniel being placed into the lions' den say, **Let's see how Amanda, Jon and Shayna colored their lions.** If a student in your class is able to read the story, invite him or her to read the story aloud, or several students may take turns reading alternate sentences.

More than Coloring!

For each coloring page, an optional enrichment idea is suggested. Additional items to draw, touch-and-feel materials to glue to the page or fun display ideas are some of the creative add-ons to this activity.

Skit Center Tips

Skits from *The Big Book of Bible Skits* can be a real benefit to older students. They enjoy reading and participating in something beyond the Bible story. You may also wish to use skits to provide a change of pace in Bible story presentation. Older students can read or even memorize the skits and wear costumes to tell the story to younger students.

Preparing for the Skit

Read the skit aloud ahead of time. Make note of vocabulary or pronunciation help you will need to give your students at the first read-through.

- ♦ Consider your students. You may want to reduce or increase the number of characters in a skit. If you have younger children who are excellent readers or older children who have difficulty reading, adjust the parts offered to them accordingly.
- ♦ Provide enough copies for all students and highlighter pens for players to mark their parts.

Using Skits with Poor Readers

Your group may include students with poor reading skills, with learning disabilities or for whom English is a second language. With a little planning and some tender loving care, your players can gain badly needed confidence while enjoying the skits!

- ♦ Highlight each character's lines on separate copies of the script. Add pronunciation pointers as needed.
- ♦ Have the entire group read through the skit in pairs before rehearsing in a larger group.
- ♦ Give everyone in the group a script to follow as selected readers read aloud. Receiving information through more than one sense helps students who are better visual than auditory learners.
- ♦ Students may write out each sentence spoken by their characters on a separate index card, making the job look smaller.
- ♦ Call a student and have him or her read the part to you over the phone for practice.
- ♦ Give permission to improvise! Students who understand the sense of a speech, and whose verbal skills are better than their reading and memorization skills, may communicate better and more freely if they paraphrase.
- ♦ When a volunteer has read as much as he or she wants, have another volunteer ready to jump in and continue reading. Another option is to let each reader choose a partner to trade with whenever necessary.

Performing Skits

If you're practicing a skit to use as part of a later lesson and you want students to memorize their parts, encourage them to make cassette recordings of their parts and replay them over and over. Students may take home the cassettes for extra practice. The repetition will be a great help to auditory learners.

- ♦ Have on hand a box of simple, inexpensive props: Bible-times costumes, pretend scrolls, a variety of hats, men and women's clothing, etc.
- ♦ Occasionally plan to have students present a skit in a worship service. Arrange to have students practice the skit in the worship area.

Bible Skills Center Tips

Give older students (third to sixth grade) the opportunity to develop skill in using and understanding God's Word as they complete the activities provided in the *Big Book of Bible Skills*. Two activities are suggested for each lesson. Lead students in either or both activities, depending on the time available and the needs and interests of your students.

For example, if students have been sitting, they will need the chance to move by participating in one of the games; if students have just completed the Active Game Center, however, they will be ready to have a quieter time to complete a fun maze or puzzle. Vary the activities from week to week so that students can participate in several different ways of learning.

Get Ready

Have several Bibles on hand for students to use as they participate in the Bible skill activities. In addition, provide several Bible dictionaries, a Bible encyclopedia and a Bible atlas for students to refer to as needed.

♦ Plan an open area for the games that require movement. If possible, play some games outdoors to provide variety for students.

♦ On the back of each worksheet is an Answer Key for reference if students have difficulty completing a page.

Getting and Keeping the Very Best Staff

One of the most important elements in staffing a successful *KidsTime* is planning how you will recruit and organize your staff. However you do it, keep in mind that the best learning and the most fun take place when there is a teacher or helper for every six to eight children.

The optimum plan for staffing is to have the same teachers in place for six months to one year. Both teachers and children benefit from regular interaction. Having long-term teachers creates a wonderful opportunity for spiritual growth in students as they build relationships with adults who are faithful in demonstrating God's love.

While it may be easier to recruit teachers to teach one session at a time, such short-term staffing creates other problems. Many churches have found that frequently rotating teachers not only makes learning and growth difficult for children, but it also creates a heavy workload in administration (distributing curriculum, orienting a constant stream of new teachers, etc.).

Here are some options if long-term commitment is difficult in your situation:

♦ Ask teachers to teach for a shorter time period—three or four months at a time instead of a year.

♦ Find two teams of teachers and helpers who will each teach for a month. Then plan to rotate the two teams so that they alternate teaching a month at a time. Over the course of a year, teachers and children become familiar with each other and can benefit from regular interaction.

♦ If you must rotate teachers more frequently (weekly or biweekly), have greeters or leaders at the Worship Center and/or the Big Picture Story Center who are present every week.

Recruiting Tips

Recruiting teachers and helpers is one of the key tasks to making *KidsTime* an effective and fun learning experience for the children of your church and community. Keep the following tips in mind as you seek the volunteers and then match their talents to the tasks to be done:

♦ Pray for guidance in finding the people God wants to serve in this ministry.

♦ Start early!

♦ Keep all the leaders of your Sunday School and other children's ministries aware of and praying about staffing needs.

♦ Develop a written job description for each *KidsTime* staff position.

♦ Make a list of potential teachers and helpers. Consider a wide variety of sources for volunteers: church membership list, new members' classes, suggestions from adult teachers or leaders, lists of previous and current teachers, survey forms and recommendations from present teachers. Don't overlook singles, senior citizens, youth and collegians. Be sure to follow your church's established procedures for screening volunteers.

♦ Look for team members with interests and abilities in specific areas. For example, the teaching team for 24 children might consist of three adults: one who prepares and leads the Big Picture Story Center each week, one who prepares and guides the Active Game Center and a third adult who prepares and leads the Worship Center. While each team member has primary responsibility to lead only one center, all team members are involved as helpers.

♦ Recruit a separate team of teachers and leaders for each center. Each team might consist of two or more adults who enjoy teaching together, or consider asking a family with teenagers to work together to form a teaching team.

♦ Prayerfully prioritize your prospect list. Determine which job description best fits each person's strengths and gifts.

♦ Personally contact the prospects. A personal letter is a good first step or send a flyer to each prospect. Follow up the letter or flyer with a phone call to answer any questions or to see if the prospect has made a decision.

♦ Provide new volunteers with all the needed materials, forms, helpful hints and training that will help them to succeed. You may want to schedule one or more training meetings for all teachers and helpers at which you distribute curriculum, review schedule and procedures, learn the songs, etc.

♦ During the volunteer's time of service, make sure the volunteer knows who will be available to answer questions or lend a helping hand. Look for specific actions and services contributed by the volunteer and offer your thanks!

♦ Plan a thank-you brunch or pizza dinner or lunch for teachers and their families. Even if they don't attend, they'll be grateful for your appreciation!

Recruiting Announcements

Your *KidsTime* teachers and helpers will appreciate clear, concise information about the program—and a little added inspiration couldn't hurt! **Here are some attention-grabbing recruiting announcements:**

EXPRESS YOURSELF!

Yes, **YOU** can fascinate, teach and amaze! Our new *KidsTime* program, *God's Big Picture,* has exciting songs, adaptable games and worship activities complete with a fun music video. But that's not all! You'll be able to keep kids on the edges of their seats with awesome art projects, amazing object talks and a terrific technique for keeping kids' attention during Bible story time.

WANT TO UNDERSTAND YOUR BIBLE BETTER?
You can! Let our new *KidsTime* program, *God's Big Picture*, be the start of expanding your understanding! What better way to learn more about God's Word than to teach it to eager kids in this kid-friendly program!

   God's Big Picture has exciting songs, adaptable games and worship activities complete with a fun music video. But that's not all! You'll be able to expand kids' minds with awesome art projects, amazing object talks and a terrific technique for keeping kids' attention during Bible story time. And all it needs to be the best is YOU! Act now to ensure your spot as a teacher of this understanding-expanding course!

Questions and Answers for a Terrific Program

What's the best way to distribute and store *KidsTime* curriculum?

When you first receive your curriculum, pull out the perforated pages and place them in a binder. Use dividers to separate the main sections of the book: planning pages, lesson pages and music resources.

At the beginning of the program, photocopy all the lesson pages, making multiple copies of the first page of each lesson (one for each teacher or helper). Also make multiple copies of the tips page for each activity center (one of the appropriate center for each teacher or helper).

Distribute the appropriate pages to teachers and helpers at a *KidsTime* orientation meeting, or mail them to teachers a week or so before the teaching assignment begins. (If pages will be distributed periodically throughout the year, store the photocopied pages in a separate notebook.)

How can we build enthusiasm for *KidsTime*?

Children of all ages will respond positively to your efforts to create interest in *KidsTime*. These special attention-getting ideas can be used to kick off the beginning of *KidsTime*, as an outreach emphasis or as "shot-in-the-arm" ideas at any time during the year.

♦ Plan theme days such as Crazy Hat Day (everyone wears a funny- or silly-looking hat), Color Day (everyone wears clothes of a certain color) or Parent Day for Sunday evening or weekday programs (as many parents or grandparents as possible attend *KidsTime* with their children or grandchildren).

♦ Design a special name tag.

♦ Make or decorate T-shirts for *KidsTime* participants to wear.

♦ Create a special name or logo for your *KidsTime* program and use it on all publicity, recruiting letters, T-shirts, name tags and classroom signs.

Susie Smith

What are some ways of keeping older kids interested in *KidsTime*?

Challenging options for older students are suggested in the centers, and the Skit Center and the Bible Skills Center are designed specifically for older students. Offer these centers while younger children are participating in another center. If your group is large enough to divide into classes, group older students in a separate class.

Involving older students in *KidsTime* can be a valuable experience for them as they explore and interact with the Bible content of *God's Big Picture*. They are more than able to develop an understanding of God's plan as demonstrated in the Bible and in the lives of Christians today. Younger students will benefit from the presence of older children who can help them when needed. Teachers also appreciate the assistance of willing hands. Older students can also be assigned to assist in specific centers:

♦ As you tell the story in the Big Picture Story Center, one or more older students can draw the suggested sketches on large sheets of paper or on a chalkboard for younger students to copy.

♦ An older student may be able to demonstrate the activity suggested in the Bible Verse Object Talk. Give the appropriate object talk page to the student before the lesson is taught so that he or she can collect the needed materials and practice the object talk. Be ready to lead the object talk conclusion yourself.

♦ In the Worship Center, older students can demonstrate the motions for the song or lead the Bible verse activity.

How can we adapt the curriculum for seasonal days like Christmas and Easter?

In order to celebrate these holidays during *KidsTime,* substitute the designated lessons at the appropriate time of year: Use Lesson 27 at Christmas and Lesson 42 at Easter. Many churches find that on these holidays children are often included in additional programs planned for the entire church family. If *KidsTime* meets on a weekday, teach the suggested seasonal lessons during the weeks closest to the actual holidays.

How can we use awards at *KidsTime*?

Many churches like to offer awards to their children. Awards have long been a fun way to motivate children. However, to avoid having children try to defeat each other and thus create a group of losers, offer awards that ensure every child can be a winner.

♦ Give award tickets for specific, predetermined actions (attendance, repeating the Bible verse, bringing a Bible or any desired positive behavior). At the end of the session (or month), award tickets can be exchanged for prizes. Distributing award tickets for specific positive behaviors allows the teacher to make sure everyone gets something.

♦ Plan a cooperative contest in which the entire class or group works together to reach a goal and everyone shares in the awards. For example, a cooperative contest might set a goal for the total number of children attending on a specific day (or over a month's time) or a total number of Bible verses to be memorized. When the goal is reached, the class is given a special award—a pizza or ice cream party, inexpensive toys or gift certificates.

What can we do to decorate our *KidsTime* room(s)?

A bit of decoration can make all the difference in creating that special, fun atmosphere!

♦ Attach a large butcher paper art frame around the door through which students enter to attend *KidsTime.* Ask a carpenter in your church to make a bright frame.

♦ Cut out large randomly shaped pieces of brightly colored butcher paper to represent paint spatters or artist palettes. Attach to classroom walls.

♦ Stand up an artist's easel in the corner of the room. Display a reproduction of a famous painting on it or show a framed picture that illustrates the session's Bible story.

♦ Create an art gallery in your room. Collect finished work from students who have participated in the Art Center. Put construction paper (or more permanent, reusable poster board frames) around the artwork and display it on classroom walls.

♦ Periodically take pictures of students participating in the various centers and display them. Another fun idea is to ask students to pose as statues during the Active Game Center, take their pictures and display the pictures as in a museum.

Introducing Kids to Adult Worship

For a few moments, let's do a little pretending. Let's pretend that we are six-year-old children and that we are sitting in the adult worship service of our church. What words do we hear that we don't understand? What books are we asked to use that we don't know how to read? What happens in front that we can't see because we are small? What are we expected to do that is confusing to us? How long do we have to sit still when we are not used to sitting?

As you think through some of the things your children experience in a typical worship service, you may come to the realization that the adult worship service sometimes becomes an uncomfortable, passive experience for a child, rather than an opportunity to praise and worship God.

However, you as *KidsTime* leader, as well as parents, pastor and others involved in leading the adult worship service, CAN take many specific actions to make the service more meaningful and enjoyable for children. Whether the children in your church are approaching the first time they will attend the service, attend the service only occasionally, frequently attend at least part of the service or are about to be promoted from their own *KidsTime* program into regular attendance at the adult worship service, here are some specific suggestions to help them enjoy and benefit from being with the grown-ups in "Big Church."

When Children Are in the Worship Service

Encourage parents to sit with their children near the front of the worship service. The children will not only see and hear better, but they will also have more of a sense that the person up front is speaking to them. Proximity encourages participation.

Arrange for those who are involved in leading worship to meet periodically with the children in fairly small groups. This can be done briefly at the end of Sunday School or as a part of another children's program. Use this time to explain one feature of the service the children are about to attend. If this is done every week or on some other regularly scheduled basis, the children can gradually be introduced to the entire spectrum of worship activities which occur in your services.

A significant bonus of this approach is that children will also get to know your leaders as friends who care about them, rather than viewing them as strangers who lead unfamiliar ceremonies at a distance. Perhaps of even greater significance, this brief time of interaction will alert these leaders to the presence of children in the worship service, helping the leaders become more effective in including children in the worship experiences.

HINT: If you invite someone to meet with the children and this person is not experienced in speaking at a child's level, structure the time as an interview which one of the children's teachers or leaders will conduct. Let your invited guest know ahead of time the specific questions that will be asked.

Provide parents with a sheet of tips of things to have the child do before, during and after the service (see p. 27) in order to gain maximum understanding and participation.

Kids in Adult Worship

Tips for Parents

Before the Service:

- ◆ Sit near the front where your child can easily see what is happening.
- ◆ If your church prints an order of service in the bulletin, help your child identify, find and mark locations of hymns and Scripture readings.
- ◆ Let your child underline all the words in the bulletin he or she can read.
- ◆ Briefly explain the meaning of any difficult words or phrases in at least the first hymn or song you will sing.
- ◆ Share your own feelings about the hymns or songs to be sung: "This is one of my favorites"; "I really like to sing this because it helps me tell God I love Him"; "This is one I've never learned. I hope it's easy to sing"; etc.

During the Service:

- ◆ Let your child help hold the hymnal or song sheet. Run your finger beneath the words being a sung to help your child follow along. If your church displays the words of a song on an overhead, make sure you sit where your child can see the words.
- ◆ Touch your child (not just when the wiggles are in action) to build a sense of warmth in being together.
- ◆ Provide writing and/or drawing materials. Encourage your child to write or draw about things he or she sees or hears during the service ("Draw a picture of something the pastor talks about in his sermon.").
- ◆ If there is a time of greeting one another, introduce your child to those around you.
- ◆ Let your child take part in passing the offering plate, registration cards or other items distributed throughout the congregation.

After the Service:

- ◆ Express your appreciation at being in church with the child.
- ◆ Commend your child for specific times when he or she was participating well ("You really did a good job singing that first hymn.").
- ◆ Talk about what went on in the service. Avoid making this sound like an exam, but ask one or two questions to let the child know that you expect him or her to be listening. A few good questions to use are "What is one thing you remember from the service?" "Which song did you like best?" "What Bible person did the pastor talk about?" and "What was the pastor trying to teach us about?"
- ◆ Share your own answers to those questions, or let your child ask you any questions he or she desires.
- ◆ Explain one or two things that happened in the service that you think your child was interested in or could have been confused by.

Tips for the *KidsTime* Leader

As the *KidsTime* leader, you can also take specific actions to make the adult worship service more meaningful for the child. Look at everything that is done through a "six-year-old's filter." Ask yourself, "What would a child understand from what we just did?" This is not a plea to conduct six-year-old-level worship services, but it will help adults become aware of the presence of children and their right to be led in meaningful worship of the Lord. The child will not understand EVERYTHING that occurs in every service, but the child deserves to understand SOMETHING in every service.

Meet with the person(s) responsible for planning the worship service and talk about ways to make the service more helpful to children. Consider these ideas:

♦ Choose at least one hymn or song with a repeating chorus, which makes it easier for children to learn and thus participate.

♦ Choose at least one hymn or song with fairly simple words and melody.

♦ Introduce at least some hymns with a brief explanation for children.

♦ Once or twice in the service, say, "Our children are worshiping with us and we want to help them know what we are singing (talking) about." This will help raise the congregation's awareness of their responsibility to guide children and will also explain some things to adults and teenagers that they might be embarrassed to ask about.

♦ Provide simple explanations of special observances (baptism, the Lord's Supper, etc.).

♦ When inviting people to greet one another, remind them to include children in their interaction. Instructions such as "Talk to at least one person from a generation other than your own" or "Greet someone who is now attending school" are enjoyable ways to alert adults without making the children feel put on the spot.

♦ Find ways to involve children in some specific aspects of the service. Many churches are familiar with occasionally having a children's choir sing, but often the children feel more like outside performers than participants in family worship. Occasionally invite children to assist in receiving the offering (perhaps have parent-child teams), handing out bulletins, reading Scripture, answering a question, etc. Some churches periodically give their choir the day off and form a family choir with moms, dads and kids singing a simple song with other families after a brief rehearsal or two.

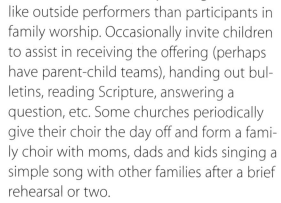

♦ If the adults in your congregation wear name tags, provide name tags for the children, too.

♦ Provide clipboards, paper and crayons for children to use during the service. Before the sermon, have the person leading the service suggest that the children listen for a particular person or event during the sermon and draw a picture about that person or event on the paper. Children may pick up the clipboards during a hymn or some other appropriate time just before the sermon.

- Make a checklist of things for the children to listen for during the service. As the children hear one of the things listed, they check it off the list.
- Several months before children are promoted from *KidsTime* into regular attendance at the adult worship service, plan to have the children participate in a portion of each service each week or the entire service once a month.
- Ask a person with video equipment to make a recording of the entire worship service. Then, occasionally during the Worship Center, choose specific parts of the service to show and explain.
- If the order of worship is printed in your bulletin, give each child a bulletin and briefly explain the order of worship. Describe in childlike terms how each part of the service helps us worship God.
- If your congregation often sings a particular song (such as the "Doxology" or "Gloria Patri"), teach it to the children. You may also help them become familiar with the Lord's Prayer or the Apostles' Creed (if they are used in your church) by repeating them from time to time in your program.
- Help children understand that worship is anything we do that shows that we love and respect God. Use your conversation in the Worship Center to help your children understand how praise, music, prayer and learning from God's Word are all important aspects of worship.

Leading a Child to Christ

One of the greatest privileges of serving in Sunday School is to help children become members of God's family. Some children, especially those from Christian homes, may be ready to believe in Jesus Christ as their Savior earlier than others. Ask God to prepare the children in your class to receive the good news about Jesus and prepare you to communicate effectively with them.

Talk individually with children. Something as important as a child's personal relationship with Jesus Christ can be handled more effectively one-on-one than in a group. A child needs to respond individually to the call of God's love. This response needs to be a genuine response to God—not because the child wants to please peers, parents or you, the teacher.

Follow these basic steps in talking simply with children about how to become members of God's family. The evangelism booklet *God Loves You!* (available from Gospel Light) is an effective guide to follow. Show the child what God says in His Word. Ask the questions suggested to encourage thinking and comprehending.

a. God wants you to become His child. (See John 1:12.) **Do you know why God wants you in His family?** (See 1 John 4:8.)

b. You and all the people in the world have done wrong things. (See Romans 3:23.) **The Bible word for doing wrong is "sin." What do you think should happen to us when we sin?** (See Romans 6:23.)

c. God loves you so much He sent His Son to die on the cross for your sins. Because Jesus never sinned, He is the only One who can take the punishment for your sins. (See 1 Corinthians 15:3; 1 John 4:14.) **The Bible tells us that God raised Jesus from the dead and that He is alive forever.**

d. Are you sorry for your sin? Do you believe Jesus died to be your Savior? If you do believe and you are sorry for your sin, God forgives all your sin. (See 1 John 1:9.)

When you talk to God, tell Him that you believe He gave His Son, Jesus Christ, to take your punishment. Also tell God you are sorry for your sin. Tell Him that He is a great and wonderful God. It is easy to talk to God. He is ready to listen. What you are going to tell Him is something He has been waiting to hear.

e. The Bible says that when you believe in Jesus, God's Son, you receive God's gift of eternal life. This gift makes you a child of God. This means God is with you now and forever. (See John 3:16.)

Give your pastor the names of those who make decisions to become members of God's family. Encourage the child to tell his or her family about the decision. Children who make decisions need follow-up to help them grow in Christ.

NOTE: The Bible uses many terms and images to express the concept of salvation. Children often do not understand or may develop misconceptions about these terms, especially terms that are highly symbolic. (Remember the trouble Nicodemus, a respected teacher, had in trying to understand the meaning of being "born again"?) Many people talk with children about "asking Jesus into your heart." The literal-minded child is likely to develop strange ideas from the imagery of those words. The idea of being a child of God (see John 1:12) is perhaps the simplest portrayal the New Testament provides.

God's True Story

Big Picture Verse

"These are written that you may believe that Jesus is the Christ, the Son of God, and that by believing you may have life in his name." John 20:31

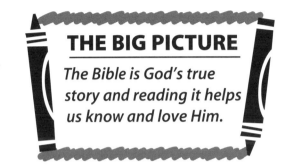

THE BIG PICTURE

The Bible is God's true story and reading it helps us know and love Him.

Scripture Background
Psalm 119:89,130

The Bible is one book, one history, one story—His story. The Bible is also a library, a collection of diverse kinds of writing. Behind 10,000 events stands God, the builder of history, the maker of the ages. Eternity bounds the one side, eternity bounds the other side, and time is in between. From the origins described in Genesis and the endings in Revelation, God is working things out. Go down into the minutest detail everywhere and see that there is one great purpose moving through the ages: the eternal design of the Almighty God to redeem a wrecked and ruined world.

Many people know the Bible characters and the principal events but are hopelessly lost when they are called upon to connect the stories in order. The Bible is one book, and you cannot read it in bits and pieces and expect to comprehend the magnificence of divine revelation. You must see it in its completeness. God has taken pains to give a progressive revelation, and we should take pains to read it from beginning to end. Don't suppose reading little scraps can ever be compensation for doing deep and consecutive work on the Bible itself. One would scorn to read any other book, even the lightest novel, in such a haphazard fashion.

Pick up the "pearls" in the Scriptures and string them into order from Genesis to Revelation so that you can "think through" the Bible story. Give the Book a chance to speak for itself, to make its own impression and to bear its own testimony. You will find a unity of thought which indicates that one mind inspired the writing of the whole series of books, that it bears on its face the stamp of its Author and that it is in every sense the Word of God.

Adapted from *What the Bible Is All About* by Henrietta C. Mears.

Big Picture Story Center

Teacher Materials
Bible Time Line, drawing materials/equipment.

Student Materials
Drawing materials.

Tell the Story
Move the *Bible Time Line* frame to highlight Picture 1. As you tell each part of the story, draw each sketch. Students copy your sketches.

What kinds of pictures do your parents frame? Today we're going to talk about the biggest picture and the oldest story ever.

1. Imagine we've walked through the door of an art gallery. We walk through and look at the framed pictures, one after another. Now we see that each picture tells part of a story, like pictures on the pages of a storybook. Some pictures are small, some are large; some are simple, some are fancy. But every picture tells part of the story.

1. Draw a door.

2. The Bible, God's Word, is like that! Its stories are like a series of pictures. Each picture tells something about who God is and what He wants us to know. As we learn more, we understand how each picture is part of God's story!

2. Draw one big frame from square and "3"s.

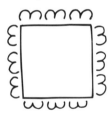

3. The very first picture in our gallery tells us how God's story begins. Since it's the biggest, oldest story ever, it begins with God. God was ALWAYS there! Before there was anything in the whole universe, God was there. He knew each of us, loved us and had plans for every one of us, even way back then.

3. Add "GOD" to frame. Add heart.

4. After God made everything we see around us, He made people, so He could love them and be loved by them. God chose certain people to listen to Him and talk with Him. First, only a few people knew God. Then those people grew into a big family that grew and grew until it was a huge

4. Draw 2 stick figures.

tribe of people, enough people to fill a country! And God loved these people and took care of them. God sent leaders to help His people. He also sent kings to lead them and prophets to tell them His messages. It was all part of God's story.

Add more figures. Add staffs and crowns to some.

5. So that everyone could understand God's story, He helped people write it down in just the way He wanted it told. That way, everyone could read it over and over and get to know Him better! God helped people write what we call the Old Testament. It's the history of God's people and the family from which Jesus came.

5. Draw eyes from sideways "D"s.

6. Later, God helped more people write down the rest of the story, the New Testament. After Jesus came to earth, four men wrote about Jesus' birth and childhood, about how Jesus helped many people and about what Jesus taught them. The four men also wrote about how Jesus died on the cross and how He lives again.

6. Write "JESUS." Add cross.

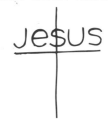

7. But God's big story in the Bible doesn't end there. The good news of Jesus spread to many places. In every place, people came together, so they could worship God and learn about Him. Jesus' followers wrote letters to help these people know more of God's story.

7. Draw arrows outward from cross.

8. God gave us the Bible with many people over hundreds of years writing different parts of God's story. And it isn't a made-up story. No, God's story is true. And YOU can learn about how YOU are part of that story, too! This story never ends because it is God's story.

8. Draw large "U." Add details to make face. Kids can finish to look like themselves.

Get the Big Picture

What part of the Bible tells the history of God's people and the family from which Jesus came? (The Old Testament.) **What part tells about Jesus and about how the good news spread?** (The New Testament.)

God's true stories help us know and love Him.

Bible Verse Object Talk: You've Got Mail!

Big Picture Verse

"These are written that you may believe that Jesus is the Christ, the Son of God, and that by believing you may have life in his name." John 20:31

The Bible is like a letter from God—written just to me and you. In this bag I've got a sample of some of the mail I received this week. As I take the mail out of the bag, let's talk about how God's letter is different from the rest of the mail.

Teacher Materials

Bag into which you have placed a Bible with bookmark at John 20:31 and a variety of mail (bill, letter, greeting card, advertising, catalog, e-mail, magazine, etc.).

Present the Object Talk

1. One at a time, hold up each piece of mail (keeping the Bible until the last) and ask volunteers to describe it. Discuss mail by asking questions such as, **Who is this mail from? What is this mail trying to get me to do? What message does this mail tell me? Why might I be excited to get this mail?**

2. Hold up the Bible. **How would you describe this letter? How is God's letter to us different from the rest of the mail I've received?** (It was written long ago. Its message is for everyone.) **What makes God's Word better than any other message to us?** (It's true. It tells the good news about Jesus.)

Conclude

Read John 20:31 aloud. **The words in the Bible help each person learn that when we believe Jesus is God's Son, we can be part of God's family.** Talk with interested students about becoming Christians, following the guidelines in the "Leading a Child to Christ" article on page 30. Thank God for sending His letter to each of us and ask His help in getting to know more about Him as we read the Bible.

Discussion Questions

1. What's your favorite kind of mail?

2. What's the best thing you've ever received in the mail?

3. When are some times you read God's letter—the Bible?

Active Game Center: Picture Puzzle Relay

Materials
Puzzles with about a dozen pieces each (one puzzle for every six to eight students).

Lead the Game
1. Divide group into teams of six to eight students.

2. Teams form lines. Mix up puzzle pieces and place them about 20 feet (6 m) from the teams, keeping each team's puzzle pieces separate.

3. At your signal, the first student from each team runs to his or her team's puzzle pieces, gets a piece, returns to his or her line and tags the next student to run to the puzzle and get a piece. Students continue until all puzzle pieces have been collected. Then students on each team work together to assemble their puzzle. Play additional rounds as time allows, trading puzzles each round.

> *We put together the pieces of a puzzle to see the picture that it makes. Reading the Bible is like putting together a puzzle. All the stories we read in the Bible help us see a true picture of what God is like, so we can know and love Him.*

Option
Borrow puzzles from students or preschool classes. If puzzles are not available, print John 20:31 on index cards, one word on each card. Play relay as instructed above, substituting index cards for puzzle pieces and having teams put cards in correct verse order.

Discussion Questions
1. What was the hardest puzzle you ever put together?

2. What was the longest story or part of the Bible you ever read?

3. What have you learned about God from the Bible? (He loves all people. He is more powerful than anyone. He is the only true God.)

Art Center: Tablets of Truth

Student Materials
Bibles, play dough, craft sticks.

Lead the Activity
1. Give each student a fist-sized lump of play dough and a craft stick. Allow students time to experiment with play dough.

2. Students flatten and shape play dough into tablets (see sketch).

The Bible is God's true story and reading it helps us to know God. A long time ago God's words were written on stone tablets. Today we will make tablets from play dough. To remind us of what we learn from God's Word, we'll write words from John 20:31 on the tablets.

3. Students use craft sticks to write words or phrases from John 20:31 on the tablets.

Options
1. Provide a piece of cardboard for each student. Students work with dough on cardboard and use cardboard to help carry home their completed tablets.

2. Provide other materials (forks, spoons, buttons, etc.) for students to use to make impressions on the borders of the tablets.

Discussion Questions
1. **What is one of your favorite Bible stories?** (David fights against Goliath. Jesus is born. Paul's shipwreck.)

2. **What have you learned about God from the Bible?** (God loves me. God's Son is Jesus.)

3. **How do you think children learned Bible stories in Bible times?** (From parents. From teachers called rabbis.)

4. **What is your favorite way to hear a Bible story?** (Video. Read a book. Teacher tells.)

Lesson 1

Worship Center

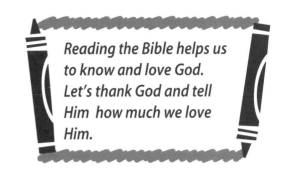

Reading the Bible helps us to know and love God. Let's thank God and tell Him how much we love Him.

Big Picture Verse

"These are written that you may believe that Jesus is the Christ, the Son of God, and that by believing you may have life in his name." John 20:31

Teacher Materials

Bible, *God's Big Picture* cassette/CD or music video and player, "Picture This!" word chart (p. 473 in this book), large sheet of paper on which you have printed John 20:31, masking tape.

Sing to God

Play "Picture This!" encouraging students to sing along with the music and do the actions shown on the word chart or music video. **What do you learn about God from this song? What has God done?**

Hear and Say God's Word

Display paper on which you have printed John 20:31. Have a volunteer read the verse to the class. Then lead students in saying the verse: all boys say the first word, all girls say the second, boys say the third, and so on. Have students repeat the verse in this manner several times, alternating which group says the first word. **What does this verse tell us about why the Bible was written? What are some stories from the Bible which help you believe that Jesus is God's Son?** (Jesus died on the cross. Jesus healed sick people. Jesus rose from the dead.) Talk with students about becoming Christians, following the guidelines in the "Leading a Child to Christ" article on page 30.

Pray to God

What are some things you have learned about God by hearing and reading the Bible? (He loves us. He answers prayer. He promises to help us.) Let volunteers pray sentence prayers, thanking God for the things they have learned about Him and asking for His help in reading the Bible to learn more about Him and His love.

Options

1. Sing "God's Holy Book" with students, leading them in actions shown on word chart (p. 459 in this book) or music video. **Why is reading God's Word so important?**

2. Invite an older student to read Psalm 150 as an invitation to children to worship.

Bible Story Coloring Center

Materials

Crayons or markers, a copy of "God gives the Ten Commandments" and "John writes good news" pictures (pp. 53 and 245 from *Bible Story Coloring Pages*) for each student.

Lead the Activity

Students color pictures. **These pictures show two ways in which God's Word was written in Bible times.**

Option

Copy pages 117 and 118 from *Coloring Pages* for each student. Explain that for many years God's Word was written on long strips of animal skin called "parchment" that were rolled up. Students color page 117; tell the story on page 118.

Skit Center

Materials

A copy of "Dot Your I's and Cross Your T's" skit (pp. 349-353 from *The Big Book of Bible Skits*) for each student; optional—highlighter pens.

Lead the Activity

Briefly tell the background information on page 349. Volunteers choose parts and read the skit, which tells the story of how the Bible was written by scribes, translated into English and later printed on a printing press. (Optional: Students highlight parts.) Ask the discussion questions on page 349.

Bible Skills Center

Materials

Materials needed for "Book Guess" and/or "Swimming Divisions" (p. 25 and/or p. 129 from *The Big Book of Bible Skills*).

Lead the Activity

Students complete activities as directed in *The Big Book of Bible Skills*.

 **Lesson 2**

Created by God's Hand

Big Picture Verse

"How great is the love the Father has lavished on us, that we should be called children of God!"
1 John 3:1

THE BIG PICTURE

The same God who made the world and us, shows His love to all who are His children.

Scripture Background
Genesis 1—2:2

As the book of Genesis begins, we see these words untarnished by the ages: "In the beginning God created the heaven and the earth" (Genesis 1:1). In these few simple words we have the Bible declaration of the origin of this material universe. God called all things into being by the word of His power. He spoke and worlds were framed (see Hebrews 11:3).

This story of creation is a hymn of praise to God, magnifying His mighty works and indicating our high relation to Him. The deeds of our God, as seen in creation, are His footprints by which we recognize His work and Himself. The creation story speaks to us of revelation and inspiration. All the nations from the very beginning have had this light from heaven; therefore, we all should study God's works as well as His Word because each throws light upon the other, and we will not truly understand either without the help of the other.

We learn from the works of creation the wisdom, power, goodness and love of God. The more we study them, the more we learn to love, to wonder and to adore. This wise and good God is our Father; we look upon His works and say, "My Father made them all." We rest in the love of the strongest. We trust in the guiding care of the wisest.

When looking up at the sky and its beauty—at the sun, the moon, the stars and their light—at our earth and at everything that fills it, in all this we recognize God. All God's creation points us to the Creator, as if taking us by the hand and leading us to the understanding and knowledge of His mercy and loving kindness. It's as if God's creations are speaking to us: "Look at us! God created us! We are here to be of help!" God's creation teaches us to love God, to search for Him alone—from whom everything good and loving comes.

Adapted from *What the Bible Is All About* by Henrietta C. Mears.

Big Picture Story Center

Teacher Materials
Bible Time Line, drawing materials/equipment.

Student Materials
Drawing materials.

Tell the Story
Move the *Bible Time Line* frame to highlight Picture 2. As you tell each part of the story, draw each sketch. Students copy your sketches. (Optional: Invite students to tell details of this familiar story.)

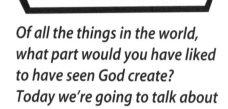

Of all the things in the world, what part would you have liked to have seen God create? Today we're going to talk about how everything came to life!

1. Before God made the world, there was nothing—no houses, no people, no animals, no sun or sky or land. It was just dark and empty. But God was there! And God decided to make something wonderful.

1. Draw dark scribbles.

2. So God said, "Let there be light!" And light shone all around! God called the light "day" and He divided the darkness from the light to make what He called "night." God saw that it was GOOD. And that's what God did on the first day!

2. Use "M"s to draw burst of light; add "1."

3. The next day, God said, "Let the sky and the water be made separate from each other." Now there was water below the sky and a sky that arched over the water. And that's what God did on the second day!

3. Sky from curved strokes; clouds from "3"s; "U"s for water. Add "2."

4. On the third day, God spoke and the waters gathered together to make rivers, lakes and oceans. Once the water was moved around, dry land appeared. Now there were mountains and hills, deep canyons and dry deserts. God had shaped a beautiful world. But God was not finished yet! There still was not anything on the earth that was ALIVE.

4. Draw "M"s for mountains. Add "3."

5. So God said, "Let there be all sorts of grasses and plants and trees." Grass sprang up. Flowers bloomed—red, yellow, pink, purple—every color you can think of! Trees of all shapes and sizes grew. Berry bushes and pumpkin vines grew beautiful fruit and bright orange pumpkins. God looked at all the work He had done. And God saw that it was GOOD!

5. Flowers and bushes from "3"s, berries and pumpkins from "O"s.

6. Next, God made a special bright light and put it in the sky to shine during the day. We call that light the sun! And He made the moon and stars to shine at night. God did a lot of things on the fourth day!

6. Sun from circle and "M"s; moon from "C"s, stars from triangles. Add "4."

7. On the fifth day, God filled the water and the sky with living creatures. He put fish and sharks, octopuses and whales into the oceans. Birds flew through the sky. Some birds were tiny; some birds were BIG. And they were every color you can think of!

7. Octopus from upside-down "U" and "S"s. Add "5."

8. On the sixth day, God made land animals. He made little mice and middle-sized anteaters and laughing hyenas—and great big polar bears and water buffalo and even dinosaurs! Now the world was a hopping, buzzing, galloping, wiggling, lively place! This was all very wonderful. But the day was not over yet. The next thing God did was even more amazing.

8. Mouse from triangle, "C," and "S." Add ears, feet and eye.

9. God created a MAN. God called the man Adam. Later, God made a woman called Eve. God made them different from the animals. They could think and make things; they could talk to each other and to God. God loved them. They were His special friends! Adam and Eve lived in a beautiful garden that was full of the wonderful things God had made.

9. Stick figures. Add heart and "6."

10. God looked at the whole world He had created. It was exactly as He wanted it to be! He looked around at everything and said, "This is GOOD!"

10. Draw eyes. Add "G" and "D."

Get the Big Picture

What did God say about the world He made? (It was good.) **What made people different from the animals and plants?** (They could love God. They could think and talk.) **How did God feel about Adam and Eve?** (He loved them.)

When we look at the animals and plants, the moon and the stars, we remember that God is very strong. He can do anything! And what we see around us helps us know He loves us. He wants us to be His special friends, like Adam and Eve were! God made this world to show His love.

Bible Verse Object Talk: Special Love

Big Picture Verse

"How great is the love the Father has lavished on us, that we should be called children of God!" 1 John 3:1

Teacher Materials

Bible with bookmark at 1 John 3:1.

Student Materials

A leaf for each student (small rocks, potatoes or other nature items may be substituted).

> When God made the world, He did many things to show His love for us. One thing God did was make each thing He created special. Try to figure out what is special about the leaf I give you.

Present the Object Talk

1. Give each student a leaf. Allow students 30 to 60 seconds to examine leaves. **What do you notice about the size of your leaf? its color? How does your leaf feel?** Students briefly compare leaves. **Look carefully at your leaf, so you can find your leaf again when they're all mixed up.**

2. Collect leaves and group them together on table or floor. Students try to find their leaves. (Note: If you have a large class, divide into groups of six to complete this segment of the activity.) **How hard was it to find your leaf? What helped you find your leaf?** Volunteers answer. **The more you knew about your leaf, the easier it was to find it.**

Conclude

Because God made each of us, He knows us and loves us. No matter how many people there are in the world, God knows and loves each person. We are so special to Him that He wants us to love Him and be in His family.

Read (or ask a volunteer to read) 1 John 3:1 aloud. **The word "lavish" means to give more than is needed. This verse reminds us of God's love. The reason God made the world and us is to show love.** Pray, thanking God for His love and for the special way in which He made the world and us.

Discussion Questions

1. What are some other things in creation that look similar but are really different from each other? (Snowflakes. Stars.)

2. What are some ways God made each person unique? (Our fingerprints. Our voices. Our smiles.)

3. What are some ways God has shown love to you and your family?

Active Game Center: Footloose Relay

Materials
Large sheet of butcher paper, pencils.

Lead the Game
1. Each student traces one of his or her feet (with shoe on) on the butcher paper.

2. Students line up across the room from the paper. (If you have more than 10 students, students form two or more teams and race against each other.)

3. At your signal, the first student(s) in line runs to the paper, finds his or her shoe outline, removes his or her shoe and leaves it in the outline. Student returns to line, hopping on the foot that still has a shoe on it. Students in line repeat the process until everyone has had a turn.

4. If you have time, play another round, with each student tracing his or her hand this time. Student runs to paper, finds his or her handprint and writes his or her initials in it with a pencil. Student then skips back to line. Students in line repeat the process until everyone has had a turn.

Option
If you have older students, play another round with students hopping back to paper to retrieve a teammate's shoe.

When God made us and the world, He showed His love for us. One of the ways He showed His love is that He created us each a little differently. Let's find out one way we are each special.

Discussion Questions
1. How did God make you the same as others? different from others?

2. If everyone in our class was created exactly alike, how might your parents find you after church?

3. How did God show His love for us when He created the earth, the animals and you? (He made the sun so that we have heat and light. He gave animals ways to protect themselves. He made our bodies in amazing ways.)

Art Center: String Animals

Student Materials

Sheet of construction paper or poster board for each student, pencils, glue, cotton swabs or glue brushes, string, scissors.

Lead the Activity

1. Each student draws a picture of a favorite animal on paper or poster board.

2. Each student spreads a thin layer of glue over one portion of the picture.

3. Students press string along lines of the pictures. Suggest students fill in the open spaces with loops and swirls (see sketch). Each student repeats process for each portion of his or her picture.

When God made the world, He wanted to show His love for us. One way He showed His love was by creating so many interesting animals for us to enjoy. Today we can make string animals as reminders of God's love.

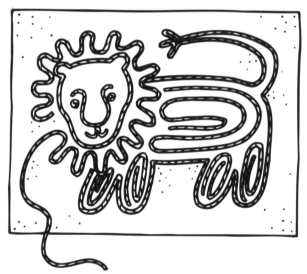

Options

1. Use a sheet of cardboard instead of construction paper or poster board.

2. Play "Promises" from *God's Big Picture* cassette/CD while students complete activity.

Discussion Questions

1. What is the name of a funny looking animal God made? a beautiful one? a tall one?

2. What is your favorite animal?

3. How did God decorate some animals?

4. What are some other things God made for us to enjoy?

Lesson 2

Worship Center

Big Picture Verse

"How great is the love the Father has lavished on us, that we should be called children of God!" 1 John 3:1

Let's tell God how thankful we are that He made the world and us to show His love.

Teacher Materials

Bible, *God's Big Picture* cassette/CD or music video and player, "Picture This!" word chart (p. 473 in this book), large sheet of paper on which you have printed 1 John 3:1, masking tape.

Sing to God

Play "Picture This!" encouraging students to sing along with the music and do the actions shown on the word chart or music video. **According to this song, what are some of the ways God shows His love to us?**

Hear and Say God's Word

Display paper on which you have printed 1 John 3:1. Lead students in repeating the verse a few times in this manner: Say the verse very quietly the first time and then louder each time you repeat the verse. Students shout the good news of this verse the last time, if it is possible in your location. **What does this verse say is the greatest way God has shown His love?** (By calling us His children.) **How do we become God's children?** (By believing that Jesus is God's Son and that God forgives us for the wrong things we do.)

Pray to God

God made this world to show His love. What are some things God made that you are thankful for? Begin prayer by saying **God, we thank You for...** and allow students to name different things God created. Conclude prayer by thanking God for all the ways He shows His love to us.

Options

1. Before the prayer, lead students on a walk outdoors. Ask students to look for things God created. If possible, complete both the Bible verse and prayer activities outdoors.

2. Sing "God Is So Strong" (p. 455 in this book) with students, asking students to name powerful things God has created.

 **Lesson 2**

Bible Story Coloring Center  FOR YOUNGER CHILDREN

Materials

Crayons or markers, a copy of "God creates the world" picture and story (pp. 9-10 from *Bible Story Coloring Pages*) for each student.

Lead the Activity

Students color page 9; read or tell the story on page 10. **How many animals do you see? How many different kinds of growing things do you see?**

Option

Provide blank paper. Students draw pictures of their favorite creation items. Display pictures on bulletin board or wall.

Skit Center FOR OLDER CHILDREN

Materials

A copy of "Love, Love, Love" skit (pp. 374-376 from *The Big Book of Bible Skits*) for each student; optional—highlighter pens.

Lead the Activity

Students form pairs and read the skit, which talks about the way in which some kids use the word "love." (Optional: Students highlight their parts.) Ask the discussion questions on page 374, asking students to compare God's love with the love described in the skit.

Bible Skills Center FOR OLDER CHILDREN

Materials

Materials needed for "Spell It!" and/or "Writing Relay" (p. 26 and/or p. 92 from *The Big Book of Bible Skills*).

Lead the Activity

Students complete activities as directed in *The Big Book of Bible Skills*.

The First Family

Big Picture Verse

"Put your hope in the Lord, for with the Lord is unfailing love and with him is full redemption."
Psalm 130:7

THE BIG PICTURE

God's love is bigger than our sin.

Scripture Background
Genesis 2:4—3

Genesis is the seed plot of the Word of God.

The title "Genesis" means "origin." The first word in Genesis is translated as "in the beginning"—words which indicate both the scope and the limits of the book. Genesis tells us the beginning of everything except God. It tells only of beginnings; there is no finality here. Upon the truths of Genesis all the future revelation of God to people is built up.

In Genesis 1 we have the account of creation in outline, and in chapter 2 part of the same is described in detail. The detail concerns the creation of humankind, for the Bible is the history of the redemption of all people.

In this beginning of the story of God's interaction with people, Adam and Eve were created in a state of innocence but with the power of choice. They were tested under the most favorable circumstances. They were endowed with clear minds and pure hearts, with the ability to do right. God gave them His own presence and fellowship (see Genesis 3:8).

Satan, the author of sin, acting as a serpent, tempted Adam and Eve to doubt God's Word. They yielded to the temptation and failed the test. Here sin entered the world. The results of Adam's and Eve's sin are enumerated in Genesis 3. They were separated from God, the ground was cursed and sorrow filled their hearts. In mercy, God promised One who would redeem us from sin (see Genesis 3:15). The seed of the woman (the virgin-born Jesus) would come to destroy the works of the devil (see 1 John 3:8).

God created us in His own image to have fellowship with Himself. We cut ourselves off from God by sin. It is only when sin is removed that we can have fellowship again. This is why Jesus Christ came to this earth: He "bore our sins in his body on the tree" (1 Peter 2:24). This promise of redemption is seen throughout God's Word—and it's a promise for each person to claim.

Adapted from *What the Bible Is All About* by Henrietta C. Mears.

Lesson 3 • Genesis 2:4—3

Big Picture Story Center

Teacher Materials
Bible Time Line, drawing materials/equipment.

Student Materials
Drawing materials.

Tell the Story
Move the *Bible Time Line* frame to highlight Picture 3. As you tell each part of the story, draw each sketch. Students copy your sketches.

What's your favorite animal God made? What was the last thing God made? Today we're going to create some stick people on paper to tell about what happened in the garden of Eden.

1. Of everything God made, He made people last. The Bible says God took dirt from the ground and formed a body from the dirt. Then, God breathed His breath into the body. And that body became a LIVING PERSON!

1. Draw stick figure. Add face.

2. God named that person Adam. He put Adam in a special garden called the Garden of Eden. And He gave Adam important work to do! Adam took care of the garden and named all the animals. That must have been fun! But God knew it wasn't good for Adam to be alone. So God made another person! When Adam saw her he said, "At last! She is someone like me! I'll call her woman."

2. Draw second stick figure; add small circles for hair.

3. Adam and Eve must have loved living in the garden. They talked with God every evening. And there was lots to eat! In fact, Adam and Eve could eat from any plant or tree in the garden except ONE. God told Adam, "Do not eat from the tree of the knowledge of good and evil. You'll die if you do!" God loved Adam and Eve and wanted them to live and be happy. So He made this one rule for them to obey.

3. Flowers and tree from "3"s.

48

4. Adam and Eve obeyed this rule UNTIL the day a beautiful snake came along. The snake was really God's enemy, Satan, in disguise. Satan wanted to destroy God's plan and the people God loved so much. The snake slyly asked Eve if God REALLY had said they couldn't eat from that one tree. The snake told Eve that it would be good to try that fruit. He said eating that fruit wouldn't make them die. It would make them like God!

4. Snake from 2 "S"s. Fruit from letter "O."

5. Eve saw the beautiful fruit; it looked DELICIOUS! She reached. She picked the fruit off the tree and took a bite. At that moment, everything changed. A person had disobeyed God's one rule. That's called sin. Eve gave the fruit to Adam and he ate some, too. Now they had BOTH disobeyed!

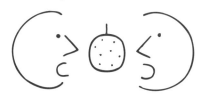

5. On either side of fruit, draw faces from "C"s and upside down "7"s.

6. When they heard God coming, Adam and Eve HID from God, who loved them and had made them to share His wonderful creation! God called to them. Finally Adam answered and told God that he was afraid. God asked if Adam had broken His one rule. Adam blamed Eve. He said it was Eve's fault. Then Eve blamed the snake.

   God was very sad. Adam and Eve were certainly sad. Adam and Eve had to leave the beautiful garden. Now thorns and weeds would grow. There would be pain and death.

6. Draw 2 sad faces.

7. But God still loved Adam and Eve! God made a VERY important promise. He promised to send a special person who would put an end to all the wrong things that Satan had brought into the world. And God's promise came true many, many years later. The person He sent was JESUS!

7. Write "PROMISE." Add "JESUS."

PROMISE JESUS

Get the Big Picture

Who convinced Eve to disobey? (Satan.) **What happened as a result? What did God promise He would do to stop sin from ruining the world He had made?** (Send Jesus—the only One who could stop Satan.)

   Even though Adam and Eve had disobeyed God, God still loved them. And even when we do wrong, it's good to know that God's love is bigger than ANY sin!

Bible Verse Object Talk: Take It Away

Big Picture Verse

"Put your hope in the Lord, for with the Lord is unfailing love and with him is full redemption." Psalm 130:7

Teacher Materials

Bible with bookmark at Psalm 130:7, clear glass, measuring cup, water, blue food coloring, bleach, spoon; optional—markers, white construction paper.

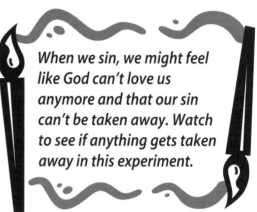

When we sin, we might feel like God can't love us anymore and that our sin can't be taken away. Watch to see if anything gets taken away in this experiment.

Present the Object Talk

1. Place one cup water in a clear glass. Add three drops of blue food coloring. **How can we take the color out of the water? Can we pour it out?** Volunteers tell ideas.

2. Add one-half cup of bleach. Stir and let stand. The water will become clear. Note: Keep bleach away from students. (Optional: Draw on white construction paper with markers. Use spoon to add several drops of bleach onto the drawings. Drawings will disappear.)

Conclude

This experiment is an example of a way color can be taken away even when it seems impossible. It reminds me that our sin can be taken away, too. God's love and forgiveness are bigger than our sin. When we ask His forgiveness, He takes away our sin.

Listen for the last word in this verse: it means something wonderful God does for us. Read Psalm 130:7 aloud. **When something is redeemed, it becomes useful or valuable. This verse reminds us that because God's love for us never ends, we can depend on Him to always treat us as valuable.** Thank God for His unfailing love.

Discussion Questions

1. How does doing wrong often make us feel?

2. Who in your family has forgiven you? How did you feel?

3. When are times kids need to remember God's forgiveness?

4. Why can we depend on God to forgive us? (Because God loves us.)

Active Game Center: String Hunt

Materials

String (or yarn), scissors, stopwatch or watch with second hand.

Prepare the Game

Cut string into varying lengths (at least two lengths for each student). Hide string in classroom or outdoor area.

Let's play a game to remind us of God's great love for us. In our game, the string we collect will get bigger and bigger to remind us that God's love is bigger than all the wrong things we have done.

Lead the Game

1. Group students in two or more teams of four or five students each.

2. At your signal, students look for and collect string, trying to find as many pieces as they can in 30 seconds.

3. After time is called, team members lay out end-to-end the pieces of string they have collected. Team who collected the longest length wins. Play additional rounds of this game as time permits. (Volunteers take turns collecting and hiding string.)

4. At the end of the game time, teams use string to spell out the words "God's Love."

Options

1. If space is limited, students roll string into balls to see who collected the most string.
2. Depending on the number of students in your class, vary the amount of time students have in which to collect string.
3. To help students become better acquainted, form new teams for each round of the game.

Discussion Questions

1. What are some big things that might remind you of how big God's love is? (The ocean. A tall redwood tree. A huge waterfall. The sky.)

2. How does God's love get rid of our sin? (Because God loves us, God forgives us. Jesus loves us so much He took the punishment we deserve.)

3. What are some ways Jesus showed God's love in the Bible? (He made sick people well. He taught others about God. He died on the cross.)

 **Lesson 3**

Art Center: Great Heart

Student Materials

6-foot (1.8-m) square of butcher paper, crayons, masking tape, variety of 3-D collage materials (Styrofoam, small boxes, different colors and textures of paper to crumple into shapes or balls, leaves, colored papers, ribbon, yarn, feathers, crepe paper, raffia), glue sticks.

God's love is bigger than our sin. Help decorate a great big heart to remind us of God's enormous love for us.

Prepare the Activity

Draw a heart as large as possible on the paper. Write the words "God's Love" in large letters in the middle of the heart. Tape butcher paper in place on the floor.

Lead the Activity

Students select collage materials and glue them onto the heart, trying to cover the entire heart, except for the letters. As students work on the collage, suggest they experiment with the different materials you have provided.

Options

1. Students crumple neon-colored paper and glue it onto the letters of the phrase "God's Love."

2. Cut smaller hearts from construction paper so that students may make individual collages.

3. Play "Promises" from *God's Big Picture* cassette/CD while students complete activity.

Discussion Questions

1. Which collage materials do you like best?

2. How would you describe God's love? Because of His love, what does God promise to do? (To hear our prayers. To help us do what's right.)

3. What are some other ways God has shown His love for you and your family? our church family?

Lesson 3

Worship Center

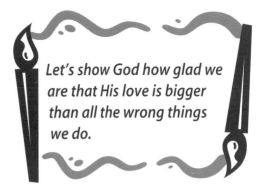

Let's show God how glad we are that His love is bigger than all the wrong things we do.

Big Picture Verse

"Put your hope in the Lord, for with the Lord is unfailing love and with him is full redemption." Psalm 130:7

Teacher Materials

Bible, *God's Big Picture* cassette/CD or music video and player, "Promises" word chart (p. 475 in this book), large sheet of paper on which you have printed Psalm 130:7, masking tape.

Sing to God

Play "Promises," encouraging students to sing along with the music and do the actions shown on the word chart or music video. **What promise did God make to Adam and Eve? Why?**

Hear and Say God's Word

Display paper on which you have printed Psalm 130:7. Point out the three times in which the verse says or refers to the Lord. Lead students in saying verse, standing up and then sitting back down each time they say "Lord" or "him." Repeat several times. **How does God show us that His love is unfailing?** (He always forgives us, no matter how many wrong things we do. He loves all people, no matter what they are like.)

Pray to God

Play the first verse of "Promises" again. **God showed His love to Adam and Eve in the garden and then to us by sending Jesus as our Savior.** Lead students in silently thanking Jesus that He came to forgive us for the wrong things we do. Talk with students about becoming Christians, following the guidelines in the "Leading a Child to Christ" article on p. 30.

Options

1. Divide the group in half. As everyone repeats the verse together, one half stands up on the first "Lord," the other half stands on the second "Lord," and the whole group stands on "him."
2. Have an older student find the definition of "redemption" in a Bible dictionary and read it to the younger students during the verse activity.

Bible Story Coloring Center

Materials
Crayons or markers, a copy of "Adam and Eve disobey God" picture and story (pp. 11-12 from *Bible Story Coloring Pages*) for each student.

Lead the Activity
Students color page 11; read or tell the story on page 12. **How did God show that He loved Adam and Eve? What rule did God want them to obey?**

Option
After pages are completed, each student cuts his or her picture into four pieces. Several students mix their pieces together and then see how fast they can find their own pieces and put pages back together again.

Skit Center

Materials
A copy of "The Savior" skit (pp. 9-12 from *The Big Book of Bible Skits*) for each student; optional—highlighter pen.

Lead the Activity
Students form pairs and read the skit, which tells about God's promise to send a Savior in the story of Adam and Eve and in the prophecies of Isaiah. (Optional: Students highlight their parts.) Ask the discussion questions on page 9.

Bible Skills Center

Materials
Materials needed for "Who's Got the Beans?" and/or "Turn and Match" (p. 41 and/or p. 131 from *The Big Book of Bible Skills*).

Lead the Activity
Students complete activities as directed in *The Big Book of Bible Skills*.

Safe in the Ark

Big Picture Verse

"If you love me, you will obey what I command."
John 14:15

THE BIG PICTURE

People who love God obey Him.

Scripture Background
Genesis 6:9—9:19

The account of the flood in the Bible is very plain and straightforward. The story is not only told because it is startling or interesting but also because it is an incident in the history of redemption.

After the fall God gave the world a new beginning, but soon wickedness increased until there remained but one righteous man, Noah. Adam and Eve had yielded to an outward temptation, but now people had yielded to temptation which was within. "The Lord saw how great man's wickedness on the earth had become, and that every inclination of the thoughts of his heart was only evil all the time" (Genesis 6:5). Evil threatened to destroy everything that was good. God had been long-suffering in His patience with people. Noah had warned his peers for 120 years while he was building the ark, but God's mercies were refused and so the wicked people had to perish. God was going to separate the righteous from the wicked. He was taking the first step toward a chosen nation.

Who was Noah? He was not a sailor or a carpenter but a farmer, a man of the soil (see Genesis 9:20). God did not choose him for his boat-building skills! But in the New Testament Peter tells us this farmer was also a preacher of righteousness (see 2 Peter 2:5). And Genesis 6:9 says that he was blameless and that he walked with God. God used Noah for this very reason: he was obedient. Noah never tried to second-guess God's instructions; he simply did everything just as God commanded as a reflection of his love and faith in the Lord of life.

Adapted from *What the Bible Is All About* by Henrietta C. Mears.

Big Picture Story Center

Teacher Materials
Bible Time Line, drawing materials/equipment.

Student Materials
Drawing materials.

Tell the Story
Move the *Bible Time Line* frame to highlight Picture 4. As you tell each part of the story, draw each sketch. Students copy your sketches.

How do you feel when someone is mean to you? Today we're going to tell about one man who was different from his mean neighbors. He obeyed God.

1. After God made the world, more and more people were born. Now there were more people than anyone could count! But people had forgotten that God had made them. They had forgotten all about obeying Him. Instead, they were disobeying God—lying, hurting and even killing each other! They didn't care what God wanted. That made God very sad.

1. Use "V"s and "C"s to draw mean faces.

2. But in all that meanness and disobeying, one person DID love and obey God. His name was Noah. When God decided to put a stop to the terrible things going on in the world, He decided to do it with a flood. God told Noah, "I'm going to send a lot of rain. It will rain until the whole earth is covered with water. But I want you to build a big boat, an ark. You, your family and all the creatures I have made will be safe there."

2. Draw as many raindrops as you can.

3. God told Noah EXACTLY how to build the ark, what kind of wood to use and how big to make it. It was going to be BIG—as long as one and a half football fields! Noah obeyed. He chopped down trees; he sawed and nailed. It was a BIG JOB! Noah and his family worked many, many YEARS to build the ark. After it was built, Noah painted it inside and out with tar to keep it from leaking.

3. Ark from sideways "D." Add roof.

4. One day God said, "Noah, take your family into the ark. And take EVERY kind of animal and bird with you—two of some and seven of others." Again, Noah obeyed! He loaded food for his family and for ALL those animals into the ark. Then God sent animals to Noah. Animals of every kind and size came to the ark! Rabbits and hippos, lions and mice, sparrows and eagles—all these and more found places in the ark. Finally Noah and his family got inside the huge boat, too. As Noah and his family got settled, they began to hear something—plink, plink, plink! Rain was coming down, faster and harder! Then God shut the door of the ark.

4. Draw two rabbits from long and round "O"s.

5. The rain fell harder. Little puddles got larger. Soon, the ground was covered with water! The ark began to FLOAT! For 40 days and 40 nights the rain fell hard and fast. OUT-SIDE, the water got DEEPER and DEEPER until even the tallest mountain on earth was COVERED. But inside the ark, Noah and his family and all the animals were snug and dry.

5. "U"s for water. Add rain clouds from "3"s, "Z"s for lightning.

6. One day, it got very quiet. The rain had stopped! But it was a LONG time before the water dried up—almost a YEAR. Then one day God told Noah to bring his family and all those animals and birds out of the ark! What an exciting day THAT must have been! At last, Noah and his family and ALL those creatures could run and stretch their legs and leap in the sunshine!

6. Add sun in front of clouds.

7. The first thing Noah did was thank God for keeping him and his family safe. God was glad that Noah remembered to thank Him. God promised, "I will NEVER again destroy the whole earth with a flood." Then to remind everyone of His promise, God put a beautiful rainbow in the sky. Even today, whenever we see a rainbow, we remember that God prom-ised NEVER again to cover the whole earth with water.

7. Draw "C"s for rainbow (7 "C"s for full rainbow). Add colors.

Get the Big Picture

Who showed love for God by obeying Him? (Noah.) **What are some ways Noah obeyed God?** (Built ark. Took care of animals. Thanked God.) **What did God do to show His promise?** (Made a rainbow.)

   We may find it hard to obey God. But He will help us obey Him if we ask Him. He loves us and wants us to show we love Him by obeying Him!

Bible Verse Object Talk: Rainbow Fun

Big Picture Verse

"If you love me, you will obey what I command."
John 14:15

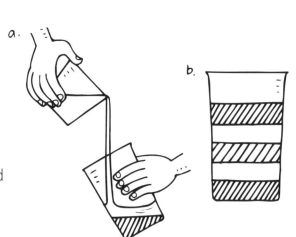

God's instructions help us know the best way to live. Watch what happens when I follow these instructions.

Teacher Materials

Bible with bookmark at John 14:15, six clear glasses, measuring cup, light corn syrup, glycerin, water, cooking oil, rubbing alcohol, blue, green, yellow and red food coloring, four spoons.

Present the Object Talk

Read directions aloud as you complete each step.

1. Set out the glasses and pour 1/2 cup of each liquid into separate glasses in the following order: light corn syrup, glycerin, water, cooking oil, rubbing alcohol.

2. Using separate spoons, stir several drops of food coloring into the liquids: red into light corn syrup, yellow into glycerine, green into water, none into cooking oil, blue into alcohol.

3. Pour about 1 inch (2.5 cm) of each liquid into the remaining glass as follows: *(a)* pour red into the center of the glass without letting liquid hit the side; *(b)* tilt the glass and pour yellow into point where red meets the side of the glass (see sketch a); *(c)* pour green liquid down the side of the tilted glass, then clear, then blue. Each liquid should float on the top of the previous liquid. Hold the glass upright to see rainbow (see sketch b).

Conclude

Following these directions helped me make a rainbow. Following God's directions or commands is even better! They help us know the best way to live. Read John 14:15 aloud. **Because I love God, I want to obey Him.** Ask God's help in obeying.

Discussion Questions

1. What would have happened if I hadn't followed the directions?

2. Being honest is a command God wants us to obey. What are some of the results of being honest? (Parents and friends trust you and like to be with you. Teachers know they can depend on you.)

3. What are some ways you can show love for God and obey His commands? (Be honest. Care about the needs of others.)

 **Lesson 4**

Active Game Center: Two-by-Two Relay

Materials
Index cards, marker.

Lead the Game

1. **What kinds of animals came on the ark with Noah?** Write each animal students suggest on a separate index card. (You may also prepare cards ahead of time.) Mix order of cards and place in a stack.

2. **Many of the animals who came onto the ark came in pairs.** Students line up in pairs.

> Noah showed his love for God by obeying Him and building the ark. The animals even obeyed by getting on board! Let's play a game about the animals getting on board the ark.

(If you have an uneven number of students, form one or more trios.) Each pair of students takes a card and quickly decides an action to imitate the animal on their card (arms down in front of face like the trunk of an elephant, hopping for a rabbit or frog, etc.). At your

signal, each pair links arms and moves across the playing area in the manner chosen. When they get to the other side of the playing area, pair stands up and makes the noise of their animal and then returns to line in the same manner.

3. If you have time, shuffle the cards and play again so that each student gets a chance to imitate more than one kind of animal. Students change partners for each round of the game.

Discussion Questions

1. *What animal would you most like to be? Why?*

2. *What animal did you have the most fun acting like?*

3. *Noah obeyed God by building an ark. What are some ways a kid your age can obey God?* (Help people in need. Speak kind words to stop an argument.)

Lesson 4

Art Center: Rainbow Art

Student Materials
Four small containers, water, measuring cup, four colors of food coloring, one or more white paper napkins or white coffee filters for each student, newspaper.

Prepare the Activity
Put one-half cup of water into each container. Put drops of food coloring into each container until colors are dark. Cover tables with newspaper.

People who love God obey Him. Because Noah loved and obeyed God, God saved the lives of Noah and his family. After Noah left the ark, God sent a beautiful rainbow as a promise of His love. Today we'll experiment with the colors of a rainbow.

Lead the Activity
1. Students fold napkins or coffee filters in half and then in half again.

2. Each student takes a turn to dip a corner or section of napkin or coffee filter into a container of food coloring, holding napkin or filter in container for several seconds (see sketch). (Note: If students hold napkins or filters in food coloring too long, the paper will become too saturated.) Students repeat process several more times, allowing the colors to mix.

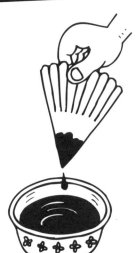

3. Students carefully open the napkins or filters and set on newspaper to dry. Suggest students take home their rainbow art creations and hang them in windows.

Options
1. Instead of dipping napkins or filters into food coloring, students use eyedroppers to drop color onto unfolded napkins or filters.

2. Plain white paper towels may be used instead of napkins or filters.

3. Display rainbow art creations in classroom.

Discussion Questions
1. What animals walk on two feet? on four feet? on no feet?

2. Which animals have hooves? toes? tails? no tails?

3. How much bigger do you think an elephant's footprint is than a mouse's?

4. What do you think might happen if an elephant and a mouse had to stay in the same stall?

 **Lesson 4**

Worship Center

Big Picture Verse

"If you love me, you will obey what I command."
John 14:15

> We show God we love Him when we obey Him. The Bible tells us to praise and thank God. Let's obey God by praising Him for who He is.

Teacher Materials

Bible, *God's Big Picture* cassette/CD or music video and player, "Promises" word chart (p. 475 in this book), large sheet of paper on which you have printed John 14:15, masking tape.

Sing to God

Play "Promises," encouraging students to sing along with the music and do the actions shown on the word chart or music video. **How can knowing God keeps His promises help us obey Him?** (He promises to always be with us and help us.)

Hear and Say God's Word

Display paper on which you have printed John 14:15. Have volunteer read verse aloud. **What are some ways we can obey God to show we love Him?** (Tell the truth. Be patient when waiting a turn.) Students stand or sit in a circle. Students repeat words of John 14:15 in clockwise order around the circle. When you clap hands, students repeat words in counterclockwise order. Continue, with students reversing the order in which they are repeating the verse each time you clap hands.

Pray to God

What are some times when it is hard to obey God? Pray, telling God we love Him and asking for His help to obey Him in the times students named.

Options

1. Before singing "Promises," group students according to the dominant color of clothing that each one is wearing. Then guide groups to stand in an order and shape similar to a rainbow while they sing the song.

2. Invite an older student to lead the prayer.

3. Record students' prayer requests and items for which they wish to thank God in a prayer journal to which you can refer each week.

 Lesson 4

Bible Story Coloring Center  FOR YOUNGER CHILDREN

Materials

Crayons or markers, a copy of "Noah builds an ark" picture and story (pp. 13-14 from from *Bible Story Coloring Pages*) for each student.

Lead the Activity

Students color page 13; read or tell the story on page 14. **Why were Noah and his family thankful? After thanking God for saving them, what do you think Noah and his family did?**

Option

Copy pages 17 and 18 for each student. Cut 1/2-inch (1.25-cm) red, yellow, orange, green, blue and purple paper squares. Students glue squares on rainbow on page 17. Read aloud the story on page 18.

Skit Center FOR OLDER CHILDREN

Materials

A copy of "Show Me" skit (pp. 19-22 from *The Big Book of Bible Skits)* for each student; optional—highlighter pens.

Lead the Activity

Four volunteers read Scene One of the skit, which tells the story of Noah's faith in God and his willingness to obey God. (Optional: Students highlight their parts. If time permits, students may also read Scene Two.) Ask the discussion questions on page 19.

Bible Skills Center FOR OLDER CHILDREN

Materials

Materials needed for "Bible Book Mix-Up" and/or "Around the Verse" (p. 37 and/or p. 63 from *The Big Book of Bible Skills)*.

Lead the Activity

Students complete activities as directed in *The Big Book of Bible Skills.*

Abraham Answers God's Call

Big Picture Verse

"For great is his love toward us, and the faithfulness of the Lord endures forever." Psalm 117:2

THE BIG PICTURE

God keeps His promises to show His faithfulness.

Scripture Background
Genesis 12:1-5; 15:1-7; 18:1-19; 21:1-7

The period of the patriarchs is the groundwork and basis of all history. It covers the time from Adam to Moses. As a result of the failures on the part of people during these early years, the period of the patriarchs begins with God calling out an individual. He chose a people to be His own and called a man, Abram, who was to become the father of the Hebrew nation. We enter into this period in Genesis 12.

In spite of the wickedness of the human heart seen in the early chapters of Genesis, God wanted to show His grace. He wanted a chosen people (1) to whom He might entrust the Holy Scriptures, (2) to be His witness to the other nations and (3) through whom the promised Messiah could come. Therefore, God called Abram to leave his home in idolatrous Ur of the Chaldeans to go to an unknown land where God would make him the father of a mighty nation.

Abram, later called Abraham, was willing to move according to God's desires because God's promises stood before Abraham as an accomplished fact. Abraham's faith in God was rooted in his belief that God would keep His promises. Wherever Abraham went, he erected an altar to God. God signally honored him by revealing Himself to him. Abraham was called a "friend of God" (see James 2:23). God made a covenant with him that he should be the father of a great nation and that through him the nations of the earth would be blessed. His family became God's special charge; God dealt with them as with no other people. Through Abraham and his descendants, the promises of God were passed down to all generations.

Adapted from *What the Bible Is All About* by Henrietta C. Mears.

Big Picture Story Center

Teacher Materials
Bible Time Line, drawing materials/equipment.

Student Materials
Drawing materials.

Tell the Story
Move the *Bible Time Line* frame to highlight Picture 5. As you tell each part of the story, draw each sketch. Students copy your sketches.

Where has someone promised to take you?
Today we're going to use shapes and letters to tell about people who trusted God's promises.

1. In the city of Ur lived a man named Abraham. Ur was a big city, with trees and fountains and buildings. Abraham and his wife, Sarah, had always lived there. But one day, God told Abraham, "I want you to leave Ur. I will show you a new land."

1. Draw fountain from 3 half circles. Add water.

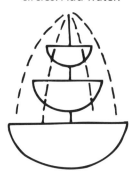

2. Abraham and Sarah and all their helpers packed pots and pans, clothes and tents, food and water, and put their bundles on camels and donkeys. Abraham, Sarah and some of their family began to walk. Traveling was hot, hard work! There were no cars or air conditioning. When they stopped, they put up tents, built a fire, cooked dinner and slept rolled up in blankets. When it was time to move on, they packed up everything, got fresh water and walked some more.

2. Tents from upside-down "V"s and trapezoids.

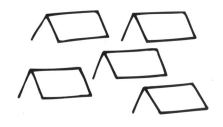

3. They must have often wondered where they were going—and if they would ever get to the land God had promised! But Abraham believed God. And one day, they came to a place of hills and valleys covered with good grass. It was beautiful! "This is the land I promised to you," God told Abraham. The land was called Canaan. God had kept His promise!

3. Small lines for grass.

4. Now God had also promised that Abraham would have many grandchildren and great-grandchildren. But Abraham and Sarah didn't have ANY children yet! And they were old! But God told Abraham again, "You will have a son. And from him there will come more grandchildren than you can imagine! Look at the stars. Can you count them? You'll have more grandchildren than there are stars in the sky!" And Abraham believed God.

4. Stars from triangles. Make as many as you can.

5. More years went by. Abraham and Sarah grew even older. But God told Abraham His promise again. And again, Abraham believed God, even though it made him laugh! Abraham wondered, *How can we have a son? I am 100 years old and Sarah is 90!*

5. Faces from "100" and "90," adding noses and mouths from "C"s.

6. Even more time went by and still no baby. But one day, three VERY important visitors came to Abraham's tent. In fact, ONE of the visitors was really God, although He looked like a man! As Abraham and the visitors talked, Sarah listened at the tent door. She heard God say that she would soon have a son! Sarah laughed! She thought, *I'm so OLD! Will I really have a child?* But God said, "NOTHING is too hard for the Lord! Sarah really will have a son!"

6. Laughing face.

7. At the EXACT time God had promised, Abraham and Sarah DID have a baby boy! They named him Isaac, which means "laughter!" Sarah and Abraham remembered God's promise every time they called Isaac's name!

7. Baby from oval and circle. Add "C"s for face.

Get the Big Picture

How did Abraham and Sarah show their trust in God? (Moved to a new land. Believed God would give them a child.) **What did Abraham and Sarah learn about God?** (He keeps promises. He is faithful.)

Sometimes it is hard to believe God's promises. But God shows us that even if we have to wait, He never forgets us. And He never, EVER forgets to keep His promises! That's why the Bible says God is faithful. He always keeps His promises. The Bible is filled with wonderful promises God makes to us.

Bible Verse Object Talk: Never-Ending Love

Big Picture Verse

"For great is his love toward us, and the faithfulness of the Lord endures forever." Psalm 117:2

Teacher Materials

Bible with Psalm 117:2 marked with a bookmark.

Student Materials

Two 12x2-inch (30x5-cm) strips of paper, scissors, tape.

God's love and His faithfulness last forever. Something that lasts forever has no end. Let's make something that doesn't have an end or a beginning—and gets bigger and bigger.

Present the Object Talk

1. Give each student two strips of paper. **Where's the beginning of these strips? the end?**

2. Student tapes strips together at one end to make one long strip. Student flips one end of the strip over (see sketch a) and tapes it to the other end, so paper loop has a twist. Make sure joined ends are completely covered with tape.

3. Student folds strip and cuts down the middle of the loop (see sketch b). (Loop will expand to double size.) Students cut down the middle of their loops at least one more time.

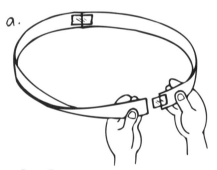

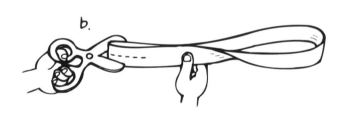

Conclude

Now our paper strips have become a big loop which has no beginning or end. What does Psalm 117:2 say lasts forever? Read Psalm 117:2 aloud. **"Faithfulness" means always keeping your promises and doing what you say you will do. God is faithful and His promises last forever.** Thank God for keeping His promises.

Discussion Questions

1. What are some things other than God's love and faithfulness that don't seem to have a beginning or end? (Sky. Ocean.)

2. What are some of God's promises to us? (Always hear our prayers. Always help us.)

3. When might someone your age need to remember one of these promises?

Active Game Center: Follow the Leader

Materials
None.

Lead the Game
Play one or both of these Follow-the-Leader games:

When we follow God, He will always keep His promises to us. We're going to play a game to try to follow each other.

Who's It
Students sit or stand in a circle. Choose one student as "It." "It" leaves the circle and covers eyes. Silently choose another player as the leader. The leader begins an action such as clapping hands, stamping feet, wiggling fingers, etc. Call "It" back to the circle while students are doing the action the leader has started. After ten seconds, the leader begins a new action. Students imitate the leader's new action while trying not to look at the leader. "It" tries to identify the leader. When the leader is correctly identified, he or she becomes "It" and a new leader is chosen. Repeat game as time permits.

Line Leaders
Students stand in a line, facing the person in front of them. The first student in line is the leader. The leader stays in one place and begins a motion (moves legs, arms, bends to the side, etc.). The second student follows the leader, the third student follows the second, the fourth student follows the third, etc. The effect will be a delayed movement like "the wave" at a sports event. Repeat several times with new leaders. If you have a large group, divide into two or more lines. The leader of one line begins a motion, immediately followed by the leader of the other line.

Discussion Questions

1. Was it easier to be the leader or the follower in these games? Why?

2. How can we show that we want to follow God? (Read God's Word. Tell others about Him. Show His love to others.)

3. What's something God has promised to do for His followers? (Hear prayers. Forgive sins. Give courage.)

 **Lesson 5**

Art Center: Starry Night

Student Materials

Black, dark blue or purple construction paper, scissors, glue; one or more of these materials—yellow, white and metallic crayons; metallic pens; glitter glue tubes; aluminum foil; foil wrapping paper; star stickers.

> *God promised Abraham he would have as many children and grandchildren as there are stars in the sky. We are going to make lots of stars to remind us that God always keeps His promises.*

Lead the Activity

Students use materials to make as many different kinds of stars as they can. Students may cut stars from construction paper and decorate them. Students may also cut stars from foil and glue them to paper. Challenge the students by making comments such as, **Let's see how much of this wall we can cover with star pictures. How many stars would we have to make to have more than we can count?**

Options

1. Tape the pictures to the underside of a table. Students climb under the table to look at their "starry night." You may want to hang a blanket over the table and give students flashlights with which to look at the stars.

2. Give students different colors of construction paper to cut out and decorate as stars. Students tape string to each star. Hang stars from the ceiling.

Discussion Questions

1. *What are some promises God has made?* (To hear and answer our prayers. To give us courage to do right. To help us know what to do when we need help.)

2. *How can we find out more about God's promises?* (Read the Bible. Listen to what other Christians say about God.)

3. *Why can we be confident that God will always keep His promises?* (God kept His promises to Bible people. We know that God doesn't lie.)

Lesson 5

Worship Center

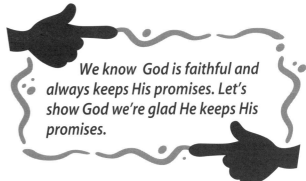

We know God is faithful and always keeps His promises. Let's show God we're glad He keeps His promises.

Big Picture Verse

"For great is his love toward us, and the faithfulness of the Lord endures forever." Psalm 117:2

Teacher Materials

Bible, *God's Big Picture* cassette/CD or music video and player, "Promises" word chart (p. 475 in this book), large sheet of paper on which you have printed Psalm 117:2, marker, masking tape.

Sing to God

Play "Promises," encouraging students to sing along with the music and do the actions shown on the word chart or music video. **When are some times you need to remember God is always with you?**

Hear and Say God's Word

Display paper on which you have printed Psalm 117:2. Have a volunteer read the verse aloud. Then mark lines on the paper to divide the verse into six phrases. Divide group into two teams. Lead one team in saying the verse one phrase at a time, stopping after each phrase to let the other team echo the phrase. Rotate which group leads and which group echoes. **What does it mean to be faithful?** (To always do what you say you are going to do.) **How does God show He is faithful?**

Pray to God

One way God shows He is faithful is by answering our prayers. List students' prayer requests on back of Psalm 117:2 paper. Close in prayer, praying for students' requests and thanking God for His love and His faithfulness that never ends.

Options

1. Videotape the students singing and doing the actions for "Promises."

2. During the Bible verse activity, discuss what it means to "endure forever." Ask students to name things they think last a long time. Explain that God's love and faithfulness lasts longer than anything we can imagine.

3. Invite students to read aloud these Bible verses which describe God's love: Psalm 103:11,12; Jeremiah 31:3; 1 John 3:16.

 Lesson 5

 Bible Story Coloring Center  FOR YOUNGER CHILDREN

Materials

Crayons or markers, a copy of "Isaac is born" picture and story (pp. 21-22 from *Bible Story Coloring Pages*) for each student.

Lead the Activity

Students color page 21; read or tell the story on page 22. **Who promised that Abraham and Sarah would have a baby? What do you think Abraham and Sarah did to take good care of their baby?**

Option

Each student begins coloring on his or her own page. After several minutes, each student signs name on page and trades page with another student. Repeat trading several times until all pages are completely colored.

 Skit Center FOR OLDER CHILDREN

Materials

A copy of "Brothers Under the Skin" skit (pp. 333-335 from *The Big Book of Bible Skits*) for each student; optional—highlighter pens.

Lead the Activity

Students form pairs and read the skit, which tells the story of two people who make a covenant, or promise, to each other. (Optional: Students highlight their parts.) **What did Toronto and Ranger promise each other? Are people always able to keep their promises to each other? Why or why not? Why can we depend on God to always keep His promises?)** Ask the discussion questions on page 333.

 Bible Skills Center FOR OLDER CHILDREN

Materials

Materials needed for "Book Traders" and/or "Amazing Ways" (p. 38 and/or p. 103 from *The Big Book of Bible Skills*).

Lead the Activity

Students complete activities as directed in *The Big Book of Bible Skills.*

Jacob Is Forgiven

Big Picture Verse

"Give thanks to the Lord, for he is good. His love endures forever." Psalm 136:1

THE BIG PICTURE

God doesn't give up on us.

Scripture Background
Genesis 25:19-34; 27—33

Jacob is one of the most interesting characters in the Bible. We see the worst side of him at the very start. He is a deceiver (his name means "he deceives") and a man who drove a hard, sharp bargain at the expense of his own brother.

In the story of the first recorded conflict between Jacob and Esau, Jacob took advantage of his brother's weakness in order to gratify his own covetousness. Esau did not offer to sell his birthright; he asked Jacob to give him something to eat. It was Jacob's opportunity to show kindness; instead, he used Esau's weakness for his advantage. Later, after Jacob defrauded his brother, one despicable thing led to another. To secure the blessing of his father, Isaac, Jacob lied to his father (with the help of his mother) and stole the blessing.

However, despite his many faults, God's love for Jacob continued through all the ups and down of his life. Jacob in his wanderings suffered for his sin and through chastening came out a great man. His name was changed to Israel, a prince with God (see Genesis 32:28), and this is the name by which God's chosen people were called—Israelites. Jacob's twelve sons became the heads of the twelve tribes of Israel.

Some wonder at the greatness of the blessings Jacob received. But Jacob's life is simply a clear reminder that every blessing—all we have—is the result of God's boundless grace! We have no merit but for the merit of the work of Christ on our behalf, for if God must wait for pure merit before He bestows His grace, not a drop of grace will ever descend to this earth. For as Paul says, "From him and through him and to him are all things. To him be the glory forever!" (Romans 11:36).

Adapted from *What the Bible Is All About* by Henrietta C. Mears.

Lesson 6 • Genesis 25:19-34; 27—33

Big Picture Story Center

Teacher Materials
Bible Time Line, drawing materials/equipment.

Student Materials
Drawing materials.

Tell the Story
Move the *Bible Time Line* frame to highlight Picture 6. As you tell each part of the story, draw each sketch. Students copy your sketches.

What are some words that have the letter O in them? Today we're going to use the letter O to tell about twins who were oh, so much trouble!

1. Abraham was a new grandfather! His son Isaac had married a woman named Rebekah. And she gave birth to TWINS! The oldest one was named Esau. The younger twin was named Jacob. But OH, were these twins different! Esau was hairy and strong. He loved to be outdoors and grew to be a hunter. Jacob was smooth-skinned and liked to work around the family tent.

2. One day after the boys were grown, Esau came in from a long day of hunting. He hadn't caught any food and he was VERY hungry. He could smell stew cooking. When he saw Jacob by the pot, he said, "Give me some stew!" Jacob slyly answered, "Sure! If you promise to give me your birthright."

   Esau's birthright meant he would inherit twice as much as Jacob because Esau was born first. But he didn't care about that birthright at all! He just wanted FOOD. (That word has two Os!) So Jacob gave him food and got Esau's birthright. OH-OH!

3. Later, Jacob tricked his father, Isaac, so he could get the special blessing that Isaac would normally have given to Esau. While Esau was gone, Jacob dressed up like Esau and made his father's favorite food. Because Isaac was now blind, Jacob was able to make him think he was Esau. Once Isaac's words of blessing were said, they couldn't be taken back! Esau was OH, SO ANGRY that he wanted to KILL Jacob! So Jacob ran away, afraid of what his brother might do to him.

1. Draw two babies from long and small "O"s. Add hair to one.

2. Bowl of stew from long "O" and "U"; add "S"s for steam.

3. Esau's angry face with 2 "V"s. Jacob's scared face from "O"s.

4. Jacob traveled and traveled. In one place, he lay his head on a rock and slept. And OH, what an amazing dream he dreamed! He saw a beautiful stairway that went up into heaven, with angels going up and down. And he heard God tell him, "I will bless you and help you. You will have many, many children and will inherit the land where you are. Your children will bless all the earth." Jacob woke up and called the place Bethel, or "house of God." He promised to honor God because of the promises God had made to him.

4. Jacob's face and body from long and round "O"s. Add pillow and facial features.

5. Jacob went to live with his uncle, far away. He became very wealthy! He got married and had children—oh, did he have a lot of children! He had 12 sons and only one daughter. He lived far from home for many years. But finally, God told Jacob it was time to go back. Jacob was still very afraid of Esau because Jacob remembered that Esau had wanted to kill him! But God promised to be with him. So Jacob and his family packed up and set out.

5. Draw 13 "0"s for children; add faces.

6. As Jacob and his family traveled, Jacob sent many presents on ahead of him for Esau—cattle and sheep and camels and goats. He kept his family far behind all of these gifts, in case Esau was still angry. At long last, he could see dust rising. Esau was coming—with 400 men! OH-OH! But God had told Jacob that He would be with him. So Jacob went on ahead. He bowed low to his brother. And Esau didn't KILL him—he KISSED him! The two brothers cried and Esau forgave Jacob for the mean tricks he had played.

6. Cow face from "U","O"s and "C"s.

Write "KILL"; change "L"s to read "KISS."

KILL

KISS

Get the Big Picture

Who was a cheater? (Jacob.) **Who didn't care about his birthright?** (Esau.) **How did Jacob's and Esau's feelings change during this story?**

When we do wrong, we sometimes think that God doesn't love us. We might think that God will give up on us. But God loves us even when we do wrong. He is always waiting for us to come to Him and ask His forgiveness. He never gives up on us!

Bible Verse Object Talk: Full of Beans

Big Picture Verse

"Give thanks to the Lord, for he is good. His love endures forever." Psalm 136:1

Teacher Materials

Bible with Psalm 136:1 marked with a bookmark, one bowl or bucket filled with several cups of beans (or dry cereal), one empty bowl or bucket, one or more tea-spoons; optional—snack.

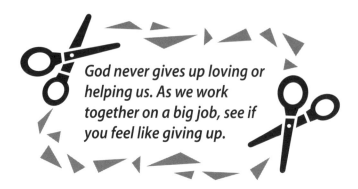

God never gives up loving or helping us. As we work together on a big job, see if you feel like giving up.

Present the Object Talk

1. Place the filled bowl on one side of the room. Place the empty bowl on the other side of the room. Students line up by the filled bowl.
2. **How long do you think it will take us to move all these beans to the empty bowl—one spoonful at a time?** Students take turns carrying beans to the empty bowl. (If you have a large group, more than one student at a time may participate.) Several times during the activity ask students how this job makes them feel and make comments such as, **Moving all these beans is a big job! A job like this might make you feel like quitting. If we don't give up on this job, it will get done!** Allow the activity to continue until all beans are moved or until students lose interest. (Optional: Give snack to students as a reward if they move all the beans.)

Conclude

One of the things I'm glad to know about God is that He doesn't give up loving us. **How does Psalm 136:1 describe God?** Read verse aloud. **God is good, and because He is so good He will never give up loving or helping us.** Thank God for His love and help.

Discussion Questions

1. What are some jobs you've felt like quitting?

2. Why do you think God doesn't quit loving us so much? (His love is so great!)

3. How has God shown love and help to you and your family?

4. When we've disobeyed God, how do we know God still loves us? (We can tell God we're sorry for our sin. He cares for us and promises to forgive us.)

Active Game Center: Ladder Leap

Materials
Masking tape, sheets of paper, marker.

Prepare the Game
1. Make a masking tape ladder on the floor, with at least ten rungs or spaces (make one ladder for every 10 students).
2. Print actions on separate sheets of paper—one for each ladder space: "touch your toes, " "turn around three times," "do five jumping jacks," "shake hands with everyone in line," etc. Place papers outside ladder outline next to each space.

God loves us even when we do wrong. Let's play a game to remind us that God doesn't give up on us!

Lead the Game
1. Students form a single line. First student hops on one foot through ladder spaces, while saying the sentence "My name is (P-E-T-E-R) and God does not give up on me!" and hopping one space for each word and for each letter of his or her name. Student hops up and down the ladder as many times as needed to complete sentence.
2. On the word "me," student stops and reads what the paper says in that space. Student leads all students in doing whatever action the paper says to do.
3. Repeat game with each student in line.

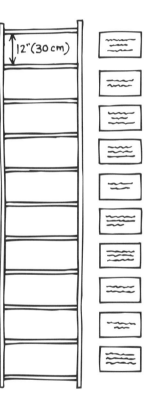

12"(30 cm)

Discussion Questions

1. When might a kid your age feel like God doesn't love him or her?

2. What should we do when we've disobeyed God? (Ask God for forgiveness and ask His help in doing right.)

3. How do we know that God will never give up loving us? (God promises to love us. God always keeps His promises.)

4. How would you describe God's love?

Lesson 6

Art Center: Fingerprint Drawing

Student Materials

Several stamp pads, white paper, tub with soapy water, paper towels, markers or pens.

Lead the Activity

1. Each student takes a turn using a stamp pad to make one or more finger or handprints in a random design on a sheet of paper. Students wash and dry hands.

2. Encourage students to compare their finger- or handprints. Then collect papers from students, mix them up and distribute to students. Make sure no student receives his or her own paper.

God loves us so much that He never gives up helping us or caring for us. One way God shows His love for us is by making each person unique. Our finger- and handprints are unique, too—they are different from each other. Let's make pictures with our prints.

3. Students draw pictures on papers using the finger- or handprints as the basis for their drawings. For example, a student may draw arms and legs to turn a fingerprint into a person (see sketch).

Option

Provide tempera paint and paint brushes. Students paint their fingers or hands and then make prints with them.

Discussion Questions

1. **What are some other ways God has made us different from others?**

2. **What are some other ways God shows His love for us?**

3. **When might a kid your age feel like God doesn't love him or her?**

4. **How do we know that God always loves us?** (He promises to love us. We read in the Bible how He has always shown love. We remember the ways in which He has already shown love for us.)

Worship Center

Big Picture Verse

"Give thanks to the Lord, for he is good. His love endures forever." Psalm 136:1

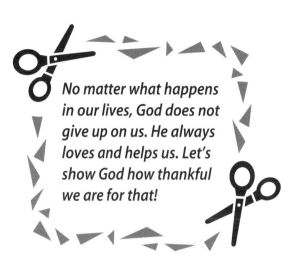

No matter what happens in our lives, God does not give up on us. He always loves and helps us. Let's show God how thankful we are for that!

Teacher Materials

Bible, *God's Big Picture* cassette/CD or music video and player, "God's Holy Book" word chart (p. 459 in this book), large sheet of paper on which you have printed Psalm 136:1, masking tape.

Sing to God

Play "God's Holy Book," encouraging students to sing along with the music and do the actions shown on the word chart or music video. **What good news do we read in the Bible?** (God's love for us. God's directions for the best way to live.)

Hear and Say God's Word

Display paper on which you have printed Psalm 136:1. Have a volunteer read the verse to the class. Lead students in saying the verse, clapping once for each word of the verse. (Variation: Students clap once for each syllable.) Repeat verse several times. If time permits, invite students to suggest other rhythmic motions (snap fingers, stamp feet, etc.). **How does God show His goodness to us?**

Pray to God

Lead students in praying aloud. Invite volunteers to tell in one word things for which they are thankful. End prayer time by thanking God that He never gives up loving us or helping us.

Options

1. Group students into two sections. Lead students in reading Psalm 136:1-9 together. Students in one section read the first phrase of each verse. Students in the other section read the second phrase.

2. If students give an offering during this worship time, explain that giving money to God is one way we can show our love and thanks to Him. Describe several ways in which your church family uses the offering to help others learn about God and His love.

 **Lesson 6**

Bible Story Coloring Center

Materials

Crayons or markers, a copy of "Jacob tricks Esau" picture and story (pp. 27-28 from *Bible Story Coloring Pages*) for each student.

Lead the Activity

Students color page 27; read or tell the story on page 28. **How did these two brothers look different from each other? In what ways can brothers and sisters show God's love to each other?**

Option

Make two copies each of pages 27, 29 and 31 for each group of six students. Students color pictures with crayons and then play a game like Concentration (place pictures facedown in mixed-up order; students turn over to find matches).

Skit Center

Materials

A copy of "There's Fruit and There's Fruit" skit (pp. 417-419 from *The Big Book of Bible Skits*) for each student; optional—highlighter pens.

Lead the Activity

Students form pairs and read the skit, which tells the story of how God causes the fruit of the Spirit to grow in the lives of His followers. (Optional: Students highlight their parts.) **What kind of "fruit" was Jacob growing in his life? What were the results? What can we do to grow the kind of fruit Galatians 5:22,23 talks about?** Ask the discussion questions on page 417.

Bible Skills Center

Materials

Materials needed for "Spelling Race" and/or "Who's Who?" (p. 40 and/or p. 101 from *The Big Book of Bible Skills*).

Lead the Activity

Students complete activities as directed in *The Big Book of Bible Skills*.

Joseph Faces Tough Times

THE BIG PICTURE

No matter how bad it looks, God is with us.

Big Picture Verse

"The Lord is with me; I will not be afraid. What can man do to me? The Lord is with me; he is my helper."
Psalm 118:6,7

Scripture Background
Genesis 37; 39—45

A very large portion of the story of Genesis is devoted to Joseph. Why? Because Joseph is the link between the family of Abraham and the nation of Israel. Up to the time of Joseph, Genesis is the record of the family of Abraham, Isaac and Jacob. After Joseph and in the opening pages of Exodus, we see that the nation of Israel has developed.

Born by the loved and favorite wife of Jacob, Joseph received an eager welcome and showed unusual promise. Joseph was endowed with very remarkable intelligence. God had a great work for Joseph to do. He knew that the Israelites needed the long discipline of residence in Egypt to prepare them to become the people of God. He knew that contact with a highly civilized people would give His people an education in arts and a discipline by law and government such as there was little prospect of their receiving in Canaan. So when Joseph's brothers banished him to life in Egypt, God overruled their crime for good. It is a comfort to know that God rules over all people and can use even the evil which is done in such a way as to thwart evil plans and bring forth good.

Most striking about Joseph is the evidence of his character. Though stripped of his coat, he had not been stripped of his character. His godly character was the spirit of his life. Joseph seemed to have filled his life with the knowledge of God and the practicing of His presence. Separation from his brothers compelled him to strike his roots deeper into the life of God. Here is inspiration and comfort for our dark hours. Joseph in the pit or as a slave could see no way in which captivity could work out well for him; and yet because of God's presence in his life, it was the road to the throne.

Adapted from *What the Bible Is All About* by Henrietta C. Mears.

Big Picture Story Center

Teacher Materials
Bible Time Line, drawing materials/equipment.

Student Materials
Drawing materials.

Tell the Story
Move the *Bible Time Line* frame to highlight Picture 7. As you tell each part of the story, draw each sketch. Students copy your sketches.

How would you feel if a brother, sister or friend got a better gift than you? Today we're going to use faces to tell our story about a boy who had a lot of trouble because his brothers were jealous.

1. Jacob had 12 sons and one daughter. Joseph was his eleventh son. And he was Jacob's FAVORITE son. This made his brothers jealous! Joseph also had dreams that he told to his family—dreams about his family bowing down to him. This made his brothers MORE jealous! And if that weren't enough, Jacob made a special coat for Joseph. That coat showed everyone that Jacob had chosen Joseph to be in charge of his brothers. WOW, were his brothers ever jealous!

1. Draw Joseph's face from "U"s. Add "Z"s for hair and "L"s for coat.

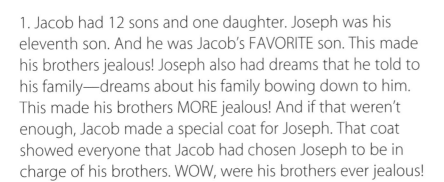

2. Joseph's brothers had gone off to find new pastures for their animals. One day, Jacob sent Joseph to check on them. When they saw Joseph coming (it was easy to spot his coat!), they decided to take his coat from him and throw him into a nearby pit.

2. Draw mean faces.

3. A traders' caravan was coming. So the brothers sold Joseph to the traders. His brothers told their father, Jacob, that Joseph was dead. But really, Joseph was now a slave in Egypt.

3. Draw a sad face.

4. But Joseph trusted God and did his best and became his Egyptian owner's most trusted servant. But the man's wife lied about Joseph. Joseph was put into JAIL! Once again, Joseph trusted God. He did his best and helped other prisoners. He even told two other prisoners what their dreams meant.

4. Write "Jail." Add face to "a," bars from other letters.

5. Some time later, Pharaoh, the ruler of all Egypt, had a dream. No one could tell him what it meant! But one of the men Joseph had helped in jail told Pharaoh about Joseph. Soon Joseph was in front of Pharaoh! He told Pharaoh that his dream meant there was going to be a famine. There wouldn't be any rain or much food.

So Pharaoh made Joseph second ruler in Egypt! Joseph had granaries built to store food to eat during the famine. He was in charge of everybody except Pharaoh!

5. Pharaoh from 2 "F"s, "V"s, and sideways "D"s.

6. But there was also a famine back where Jacob and all of Joseph's brothers lived. Soon the brothers came to Egypt and bowed low before Joseph. They begged him to sell them food. Joseph didn't tell them who he was just yet. But he gave them lots of grain and sent them home. He also kept one brother with him, just to be sure they would come back!

6. Bowing man: sideways "L" and 3 "C"s; "7" for nose.

7. Joseph's brothers did come back. And finally, he told them who he was! His brothers were afraid he would punish them all, but Joseph told them that even though they had meant to hurt him, God had used it for good! Now Joseph forgave his brothers and invited them all to come and live in Egypt.

7. Draw happy face.

Get the Big Picture

Who had the most trouble in this story? (Joseph.) **Why were his brothers mean to him?** (They were jealous.) **How did God turn the brothers' mean actions into something good?** (Joseph was in Egypt, so they could get food and move there.)

When things are hard for us, it's easy to forget that God is with us. But He never forgets where we are or what we need. Even in the worst times, He loves us and will help us!

Bible Verse Object Talk: Mirror Talk

Big Picture Verse

"The Lord is with me; I will not be afraid. What can man do to me? The Lord is with me; he is my helper." Psalm 118:6,7

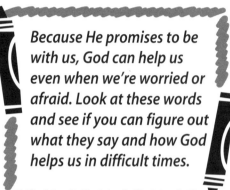

Because He promises to be with us, God can help us even when we're worried or afraid. Look at these words and see if you can figure out what they say and how God helps us in difficult times.

Teacher Materials

Bible with bookmark at Psalm 118:6,7, one or more hand mirrors, paper on which you have printed the sentence "The Lord is with me" backwards (see sketch).

Student Materials

Paper, pencils.

ᴙꙅᴙ. (The Lord is with me. — printed backwards)

Present the Object Talk

1. In class, show words you printed to one or more volunteers and ask them to try to read the words. **How hard is it to read these words? Why don't they make sense when you first look at them?**

2. Hold words up to a mirror and invite several volunteers to read the words. Students write sentence backwards and use mirrors to read words.

Conclude

Sometimes we might feel like all the wrong things are happening to us. We might feel like we can't understand why sad things happen to us or to others. But if we remember that God is with us, we can ask Him to help us know what to do. Read Psalm 118:6,7 aloud. Thank God for promising to be with us even in difficult times.

Discussion Questions

1. *When is a time kids your age might feel afraid or worried?*

2. *What are some of the ways God helps us?* (Gives us parents and friends. Promises to hear and answer our prayers.)

3. *What other promises does God give us?* (To forgive us when we do wrong. To give us courage.)

Active Game Center: Colorful Costumes

Materials
Colored newspaper comics, colored construction paper, colored tissue paper, rolls of tape.

Lead the Game
1. Divide class into groups of no more than four. Give each group a roll of tape and some comics, construction paper and tissue paper.

2. Each group chooses one student to dress in a costume that will look like a "coat" of paper. **Make your coats by taping together paper. Each coat must have a front, a back and two sleeves.** Groups dress volunteers. As time permits, groups make coats for other volunteers.

Options
1. If you have older students, students compete to see which group can make the best coat costume in five minutes.
2. Take instant photo of each student wearing a coat.
3. Invite students wearing coats to participate in a "fashion show" of coats; describe the coats as students walk in front of group, commenting on the ways coats have been constructed.

Getting a coat of many colors was the beginning of a long adventure for Joseph. There were times when Joseph had to go through hard times in that adventure, but God was still with him. We're going to have an adventure making our own colorful costumes that look like coats.

Discussion Questions

1. No matter what happened to him, Joseph remembered that God was with him. When are some times kids your age need to remember that God is with them?

2. When has God helped you or your family in the past?

3. When do you need to remember God's love and help?

Art Center: Fabric Collages

Student Materials

Construction paper, glue, scissors, variety of collage materials (fabric, thread, yarn, ribbon).

Lead the Activity

Students create fabric collages by choosing, cutting and gluing materials to construction paper. Encourage students to experiment by cutting fabric into a variety of shapes, by gluing yarn or thread designs onto fabric pieces and by braiding ribbon or yarn before adding to collage.

Joseph was given a colorful coat. Let's make a fabric collage to remind us of Joseph and his coat. No matter what happened to him, Joseph remembered that God was with him.

Options

1. Instead of using construction paper, cut vests from paper grocery bags. Students glue collage materials onto the vests.

2. Instead of fabric collages, students tear shapes from construction paper, newsprint, wrapping paper and magazine pictures. Students glue shapes as the "fabric" on their collages.

3. Older students may glue fabric to make scenes picturing places where God is with them.

4. On large sheet of butcher paper, draw a large coat outline. Students fill in coat outline with collage materials.

Discussion Questions

1. How many different colors are you using on your collage?

2. Joseph remembered that God is always with him. Where are some places you go? How does God help you at those places?

3. How might God help you when you have a problem or feel worried? (Help you know what to do. Remind you of an encouraging Bible verse. Provide someone to help you.)

Lesson 7

Worship Center

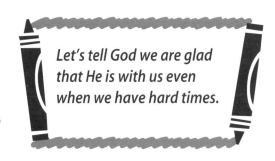

Let's tell God we are glad that He is with us even when we have hard times.

Big Picture Verse

"The Lord is with me; I will not be afraid. What can man do to me? The Lord is with me; he is my helper." Psalm 118:6,7

Teacher Materials

Bible, *God's Big Picture* cassette/CD or music video and player, "God Is So Strong" word chart (p. 455 in this book), large sheet of paper on which you have printed Psalm 118:6,7, masking tape.

Sing to God

Play "God Is So Strong," encouraging students to sing along with the music and do the actions shown on the word chart or music video. **What are some other words that describe God?** (Loving. Helper. Shepherd.)

Hear and Say God's Word

Display paper on which you have printed Psalm 118:6,7. Have a volunteer read the verse aloud. **What do these verses tell us about God? What do these verses say about us?** Divide students into several groups. Assign each group one of the phrases of the verses. Lead groups in saying phrases in order, standing up as they say the phrases.

Pray to God

What are some situations in which you or kids your age might be afraid? Volunteers answer. Lead students in prayer; volunteers thank God that He is with them and helps them through specific situations mentioned.

Options

1. During the Bible verse activity, ask older students to pantomime words of the verses.
2. Invite a guest to briefly tell students about a way in which God has helped him or her during a hard time.

 Lesson 7

Bible Story Coloring Center

 FOR YOUNGER CHILDREN

Materials
Crayons or markers, a copy of "Joseph's brothers sell him" picture and story (pp. 33-34 from *Bible Story Coloring Pages*) for each student.

Lead the Activity
Students color page 33; read or tell the story on page 34. **How do you think Joseph felt? How do you think his brothers felt? Even when his brothers sold him, why do you think Joseph trusted God?**

Option
Students glue completed pictures onto cardstock. Help students cut apart pictures into five or six puzzle pieces. Students trade puzzles and put puzzles together. Provide plastic bags in which to store puzzles.

Skit Center

 FOR OLDER CHILDREN

Materials
A copy of "Unfair" skit (pp. 420-421 from *The Big Book of Bible Skits*); optional—highlighter pens.

Lead the Activity
Students form pairs and read the skit, which tells the story of a gymnast who feels she has been treated unfairly. (Optional: Students highlight their parts.) **Who in today's Bible story might have felt like Julie? Why?** Ask the discussion questions on page 420.

Bible Skills Center

 FOR OLDER CHILDREN

Materials
Materials needed for "Promise Search" and/or "Tower to Remember" (p. 55 and/or p. 88 from *The Big Book of Bible Skills*).

Lead the Activity
Students complete activities as directed in *The Big Book of Bible Skills*.

Moses Leads the Escape

Big Picture Verse

"Teach me knowledge and good judgment, for I believe in your commands." Psalm 119:66

THE BIG PICTURE

God helps us do what's right, even when it's hard.

Scripture Background
Exodus 1—20

Exodus follows Genesis in just the same relation as the New Testament stands to the Old Testament. The story is just continuing. Genesis tells of human failure under every test and in every condition; Exodus is the thrilling epic of God hastening to the rescue of all people. It tells of the redeeming work of a sovereign God. The New Testament continues the story of redemption as it recounts the life of Christ.

Exodus is preeminently the book of redemption in the Old Testament. It begins in the darkness and gloom, yet it ends in glory; it commences by telling how God came down in grace to deliver an enslaved people, and it ends by declaring how God came down in glory to dwell in the midst of a redeemed people.

The book gives us the story of Moses, the great hero of God. D. L. Moody said that Moses spent "forty years thinking he was somebody, forty years learning he was nobody, forty years discovering what God can do with a nobody."

As this book opens, three and a half centuries have passed since the closing scene of Genesis. There were only 70 persons that went down into Egypt, but before they left Egypt the people had grown into a nation of 3 million. At this time, the wealth and great number of the children of Israel made them objects of suspicion in the eyes of the Egyptians. The pharaohs, wishing to break with them, reduced them to a slavery of the worst sort. This was hard for a people who had lived as free, with every favor upon them. They remembered the promises God had given to Abraham and his descendants, and it made this bondage doubly hard to understand. The story told in the book of Exodus, however, shows that God did not forget the promise which He made to Abraham. The obedience of His people was rewarded with freedom.

Adapted from *What the Bible Is All About* by Henrietta C. Mears.

Big Picture Story Center

Teacher Materials
Bible Time Line, drawing materials/equipment.

Student Materials
Drawing materials.

Tell the Story
Move the *Bible Time Line* frame to highlight Picture 8. As you tell each part of the story, draw each sketch. Students copy your sketches.

What is something hard you are learning to do? Today we're going to use letters and numbers to tell about someone who learned to do right even when it was hard.

1. Joseph's brothers had gone to live in Egypt. Their families had children. Those children had MORE children. The family grew to be thousands of people! Many years later, something awful happened to this family called the Israelites.

The king of the Egyptians was called Pharaoh. Egyptian pharaohs (or kings) had been kind to the Israelites because of the way Joseph had helped Egypt. But now there was a new pharaoh. He didn't care about what Joseph had done. What he DID care about was that there were so many of those Israelites! He was worried that the Israelites might take over his country.

2. So Pharaoh made the Israelites slaves. They were forced to build cities. They had to make bricks out of mud and straw. It was hard, hot work. The Israelites were sad and angry at the way they were being treated. Then life got even worse. Pharaoh made a law that all Israelite baby boys were to be killed. But one baby boy was saved—Moses. His mother floated him on the river in a basket. The daughter of Pharaoh found him and raised him.

3. When Moses grew up, he had to leave Egypt. For many years he lived in the desert tending sheep. One day he saw a bush that was on fire, but it didn't burn up. Moses came closer; then he heard a voice. It was GOD! God told Moses that He had heard the Israelites's cries for help. And Moses was going to be the one to lead the people out of Egypt, so they wouldn't be slaves anymore. Moses wasn't sure he

1. Draw Pharaoh from 2 "F"s, "V"s, sideways "D"s.

2. Baby in basket: long "O," "C" for bottom. Face: "M"s and "C"s.

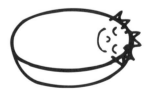

3. Bush: "3"s, "M"s. Add "I"s for trunk.

could do this job! But God told Moses He would be with Moses and that his brother, Aaron, would go with him to help him.

Moses and Aaron obeyed God and went to talk to Pharaoh. They told him God wanted the Israelites to leave Egypt. But Pharaoh kept saying no. So God sent the Egyptians 10 troubles—called plagues—to make Pharaoh obey God!

4. One trouble God sent was frogs! Frogs were everywhere! They were in beds and cooking pots and jumping out of trees onto people's heads. There were nine other awful things God sent, too. After all 10 plagues were sent, Pharaoh finally said the Israelites could leave. In fact, now he WANTED them out of his sight!

4. Frog: "P"s and "C"s for body. Add "I"s, "V"s and "W"s for legs and feet.

5. So Moses led the people away from Egypt, following God's instructions exactly. By the time the Israelites reached the Red Sea, however, Pharaoh had changed his mind. He sent an army to capture them!

God told Moses to hold up his walking stick. Moses obeyed and God sent a wind. The wind was so strong that it blew a path through the sea. Moses led the people to safety on the other side of the sea. When the Egyptian army tried to follow, the sea went back to its place! But the Israelites were safe!

5. Draw many "C"s. Tall "C"s for water. Add Moses' stick.

6. Moses led the people into the desert to a mountain called Mount Sinai. God gave Moses 10 special commands to teach all the people to follow. They are called the Ten Commandments. God gave many other instructions that Moses wrote down. Now Moses and all the Israelites knew God's instructions for them.

6. Draw sideways "B." Add details and "10."

Get the Big Picture

Who obeyed God and did what was right? (Moses. Aaron.) **How?** (Talked to Pharaoh. Led the people.) **When do you think it might have been hard for Moses to do what was right?**

Sometimes you might think that it's just too hard for a kid to do what God wants or that God only cares about the lives of grown-ups like parents, teachers or coaches. But God wants everyone to do what's right. Ask God to show you what's right. And ask Him to help you do it. He will help you do it. He'll even give you family and friends who will make it easier—just like He did for Moses.

Bible Verse Object Talk: Emergency Kit

Big Picture Verse

"Teach me knowledge and good judgment, for I believe in your commands." Psalm 119:66

Teacher Materials

Large bag with these objects inside: Bible with bookmark at Psalm 119:66, eraser and a framed photo of a friend and/or family member.

A first aid or emergency kit usually has bandages and medicine in it. This bag is like an emergency kit for people who love God. Let's find out what's in the bag.

Present the Object Talk

1. Show bag to students and shake it slightly, so students hear objects inside. Invite one or more volunteers to feel the bag and try to guess what the objects might be.

2. As you take each item out of the bag one at a time, explain how the object reminds us of what it means to do what's right.

This eraser reminds us of making mistakes. Obeying God doesn't mean we'll never make mistakes. God erases our wrong actions by forgiving our sins when we ask Him to.

This picture of a friend reminds us that God gives us moms and dads, grandmas and grandpas, sisters and brothers and friends who will pray for us and help us know what God wants us to do.

Conclude

The best part of obeying God is that God gives us the Bible to help us obey Him. Read Psalm 119:66 aloud. **To have good judgment means to be wise and know the right things to do and say. We know that we can depend on God to help us be wise and make good choices.** Ask God's help in doing what's right.

Discussion Questions

1. What promises in God's Word do you remember? instructions? Tell an example of a promise or instruction that has helped you obey God. Older students may find and read a promise or two: Joshua 1:9; Psalm 23:1; Proverbs 3:5,6.

2. Who is someone God has given you to help you learn what God wants you to do?

 **Lesson 8**

Active Game Center: "Pharoah, Pharoah, Can We Go?"

Materials
Masking tape or chairs.

Prepare the Game
Use masking tape or chairs to mark a "safe" area either indoors or outdoors.

Lead the Game
1. Choose a volunteer to be Pharaoh. All the other students act as Moses and the Israelites.

2. Explain to the students where the safe area is. Pharaoh should start walking around the safe area. Other students follow him and ask in unison, "Pharaoh, Pharaoh, can we go?" If Pharaoh answers "No," students continue following and keep repeating the question. If Pharaoh answers "Yes," Pharaoh turns and chases the students back to the safe area. The first student Pharaoh tags becomes Pharaoh for the next round of play. If all students reach the safe area before they are tagged by Pharaoh, Pharaoh continues in his position or a new volunteer is chosen.

> Today we're learning that Moses kept going to Pharaoh to ask him to let the Israelites leave Egypt. It was hard to keep asking Pharaoh, but God helped Moses. Let's play a game to act out what happened.

Discussion Questions

1. What are some things kids your age do to love and obey God? (Be patient. Help an older neighbor.)

2. Why might it be hard for a kid your age to do what's right? (No one else is doing right. Afraid of what friends might think.)

3. How might God help someone your age do what's right? (Give courage. Help the person think of a right action.)

 **Lesson 8**

Art Center: Sandpaper Art

Student Materials
Crayons, a 10-inch (25-cm) square of sandpaper for each student.

Prepare the Activity
Write the word "desert" in large letters on a sandpaper square.

Lead the Activity
Students draw pictures or write words on the sandpaper about events in today's Bible story, or students draw pictures and write words about things often seen in the desert (cactus, sun, lizards, rocks, sunset, etc.).

Our story about Moses in the desert shows how God helps us do what is right even when it is hard. We're going to draw desert scenes on sandpaper.

Options
1. Bring in books or magazines with pictures of desert life.

2. Play "Who Is Like You, Lord?" from *God's Big Picture* cassette/CD while students complete art activity.

3. If sandpaper is not available, provide sand, glue and paper. Students make designs with glue on paper and sprinkle sand on the glue. Allow time to dry.

Discussion Questions
1. What would you have liked about living in the desert? disliked?

2. How do you think people might have cooked their food in the desert? washed their hands?
   (Carried wood to build cooking fires. Carried water in jars to wash hands.)

3. Moses did what was right, even when it was hard. What are ways we can learn how to do what is right? (Ask God for help. Follow example of other Christians.)

4. When are some times it is hard for a kid to do what is right?

Lesson 8

Worship Center

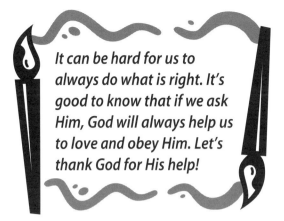

It can be hard for us to always do what is right. It's good to know that if we ask Him, God will always help us to love and obey Him. Let's thank God for His help!

Big Picture Verse

"Teach me knowledge and good judgment, for I believe in your commands." Psalm 119:66

Teacher Materials

Bible, *God's Big Picture* cassette/CD or music video and player, "Who Is Like You, Lord?" word chart (p. 481 in this book), large sheet of paper on which you have printed Psalm 119:66, masking tape.

Sing to God

Play "Who Is Like You, Lord?" encouraging students to sing along with the music and do the actions shown on the word chart or music video. **According to this song, why can we depend on God?**

Hear and Say God's Word

Display paper on which you have printed Psalm 119:66. Have a volunteer read the verse aloud. **When a person has knowledge and good judgment, it means he or she is able to make good choices in difficult situations. What other things could we ask God to teach us besides "knowledge" and "good judgment"?** (Patience. Kindness. To be a good friend.) List student's ideas on paper under Psalm 119:66. Repeat the verse together several times, each time substituting two of the words students have suggested for "knowledge" and "good judgment."

Pray to God

Who are some people you know who show by their actions that they want to do what is right? Students answer. Then lead volunteers to pray by completing this prayer starter: **Dear God, thank You for these people who do what's right. Thank You for....** Conclude by asking for God's help to follow the example of those people and the commands He gives us.

Option

If you have older students, during the Bible verse activity ask them to find and read aloud these Bible commands: Joshua 1:8, Galatians 6:10, Ephesians 4:29,32.

 **Lesson 8**

Bible Story Coloring Center  FOR YOUNGER CHILDREN

Materials

Crayons or markers, a copy of "Moses leads the people out of Egypt" picture and story (pp. 47-48 from *Bible Story Coloring Pages*) for each student.

Lead the Activity

Students color page 47; read or tell the story on page 48. **How many people and animals are going on this trip? How would you travel today if your family was going on a long trip?**

Option

Choosing from pages 39-53 in *Bible Story Coloring Pages*, give each student a different page to color. After pages are colored, guide students to put the pages in order. Mix up the pages, and see how fast students can reorder them.

Skit Center FOR OLDER CHILDREN

Materials

A copy of "Passover Me By" skit (pp. 23-26 from *The Big Book of Bible Skits*) for each student; optional—highlighter pens.

Lead the Activity

Students form pairs and read the skit, which tells the story of the plagues in Egypt. (Optional: Students highlight parts.) Ask the discussion questions on page 23.

Bible Skills Center FOR OLDER CHILDREN

Materials

Materials needed for "Command Talk" and/or "Word Works" (p. 49 and/or p. 107 from *The Big Book of Bible Skills*).

Lead the Activity

Students complete activities as directed in *The Big Book of Bible Skills*.

Joshua Takes Charge

Big Picture Verse

"Be strong and courageous. Do not be terrified; do not be discouraged, for the Lord your God will be with you wherever you go." Joshua 1:9

THE BIG PICTURE

God encourages us when we're afraid.

Scripture Background
Joshua 1; 3; 6

When we open the book of Joshua, we are beginning the second division of the Old Testament, the books of History. No book has more encouragement and wisdom for the followers of God than this book of Joshua.

In this book, Israel not only overcomes the enemy but also occupies the land which God promised them. This book bears the name of Joshua, the hero of this great conquest. The name "Joshua" was originally *Hoshea,* meaning salvation, or *Jehoshua,* the Lord's salvation.

Picture the opening scene: We find the children of Israel right on the border of the land of promise, near the banks of the Jordan. The poor Israelites were ready to turn back into the desert and dig their graves among the sand dunes where the bones of their fathers were buried. They could not invade this land filled with giants and take their walled cities. The conquest of the land seemed impossible! Can you picture the row on row of tents and all the people wondering what their leader would do?

Joshua was the leader of these fearful Israelites now. Moses was dead! Joshua stood with bowed head and a lonely heart, for his wise counselor and friend had gone. But God spoke reassuringly. Joshua sent men through the camp to tell them that in three days they would cross the Jordan and to be prepared for the journey. Unless they obeyed and crossed the river, they'd be left on the far side during flood season, with no way to cross. This was their one chance to go, believing in God's power and help—or stay in unbelief as their parents had.

God called Joshua to lead the children of Israel into the promised land. God calls us to follow Him in fearful situations, too. We have the words which must have come to Joshua in answer to a prayer for help in his great undertaking, "I will be with you; I will never leave you nor forsake you" (Joshua 1:5). These words are just as true for us!

Adapted from *What the Bible Is All About* by Henrietta C. Mears.

Big Picture Story Center

Teacher Materials
Bible Time Line, drawing materials/equipment.

Student Materials
Drawing materials.

Tell the Story
Move the *Bible Time Line* frame to highlight Picture 9. As you tell each part of the story, draw each sketch. Students copy your sketches.

What are some street signs you see on your way to school or church?
Today we'll draw some signs to tell our story!

1. The Israelites were camped by the Jordan River. Moses, their leader, had died. Now Joshua was their leader. Leading God's people was a big job. Joshua must have felt afraid! But God told him over and over, "Be strong and courageous. Don't be afraid. I am giving you this land." God told Joshua to get all the people ready to cross the Jordan River.

1. Draw sign: "FEAR" with "no" slash.

2. God's people were excited! After many years, they were going to enter the Promised Land. But the river was so high and moving so fast, it looked dangerous.

2. Sign: 2 "V"s, "DANGER." Add water behind sign.

3. Now God had told Joshua exactly what to do. Joshua told the people, "Follow the Ark of the Lord!" (The Ark of the Lord was a big, beautiful box covered with gold. It was set on poles and had God's laws inside it.) The priests carried the Ark to the edge of the rushing river. God had that wild river under control, for as the priests' feet touched the water, it stopped upstream! All the people walked across the riverbed without getting their feet wet!

3. Sign: "RR" crossing; add "IVE."

Footprint: "J," backward question mark, "O"s. Students add more footprints.

4. The leader of each family picked up a big, smooth stone from the riverbed. When everyone except the priests were safely across, God told Joshua, "Tell the priests to come up out of the Jordan." As the priests stepped out—CRASH!— the water roared back in place! God's people stacked up the

4. Draw 12 stones from "O"s. Students add details.

stones from the riverbed as a sign to remind them how God helped them cross that scary river!

5. God's people were finally in the Promised Land. But other people lived in that land already. These people had known that God's people were coming for a long time. And their strong armies wanted to keep God's people out!

5. Sign: "STOP."

6. Jericho was the first big city. A huge stone wall was around it. When the city gates closed, no one could get in or out. That wall looked like it would NEVER come down!

But God told Joshua that He would help His people take over the city of Jericho. God told Joshua, "March around Jericho with your army once a day for six days while the priests blow trumpets made from sheep horns.

"On the seventh day, march around the city SEVEN times. That day, have the priests blow one long, loud blast on the horns. When everyone hears it, tell them to SHOUT! The walls of the city will fall down. They can walk right in!"

6. Sign: "DO NOT ENTER."

7. Joshua told the people all about God's plan. That big wall looked strong, but God had said it would fall! So the Israelites did EXACTLY what God had told them to do. For six days, the army, the priests and all the Israelites marched around Jericho. There was no sound but the horns and the STOMP, STOMP, STOMP of marching feet. The people marched like a big parade for six days.

7. Horn: "6," "C"s.

8. On the seventh day, everyone came together to march around that huge high wall. The first six times around there was no sound but the priests' horns and the marching feet. Nothing happened—yet!

But the SEVENTH time around, the priests blew their horns long and loud together. Joshua called, "SHOUT! The Lord has given you the city!"

The Israelites SHOUTED! The high, strong wall rumbled. It CRACKED! And then—CRASH!—the wall came down. And the Israelites marched right in, just as God had promised!

8. Sign: "PROBLEM" with a "no" slash.

Get the Big Picture

Who was the new leader? (Joshua.) **What river did the Israelites cross?** (Jordan.) **What did God tell the people?** (Don't be afraid. I will make the wall of Jericho fall.) **What do you think the people learned about God?**

When we are afraid, God encourages us and promises to be with us. He will help us by giving us courage and by giving us good ideas of what to do.

Bible Verse Object Talk: Mission Impossible?

Big Picture Verse

"Be strong and courageous. Do not be terrified; do not be discouraged, for the Lord your God will be with you wherever you go." Joshua 1:9

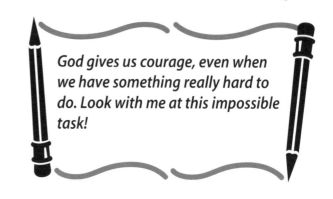

God gives us courage, even when we have something really hard to do. Look with me at this impossible task!

Teacher Materials

Bible with Joshua 1:9 marked with a bookmark, 8½ x 11-inch (21.5 x 27.5-cm) paper, scissors.

Prepare the Object Talk

Practice cutting paper, following directions below.

Present the Object Talk

1. Show paper and ask, **How might I fit my whole body through this paper?**

2. After students conclude that the task is impossible, fold the paper lengthwise. Cut the paper as shown in Sketch a, making an uneven number of cuts approximately ½ inch (1.25 cm) apart. Cut on the fold between the first and last sections as shown in Sketch b. Then carefully open up the folds and step through the circle you have made.

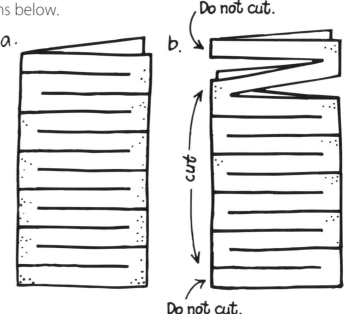

Conclude

When something seems too hard to do or we're discouraged, God can help us by giving us courage and helping us know what to do. What does God promise to do? Read Joshua 1:9 aloud. Thank God for encouraging us when we're afraid.

Discussion Questions

1. What might make a kid your age feel discouraged?

2. When is a time a kid your age might feel afraid and need to ask God for courage?

3. What are some ways in which God encourages us? (Gives us friends and parents. Gives us promises of help in the Bible.)

Active Game Center: Battle of Jericho

Materials

God's Big Picture cassette/CD and player, a chair for each student less one, wooden or cardboard blocks.

Prepare the Game

Place chairs in a circle, facing out. Several feet away from the chairs, stack blocks to make a wall.

What happened when Joshua and the Israelites walked around the walls of Jericho? Even though what they were doing seemed impossible, God was with them and gave them courage. We're going to play a game to act out what happened.

Lead the Game

1. Students walk around the chairs as you play "God Is So Strong" from *God's Big Picture* cassette/CD.

2. When you stop the music, each student tries to sit in a chair. The student without a chair removes one of the blocks from the wall. Continue playing until wall has been dismantled. Student to remove last block says Joshua 1:9 or answers one of the Discussion Questions below. Play additional rounds of the game as time permits.

Options

1. If wooden or cardboard blocks are not available from preschool classes, draw a block wall on chalkboard or whiteboard. Students erase blocks as game is played.

2. If possible in your location, student without a chair knocks down the entire wall instead of removing a block. Student and another volunteer quickly rebuild the wall before the next round of the game.

Discussion Questions

1. When are some times kids your age need encouragement?

2. Why might someone forget to depend on God and His encouragement?

3. God provides people to encourage us. If you needed courage, what could someone do or say to help you?

4. When might you be able to encourage someone else?

Art Center: Crayon Resist

Student Materials
White paper, light-colored crayons, washable markers.

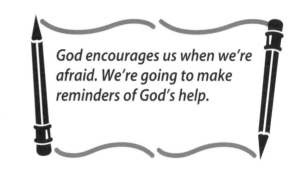

God encourages us when we're afraid. We're going to make reminders of God's help.

Prepare the Activity
Print the words "God will be with you wherever you go" on paper and place paper in a visible place.

Lead the Activity
1. Students refer to paper you prepared and write the words on their papers, using crayons and pressing firmly. Students may also add other designs or symbols and drawings.

2. With markers, students color over the crayon writing and drawings. Suggest students use markers in colors that contrast with crayon colors. The crayon writing and drawings will resist the marker color and stand out.

3. As time permits, invite students to suggest additional sentences and/or slogans which remind them of God's encouragement in fearful situations. Students make additional crayon resist drawings. Invite each student to think of a person to whom drawing may be given.

Option
Use tempera paint instead of markers.

Discussion Questions
1. When might a kid feel afraid?

2. We all feel afraid or worried sometimes, but what helps us when we feel afraid? What do you do when you are afraid?

3. Name a time or a place when it helps to remember that God is with you.

Lesson 9

Worship Center

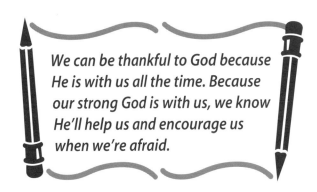

We can be thankful to God because He is with us all the time. Because our strong God is with us, we know He'll help us and encourage us when we're afraid.

Big Picture Verse

"Be strong and courageous. Do not be terrified; do not be discouraged, for the Lord your God will be with you wherever you go." Joshua 1:9

Teacher Materials

Bible, *God's Big Picture* cassette/CD or music video and player, "God Is So Strong" word chart (p. 455 in this book), large sheet of paper on which you have printed Joshua 1:9, masking tape.

Sing to God

Play "God Is So Strong," encouraging students to sing along with the music and do the actions shown on the word chart or music video. **How would you describe God? What do you want others to know about Him?**

Hear and Say God's Word

Display paper on which you have printed Joshua 1:9. Have a volunteer read the verse to the group. **When are some times you or kids your age get scared and would be glad to hear this verse?** Volunteers answer. **The words in this verse are ones we can never get tired of hearing. I'll say a part of the verse, and you echo it after me, so we hear the words twice!** Repeat the verse in this manner several times, inviting different students to lead the echo.

Pray to God

Lead students in a prayer to thank God that He is with us and helps us when we are afraid. If your students are hesitant to pray aloud, lead them in a short prayer which they can repeat after you.

Option

During the prayer, have students suggest sentences for a prayer, thanking God that He is with us and helps us when we are afraid. Print the words on the back of the Bible verse paper. Students read words together as a prayer.

 **Lesson 9**

Bible Story Coloring Center

 FOR YOUNGER CHILDREN

Materials
Crayons or markers, a copy of "The walls of Jericho fall down" picture and story (pp. 63-64 from *Bible Story Coloring Pages*) for each student.

Lead the Activity
Students color page 63; read or tell the story on page 64. **What did God do to help the Israelites? How do you think the Israelites felt when the walls fell down?**

Option
Tape a large sheet of butcher paper onto table top. Students draw and then color walls on the paper.

Skit Center

 FOR OLDER CHILDREN

Materials
A copy of "Problems, Problems, Problems" skit (pp. 31-34 from *The Big Book of Bible Skits*) for each student; optional—highlighter pens.

Lead the Activity
Students choose parts and read the skit, which tells the story of the crossing of the Jordan River. (Optional: Students highlight parts.) Ask the discussion questions on page 31.

Bible Skills Center

 FOR OLDER CHILDREN

Materials
Materials needed for "Leader Hunt" and/or "Lands of the Bible" (p. 51 and/or p. 161 from *The Big Book of Bible Skills*).

Lead the Activity
Students complete activities as directed in *The Big Book of Bible Skills*.

Deborah Calls for Courage

Big Picture Verse

"Encourage the timid, help the weak, be patient with everyone." 1 Thessalonians 5:14

THE BIG PICTURE

Encouraging others can help them trust in God, too.

Scripture Background
Judges 4:1-16; 5:1-23

The book of Judges begins a new hour in the history of Israel. Remember, Israel had come from a long era of bondage in Egypt to a period of 40 years when she lived in tents and wandered in the wilderness. Now the march was over. The nomads were to become settlers in a land of their own. The change was not as easy for them as they expected it to be. The book of Judges is, in a way, another book of beginning where we see a new nation adjusting her national life.

Someone has called the book of Judges the account of the Dark Ages of the Israelite people. The people turned away from God, and God gave them over to their enemies (see Judges 2:13,14). But Judges also tells us of the leaders whom God raised up to deliver His oppressed people. There is a decided monotony in the description of each successive stage of sin in Israel, but there is an equally remarkable variety in the instruments and methods of deliverance which God used. There is something different in the story of each judge.

One of these judges was the prophetess, Deborah. She was one of those rare people whose heart burns with enthusiasm when other's hearts are despondent. Many a queen, like England's Elizabeth II, has reigned with honor and wisdom, and often a woman's voice has struck a deep note that has roused nations.

Israel had been terribly oppressed for 20 years under Sisera. Deborah, the daughter of the people, had gained the confidence of the people to such a degree that they had appointed her as judge. Deborah called Barak to help her. Together they delivered Israel from their oppression. War was everywhere, and the Israelites were defenseless and crushed; but God delivered them. The tribes should have known by now the danger of leaving God. Without God they were as weak as babes. But even after the victory over Sisera, did they bend themselves to Him? Not yet. Not for more than 40 years.

Adapted from *What the Bible Is All About* by Henrietta C. Mears.

Big Picture Story Center

Teacher Materials
Bible Time Line, drawing materials/equipment.

Student Materials
Drawing materials.

Tell the Story
Move the *Bible Time Line* frame to highlight Picture 10. As you tell each part of the story, draw each sketch. Students copy your sketches.

What makes you feel better when you're scared? Today we're going to talk about a woman who was very wise. She knew how to encourage someone who was afraid.

1. The Israelites were disobeying God by worshiping idols (gods who weren't real). And so the Israelites had trouble! The trouble was that for 20 YEARS a man named Sisera had been attacking Israel. Sisera's army had 900 iron chariots! Things looked bad. But in the middle of all this trouble, the Israelites finally remembered that God had helped them before. They began to pray to Him to help them again.

2. A woman named Deborah was a judge for the Israelites. She helped people settle their arguments. People came from all over to a palm tree near her home to get her help. Deborah sat under the palm tree while she helped people. She loved God and listened to Him. She was also a prophetess. That means God gave her messages to tell the Israelites.

3. One day Deborah sent for a man named Barak (BEAR-uk). When Barak came, she said, "The Lord has a job for you. God says, 'Get 10 thousand men and go to Mount Tabor.' God will bring Sisera, his chariots and his army to the river there. God will help you defeat Sisera."

4. Barak was afraid! *Was this really God's plan?* he wondered. Barak said, "Deborah, if you go with me, I will go. But if you don't go, I'm not going either." Deborah was not afraid. And she wanted Barak to trust God, too. So she said, "Very well. I will go with you."

1. Draw chariot from triangle, circle and straight line. Add stick-figure driver.

2. Palm tree from "W"s and "C"s. Deborah from upside-down "U" and "B." Add face.

3. Draw Barak.

4. Draw scared faces and "3"s for hair.

5. Barak and Deborah went together to Mount Tabor. Barak sent messengers to the Israelites to ask them to join his army. Soon 10 thousand men were hiking up that mountain. But they weren't the ONLY ones getting ready for a battle!

5. Draw large "M" for mountain.

6. Sisera had heard about all the people coming to Mount Tabor. He prepared for battle, too. And he was sure he'd win. After all, he had the chariots! But Sisera didn't know that the Israelites had GOD'S help!

One morning, Deborah and Barak looked out across the wide, flat valley below. First, they saw a little cloud of dust. It became a BIG cloud of dust! It was the chariots of Sisera and his men! They came closer and CLOSER, until Sisera's army filled the valley below Mount Tabor.

6. Below mountain add wide "U" for valley; add sideways "C"s for people.

7. Deborah turned to Barak and smiled! "Go!" she said. "God will help you defeat Sisera's army!" Deborah encouraged Barak just when he needed it! So Barak and his men came down the mountain. And what do you think happened? God sent a THUNDERSTORM! Lightning flashed. Rain poured down.

7. "Z"s for lightning; add raindrops and "3"s for clouds.

8. Sisera and his chariots were in the wide, flat valley where they could go very fast—over dry ground. But they hadn't counted on RAIN! Soon, water was everywhere! The ground was thick mud! And those horses and chariots were stuck. Sisera and his men left their chariots in the mud and ran! All Barak's army had to do was to chase the enemy until there was no one left to chase! God had won the battle, just as Deborah had told Barak

8. Draw running stick figures.

9. Deborah and Barak made up a song about how God won the battle! This song is written in Judges chapter 5. Deborah showed how encouraging someone can help that person trust God.

9. Draw musical notes.

Get the Big Picture

What was Deborah like? (Prophetess. Wise. Believed God.) **Why do you think Barak needed her help?** (He was afraid.) **When God sent a storm, what happened?** (The chariots were stuck in mud. The soldiers ran.)

Sometimes we might be afraid to obey God, like Barak was. One way God helps us is by giving us people to encourage us like Deborah encouraged Barak to trust God. We can be encouragers, too—by our kind words and the things we say!

Bible Verse Object Talk: Paper Challenge

Big Picture Verse

"Encourage the timid, help the weak, be patient with everyone." 1 Thessalonians 5:14

Teacher Materials

Bible with 1 Thessalonians 5:14 marked with a bookmark, one or more of these materials: toilet tissue, crepe paper strip, yarn, curling ribbon, narrow fabric strip.

God tells us in His Word that He wants us to help people who are weak. Watch to see what is weak in this experiment and what makes the weak item become strong.

Present the Object Talk

1. Invite a volunteer to come forward. Ask the volunteer to hold wrists together in front of him- or herself as you wrap one strand of toilet tissue around the wrists. Challenge the volunteer to break free.

2. Repeat several times, each time adding one or two strands of tissue before the volunteer tries to break free. Comment, **One or two strands of tissue are weak and we can break them easily. The more strands of tissue we add, the stronger the tissue becomes.** Repeat with other volunteers and/or materials.

Conclude

When we try to trust in God by ourselves, it's like we are as weak as one strand of tissue. We might find it hard to do what God says. But when others help us and encourage us, it's easier to trust God. We are stronger together—just as the tissues were stronger when they were put together. Count the ways this verse says we can help others. Read 1 Thessalonians 5:14 aloud. Pray, asking God to show students ways of helping others to trust Him.

Discussion Questions

1. When might it be hard for a kid to do what God wants? How could a friend help him or her to obey?

2. What's something you know God wants you to do? (Be honest. Stand up for someone who needs help.) *How could you help a friend obey God in that way too?*

3. Who has helped you learn about God and trust in Him?

Active Game Center: Partner Relay

Materials
Sheets of newspaper, masking tape.

Prepare the Game
Use masking tape to make a starting line on one side of the playing area.

Lead the Game
1. Divide class into teams of six to eight. Teams line up behind masking-tape line. Students on each team form pairs. Give each pair two sheets of newspaper. (Partner with a student if needed.)

2. To move, student's partner places newspaper sheets on floor for student to walk on. First student in each line moves across the room and back, stepping only on sheets of newspaper. Each pair completes the relay twice with a different student moving the newspaper sheets the second time.

3. Repeat relay as time permits, forming new teams and new pairs.

Sometimes others need our help to trust God and obey Him. It's good to work with others to do good things. Let's play a game to practice helping each other.

Options
1. Rectangles made from large paper grocery bags may be used instead of newspapers.
2. If playing this game outdoors, use yarn or string to mark the starting line.

Discussion Questions
1. What are some other games you like to play with friends?

2. How can you help or encourage someone who has something hard to do? (Pray for him or her. Offer to help or go with the person.)

3. When has someone helped or encouraged you to obey God? How?

Art Center: Talking Collage

Student Materials
Large sheet of paper, pencil, scissors, magazines, glue, construction paper, markers.

Prepare the Activity
Draw an outline of a person on a large sheet of paper. Cut out the outline.

Lead the Activity
1. Distribute magazines. Students cut out pictures of as many different people (faces or whole bodies) as they can find.

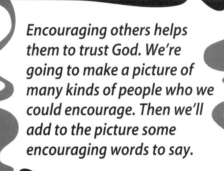

Encouraging others helps them to trust God. We're going to make a picture of many kinds of people who we could encourage. Then we'll add to the picture some encouraging words to say.

2. Students glue pictures of people onto the person outline, fitting the pieces together to form a collage.

3. Then give each student a sheet of construction paper. Students cut paper into large conversation balloons, lettering in the balloons encouraging words or phrases ("Thank you." "Please." "Thanks for your help." "You're good at that." "You can do it.").

4. Display person outline and conversation balloons on classroom wall.

Options
1. Students make individual collages.

2. If you have a large group of students, make more than one person outline on which to make a collage.

Discussion Questions
1. How can you help or encourage someone older than you? younger than you? the same age as you?

2. What kind of help or encouragement do the people in your family need? in your neighborhood? in your school?

3. What might make it hard to encourage or help someone?

Lesson 10

Worship Center

Let's thank God that He is so strong. We can trust in Him and encourage others to trust in Him, too.

Big Picture Verse

"Encourage the timid, help the weak, be patient with everyone." 1 Thessalonians 5:14

Teacher Materials

Bible, *God's Big Picture* cassette/CD or music video and player, "Who Is Like You, Lord?" word chart (p. 481 in this book), large sheet of paper on which you have printed 1 Thessalonians 5:14, masking tape.

Sing to God

Play "Who Is Like You, Lord?" encouraging students to sing along with the music and do the actions shown on the word chart or music video. **How does learning about God's power encourage you?**

Hear and Say God's Word

Display paper on which you have printed 1 Thessalonians 5:14. Have a volunteer read the verse to the group. Help students think of hand motions for the words "encourage," "timid," "help," "weak," "patient" and "everyone." Say the verse together a few times, doing the hand motions for words as you say them. **In what ways can you help someone who is timid or fearful? weak? How can you be patient with others?**

Pray to God

Praying for people is a way to help them. Telling them you're praying for them is also a way to encourage them. Ask volunteers to tell prayer requests for others. Lead students in prayer, mentioning their requests.

Options

1. As students sing "Who Is Like You, Lord?" ask them to find and then name reasons to trust God that are mentioned in the song (Because He is holy and pure and awesome. Because He helped Moses. Because Jesus died for us, etc.).

2. Invite volunteers to suggest hand motions for several of the words in Joshua 1:9. Say the verse together several times, leading students to do the suggested motions.

 **Lesson 10**

Bible Story Coloring Center

FOR YOUNGER CHILDREN

Materials

Crayons or markers, a copy of "Deborah helps Barak" picture and story (pp. 65-66 from *Bible Story Coloring Pages*) for each student.

Lead the Activity

Students color page 65; read or tell the story on page 66. **Do Deborah and Barak look sad or glad? Why? What do you think they said to God for helping them?**

Option

Provide glue and small fabric pieces. Students glue fabric onto clothing of Deborah and Barak.

Skit Center

FOR OLDER CHILDREN

Materials

A copy of "Canaan TV News" skit (pp. 46-50 from *The Big Book of Bible Skits*) for each student; optional—highlighter pens.

Lead the Activity

Students choose parts and read the skit, which tells the story of the Israelite victory. (Optional: Students highlight their parts.) Ask the discussion questions on page 46.

Bible Skills Center

FOR OLDER CHILDREN

Materials

Materials needed for "Division Match-Up" and/or "Ball Toss" (p. 39 and/or p. 67 from *The Big Book of Bible Skills*).

Lead the Activity

Students complete activities as directed in *The Big Book of Bible Skills*.

 **Lesson 11**

Gideon's Hiding Place

Big Picture Verse

"Surely God is my salvation; I will trust and not be afraid. The Lord, the Lord, is my strength and my song; he has become my salvation."
Isaiah 12:2

THE BIG PICTURE

God's love and power are bigger than the biggest fear.

Scripture Background
Judges 6; 7

In reading Judges you may think that the whole of these possibly 350 years was spent in rebellion and sin. But if you read it carefully, you will see that only about 100 of these years were spent in disloyalty to God. One thing we learn in the book of Judges is that a people who spend much of their time in disobedience to God make little progress during their lifetimes.

In one of these times of disobedience, the deliverer was Gideon, a humble farmer. The Midianites had held the Israelites under bondage for seven years. So terrible was their persecution that the people fearfully hid themselves in caves and dens and were hunted in the mountains (see Judges 6:2). Again the people of Israel cried unto the Lord. God's answer was to call Gideon to act as deliverer. Gideon broke down the altar of Baal and restored the worship of God. The story of the conflict is one of the most fascinating in history. Gideon and his band of 300 with their pitchers and horns relied on God's power and defeated their enemies.

After the great victory over the Midianites, the Israelites sought to make Gideon king. He refused. Gideon was not perfect; his initial response to God's call was one of fear and worry. We find in the record some things that he should not have done; but his faith in Jehovah, despite his fears, was one God could honor. God gave Gideon's name a place in the Hall of Faith (see Hebrews 11:32).

Adapted from *What the Bible Is All About* by Henrietta C. Mears.

Big Picture Story Center

Teacher Materials
Bible Time Line, drawing materials/equipment.

Student Materials
Drawing materials.

Tell the Story
Move the *Bible Time Line* frame to highlight Picture 11. As you tell each part of the story, draw each sketch. Students copy your sketches.

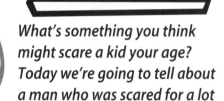

What's something you think might scare a kid your age? Today we're going to tell about a man who was scared for a lot of different reasons!

1. Gideon was threshing grain—tossing it into the air to separate the hulls from the grain. Usually people do this in the open air, so the breeze carries off the hulls. But Gideon was doing it while he HID! He was down in a large pit under an oak tree! You see, the Midianites were everywhere. And they were taking everything! Gideon was scared and was hiding and hoping the Midianites wouldn't find him and take his grain! But someone DID find him.

1. Draw 2 "I"s and add "3"s for oak tree. Add figure in "U" for pit.

2. Gideon looked up. A stranger looked down at him and said, "The Lord is with you, mighty warrior!" **How do you think Gideon felt, hearing that?** The stranger said that Gideon was going to defeat the Midianites! Gideon didn't see how THAT could happen! He wasn't brave or strong—he was scared! But the stranger said, "I will be with you." The stranger was God. GOD would help Gideon!

2. Draw scared face.

3. So Gideon blew a ram's horn and sent messengers to call warriors from all over the country of Israel. Thousands of Israelites came to help defeat the Midianites!

3. Horn from "6" and "C"s.

4. But Gideon was still afraid. He asked God to do something to prove he would really defeat the Midianites. Gideon laid a sheepskin out at night and asked God to make the ground around it dry but the sheepskin wet. Well, God did just that! And God did it again in a different way, just so Gideon would know God was helping him.

4. Draw sheepskin from "C"s, "L"s and "3"s.

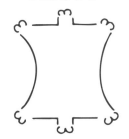

5. Next, God told Gideon, "There are too many soldiers. With so many, Israel might think they beat the Midianites by their own strength. Send anyone home who is afraid!" Gideon obeyed, and all but 10,000 men went home. And Gideon obeyed again when God told him to send even MORE people home! Now there were only 300 soldiers. There were THOUSANDS of Midianites! But God had told Gideon that He would defeat the enemy.

5. Draw scared face. Add "Z"s for legs and "I"s for arms.

6. Gideon and his men got ready. Instead of weapons, they carried horns and torches inside clay jars. Gideon told them, "God has said we will defeat the Midianites. Now watch me and do what I do!" In the middle of the night, they made a big circle around the valley where the Midianites were sleeping. They blew their horns, broke their jars, lifted their torches and shouted!

6. Make "V"s for torches.

7. The shouting and bright lights woke the Midianites. Scared and confused, they began to fight EACH OTHER! They began to RUN! All Gideon and his men had to do was CHASE them! Gideon had trusted God and obeyed, even when he was afraid. And God HAD defeated the Midianites!

7. Write "FEAR." Add circle and "no" slash.

Get the Big Picture
What did God tell Gideon to do? (Defeat the Midianites.) **When Gideon was afraid, what did he do? What did God do?** (Asked God to prove He would help; God proved to Gideon He would help him.)

Even when we are afraid, we can still obey. God's love and power are bigger than all our fears. We can tell Him when we are afraid, like Gideon did. He knows we need His help. And He hears us when we pray to Him!

Bible Verse Object Talk: Bigger Than All

Big Picture Verse

"Surely God is my salvation; I will trust and not be afraid. The Lord, the Lord, is my strength and my song; he has become my salvation."
Isaiah 12:2

Teacher Materials

Bible with Isaiah 12:2 marked with a bookmark, a variety of classroom or household objects ranging in size from very small to very large.

When we feel worried or afraid because of problems at school or in our neighborhoods, it helps to remember that God's love and power are bigger than our biggest fears. Let's name some things that are bigger than others.

Present the Object Talk

1. Invite one or more volunteers to arrange objects in order of size.

2. Beginning with the smallest object, invite volunteers to name a variety of objects which are bigger than the smallest object but smaller than the next object. For example, a pencil is bigger than a penny but smaller than a book. Continue until all objects have been discussed. **What are the biggest objects you can think of?** (Redwood tree. Skyscraper. Bridge.)

Conclude

We've been talking about a lot of things that are bigger than others. Listen to Isaiah 12:2 to find out what we can remember about God when we're afraid or worried. Read Isaiah 12:2 aloud. **We can remember that God's strength and His help for us are bigger than our fears or worries.** Thank God for His love and help when we're worried or afraid.

Discussion Questions

1. *What's a worry a kid your age might have? a fear?*

2. *Why might someone who's afraid forget about God's love and help?*

3. *How has God helped you when you've felt afraid?*

4. *What worry or fear do you want to talk to God about?*

Active Game Center: Question Contest

Materials

Two chairs, list of yes-or-no questions (see step 3 below).

Lead the Game

1. Divide the class into two equal teams. Have each team sit in a row on the ground so that the two teams are facing each other with about 4 feet (1.2 meters) between them. Place chairs as shown in sketch. Designate one chair to be the "yes" chair, and the other chair to be the "no" chair.

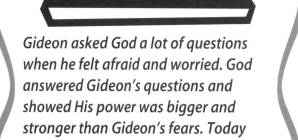

Gideon asked God a lot of questions when he felt afraid and worried. God answered Gideon's questions and showed His power was bigger and stronger than Gideon's fears. Today we're going to play a game with questions.

2. Assign a number to each student, assigning the same series of numbers to both teams so that there is a number one on each team, etc.

3. Ask a question from a list of prepared questions, all of which can be answered "yes" or "no." They may be Bible story review questions, questions that only kids in your town would know or general questions. For example, "Did Gideon and his men win the battle?" "Is there a basketball hoop at Manning Park?" or "Is the sky blue?"

4. After you ask a question, call out a number. Students with those numbers get up and try to be the first to sit in the chair that represents the correct answer. The student who sits in the correct chair first scores a point for his or her team. (Note: If you have mostly younger students, give each student his or her own number. When you ask a question, call out one of the assigned numbers. Student with that number sits in the appropriate chair to answer the question.)

Discussion Questions

1. What questions would you ask God?

2. Why is it good to talk to God when you are afraid or worried?

3. What has God given to help us when we're afraid? (Promises of His help found in the Bible. Parents. Friends.)

Art Center: Designer T-Shirts

Teacher Materials

One or more T-shirts with slogans printed on them.

Student Materials

Large sheets of white construction paper, pencils, scissors, markers.

Prepare the Activity

Draw the outline of a T-shirt on construction paper, making one for each student (see sketch).

Whenever we're worried about big or little things, God is always ready to help us. God's love and power are bigger than the biggest fear. We're going to design T-shirts as reminders of God's help when we're afraid.

Lead the Activity

1. One at a time, show T-shirt(s). **What does this T-shirt tell or show you? What does this T-shirt remind you of?** Volunteers answer.

2. Invite students to tell words or pictures which remind them of God's love and power.

3. Each student cuts out a T-shirt outline and draws pictures or writes words on the outline as a reminder of God's love and power.

Options

1. If you have older students, they may draw their own T-shirt outlines.

2. Purchase (or ask students to bring) white fabric T-shirts. Students draw pictures and write words on the T-shirts with fabric markers.

3. Display completed T-shirts in your classroom.

Discussion Questions

1. What's something that might frighten someone younger than you? someone your age? someone older than you?

2. What words would you use to describe God?

3. What pictures remind you of God's strength and power?

Worship Center

No matter how afraid we feel, God's love and power are bigger than whatever we are afraid of. His help and love are stronger than our fears. Let's thank God for His promises of help and love.

Big Picture Verse

"Surely God is my salvation; I will trust and not be afraid. The Lord, the Lord, is my strength and my song; he has become my salvation." Isaiah 12:2

Teacher Materials

Bible, *God's Big Picture* cassette/CD or music video and player, "God Is So Strong" word chart (p. 455 in this book), large sheet of paper on which you have printed Isaiah 12:2, masking tape

Sing to God

Play "God Is So Strong," encouraging students to sing along with the music and do the actions shown on the word chart or music video. **What are some of the strong things God can do?**

Hear and Say God's Word

Display paper on which you have printed Isaiah 12:2. Have a volunteer read the verse to the group. **Why do you think the verse says "The Lord" twice?** (To emphasize that God is the One who helps us.) **What reasons does this verse give us for not being afraid?** Draw lines to divide the verse into four sections. Divide the class into two groups. Groups alternate reading sections of the verse in order. Say the verse several times in this manner. (Variation: Divide class in different ways: boys and girls, grade level, teacher(s) and students, etc.) **"Salvation" means to be rescued from the punishment we deserve for our sin.** Talk with students about becoming members of God's family, following the guidelines in the "Leading a Child to Christ" article on page 30.

Pray to God

Why should we trust in God? How has He helped you or your family in the past? Volunteers answer. Lead students in prayer, thanking God for His love and help when we're afraid.

Options

1. After singing "God Is So Strong," invite volunteers to complete the sentence "God is..." in as many different ways as possible ("loving," "forgiving," "powerful," "great").
2. During the Bible verse activity, students vary the level of their voices. If one group says its part of the verse loudly, then the other group responds by saying its part of the verse loudly. If a group says its part quietly, then the other group responds by speaking quietly.

 Bible Story Coloring Center FOR YOUNGER CHILDREN

Materials

Crayons or markers, a copy of "God helps Gideon defeat the Midianites" picture and story (pp. 69-70 from *Bible Story Coloring Pages*) for each student.

Lead the Activity

Students color page 69; read or tell the story on page 70. **What are the soldiers doing? What weapons are they using? Who helped them win the battle? What did they learn about God?**

Option

Students glue orange or red pieces of tissue paper to flames and add gummed stars to the sky.

Skit Center FOR OLDER CHILDREN

Materials

A copy of "The Call of Gideon" skit (pp. 51-56 from *The Big Book of Bible Skits*) for each student; optional—highlighter pens.

Lead the Activity

Students form pairs and read the skit, which tells the story of the angel's visit to Gideon. (Optional: Students highlight their parts.) Ask the discussion questions on page 51.

Bible Skills Center FOR OLDER CHILDREN

Materials

Materials needed for "Content Concentration" and/or "Hidden Word" (p. 45 and/or p. 121 from *The Big Book of Bible Skills*).

Lead the Activity

Students complete activities as directed in *The Big Book of Bible Skills*.

The Strongest Man Fails the Test

Big Picture Verse

"Blessed are they who keep his statutes and seek him with all their heart." Psalm 119:2

THE BIG PICTURE

Ignoring God's instructions always leads to trouble.

Scripture Background
Judges 13—16

The story of Samson begins with the words, "Again the Israelites did evil in the eyes of the Lord" (Judges 13:1). This time they were disciplined by the Philistines under whose awful oppression they lived for 40 years. Here in this story, we read about Samson—the man appointed by God before birth to begin to deliver Israel from the Philistines (see Judges 13:5). It is a story filled with opportunity—and failure.

In those days physical strength was often what made a leader great. In this case, God used Samson's incredible strength to begin the deliverance from the Philistines. Everything should have been in Samson's favor, but he entered into an unholy alliance which resulted in his downfall. The final fall occurred at Gaza. Nothing is more pathetic than Samson, blind and bound, grinding in the house of the Philistines, when he ought to have been delivering his nation from them. Samson's failure illustrates the fact that no person who does not fear God and love righteousness can do real service.

This principle of Godly obedience is the real lesson of the book of Judges. There is a phrase that runs through the book: "Everyone did as he saw fit" (Judges 17:6). We find the people repeatedly turning away from Jehovah and disobeying as they worshiped the gods of the nations round about them. They forgot that God had chosen them for a purpose—to tell the world the truth that there is but one true God. And so the book is full of rebellion, punishment and misery.

The book of Judges begins with compromise and ends with confusion. This is what happens in every unsurrendered life of disobedience to God. But God hears our cry of repentance, even as He heard Samson's cry, and restores us to favor again.

Adapted from *What the Bible Is All About* by Henrietta C. Mears.

Big Picture Story Center

Teacher Materials
Bible Time Line, drawing materials/equipment.

Student Materials
Drawing materials.

Tell the Story
Move the *Bible Time Line* frame to highlight Picture 12. As you tell each part of the story, draw each sketch. Students copy your sketches.

What might happen if a person didn't follow instructions while baking a cake? Today we're going to tell about a person who ignored some of God's instructions.

1. Once again God's people forgot to obey God's instructions. And once again, God had a plan to get them out of all the trouble they had caused by doing evil instead of doing good. One day God sent an angel to a woman. He told her that she would have a son who would obey God in some special ways. The angel told her some special rules for her son to obey: not to eat any grapes or drink any wine, not to touch anything dead and never EVER to cut his hair.

1. Draw circles for grapes. Head from a wiggly upside-down "U" and knife from 2 "D"s. Add "no" slash over grapes and knife.

2. So Samson was born. He grew up to be VERY strong. His hair was very long and braided into seven braids. But although he was strong, he was not always wise.

2. Face from "7" and "C"s. Add 7 rows of "X"s for hair.

3. You see, the Philistines lived nearby. They had made trouble for the Israelites for years. And God had told the Israelites never to marry Philistines because the Philistines worshiped false gods. But Samson wanted to get married—to a Philistine girl!

3. Draw "P"s for Philistines. Add faces and details for man and girl.

4. This led to lots MORE trouble with the Philistines. When the Philistines fought with Samson, he destroyed their fields. When their army came to kill him, he killed them all. He pulled down the gates of a town! No one could stop him! This really scared the Philistines. They began thinking they had better not attack Israel while Samson was around!

4. Gates from upside-down "U"s and lines.

5. Well, all this trouble didn't keep Samson from liking those Philistine ladies! He fell in love with another lady named Delilah. The Philistines paid her to find out how to make Samson as weak as other men. Delilah asked and asked, and Samson told her one story after another. But she nagged him until he told her that if she cut his hair, he'd be like other men. Guess what she did?

5. Knife from 2 "D"s.

6. Sure enough, with no hair Samson had broken the promise he had made to God and God's power left him. He became as weak as other men. The Philistines tied him up and made him a slave. They even blinded him and forced him to grind grain every day in prison. But slowly, Samson's hair began to grow back.

6. Draw face with sad eyes made from "C"s Add growing hair.

7. One day, many Philistines had a big party at their temple to honor their idol! They brought Samson into the temple and put him between the two main pillars that held up the roof. The Philistines wanted to make fun of their once-great enemy. But Samson wanted to stop the Philistines one more time. So he prayed.

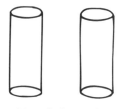

7. Draw ovals and lines to make temple pillars, leaving space between the pillars.

8. He prayed, "God, let me be strong once more, so I can knock down this temple full of Philistines." He began to push on the pillars! Soon, WHAM! the whole BUILDING fell down! Samson died, too. But the Philistines left Israel alone for a long time.

8. Add stick-figure Samson between pillars.

Get the Big Picture

What was Samson like? (Strong. Chosen by God for a special job.) **What kind of choices did he make?** (Disobeyed God.) **What were the results of Samson's disobedience?** (Lots of trouble.)

Sometimes we think we can get away with doing wrong, like Samson did. But disobeying God always causes problems. God loves us and knows what is best for us. That's why we obey Him!

 Lesson 12

Bible Verse Object Talk: Seek and Find!

Big Picture Verse

"Blessed are they who keep his statutes and seek him with all their heart." Psalm 119:2

Teacher Materials

Bible with Psalm 119:2 marked with a bookmark, blindfold.

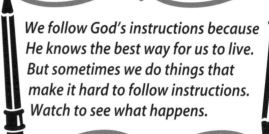

We follow God's instructions because He knows the best way for us to live. But sometimes we do things that make it hard to follow instructions. Watch to see what happens.

Present the Object Talk

Invite a volunteer to wear a blindfold. Then instruct the volunteer to complete a task in the classroom: "Walk to the table across the room and pick up the Bible," "Find the chalk and

write your name on the chalkboard" or "Play a music tape in the cassette player." Repeat with other volunteers and additional tasks. Occasionally ask volunteers, **What would make it easier to find what you're looking for? If you really wanted to do what I asked you to do, what would make it easier?** (Take off the blindfold.)

Conclude

Wearing a blindfold makes it difficult to find what you're looking for. Ignoring or disobeying God's instructions is like wearing a blindfold, and it gets us into lots of trouble. Listen to Psalm 119:2 to find what happens to people who learn about and follow God's instructions. Read verse aloud. **"Statutes" is another word for God's instructions. When we seek or try to follow God's instructions, we can find the best way to live**

Discussion Questions

1. What are ways kids your age might be tempted to disobey God? What might be the results? What kind of trouble might happen?

2. Why is it so important to God that we obey His commands? (He loves us so much, He wants us to have the good things that result from obeying Him.)

3. When can you obey God?

Active Game Center: Human Obstacle Course

Materials

None.

Lead the Game

1. Divide the group into two teams.

2. Each team plans a human obstacle course for the other team to move through. Obstacles might be a student on hands and knees to hop over, a student standing with legs apart to form a tunnel to crawl through or two students lying next to each other to jump over.

Samson kept doing things that made it hard for him to follow the instructions God had given him. His wrong actions were obstacles—things that kept him from obeying God. We're going to play a game where we form an obstacle course with our bodies.

3. In the playing area, first team forms the course. Volunteer from first team demonstrates how to move through the course. Then each member of the second team gets a turn to complete the course. Human obstacles are not allowed to move while a team is going through the course. After completing the course, second team forms their obstacle course for members of first team to complete.

Option

Students use classroom or outdoor objects to create obstacle courses.

Discussion Questions

1. When do kids your age sometimes find it hard to obey God's instructions?

2. What are some obstacles (problems, people, etc.) that sometimes get in the way of obeying God?

3. What can we do when we need help to obey? when we have disobeyed and need to be forgiven?

Art Center: Origami Shapes

Student Materials

6-inch (15-cm) squares of paper (several for each student), markers; optional—water.

Prepare the Activity

Following the directions below, make each origami shape you plan to teach students.

Our Bible story today is about someone who got in trouble because he ignored God's instructions. We're going to fold papers and if we follow the instructions just right, we'll make some fun shapes.

Lead the Activity

Lead students in following your instructions to make one or more of these origami shapes.

Dog

1. Fold paper in half diagonally.
2. Fold down the points.
3. Draw face.

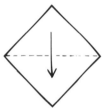 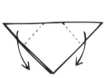 

Cat

1. Fold paper in half diagonally.
2. Fold down points.
3. Fold ears up.
4. Turn paper over. Draw face.

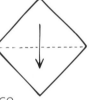 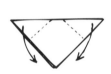 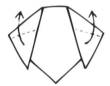 

Cup

1. Fold paper in half diagonally.
2. Fold left flap to right edge. Fold right flap to left edge.
3. Fold down the top flaps on each side. (Optional: Students drink water with cups.)

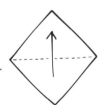 

Discussion Questions

1. When have you followed instructions in order to make or do something?

2. When you don't follow instructions, what might happen?

3. Why is it important to follow God's instructions? (God's instructions tell us how to love and obey Him. They tell us important things about how to live.)

Lesson 12

Worship Center

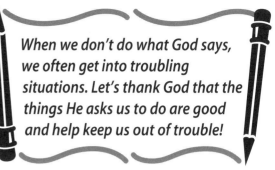

When we don't do what God says, we often get into troubling situations. Let's thank God that the things He asks us to do are good and help keep us out of trouble!

Big Picture Verse

"Blessed are they who keep his statutes and seek him with all their heart." Psalm 119:2

Teacher Materials

Bible, *God's Big Picture* cassette/CD or music video and player, "God's Holy Book" word chart (p. 459 in this book), large sheet of paper on which you have printed Psalm 119:2, masking tape.

Sing to God

Play "God's Holy Book," encouraging students to sing along with the music and do the actions shown on the word chart or music video. **What are some of the true things the Bible tells about?** (God's love. God answers prayer. Jesus' life.)

Hear and Say God's Word

Display paper on which you have printed Psalm 119:2. Ask a volunteer to read the verse aloud. **What does Psalm 119:2 say is the result of obeying God? What do you think it means to be blessed?** (To know the best way to live. To enjoy God's gifts.) **What does it mean to follow God with all your heart?** (To do your best to love and obey Him. To believe God is more important than anyone or anything.) Sing the song "Mary Had a Little Lamb" with the students to review the tune. Then sing Psalm 119:2 to the same tune:

"Blessed are they who keep his statutes, keep his statutes, keep his statutes
Blessed are they who keep his statutes and seek him with all their heart."

Practice singing the song several times until students are familiar with it. **Another word for "statutes" is "laws," or "instructions."** Sing the verse substituting one of those words for "statutes."

Pray to God

What are some of God's instructions that you are thankful for? (Pray to God. Be patient with others. Be honest.) Close in prayer, thanking God for His laws and asking for His help in following them.

Options

1. Allow students to experiment with singing the verse to other familiar tunes.

2. Ask an older student to lead the closing prayer.

 **Lesson 12**

Bible Story Coloring Center

FOR YOUNGER CHILDREN

Materials

Crayons or markers, a copy of "Samson is strong" picture and story (pp. 75-76 from *Bible Story Coloring Pages*) for each student.

Lead the Activity

Students color page 75; read or tell the story on page 76. **How does this picture show Samson's strength? What happened because Samson disobeyed God?**

Option

Students glue string or yarn to rope pictured on page 75.

Skit Center

FOR OLDER CHILDREN

Materials

A copy of "Samson: The Early Years" skit (pp. 63-68 from *The Big Book of Bible Skits*) for each student; optional—highlighter pens

Lead the Activity

Students choose parts and read the skit, which tells the story of Samson's birth and his disobedient choices. (Optional: Students highlight their parts.) Ask the discussion questions on page 63.

Bible Skills Center

FOR OLDER CHILDREN

Materials

Materials needed for "Book Pass" and/or "Poetry Puzzler" (p. 29 and/or p. 139 from *The Big Book of Bible Skills*).

Lead the Activity

Students complete activities as directed in *The Big Book of Bible Skills*.

Lesson 13
Ruth's Reward

Big Picture Verse

"I have chosen the way of truth; I have set my heart on your laws." Psalm 119:30

THE BIG PICTURE

We show our faithfulness to God by making good choices.

Scripture Background
Ruth

The delightful story of Ruth gives us an idea of the domestic life of Israel during this time period. This book, written on a separate scroll, was read at Pentecost, the harvest festival of the Israelites.

Ruth was the great-grandmother of David. This book establishes the lineage of David, the ancestor of Christ. It tells of the beginning of the Messianic family within the Messianic nation into which, over a thousand years later, the Messiah was to be born.

There are some interesting things to notice in this book. Ruth was a Moabitess. These people were descendants of Lot. They worshiped false gods. God, in establishing the family which was to produce the world's Savior, chose a beautiful Gentile girl, led her to Bethlehem and made her the bride of Boaz. This is God's grace. He adopted the Gentiles into Christ's family. Of course we know that although Ruth was born a non-Jew, through her first husband or Naomi, her mother-in-law, she learned of the true God. She was led to her choice of God and religion through human affection. She chose irrevocably. It was a life choice.

In her decision to accompany Naomi back to Bethlehem, Ruth chose well. She made the best possible choice in full view of all consequences. It was a well-considered choice—a choice of spiritual good, of right, and duty and religion. She made this choice at the cost of poverty and friendlessness and toil.

As a result of her self-denying love and giving up all to God, however, Ruth found a means of supporting her mother-in-law. Ruth won the respect and favor of the people among whom she lived. She gained a most excellent husband and home. She received the sure reward of devotion to family and trust in the Lord.

Adapted from *What the Bible Is All About* by Henrietta C. Mears.

© 1999 Gospel Light. • Permission to photocopy granted. • *God's Big Picture Leader's Guide*

127

Big Picture Story Center

Teacher Materials
Bible Time Line, drawing materials/equipment.

Student Materials
Drawing materials.

Tell the Story
Move the *Bible Time Line* frame to highlight Picture 13. As you tell each part of the story, draw each sketch. Students copy your sketches.

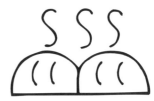

What's your favorite thing that begins with the letter B? Today we're going to Bethlehem, to tell a story that's just full of Bs!

1. This is the story of the family of a woman named Naomi. She had a husband and two sons. They lived in Bethlehem. That name means "house of bread."

1. Draw a "B" on its back; add lines for bread.

2. There was only one problem with living in Bethlehem— there was NO BREAD! No food grew because there had been no rain. That's called a famine.

2. Draw circle and "no" slash over bread.

3. So Naomi's family went to live in Moab to find food. While they lived there, the boys grew up and got married. But a while later, the boys died. Their father died, too. Naomi and her daughters-in-law, Ruth and Orpah, cried. But Naomi heard that there was food in Bethlehem again. She decided to go back there. Orpah decided to stay with her own family in Moab. But Ruth said, "I will go with you, Naomi. I won't leave you! Your people will be my people and your God will be my God."

3. Write "boo hoo." Turn "OO"s into crying eyes.

4. Ruth and Naomi arrived during the barley harvest. Ruth went to the field of a man named Boaz. She gleaned there. That means she took leftover barley off the ground and put the grains into her basket. It was hard work out in the hot sun. But Ruth was determined to help Naomi no matter what.

4. Barley grains from lines and "B"s.

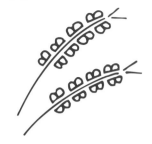

5. Boaz was kind to Ruth. He said she could come to his field any time. He told his workers to leave extra grain for her to pick up. He cared about Ruth and knew how kind Ruth had been to Naomi. Naomi was glad Ruth was working in Boaz's field. Boaz was actually a relative of her husband's! And Naomi had a plan. She told her plan to Ruth.

5. Write "Boaz"; add "3"s and lines for face.

6. Naomi told Ruth to go to Boaz at night when he would be sleeping outdoors to guard his grain. She told Ruth just how to ask Boaz to be her protector and buy back her family's land. And according to the law, if Boaz would agree, it also meant he would marry Ruth!

6. Draw rectangle to represent field. Letter "Buy Back."

7. Ruth did just what Naomi told her to do. She talked with Boaz and Boaz was glad to help—and marry her, too!

7. Letter "bride," Draw happy face.

8. So Ruth became Boaz's bride. Later, she and Boaz had a baby! Naomi had a family once again! They named the baby Obed. Now Naomi had a grandson who would keep her land in the family. And best of all, Obed would grow up and many years later, he would become a grandpa. He was the grandfather of King David—one of the ancestors of Jesus!

8. Write "Obed" and add details to make baby.

Get the Big Picture

What good choices did Ruth make? (Chose to go with with Naomi. Worked hard to get food.) **How did Ruth treat Naomi?** (Kindly. Took care of her.) **What were the results of Ruth's good choices?** (Boaz helped her and married her.)

When we make good choices, we show that we are faithful to God. Faithful means that because we love God we want to obey Him—not just when we're at church and not just when our parents or teachers are watching us, but all the time. God knows it's not always easy to make good choices, but He promises to help us.

Lesson 13

Bible Verse Object Talk: Who's First?

Big Picture Verse

"I have chosen the way of truth; I have set my heart on your laws." Psalm 119:30

Teacher Materials

Bible with Psalm 119:30 marked with a bookmark, coin, two straws or paper strips of different lengths, baseball bat or stick.

Every day we make many choices— what we're going to wear and what we're going to eat. Some choices, however, are more important than others and show our faithfulness to God. Let's talk about some of the ways we make choices.

Present the Object Talk

1. **How do you and your friends choose who will take the first turn in a game?** Volunteers answer.

2. Lead volunteers to take turns participating in one or more of these ways of choosing: *(a)* Toss a coin in the air. Two students call heads or tails. *(b)* Hold straws or paper strips with lower end inside hand so that they appear to be the same length. Two students choose straws or paper strips to see which is the longest. *(c)* Beginning at one end of a bat or stick, two students alternate grasping hold of the bat or stick to see whose hand is the last hand placed at the other end of the bat. *(d)* Choose a number between one and twenty. Two or more students guess number. *(e)* Place hands behind back holding a coin in one hand. Two students choose which hand they think holds the coin.

Conclude

These kinds of choices help us when we're playing games. But the Bible talks about the most important choice of all: whether or not we will be faithful to God. What does Psalm 119:30 say about this important choice? Read verse aloud. **Choosing the way of truth means to choose to believe in and obey God. When we make good choices, we show that we want to love and obey God.** Ask God for help in making good choices.

Discussion Questions

1. Who is someone you think makes good choices? Why?

2. What are some good choices kids your age can make at school? at home? How do these choices show love and obedience to God?

3. What might make it hard to make a good choice? Who does God provide to help you make good choices and show faithfulness to God?

Active Game Center: Balloon Carry

Materials
A balloon for each pair of students, large plastic bag.

Prepare the Game
Inflate and tie the balloons. Place them in plastic bag.

Lead the Game
1. Students form pairs. Pairs stand at one side of playing area. Give each pair a balloon.

When we make good choices in the things we do and say, we show our faithfulness to God. Sometimes other people can help us make good choices. Today you and your partner can choose the best way to carry a balloon.

2. Pairs experiment with a variety of ways in which to carry the balloon to the other side of playing area without using their hands to hold the balloon. For example, students may hold balloon between shoulders, heads or hips (see sketch).

3. After students have had time to try several methods of carrying the balloon, ask all pairs to line up at one side of playing area. Each pair chooses the method of carrying the balloon they think will be the fastest. At your signal, pairs carry balloons to the other side of the playing area and back, trying to see who can complete the task first.

Discussion Questions

1. Ruth helped her mother-in-law even when it was hard work. How has someone helped you when you had hard work to do?

2. Who is someone you can help when they have hard work to do? How?

3. What is one way God helps you when you have hard work to do? (Gives courage. Listens to and answers prayers.)

Art Center: Grab-Bag Art

Student Materials

Large paper bag in which you have placed a variety of art materials (crayons, markers, ribbon, sticker sheets, stamp and color markers, yarn, metallic pens), constuction paper, glue, scissors.

Lead the Activity

1. Show paper bag. **As this grab bag is passed to you, choose one of the art materials in it to begin creating your picture. You'll get a chance to use most of the mate-**

When a person tries to love and obey God every day, we say that the person is faithful to God. We show our faithfulness to God by making good choices. Today we're going to make some fun choices from a grab bag.

rials in the bag. Give each student a sheet of construction paper.

2. As students pass paper bag around the table, each student chooses one art material from the bag. Allow students several minutes in which to begin creating their pictures. (Note: Glue and scissors may be used as needed.) After one to two minutes, call time and collect art materials in the grab bag again. (Replace sticker sheets if needed.) Pass the grab bag again, inviting students to choose different art materials from the ones they had before. Continue procedure as time permits. As students create pictures, comment about the different ways in which they are using the art materials.

Options

1. Make a separate bag of materials for each group of eight to ten students.

2. If students have difficulty choosing, make a rule that students must close their eyes and take the first item they grab; or establish a five-second time limit and invite other students to count aloud to five.

Discussion Questions

1. Which of these art materials was your favorite?

2. What are some of the good choices kids your age can make to show their faithfulness to God?
(Read God's Word. Talk to God. Plan ways to obey Him.)

3. Who helps you make good choices?

Lesson 13

Worship Center

Big Picture Verse

"I have chosen the way of truth; I have set my heart on your laws." Psalm 119:30

Teacher Materials

Bible, *God's Big Picture* cassette/CD or music video and player, "Promises" word chart (p. 475 in this book), large sheet of paper on which you have printed Psalm 119:30, masking tape.

It's good to know that God is faithful and will always keep His promises to help us make good choices. We show our faithfulness to God by making good choices.

Sing to God

Play "Promises," encouraging students to sing along with the music and do the actions shown on the word chart or music video. **In what ways does this song say that God is faithful?**

Hear and Say God's Word

Display paper on which you have printed Psalm 119:30. Have a volunteer read the verse to the group. **What does it mean to choose the way of truth?** (To believe that God is the one true God. To choose to love and obey God.) **to set our hearts on God's law?** (To make good choices, following God's commands.) Invite volunteers to repeat the verse, inserting their names into the verse ("Jake has chosen the way of truth; Jake has set his heart on your laws").

Pray to God

Lead volunteers in completing this sentence: **Dear God, thank You for....** End the prayer time by thanking God for His faithfulness to us and asking for His help in being faithful to Him.

Option

Students sing and do actions for "Picture This!" (p. 473 in this book). Older students may make up additional actions.

 **Lesson 13**

Bible Story Coloring Center

Materials

Crayons or markers, a copy of "Ruth helps Naomi" picture and story (pp. 73-74 from *Bible Story Coloring Pages*) for each student.

Lead the Activity

Students color page 73; read or tell the story on page 74. **What was Ruth like? What good choices did she make? What are some good choices you can make to show love and faithfulness to God?**

Option

Provide a copy of page 71 for students to color as you read or tell the story on page 72.

Skit Center

Materials

A copy of "I've Been Working" skit (pp. 76-78 from *The Big Book of Bible Skits*) for each student; optional—highlighter pens.

Lead the Activity

Students choose parts and read the skit, which tells the story of Ruth and Boaz. (Optional: Students highlight their parts.) Ask the discussion questions on page 76.

Bible Skills Center

Materials

Materials needed for "Book Collections" and/or "Charades" (p. 27 and/or p. 70 from *The Big Book of Bible Skills*).

Lead the Activity

Students complete activities as directed in *The Big Book of Bible Skills*.

 **Lesson 14**

Samuel Listens Up

Big Picture Verse

"Listen carefully to the voice of the Lord your God and do what is right in his eyes." Exodus 15:26

THE BIG PICTURE

Listen to God and obey Him your whole life.

Scripture Background
1 Samuel 1—2:11,18-21,26; 3:1-19

Biblical royal history begins with the book of Samuel. The long period of the rule of the judges ends with Samuel—the last of the judges, the first of the prophets and the founder of the monarchy.

Through Samuel, God introduced a new way of dealing with Israel. He called prophets through whom He would speak. It was with Samuel that prophecy became an integral part of the life of Israel.

Throughout Samuel's long and useful life, he was God's man. Even his name—"heard of God"—bears witness to this quality of his life. Samuel was preeminently a man of prayer, not only seeking God's direction but also listening to and obeying God's commands. First Samuel is a marvelous study of the place and power of prayer.

Samuel's very life began with a prayer. It was in the dark and troubled times of Israel that we hear the prayer of faith from the lips of a simple trusting woman, Hannah. She asked God for a son whom she could dedicate to Him for service. When Samuel was born, Hannah brought him to the Tabernacle at Shiloh. Although the corruption of the priesthood was appalling, Samuel was protected and grew as a boy in the fear of the Lord. He was a child of prayer (see 1 Samuel 3:1-19); he brought victory to God's people through prayer (see 7:5-10); when the nation wanted a king, Samuel prayed to the Lord (8:6). Intercessory prayer was the keynote of his life.

God always gives us the best we will take. We are free human agents. We can choose for ourselves, but we may well tremble at the consequences. We must choose God's best or our own way. As Samuel grew into manhood and assumed the leadership for which he had been born, he chose the path of obedience and love for God.

Adapted from *What the Bible Is All About* by Henrietta C. Mears.

Big Picture Story Center

Teacher Materials

Bible Time Line, drawing materials/equipment.

Student Materials

Drawing materials.

Tell the Story

Move the *Bible Time Line* frame to highlight Picture 14. As you tell each part of the story, draw each sketch. Students copy your sketches.

Who is someone you know very well?
Today we'll use the letter U to tell about a boy who grew to know God better and better.

1. There was a lady in Israel named Hannah. She had no children and this made her very sad. One day she went to the Tabernacle—the place where God's people worshiped Him—and asked God to give her a son. She promised to let her son serve Him. God heard and answered Hannah's prayer. She had a baby and named him Samuel. His name means "God hears."

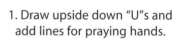

1. Draw upside down "U"s and add lines for praying hands.

2. Baby Samuel grew and grew! When he was old enough, Hannah took him to the Tabernacle where she had prayed. Samuel stayed there with Eli, the priest. Hannah loved and missed Samuel. Every year, she visited Samuel and brought him a special coat she had made him, just to remind him of her love.

2. Draw "U"s and add faces for Hannah and Samuel.

3. As Samuel grew, he helped Eli take care of the Tabernacle. By now Eli was old and he couldn't see well, so he must have been very glad to have Samuel's help! Samuel made sure there was oil for the lamps and wood for the fire. He opened the Tabernacle doors in the morning, closed them at night and probably helped Eli do many other things, too!

3. Draw lamp and wide "U"s for oil. Add wick.

4. One night, Samuel finished all his chores as usual. He got into bed, lay down and closed his eyes as usual. Suddenly, he heard a voice. Someone was calling his name. "Samuel! Samuel!" *Who was it?* Samuel thought. *Was it Eli?*

4. Draw face of sleeping Samuel.

5. Samuel sat up. Maybe Eli needed him. He ran to where Eli lay asleep. He shook Eli. "Here I am!" he said.

5. Add open eyes and mouth to Samuel.

6. Eli woke up and looked at Samuel. He said, "I didn't call you, Samuel. Go back to bed." Now Samuel KNEW there was NO ONE else in the Tabernacle. He had checked when he shut the doors! But after Samuel went back to bed, he heard the same voice calling his name. Samuel got up again and went back to Eli. "Here I am!" he said. And again, Eli said, "I didn't call. Go back to bed."

6. Draw second sleeping face. Add details for Eli's face.

7. When Samuel heard the voice call his name a THIRD time, he went to Eli and said, "Here I am! I KNOW you called me!" *Was Eli playing tricks on him?* Samuel wondered.

Suddenly, Eli realized what was going on: GOD was calling Samuel! Eli said, "Samuel, go back to bed. When you hear the voice again say, 'Speak, Lord. Your servant is listening.'"

7. Turn closed eyes to surprised face.

8. So Samuel went back to bed. But he probably wasn't sleepy! Amazed and excited, he waited quietly, straining to hear. Then, he heard it—the voice calling his name! Samuel said, "Speak, Lord! Your servant is LISTENING."

8. Add head and large ears to Samuel.

9. The Bible says that God talked with Samuel. He told Samuel important things that were going to happen. After that night, God often talked with Samuel. And Samuel always listened and obeyed. As Samuel grew up, God helped him to become a person everyone in Israel respected. All the people of Israel knew that Samuel was a person who listened to God! He became the priest and was the leader of God's people for many years.

9. Write "SAMUEL." Add "LISTENS" and "OBEYS."

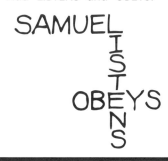

Get the Big Picture

What does Samuel's name mean? (God hears.) **How would you describe Samuel? Why do you think Samuel chose to listen to God?**

Because Samuel listened to God, he knew how to obey God. We can listen and obey, too—from the time we're young until we're old!

Bible Verse Object Talk: Quick Change

Big Picture Verse

"Listen carefully to the voice of the Lord your God and do what is right in his eyes." Exodus 15:26

Teacher Materials

Bible with bookmark at Exodus 15:26, watch with second hand.

Present the Object Talk

1. Ask students to look at you for 10 seconds, paying attention to the details of how you are dressed.

2. Ask students to close their eyes (or you may briefly step out of the room). Quickly change one detail about how you are dressed (remove glasses, take off a sweater, roll up sleeves, etc.).

Sometimes you might think that only grown-ups need to listen to God. But God wants everyone—for their whole lives—to listen to Him. When you listen to someone, it's important to pay careful attention to what the person says and does. Let's find out how good we are at paying attention.

3. Ask students to carefully look at you again, trying to identify the change you made. After change is identified or after 30 seconds, repeat activity with yourself or with student volunteers. Vary the difficulty of changes made according to the age of students. As students are guessing changes, comment occasionally about the way in which they are paying careful attention.

Conclude

What does this verse say about listening and paying careful attention? Read Exodus 15:26 aloud. **Listening to God's voice helps us know how to love and obey Him. We can listen to God's voice as we read and hear Bible stories and as we pray to Him.** Lead students in prayer, asking God's help in listening to Him.

Discussion Questions

1. Who are some people you listen to?

2. When might it be hard to remember to listen to God? (When someone wants you to do wrong.)

3. Who are some people who help you listen to God?

4. How can you help others listen to God? (Pray for them. Talk with them about what you read in God's Word.)

Active Game Center: "Here I Am"

Materials
Blindfold.

Lead the Game

1. Play a game like Marco Polo. Ask a volunteer to stand on one side of the playing area. Blindfold the volunteer. Students quietly position themselves at random around the playing area. Volunteer begins calling, "Samuel, Samuel." Rest of students answer with the phrase, "Here I am."

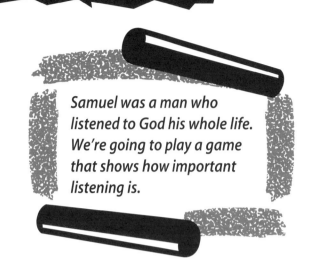

Samuel was a man who listened to God his whole life. We're going to play a game that shows how important listening is.

2. Blindfolded volunteer moves toward students by listening to their voices. As he or she continues calling, "Samuel, Samuel," students around the room must respond each time.

Depending on the size of your playing area, the students who respond to the blindfolded volunteer may stay frozen in one spot or may move around as they respond. (If you have a large playing area or a large number of students, students should stay frozen.)

3. When the volunteer finds and tags a student, that student (or a student who hasn't had a turn yet) is blindfolded for the next round. Continue game as time permits.

Discussion Questions

1. *What are ways we can listen to God and find out what He wants us to do?* (Read the Bible. Listen to Bible stories. Pray. Talk with adults who know and love God.)

2. *What do you think a person is like who listens to and obeys God?* (Treats others in kind ways. Is honest. Reads God's Word.)

2. *What's one way you have listened to God today?*

 **Lesson 14**

Art Center: It Takes Each Little Dot

Student Materials
Butcher paper, markers in a variety of colors.

Prepare the Activity
Draw the outline of one or more large scenes (park, forest, ocean) on butcher paper (see ideas in sketch a). Make at least one scene for each group of six to eight students.

Loving and obeying God is something we can do day after day throughout our whole lives! Today we are going to paint one dot after the next until we have created a whole picture by using dots.

Lead the Activity
Students fill in the scene by making dots with markers (see sketch b). As students are working on the scenes, talk with them about their work. Make comments such as, **Each dot is important to make the whole scene look good. What would the scene look like if one section didn't have any dots at all? What does a section look like with just a few dots? with many dots? Why might someone get tired of making lots of dots? When we keep on loving and obeying God, we are able to enjoy all the good things God has given us.**

a.    b.

Options
1. Use tempera paint and paint brushes or chalk dipped in milk to create the dots of color.

2. Older students may draw their own scenes.

3. Purchase ministampers for students to use in making dots.

Discussion Questions

1. What are some ways that you have seen people listen to and obey God?

2. What are some ways that kids can show they want to listen to and obey God? (Read Bible. Pray. Go to Sunday School.)

3. The Bible tells us God wants us to do good to others. What's one way you can obey this message you've heard from God's Word?

 **Lesson 14**

Worship Center

Big Picture Verse

"Listen carefully to the voice of the Lord your God and do what is right in his eyes." Exodus 15:26

Teacher Materials

Bible, *God's Big Picture* cassette/CD or music video and player, "Picture This!" word chart (p. 473 in this book), large sheet of paper on which you have printed Exodus 15:26, masking tape.

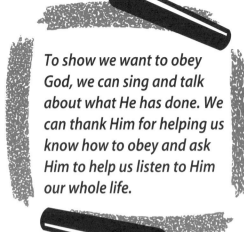

To show we want to obey God, we can sing and talk about what He has done. We can thank Him for helping us know how to obey and ask Him to help us listen to Him our whole life.

Sing to God

Play "Picture This!" encouraging students to sing along with the music and do the actions shown on the word chart or the music video. **According to this song, how long has God helped people to do good and know how to live?** (From the beginning when He created the world all the way until now when we are a part of "God's gallery.")

Hear and Say God's Word

Display paper on which you have printed Exodus 15:26. Have a volunteer read the verse aloud. **What are the two things this verse asks us to do?** (Listen carefully to God and obey His commands.) Invite students to participate in a choral reading of the verse. Divide the verse into four or five phrases. Read phrases as solos, duets or trios, assigning each part to a different student or group of students.

Pray to God

What are some ways we can listen to God? (Read the Bible. Listen to parents and teachers who love God.) On the Bible-verse paper, rewrite the words to read "God, please help us to listen carefully to Your voice and do what is right in Your eyes all of our life." Read the sentence together as a prayer.

Options

1. Students sing "Love and Power" (p. 469 in this book). Encourage students to do the actions shown on the word chart or the music video.
2. Ask an older student to lead the Bible verse activity.
3. At the beginning of this worship time, invite several students to read Psalm 108:1-5 in unison (or alternating verses) as an invitation to students to worship.

 **Lesson 14**

Bible Story Coloring Center

FOR YOUNGER CHILDREN

Materials

Crayons or markers, a copy of "God speaks to Samuel" picture and story (pp. 79-80 from *Bible Story Coloring Pages*) for each student.

Lead the Activity

Students color page 79; read or tell the story on page 80. **What is Samuel doing? How is his bed different than yours?**

Option

Students draw additional pictures of how they think Samuel may have looked when he was a teenager, a young man and an old man.

Skit Center

FOR OLDER CHILDREN

Materials

A copy of "You Were Saying?" skit (pp. 79-81 from *The Big Book of Bible Skits*) for each student; optional—highlighter pens.

Lead the Activity

Students form pairs and read the skit, which tells the story of Samuel and Eli. (Optional: Students highlight their parts.) Ask the discussion questions on page 79.

Bible Skills Center

FOR OLDER CHILDREN

Materials

Materials needed for "Get a Clue!" and/or "Ferris Wheel Definitions" (p. 46 and/or p. 113 from *The Big Book of Bible Skills*).

Lead the Activity

Students complete activities as directed in *The Big Book of Bible Skills*.

Lesson 15

Saul's Excuses Don't Count

Big Picture Verse

"To God belong wisdom and power; counsel and understanding are his." Job 12:13

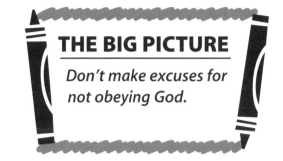

THE BIG PICTURE

Don't make excuses for not obeying God.

Scripture Background
1 Samuel 8—10; 13:1-14; 15

God never intended Israel to have any king but Himself. He would send them great leaders and these in turn would receive their orders directly from Him. But Israel, in her falling away, had become restless. The people of Israel wanted a king like the other surrounding nations. We find God granting their request.

Saul, their first king, started out splendidly. He was handsome to look at and he was tall and of a noble appearance. He proved to be an able military leader. He defeated the enemies about him—the Philistines, the Amalekites and the Ammonites. Despite his accomplishments, Saul was humble at first. But we soon find him becoming proud and disobedient to God. No man had a greater opportunity than Saul and no man ever was a greater failure.

Inasmuch as Saul was granted to Israel as king in response to Israel's sinful demand for a king, did Saul ever really have a chance to "make good" in God's sight? Could he possibly have succeeded under such circumstances? Was he not condemned by God to failure even before he started as king?

We find the answer clearly in God's Word. In 1 Samuel 12:12-15, the prophet of God tells Israel that, although they had demanded their king in defiance of God, if both they and their king would fear Jehovah and serve Him, all would be well. The only reason why any soul is ever rejected by God is because that soul has first rejected God. God takes the initiative in love. We take the initiative in sin.

Eventually, in a battle with the Philistines, Saul and his three sons met death. Here a life so full of promise ended in defeat and failure. Saul had not obeyed God absolutely. Think of the difference between the end of Saul of Tarsus (the apostle Paul) and Saul the king! One put God first, the other himself. God shows that He must be all in all, that His children have no blessing apart from Him.

Adapted from *What the Bible Is All About* by Henrietta C. Mears.

Big Picture Story Center

Teacher Materials
Bible Time Line, drawing materials/equipment.

Student Materials
Drawing materials.

Tell the Story
Move the *Bible Time Line* frame to highlight Picture 15. As you tell each part of the story, draw each sketch. Students copy your sketches.

What is something you've made an excuse for not doing? Today we're going to hear about Israel's first king who made some excuses for not obeying God.

1. Samuel had been God's leader, or judge, for a long time and now he was old. Although his sons were helping him judge, they weren't honest. So the people told Samuel, "You are old. Your sons are NOT good judges. Find a king for us instead!"

2. Samuel was upset because he knew that God was really their king! But God told Samuel, "Warn them. Tell them a king will take their children, their food, their land and their animals. They will be like slaves!" Samuel told the people God's warning. But the people wanted a king ANYWAY, so God told Samuel He would give them a king.

3. Now about this time, a young man named Saul was looking for his father's lost donkeys. He and his helper came to ask Samuel if he knew where the donkeys were. When Saul came toward Samuel, God said, "Here's the man who will be king." Samuel invited Saul and his helper to a special dinner. Later Samuel poured olive oil on Saul's head and said, "God has chosen you to be the leader of His people."

4. Not long after that, Samuel called all of Israel together and brought Saul to the front. Samuel said, "Here is the king God has chosen." God let the people have what they wanted, but God's warning about the trouble from a king came true.

1. Write "old." Add face.

2. Draw "O" and "V"s for crown.

3. Donkeys from "U"s, "V"s and lines.

4. Add "Saul" to crown.

5. King Saul seemed to want to do everything his own way instead of God's way. God was patient with him. But one day, God gave Samuel a message for King Saul. Samuel told Saul, "God will help you win your battle against the enemy. But God says that after the battle, you must get rid of EVERY-THING that belongs to the enemy." God had good reasons for His rule. And God expected Saul to obey!

5. Write "ENEMY." Add "no" slash.

6. Soon, Saul and the Israelite army charged into battle. They won, just as God had said they would. But Saul decided to bring home some of the best cattle and sheep. Saul disobeyed God's command! God told Samuel what had happened. The next morning, Samuel went to meet Saul who was returning from the battle. Sure enough, cows and sheep were coming along behind—cows and sheep that proved Saul had disobeyed!

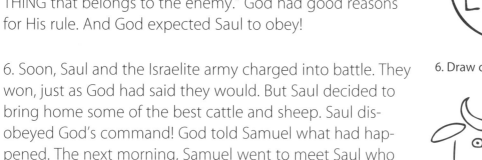

6. Draw cow and sheep from "U"s and "O"s.

7. Saul made excuses. He said that disobeying was the soldiers' idea. Then he said the soldiers wanted to offer the animals to God! Then he said he was so afraid of the soldiers that he disobeyed! Samuel told Saul that NOTHING is more important than obeying God—not even gifts! He said, "Because you no longer obey God, you will not be king."

7. Conversation balloon for excuses. Add "no" slash.

8. As Samuel walked away, Saul grabbed Samuel's robe, trying to stop him. A piece of the robe tore off. Samuel said, "Just like you tore a piece off my robe, God has torn the kingdom from you. God doesn't lie or change His mind. When He tells you something, He means it!" Saul was sorry for what he had done, but he couldn't undo it! God still loved Saul, but he was not going to be king for much longer.

8. Add "no" slash over Saul's crown.

Get the Big Picture

Why did God make Saul king? (The people wanted their own way.) **Why do you think Saul disobeyed God? How do you think Saul felt when he heard he would no longer be king?**

Sometimes we make excuses for not obeying God. Our excuses may even seem **pretty good! But deep down we know we are not obeying. God wants us to obey Him, not make excuses—not even good excuses! Nothing is more important than obeying Him.**

Bible Verse Object Talk: Circle Pass

Big Picture Verse

"To God belong wisdom and power; counsel and understanding are his." Job 12:13

Teacher Materials

Bible with bookmark at Job 12:13, several small objects (quarter, eraser, walnut, plastic letter, etc.—one of each object for each group of six to eight students); optional—bell.

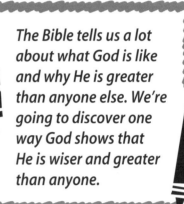

The Bible tells us a lot about what God is like and why He is greater than anyone else. We're going to discover one way God shows that He is wiser and greater than anyone.

Present the Object Talk

1. Groups of six to eight students sit in circles, with their hands placed behind their backs.
2. Secretly give one student in each circle an (eraser).
3. Allow time for student to feel the object with his or her hands, trying to identify the object but keeping its identity a secret. At your signal, student passes the object behind his or her back to the next student in the circle, keeping the object hidden in his or her hands.

 (Optional: Ring bell as signal.) Continue process until all students have had an opportunity to feel the object. Then identify the object aloud. Repeat with a variety of objects.

Variation: Bring a variety of scents for students to smell while blindfolded (orange peel, cotton ball sprinkled with vanilla flavoring, onion slice, etc.).

Conclude

How did we figure out what each object was? Volunteers answer. **The awesome way in which God made us shows how great and wise He is. How does Job 12:13 describe God?** Read verse aloud. **The words "counsel" and "understanding" mean that God's knowledge is greater than anyone else's. Discovering how great God is helps us see why it's so important to obey Him and never think that our ideas are better than His.** Thank God for His wisdom and power.

Discussion Questions

1. What are some other ways our sense of touch helps us?

2. What other senses did God give us? How do they help us? (Sense of smell helps us smell fire.) *How would our lives be different if we didn't have these senses?*

3. What are some other ways we see God's greatness and wisdom?

4. How can you obey this wise and great God? (Be kind to others. Help friends. Be honest.)

Active Game Center: Coin Toss Relay

Materials
Masking tape, coins.

Prepare the Game
Use masking tape to make two curvy paths on the ground or floor in your playing area, leaving room for students to line up behind the paths.

God wants us to obey Him because He knows His commands are the best way to live. We are going to do a coin toss relay to remind us of the difference between choosing our own way and obeying God's way.

Lead the Game
1. Group students into two teams. Each team lines up behind one of the masking-tape paths. **In this game, when your coin lands heads up, you'll get to move along the path in an easy way to**

remind you of how good it is to obey God's wise commands. If your coin lands tails up, you'll have to move along the path in a harder way to remind you that disobeying God causes trouble.

2. Student at front of each line flips a coin. If the coin lands heads up, tell the student(s) to move along the masking-tape path in an easy manner (skipping or walking). If the coin lands tails up, tell the student(s) to move along the path in a more difficult manner (crabwalking or putting one foot behind the other to move backwards).

   After first student has completed the path, next student in line flips the coin and moves along the path. Continue play until all students on one team have completed the path. If time allows, begin a new round of the relay with students doing new movements.

Options
1. Vary the complexity of the path according to the age of most of your students.
2. Suggest alternative movements for students to use, making sure to suggest an easy motion for a heads toss and a more difficult motion for a tails toss.

Discussion Questions
1. What are some commands God wants us to obey? (Forgive others. Help needy people.)

2. What is one way you can obey one of these commands?

3. What excuse might a kid your age give for not obeying God? (It's too hard. No one else obeys.)

Art Center: Crown Construction

Student Materials

Pencils, scissors, 6x22-inch (15x55-cm) sheet of construction paper (or poster board) for each student, foil wrapping paper, glue, glitter glue, tape.

Lead the Activity

1. Students draw and cut points or scallops for crowns along one long edge of paper (see sketch a).

2. Help students fit paper around heads, leaving a 1-inch (2.5-cm) overlap at ends. Cut off excess paper.

3. Students decorate crowns with foil wrapping paper and glitter glue.

4. Tape ends of each crown together (see sketch b).

Today we're making crowns to remind us of the first king in the Bible. This king disobeyed God because he thought his ideas were better than God's. But God is wiser and greater than anyone—even kings and queens.

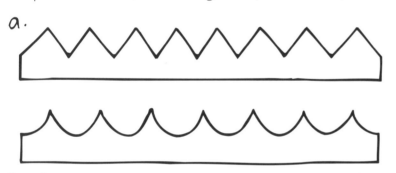

Option

Bring additional items for decorating crowns: sequins, plastic jewels, metallic or glitter pens.

Discussion Questions

1. What are some ways God has shown how great He is?

2. How does following God's commands help us? (Commands help us know what to do and how to treat others.)

3. What are some ways kids can show that they believe God is greater than anyone? (Pay attention to what His Word says to do. Don't make excuses for disobeying Him.)

Lesson 15

Worship Center

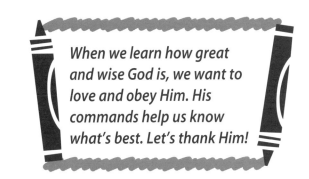

When we learn how great and wise God is, we want to love and obey Him. His commands help us know what's best. Let's thank Him!

Big Picture Verse

"To God belong wisdom and power; counsel and understanding are his." Job 12:13

Teacher Materials

Bible, *God's Big Picture* cassette/CD or music video and player, "I Know the King" word chart (p. 463 in this book), large sheet of paper on which you have printed Job 12:13, masking tape.

Sing to God

Play "I Know the King," encouraging students to sing along with the music and do the actions shown on the word chart or the music video. **What does a king do? How is God like a king? What can we do to show Him we want Him as our King?** (Obey what He says to do. Don't make excuses for not obeying His commands.)

Hear and Say God's Word

Display paper on which you have printed Job 12:13. Have a volunteer read the verse aloud. Say the verse together as a group a few times. **How has God shown how powerful and wise He is?** (Created the world. Answered prayers.) Say Job 12:13 as a group and then have students form a circle. Each student says one word of verse in order around the circle. Repeat the verse in this manner several times, making sure each student gets to say a word at least two different times.

Pray to God

When might kids your age feel like they don't want to obey God? (When it's hard to tell the truth. When they don't want to be patient toward a brother or sister.) Lead students in a prayer, asking God to help you and your students obey His commands.

Options

1. Invite older students to create their own sign language motions for the words of Job 12:13. Students demonstrate motions while repeating verse.

2. During the discussion in the prayer activity, share an age-appropriate example about a time you made an excuse for not obeying God.

3. Play "God's Holy Book" (p. 459 in this book), encouraging students to sing along with the music and do the actions shown on the word chart or the music video.

Bible Story Coloring Center FOR YOUNGER CHILDREN

Materials
Crayons or markers, a copy of "Samuel chooses a king" picture and story (pp. 81-82 from *Bible Story Coloring Pages*) for each student.

Lead the Activity
Students color page 81; read or tell the story on page 82. **Why is Samuel pouring oil on Saul's head? What should a good king be like?**

Option
Students draw pictures of kings and queens. Explain that because God is so great and wise, even kings and queens need to obey Him.

Skit Center FOR OLDER CHILDREN

Materials
A copy of "Grudge Match" skit (pp. 85-88 from *The Big Book of Bible Skits*) for each student; optional—highlighter pens.

Lead the Activity
Students form trios and read the skit, which tells the story of Saul's disobedience. (Optional: Students highlight their parts.) Ask the discussion questions on page 85.

Bible Skills Center FOR OLDER CHILDREN

Materials
Materials needed for "Power Search" and/or "Listen Up!" (p. 53 and/or p. 75 from *The Big Book of Bible Skills*).

Lead the Activity
Students complete activities as directed in *The Big Book of Bible Skills*.

 **Lesson 16**

A Man After God's Own Heart

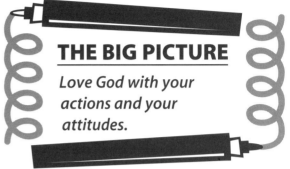

THE BIG PICTURE
Love God with your actions and your attitudes.

Big Picture Verse

"Love the Lord your God with all your heart and with all your soul and with all your mind."
Matthew 22:37

Scripture Background
1 Samuel 16—18:16; 2 Samuel 5:1-10; 6:1-19

David, "the apple of God's eye," was one of the greatest men of all times. He made great contributions to the history of Israel both spiritually and nationally.

David, Jesse's son and the great-grandson of Ruth and Boaz, was born in Bethlehem. He was the youngest of eight sons. When David was only eighteen, God told Samuel to anoint him king to succeed Saul. Second Samuel describes the enthronement of God's king, David, and the establishment of the "House of David" through which the Messiah, Jesus Christ, should later come.

There is no one found anywhere in God's Word who was so versatile. In the books of Samuel we see David as a shepherd lad, a minstrel, an armorbearer, a captain, the king's son-in-law, a writer of psalms and a fugitive. Throughout his life David was known as the lover of God. David was a man after God's own heart—not because of boasted perfection but because of confessed imperfections. He hid himself in God.

Both Saul and David reigned about the same length of time—40 years. Both had the loyal support of the people, and both had the promise of God's power to back them. Yet Saul was a failure and David was a success. Saul's name is a blot on Israel's history, and David's name is honored today both by Jews and Gentiles.

What is the reason for the differences? Saul chose the way of self; David chose God's way. David had faith in God. He was patient and was willing to wait for God to lead. He was humble before God and His people, and when he sinned he genuinely repented. David used every talent God gave him for the glory of his Creator, leaving a rich heritage to his race. But above all, he left an example of complete love and loyalty to God.

Adapted from *What the Bible Is All About* by Henrietta C. Mears.

Big Picture Story Center

Teacher Materials
Bible Time Line, drawing materials/equipment.

Student Materials
Drawing materials.

Tell the Story
Move the *Bible Time Line* frame to highlight Picture 16. As you tell each part of the story, draw each sketch. Students copy your sketches.

What's a way you show love to a person you care about? Today we're going to find out some ways one man showed his love for God.

1. King Saul had not obeyed God. He had done things his own way. Although Saul was still the king, God had chosen a new king. God sent Samuel to Jesse's house in Bethlehem, so He could show Samuel the next king. Samuel met seven fine-looking sons of Jesse, but God said NONE of them was the one He had chosen. Jesse had one more son—his youngest son David, who was out watching the sheep. When Samuel met him, God told Samuel, "HE is the one!" Samuel poured olive oil on David's head to show that God had chosen David as king.

1. Draw seven circles; add faces.

Write "8." Add details for David.

2. Some time later, King Saul needed a person to play soothing music for him. Someone told the king about this young man named David, so David was brought to the palace to play his harp for Saul. David was soon living in the palace some of the time.

2. Harp from "D."

3. One day, enemies called Philistines came to fight Israel. The Israelites were afraid! The Philistine giant named Goliath was over 9 feet (2.7 m) tall! NOBODY could fight him! Then David came. And he WANTED to fight Goliath. David took five stones from the stream. He told Goliath, "You have a spear, but I have the Lord God with me! God doesn't need a sword or a spear. The battle is His!" David whipped his sling around his head and then let it go. WHAP! The stone hit

3. Goliath from "9."

Goliath squarely between his eyes and he fell to the ground! The Philistines ran! The Israelites chased them away. David became a hero!

Write 2 "5"s; add details for David's head.

4. David married King Saul's daughter and lived in the palace. But Saul was jealous that everyone in Israel loved David. Saul even tried to KILL David. David ran from Saul, but he never tried to hurt Saul. David showed by his attitude and his actions that he trusted God to make him king at just the right time. After Saul died, the people came to David and made him their king.

4. Add stick body, "N" legs to David.

5. Now that David was king, he didn't want to be like Saul, doing things his own way. Instead, David wanted to honor God and help the Israelites remember that God was their real King! One way David helped his people was by helping them worship God. David loved to worship God. He had made up songs for God when he was a shepherd boy. Now he wrote many songs, called psalms, to help the people worship God. He also chose people to sing and play instruments, so everyone could praise God together!

5. Draw new David; add crown. Add musical notes; harp from "D."

6. David did many other things, too. He fought many battles so that there would be peace in his country. He helped people who had problems. Sometimes, David did wrong things. But David always talked to God. He asked God for help with his hard choices and asked for God's forgiveness when he had done wrong. David showed his love for God by praying whether he was glad or sad. And because David showed his love for God in the things he did and said, the people of Israel learned to honor and obey God.

6. Draw new crowned David with eyes closed. Add praying hands from "U" and "W."

Get the Big Picture

How did David show that he loved God and wanted to please God? (Trusted God when he fought Goliath. Obeyed God when he was king. Wrote songs to worship God. Prayed.)

It's easy to say we love God. But God wants us to show our love for Him by our attitudes and actions, too.

Bible Verse Object Talk: Choose That Gift!

Big Picture Verse

"Love the Lord your God with all your heart and with all your soul and with all your mind." Matthew 22:37

Teacher Materials

Bible with bookmark at Matthew 22:37, one large box, one small box, penny, dollar bill, heavy nonbreakable item (book, brick, etc.), wrapping paper, scissors, tape, ribbon.

Prepare the Object Talk

Place the penny and nonbreakable item in the large box and wrap it. Place the dollar in the small box and wrap it.

Loving God is something we can show not only with our actions, but also in our attitudes—the way we think about things. Sometimes a person might say and do one thing but think something totally different. See if you can figure out what's really on the inside of these gifts.

Present the Object Talk

1. Place wrapped boxes on table or floor, so students can see them.
2. Invite several volunteers to take turns examining and shaking boxes.

3. Ask students to raise hands showing which of the two boxes they would like to receive. Ask several students to tell why they chose the boxes and what they think is inside.
4. Have two students open boxes and show the contents.

Conclude

What made some people think the biggest box was best? What made some people think the smallest box was best? Sometimes the way people or things look on the outside isn't the same as how they are on the inside. Listen to what Matthew 22:37 says about what should be on the inside—or in the attitudes—of God's followers. Read verse aloud. **When we love God with our attitudes, we want to please Him in everything we do. Loving and obeying God is what's most important to us.** Pray, expressing your love for God and thanking Him for His love for all people.

Discussion Questions

1. When have you been given a gift that was better than it looked on the outside?

2. How do people show love for their friends and family members?

3. What are some ways in which people show their love for God?

4. How has God shown He loves you? How can you show your love for Him?

Lesson 16

Active Game Center: Friend Fun

Materials
Paper, pencils, kitchen timer or stopwatch.

Lead the Game

1. Each student traces one of his or her hands on a sheet of paper.

2. Assign students an action such as high five, shake hands or pat on the back. Set the timer or stopwatch for 60 seconds. (If you have a larger group, you may want to set the timer for a longer amount of time.)

David loved God so much. He talked to God as if God was his best friend. Let's play a fun game with our friends to find out what kinds of things we like to do with our friends.

3. Students move around the room and do the action with as many other students as they can before time is up. When two students have done the action together, they initial the hand on each other's paper. The goal is to collect as many initials as possible.

4. When time is up, students count the number of initials on his or her "hand." Student with most initials tells something he or she likes to do with friends and suggests an action for the next round. Students use reverse side of paper (or new sheet if playing more than two rounds) to trace hand and collect initials for the next round.

Option
Rather than using papers and pencils, students use washable markers to write initials on each other's hands.

Discussion Questions

1. How has a friend shown love for you?

2. What are some ways you show love to your friends?

3. What are some ways we can show God we love Him with our actions and attitudes? (Talk to Him every day. Tell other people about His love. Believe what He says in the Bible.) **One way to show love to God is to become a member of His family.** Talk with students about becoming Christians, following the guidelines in the "Leading a Child to Christ" article on page 30.

Art Center: Beautiful Words

Student Materials
Markers, white paper, gold or silver metallic pens, large piece of butcher paper, glue, masking tape.

Prepare the Activity
Use a marker to print each letter of the phrase "We Love the Lord" on separate sheets of white paper.

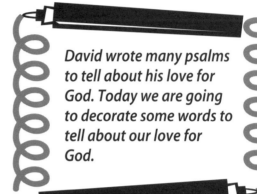

David wrote many psalms to tell about his love for God. Today we are going to decorate some words to tell about our love for God.

Lead the Activity
1. Without identifying the phrase "We Love the Lord," lead each student to choose a letter to decorate with markers and pens.

2. Students put decorated letters in order and then glue decorated letters to large piece of butcher paper. Display paper in your classroom.

Options
1. Older students may create their own slogans telling of their love for God.

2. If you know someone who does calligraphy, ask him or her to write Psalm 31:23,24 in calligraphy on a sheet of paper, making several letters larger with open space. Make a photocopy of the calligraphy for each student. Students decorate the larger letters and the border of the paper with markers and metallic pens.

Discussion Questions
1. What are some reasons we love God?

2. What are some ways to show love to God?

3. What are some ways of treating others to show we want to love and obey God? (Be fair. Be patient.)

Worship Center

Let's thank God that we can show our love for Him with our actions and our attitudes.

Big Picture Verse

"Love the Lord your God with all your heart and with all your soul and with all your mind."
Matthew 22:37

Teacher Materials

Bible, *God's Big Picture* cassette/CD or music video and player, "I Know the King" word chart (p. 463 in this book), large sheet of paper on which you have printed Matthew 22:37 with five to seven incorrect words, masking tape.

Sing to God

Play "I Know the King," encouraging students to sing along with the music and do the actions shown on the word chart or the music video. **How does this song say that David loved God with his attitude and actions?** (Trusted God with everything. Cared for his friends.)

Hear and Say God's Word

Display paper on which you have printed Matthew 22:37. **Some of the words on this paper are wrong.** Read the verse aloud from the Bible. Volunteers take turns crossing off wrong words. Print the correct words on the paper and read the verse together. **What does it mean to love God with all your heart?** (Love Him more than anything.) **What are some ways you can show God you love Him?** (Believing God's words in the Bible. Being patient with others. Avoiding arguments.)

Pray to God

Let's tell God why we love Him. Allow students a minute or so to pray silently or aloud. Conclude prayer time by thanking God for His love for us.

Options

1. Invite older students to read one or more of these well-known psalms written by David: Psalm 23; 46:1-3; 95:1-7; 100. After each psalm is read ask, **What did David say about God? What did David say to express his love for God?**
2. During the Bible verse activity, distribute paper and pencils so that students can write the words of Matthew 22:37 with a few incorrect words. Students then trade papers and correct the wrong words.

 **Lesson 16**

Bible Story Coloring Center

Materials

Crayons or markers, a copy of "David fights Goliath" picture and story (pp. 85-86 from *Bible Story Coloring Pages)* for each student.

Lead the Activity

Students color page 85; read or tell the story on page 86. **What was David able to do because he believed in God's love and care for him?**

Option

Choosing from pages 83-92 in *Coloring Pages*, give each student a different page to color. After coloring pages, guide students to put the pages in order of David's life. Briefly summarize or tell each story. Mix up the pages and see how fast students can put them back in order.

Skit Center

Materials

A copy of "Shepherd's Psalm" skit (pp. 121-124 from *The Big Book of Bible Skits)* for each student; optional—highlighter pens.

Lead the Activity

Students form pairs and read the skit, which tells the story of David writing Psalm 23. (Optional: Students highlight their parts.) Ask the discussion questions on page 121.

Bible Skills Center

Materials

Materials needed for "Ball Toss" and/or "King Quiz" (p. 28 and/or p. 93 from *The Big Book of Bible Skills*).

Lead the Activity

Students complete activities as directed in *The Big Book of Bible Skills.*

 **Lesson 17**

The Wisest Man on Earth

THE BIG PICTURE

God's wisdom helps us know what's best to do.

Big Picture Verse

"If any of you lacks wisdom, he should ask God, who gives generously to all without finding fault, and it will be given to him." James 1:5

Scripture Background
1 Kings 3; 4:29-34; 5—9:9

In the last days of David's reign, David saw that Solomon was the most fit of his sons to succeed him. Solomon was God's choice.

Solomon's reign began in a blaze of glory. First, Solomon organized his leaders. He gathered around him a wise company of officers of state, each having his own department for which he was responsible. Solomon's leadership led to days of tremendous prosperity in the kingdom.

The greatest undertaking of Solomon's reign was the building of the Temple. This was what his father, David, had longed to do. The immense foundation of great hewn stones upon which Solomon's Temple was built remains till this day under the Dome of the Rock.

Solomon was a magnificent king; his throne was the grandest the world had ever seen and his life was filled with happenings of marvelous significance. The size of his kingdom was ten times as great as that which his father had inherited. However, governing is a serious business; and because Solomon realized its seriousness as a young man, he began his reign with prayer.

God appeared to Solomon in a dream early in his reign and asked him to make a choice of anything that he might wish. The young king's wise choice revealed his feeling of inability to do all that was put upon him. God gave him the wisdom for which he asked. Solomon was the wisest man the world ever saw until the coming of Christ who could say about Himself "one greater than Solomon is here" (Matthew 12:42).

God's promise of wisdom is given to us, too. Read it in James 1:5. This is the high privilege of every person: to ask of God. Each one's life tells what he or she has asked for. What is your choice?

Adapted from *What the Bible Is All About* by Henrietta C. Mears.

Big Picture Story Center

Teacher Materials
Bible Time Line, drawing materials/equipment.

Student Materials
Drawing materials.

Tell the Story
Move the *Bible Time Line* frame to highlight Picture 17. As you tell each part of the story, draw each sketch. Students copy your sketches.

When is a time you and a friend both wanted the same thing? Today we're going to hear about a king who asked God to help him solve a problem between two women who wanted the same thing.

1. King David lived to be a very old man. Before he died, he chose his son Solomon to be the next king. Solomon loved God and wanted to obey Him. And God loved Solomon! One night, while Solomon slept, God talked with him in a dream. He told Solomon to ask for whatever he wanted God to give him! He could ask for money or power or for God to get rid of all his enemies! But Solomon told God that to be a good king he needed wisdom to know right from wrong. God was glad to answer that prayer! Besides wisdom, God gave Solomon riches and respect, too.

1. Draw "C"s to make sleeping Solomon.

2. Solomon soon had a chance to see if he REALLY had wisdom. Two women who were having a terrible fight came to see Solomon. They lived in the same house and both had new babies. One woman's baby died. While the other woman slept, she traded babies. When the other woman woke, she thought her baby had died! But in the morning light, she could see it wasn't her baby at all. The first woman argued that the other woman was lying!

2. Woman's face from "2." Add 2 "U"s for scarf.

3. Solomon didn't argue with either woman. Instead, he had his servant bring a sword. Loudly, Solomon told the servant to cut the baby in half! Of course, the baby's REAL mother said, "Oh, no! Give the baby to the other woman! Don't hurt him!" Then Solomon knew that this woman was the baby's real mother and gave the baby to her. Everyone in Israel soon heard how Solomon had been very WISE!

3. Write a large "1/2." Add sword.

4. Solomon loved God very much. He was grateful for all the gifts God had given him. God had made him very rich. So Solomon wanted to give a gift to God. He decided to use his riches to build a beautiful Temple to show his love for God. The Israelites could come to the Temple to worship God.

4. Draw a gift box.

5. Solomon had the strongest wood brought in. He hired many workers and famous artists. The workers made the Temple of white stone that sparkled in the sunlight. The floors were covered with gold. It took seven years to build the Temple—not because it was so big, but because it was so beautiful!

5. Add "7"s to sides of box to make Temple. Add other details.

6. When the Temple was finally finished, Solomon led a joyful parade to bring the Ark of the Covenant to its permanent home in the Temple. (The Ark was a special wooden chest that reminded people that God was with them.) A huge crowd of people joined in the parade. Everyone wanted to see the beautiful new Temple.

6. Add "C"s in front of Temple for people.

7. After the Ark was placed in the Temple, an amazing thing happened. The whole Temple filled with a bright cloud. Solomon knew the cloud was God's way of saying that He was there and that He was very, very pleased with this Temple. Solomon stood in front of the Temple and thanked God for keeping His promises to Israel. He also asked God to take care of all the people forever. God listened to Solomon's prayer. The people were so happy! They all stayed at the Temple and celebrated for 14 days! Because of his wisdom and his love for God, Solomon helped the people worship Him.

7. Add "3"s above Temple for cloud.

Get the Big Picture

How did Solomon show his wisdom? (Solved argument over baby. Built Temple.) **How did he get this wisdom?** (Asked God.)

As long as Solomon paid attention to God's wisdom, God helped Solomon know what was best to do. God helped him do many wonderful things. When we don't know what is best to do, God promises to give us wisdom, too. We only need to ask!

Bible Verse Object Talk: More Than Enough!

Big Picture Verse

"If any of you lacks wisdom, he should ask God, who gives generously to all without finding fault, and it will be given to him." James 1:5

We're talking today about wisdom—knowing what's best to do and say. God promises to give us wisdom if we ask Him. Watch what I do to discover a word that describes the way in which God gives us wisdom.

Teacher Materials

Bible with bookmark at James 1:5, table, one or more of the following: room freshener spray; electric fan with several settings; pitcher of water, small cup and plastic dishpan; snack divided into both bite-size and larger portions.

Present the Object Talk

1. One at a time complete one or more of these demonstrations to illustrate what it means to do something generously:

   (a) Ask students what they smell as you first spray a small amount of room freshener and then spray a larger amount.

   (b) Ask students what they feel as you first turn on fan at lowest speed and then turn fan to highest speed.

   (c) Ask students what they see as you first pour a tiny amount of water into cup and then pour water into cup until it overflows into the dishpan.

   (d) Ask students what they taste as you first serve bite-size portions of snack to students and then serve larger portions to students.

2. **Of the actions I just did, which one(s) would you describe as generous? Which one(s) were not? Why? How do you know if someone is generous or not?**

Conclude

Listen to what the Bible says about God's promise of wisdom. Read James 1:5 aloud. **What should we do if we need wisdom?** Pray, asking God for wisdom and thanking Him for giving wisdom generously.

Discussion Questions

1. Who are some wise people you know? What do you think makes them wise?

2. When is a time a kid your age needs to be wise? Why?

3. Why can we be sure God will give us wisdom if we ask for it?

4. How can you be wise today?

Active Game Center: Wise Words

Materials

Paper bags, alphabet magnets; optional—sandpaper or index cards, scissors.

Prepare the Game

Collect magnet letters that spell "wisdom." (Optional: Cut letters out of sandpaper or index cards.) Place the letters in a paper bag. Make one bag and set of letters for every six students.

God gave Solomon a great gift—wisdom. Because Solomon was wise, he did many good things when he was king. We can ask God for wisdom, too. Let's play a game to remind us of wisdom.

Lead the Game

Divide class into equal teams of six or fewer. Each team lines up across the playing area from a paper bag you prepared. At your signal, first student from each team runs to his or

her team's bag and picks a letter without looking into the bag. Student returns to line with the letter and next student runs to bag. As students return to line with the letters, team uses letters to form the word "wisdom." First team to complete the word answers one of the questions below. Repeat game as time permits.

Options

1. If you have mostly older students, put a variety of letters into the bag, including the ones needed to spell "wisdom." On each turn, student reaches into bag and feels for a letter still needed by his or her team.

2. Make letters for more than one word or phrase from the verse: "ask God," "generously" and "will be given."

Discussion Questions

1. What does the word "wisdom" mean? (Knowing the right and best things to do or say. The ability to figure out what to do to solve problems in our lives.)

2. What are some of the ways in which God give us wisdom? (In the Bible. Listening to people who know and love God.)

3. What are some good things God's wisdom can help us to do? (Treat others in good ways. Get along with friends and family members.)

 **Lesson 17**

Art Center: Gift Wrap

Student Materials
Cookie cutters, markers or crayons, butcher paper sheet for each student.

Lead the Activity
1. Students take turns placing cookie cutters on paper and tracing around them.
2. Students color in shapes to decorate paper.

God gave an important gift to someone in our Bible story today. It was the gift of wisdom. God promises to give us wisdom, too, when we ask Him. Today we are going to make wrapping paper for gifts we can give to others.

Options
1. Provide paint smocks for students to wear. Students make wrapping paper by carefully laying tree branches and/or pine cones into shallow pans of green paint and then pressing branches and cones onto paper.

2. Provide paint smocks for students to wear. Students dip cookie cutters in shallow container of paint and press cookie cutters onto paper to make shapes.

Discussion Questions
1. What is one gift you were glad to receive for your birthday or for Christmas?

2. What is a gift you were glad to give someone?

3. What are some of the good things God gives us? (Families. Friends. Wisdom.)

4. When is a time you or someone you know needs God's gift of wisdom? (When an argument needs to be stopped. When someone wants to disobey God.)

Lesson 17

Worship Center

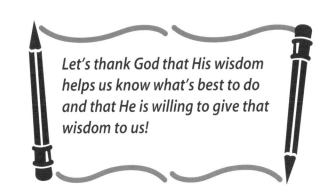

Let's thank God that His wisdom helps us know what's best to do and that He is willing to give that wisdom to us!

Big Picture Verse

"If any of you lacks wisdom, he should ask God, who gives generously to all without finding fault, and it will be given to him." James 1:5

Teacher Materials

Bible, *God's Big Picture* cassette/CD or music video and player, "Love and Power" word chart (p. 469 in this book), large sheet of paper on which you have printed James 1:5, masking tape.

Sing to God

Play "Love and Power," encouraging students to sing along with the music and do the actions shown on the word chart or the music video. **What does this song say we can do when God's wisdom and power live in us?** (Care for others. Show God's love in our actions. Show love to our families. Show love to our enemies.)

Hear and Say God's Word

Display paper on which you have printed James 1:5. Have a volunteer read the verse aloud. **What does this verse say God will give us if we ask Him?** (Wisdom.) **What is wisdom?** (The ability to make good decisions and choices that show our love for God and others.) Students form three groups. Assign each group one phrase of the verse. All students say reference. Repeat the verse several times, each group saying its phrase while doing one of these motions: clapping, stomping or finger snapping. You may assign the motions the first time students say verse; then let groups choose different motions for succeeding repetitions.

Pray to God

Students repeat this prayer after you: **God, please give us Your wisdom so that we will choose the right way to live and follow You.** Conclude prayer by thanking God that He promises to give us His wisdom when we ask.

Options

1. During the Bible verse activity, older students may want to make up a rhythm pattern (such as two claps and a snap) to use when saying James 1:5.
2. If you collect an offering, introduce it by saying, **Giving money to our church family is one way to show love for God.** Then briefly describe one or more ways in which the money is used.

 **Lesson 17**

Bible Story Coloring Center

Materials

Crayons or markers, a copy of "King Solomon is wise" picture and story (pp. 93-94 from *Bible Story Coloring Pages*) for each student.

Lead the Activity

Students color page 93; read or tell the story on page 94. **What is King Solomon doing?** (Praying to God.) **What can you talk to God about?**

Option

Also provide pages 95-96 from *Coloring Pages* and let children choose which pictures they wish to color.

Skit Center

Materials

A copy of "Make a Wish" skit (pp. 133-136 from *The Big Book of Bible Skits*) for each student; optional—highlighter pen.

Lead the Activity

Four volunteers read the skit, which tells the story of the way in which Solomon solved the problem of the two mothers and one baby. Repeat skit with other volunteers. (Optional: Students highlight their parts.) Ask the discussion questions on page 133.

Bible Skills Center

Materials

Materials needed for "Order Up!" and/or "Old Testament Surprise" (p. 32 and/or p. 123 from *The Big Book of Bible Skills*).

Lead the Activity

Students complete activities as directed in *The Big Book of Bible Skills*.

Lesson 18

God Protects Elijah

Big Picture Verse

"The Lord is good, a refuge in times of trouble. He cares for those who trust in him." Nahum 1:7

THE BIG PICTURE

God is great enough to care for us in all situations.

Scripture Background
1 Kings 17—19

In 1 Kings we see the kingdom of Israel falling apart, filled with pride and arrogance. The people had forgotten God and refused to listen to the warnings of the prophets. As a result, God wanted His people to learn the lesson of obedience and dependence upon Him.

Elijah was a bolt of fire that God let loose upon wicked Ahab and idolatrous Israel. Elijah flashed across the page of history as sudden and terrible as a flash of lightning.

He was a striking personality from the highlands of Gilead. Jehovah sent Elijah to do away with the awful worship of Baal during the reign of Ahab, who had married the wicked heathen princess, Jezebel. Suddenly emerging from the desert and standing before the corrupt king in the splendor of his court, the stern prophet boldly said, "As the Lord, the God of Israel, lives, whom I serve, there will be neither dew nor rain in the next few years except at my word" (1 Kings 17:1). Elijah was given the power to shut the heavens, so there would be no rain for three and a half years. He called down fire from heaven before the prophets of Baal at Mount Carmel. He was the evangelist of his day, thundering out warnings to these idolatrous people. The events in his great career will intrigue you and teach you. Follow his sudden appearance, his undaunted courage, his zeal, the heights of his triumph on Mount Carmel, the depths of his despondence, the glorious rapture into heaven in the whirlwind and then his reappearance with Jesus on the Mount of Transfiguration.

The name Elijah means "Jehovah is my God." It fit him perfectly. He was the most outstanding of the prophets—outstanding in the dramatic events of his life and outstanding in the picture of God we gain from him.

Adapted from *What the Bible Is All About* by Henrietta C. Mears.

Big Picture Story Center

Teacher Materials
Bible Time Line, drawing materials/equipment.

Student Materials
Drawing materials.

Tell the Story

Move the *Bible Time Line* frame to highlight Picture 18. As you tell each part of the story, draw each sketch. Students copy your sketches.

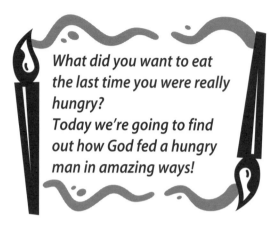

What did you want to eat the last time you were really hungry?
Today we're going to find out how God fed a hungry man in amazing ways!

1. After King Solomon died, his son became king and caused big, big problems! Soon, there was so much fighting that Israel split into two kingdoms: Israel in the north and Judah in the south. Both kingdoms had many rulers through the years, but they usually weren't wise like Solomon or loving toward God like David. God often sent prophets to these rulers with warnings for them.

1. Draw zigzag lines; add names.

2. When King Ahab ruled Israel, he worshiped false gods like Baal instead of the true God. So God gave His prophet Elijah an important message for King Ahab. Elijah declared that there would be no rain for the next few years. Without rain, no food would grow. Everyone in Israel was going to be hungry!

2. Draw raindrop and hamburger. Add "no" slash to each.

3. God promised He would take care of Elijah, so God sent Elijah to live by a little stream of water. And God sent birds called ravens to bring food to Elijah every morning and evening. Elijah drank water from the stream and ate what the ravens brought him. But finally, the stream dried up.

3. "U"s for water. Sideways "3"s for birds. Add "no" slash to water.

4. God told Elijah to go to a faraway town. Elijah met a widow at the town gate. He asked her for water—and for bread, too. But she said she had only flour and oil to make one last loaf of bread for herself and her son. Elijah told her God had promised there would be enough flour and oil for all of them. So she fed Elijah first. Then she looked in her flour jar to make more bread. She saw more flour! And there was more oil in the oil jar!

4. "U" and "O" for flour jar. Teardrop shape and "O" for oil jar. Add oil and flour spilling out.

5. After that, there was always enough flour and oil to make more bread. The flour and oil NEVER ran out! The Lord had taken care of Elijah again! And He helped this family who had nothing. Later, when the widow's son got sick and died, God brought him back to life!

5. Draw "D"s for loaves of bread.

6. Now it had been three YEARS without rain. God sent Elijah to see King Ahab again. Elijah told King Ahab to call the prophets of Baal and all the people together for a contest at Mount Carmel. When the crowd was there, Elijah told the false prophets, "Call on your god, Baal. If he is really a god, he can send fire down to burn up your offering. I will call on the Lord. If He is really God, He will send fire down to burn up my offering. We will see who is the true God!" Everyone agreed.

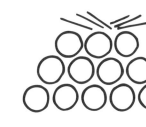

6. Draw "O"s for stone altar; add lines for wood.

7. The test began. The priests and prophets of Baal prayed and cried and even cut themselves all day long, trying to get Baal to send fire down. But nothing happened! When evening came, Elijah had people pour water three times over the offering he had prepared! He wanted everyone to know that he hadn't hidden any fire or tried any tricks. Elijah prayed, "Lord, answer me so that everyone will know that You, O Lord, are God."

7. Add water drops and wavy lines.

8. God's fire fell! It didn't just burn up the offering; it burned up the stones, the dirt and even the WATER! When the people saw this miracle, they said, "The Lord is God!" That day, the people got rid of the false prophets. The rain came again and food began to grow. But the queen was very angry at Elijah and wanted to kill him. So Elijah ran away. God fed him again and told him what to do next. Even as Elijah hid in a cave, God talked with him and showed him that He would care for him.

8. Draw blackened "O."

Get the Big Picture

How did God care for Elijah? (Fed him. Sent fire.)

God cared for Elijah in amazing ways. God is big enough to care for us in any situation! He'll give us what we need.

Bible Verse Object Talk: Animal Talk

Big Picture Verse

"The Lord is good, a refuge in times of trouble. He cares for those who trust in him." Nahum 1:7

Teacher Materials

Bible with a bookmark at Nahum 1:7, large sheet of paper, marker; optional—pictures of the animals discussed below.

A refuge is a place of safety. Because God is so great, He is like a refuge for us. He also cares for His creation by making ways for them to be safe. Let's discover some ways in which God made refuges for animals.

Present the Object Talk

1. Draw nine blank lines, one for each letter of the word "porcupine." Students guess letters of the alphabet. As each correct letter is guessed, write it on the appropriate blank line. When an incorrect letter is guessed, write it below the blank lines. Students keep guessing letters until the word is identified. **What did God give a porcupine to help keep it safe?** (Quills that stand up when a porcupine is afraid.)

$$\_\ \_\ r\ \_\ U\ \_\ \_\ \_\ E$$

$$z\ ^T S\ A$$

2. Repeat game with other animals: chameleon—able to change skin color, so it is less noticeable; gorilla—usually peaceful and shy but beats chest and screams when afraid; ostrich—largest bird in the world and can protect itself with a very powerful kick; snowshoe hare—grows white coat in winter to help it hide from attackers; alpine marmot—hides in rocks, whistles to other marmots when danger is present; mountain goat—special pads on hoofs stop it from slipping on steep rocks; sea otter—two layers of fur which give warmth in cold ocean water.

Conclude

God made these animals in special ways to help them stay safe when they are in danger. God is like a refuge for us, too. Read Nahum 1:7 aloud. **What does God do for the people who believe and trust in Him?** (Promises to answer prayers. Gives courage.) Thank God for His loving care and for helping us when we are in danger or feel afraid.

Discussion Questions

1. What are some other ways in which God made animals so that they are protected from danger?

2. When are some times people need God's help to keep them safe?

3. Who are some people God has given you to help you stay safe?

4. What are some other ways God shows His care for you?

Active Game Center: Take the Challenge!

Materials
Materials for one or more of the challenges suggested below.

Lead the Game
Lead students to participate in one or more of the following challenges:

Balloon Challenge
Give each student a balloon. Student writes initials on balloon. Student blows up balloon and pinches end to make sure no air escapes. All students stand shoulder-to-shoulder on one side of the playing area. At your signal, students let go of balloons and watch to see where balloons land. Student whose balloon lands farthest from the group gets to give the signal for the next round. (Variation: Blow up and tie balloons ahead of time. Students write their initials on balloons. Students hit the balloons as far as possible with one hit.)

When Elijah wanted to show that God was the one true God, he set up a challenge with the worshipers of Baal. God cared for Elijah by showing His power when Elijah asked Him to. Let's try some challenges today and then talk about ways God helps us meet much harder challenges.

Ping-Pong Challenge
Students form teams of four and hold a towel stretched out between them. Students work as a team to bounce a ping pong ball up into the air without the ball falling onto the floor. Teams challenge each other to see who can keep the ball off the ground the longest.

Feather-Blowing Challenge
Students kneel around a table. Students on each side of the table form a team. Set a craft feather (or cotton ball) in the middle of the table. Students blow the feather toward the other side of the table while trying to keep the feather from falling off their own side of the table. (Variation: If you have small tables, students form pairs or trios. Teams rotate as in a tournament so that winners are challenging winners and vice versa.)

Discussion Questions

1. What made the challenge(s) hard? How did you feel if your team won?

2. How do you think Elijah felt when God showed His power and answered Elijah's prayer in the challenge with the Baal worshipers? (Thankful to God. Glad that God proved He is the one true God.)

3. What kinds of challenges might a kid your age need God's help to overcome? (Telling the truth. Being patient with a brother or sister.)

Art Center: Prayer Place Mats

Student Materials

Scissors, 8½x11-inch (21.5x27.5-cm) colored paper, 12x18-inch (30x45-cm) construction paper in a variety of colors, clear adhesive-backed paper, glue, markers.

Prepare the Activity

1. Make a sample place mat following directions below.

2. Cut adhesive-backed paper into 12x18-inch (30x45-cm) sheets, making one sheet for each student.

God can help us in any situation. One of the ways God provides for us is by giving us food to eat. Today you can make and decorate place mats which you can use at home when you eat.

Lead the Activity

1. Demonstrate to students how to fold colored paper into fourths and cut designs in the paper (see sketch a). Allow time for students to experiment with cutting designs. If time permits, students make place mats for all people in their families and write names of family members on the place mats.

2. Students open papers and glue them to separate sheets of construction paper. Within the design areas, students write prayers thanking God for taking care of them (see sketch b).

3. Help students cover top of place mats with clear adhesive-backed paper. Students take place mats home.

Option

Provide stickers or magazine pictures which students can glue onto place mats in a addition to or instead of the cut papers.

Discussion Questions

1. God sent a raven with food for Elijah. How do you think Elijah felt when the bird brought his food?

2. What kind of food do you like to eat?

3. What are some others ways in which God has helped you or someone in your family? someone in our church?

4. Who does God provide to help you? (Parents. Teachers. Friends.)

 **Lesson 18**

Worship Center

Big Picture Verse

"The Lord is good, a refuge in times of trouble. He cares for those who trust in him." Nahum 1:7

Let's thank God that He is great enough to care for us in all situations!

Teacher Materials

Bible, *God's Big Picture* cassette/CD or music video and player, "People of Courage" word chart (p. 471 in this book), large index cards on which you have printed Nahum 1:7, one word per card; large sheet of paper, masking tape, index cards, crayons, shoebox or other small box.

Sing to God

Play "People of Courage," encouraging students to sing along with the music and do the actions shown on the word chart or music video. **In what ways did the people in this song show courage? How does knowing God will care for you in all situations give you courage?**

Hear and Say God's Word

Hand out index cards on which you have printed the words of Nahum 1:7. Read Nahum 1:7 aloud from your Bible. As student hears the word on his or her card, student tapes his or her card onto large sheet of paper in the correct order. Read the verse as slowly or as many times as needed for students to correctly order and tape cards. **A refuge is a safe place or a hiding place. How does God act as our refuge when we feel scared or have troubles?** (He makes us feel safe because He is stronger than any bad thing. He listens to our prayers. He gives us people to care for us.)

Pray to God

On index cards, students draw pictures of situations in which they need God's help and care. Students put index cards in box. **God promises us He will care for us in all these situations. One way God helps us when we pray is to help us think calmly and clearly of what to do or who to ask for help.** Each student chooses a card from the box. Lead students in prayer. Each student asks God's help in the situation pictured. End the prayer time by asking God to help students trust in Him.

Options

1. If your students have already heard the story, after singing "People of Courage," talk about the ways in which Elijah showed courage.

2. During the Bible verse activity, after students have said the verse a few times, redistribute the index cards and time students to see how quickly they can tape the verse cards in order.

 **Lesson 18**

Bible Story Coloring Center

Materials

Crayons or markers, a copy of "God sends ravens with food for Elijah" picture and story (pp. 97-98 from *Bible Story Coloring Pages*) for each student.

Lead the Activity

Students color page 97; read or tell the story on page 98. **How is Elijah getting food to eat and water to drink? In what way does God give you food and water?**

Option

Provide a copy of "God answers Elijah's prayer" picture (p. 99 from *Coloring Pages*) for children to color.

Skit Center

Materials

A copy of "Ahab's Mount Carmel Press Conference" skit (pp. 144-149 from *The Big Book of Bible Skits*) for each student; optional—highlighter pens.

Lead the Activity

Students form trios and read the skit, which tells the story of King Ahab's response to the warnings given by God's prophet, Elijah. (Optional: Students highlight their parts.) Ask the discussion questions on page 144.

Bible Skills Center

Materials

Materials needed for "Hands on Leaders" and/or "Secret Pass" (p. 50 and/or p. 84 from *The Big Book of Bible Skills*).

Lead the Activity

Students complete activities as directed in *The Big Book of Bible Skills*.

 **Lesson 19**

Elisha Shows God's Love

Big Picture Verse

"We love because he first loved us." 1 John 4:19

THE BIG PICTURE

Because God loves us, we can show His love to others—even to people who don't care about Him.

Scripture Background

1 Kings 19:19-21; 2 Kings 5; 6:8-23

The history of the Jews is a record of God's dealings with disobedient children. Nowhere is this seen more clearly than in 2 Kings when Israel is sent into captivity. The way of the transgressor is hard! The secret of the downfall of the Jewish people is found in 2 Kings 3:2, "He did evil in the eyes of the Lord." Be loyal and true to God. It does not pay to do evil. In all God's punishment, however, God is kind and merciful, for He loves us still.

God's love is evident in the life of Elisha who succeeded Elijah. Elijah trained Elisha as his successor, and Elisha's ministry lasted 50 years. Consider the actions of Elisha: He willingly took the prophet's mantle from Elijah and learned from him. Elisha's ministry, however, seems to be in marked contrast to Elijah's. Elijah was the prophet of judgment, law and severity. Elisha was the prophet of grace, love and tenderness. He was benevolent in contrast to the fiery Elijah. Most of his miracles were deeds of kindness and mercy. Elisha had a great influence upon the kings of the day and although he did not approve of what they did, he was always coming to their rescue.

Elisha's caring for others began with the needs of a woman and her son, then extended to the needs of Naaman—a military leader of an enemy country—and then to the soldiers sent from the enemy king of Aram. Elisha's actions bore fruit first in his own character and in his example to others and then later in their effect upon Naaman. For at least a while, the peace of Elisha's country was ensured because Naaman's gratitude prevented further enemy raids.

In Elisha's life we see that the true servant of God is ready to help in every kind of need. Our caring actions express the goodness and love of God to all those who come in contact with us. God's desire is that all people would find their chief hope and joy and blessings in Himself and in a character and life like His.

Adapted from *What the Bible Is All About* by Henrietta C. Mears.

Big Picture Story Center

Teacher Materials
Bible Time Line, drawing materials/equipment.

Student Materials
Drawing materials.

Tell the Story
Move the *Bible Time Line* frame to highlight Picture 19. As you tell each part of the story, draw each sketch. Students copy your sketches.

When have you seen or swum in a river? Today we're going to meet a man who told a sick man to wash in a river he didn't want to get into!

1. Elisha was out working hard in his father's field when Elijah the prophet came by. Elijah came up and threw his cloak over Elisha. He did this to show that God had chosen Elisha to follow Elijah and learn from him. Elisha left home to learn from Elijah and help him. Years later, God brought Elijah to heaven! Elisha was now the prophet of God.

1. Draw "M" and lines for cloak.

2. God gave Elisha power to do amazing things, even to help people who didn't believe in or care about God. One man who didn't care about God was the commander of the Aramean army (Israel's enemy). This man, Naaman, got a terrible skin disease called leprosy. He tried everything he could think of to get rid of his disease. But nothing worked!

2. Hand and arm from "U"s. Add spots to arm.

3. Living in Naaman's house, however, was a a girl who had been taken from Israel as a slave. Even though Naaman was really an enemy of her people, the slave girl helped him. She told Naaman's wife that God's prophet in Israel could help her husband! So Naaman traveled to Israel to see Elisha. Elisha sent a messenger to tell Naaman to go to the Jordan River and wash himself seven times. Then he would be well. Naaman didn't like this advice at first, but finally he did what Elisha said. And God made Naaman completely well!

3. Water from wide "U"s. Add stick figure and "7."

4. Another time, the Arameans were at war with Israel. And God kept telling Elisha all of the Arameans' battle plans! Finally, one officer told the king that Elisha the prophet was the one who was finding out all the king's plans. So the king sent soldiers to CAPTURE Elisha.

4. Sideways "C"s and lines for helmets of soldiers.

5. When Elisha's servant got up early the next morning, there were Aramean soldiers all around the city! Elisha's servant was AFRAID! But Elisha knew God had armies of His own all around them! Elisha asked God to show his servant that the hills all around them were full of soldiers and horses and chariots of fire! God was ready to protect them!

5. Amazed face from "O"s.

6. As the enemy soldiers came to capture him, Elisha asked God to make them blind. Suddenly, they couldn't see! Elisha told them that they weren't on the right road to the right place. He invited them to follow him. What else could the soldiers do? The whole Aramean army followed Elisha—all the way into the Israelite city of Samaria!

6. Draw closed eyes on soldiers drawn in #4.

7. Once the soldiers were inside the gates of the city, the Lord took away their blindness. NOW the Arameans could see they were in TROUBLE—surrounded by Israelites! The king of Israel thought this was the perfect time to get rid of these enemies. He wanted to kill the Aramean soldiers! But Elisha told the king God's plan: to feed the soldiers and send them home.

7. Draw gates behind soldiers. Make eyes wide. Add "O" mouths.

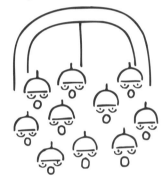

8. So the people of Samaria prepared a big feast for the soldiers. When the soldiers were full, they were allowed to go home. And for a very long time, the Arameans didn't bother the Israelites at all! Elisha had helped show God's love and care for people who didn't care about Him.

8. Add crowd around soldiers.

Get the Big Picture

How did Elijah show Elisha that God had chosen him to be his helper? (Threw his cloak over Elisha.) **What did Elisha do to help Naaman?** (Told him to wash seven times in the Jordan.) **What did Elisha do for the Aramean army?** (Fed them. Sent them home.)

   Elisha showed God's love to many people. Some of these people didn't care about God, but God cared about them because God loves all people. When we are kind to others, even those who don't know or care about God, we help them learn about God's love, too.

Bible Verse Object Talk: Link Up!

Big Picture Verse

"We love because he first loved us." 1 John 4:19

Teacher Materials

Bible with bookmark at 1 John 4:19, pencils, 1x6-inch (2.5x15-cm) strips of paper (several for each student), tape.

Present the Object Talk

Our love and caring for others begins with God's love for us. Let's help each other make a paper chain that shows some of the people we can show God's love to.

1. Print the name of one student on your own paper strip and say the name aloud. Tape the ends of the strip together, forming a link.

2. Ask for volunteers to suggest another student's name (or the name of a friend or family member) that begins with the last letter of the name you wrote. One volunteer writes one of the suggested names on a paper strip, inserts it through your link and tapes the ends together, forming a second link (see sketch).

3. Continue process, making paper chain as long as possible. Students may also make a paper chain with words of 1 John 4:19, repeating the verse until each student has added a word.

Conclude

When our names are linked together in this chain, it reminds us that we can show God's love to each other. Read 1 John 4:19 aloud. **What does 1 John 4:19 say about God? How does knowing about God's love help us?** Thank God for His love and ask His help in showing care to others.

Discussion Questions

1. What are some ways God has shown His love to us?

2. How has someone shown God's love to you?

3. How can you show God's love to others?

4. When might it be difficult to show God's love to someone?

Active Game Center: Three-Legged Race

Materials

Scarves or fabric strips at least 21 inches (52.5 cm) in length.

Lead the Game

1. Group students into pairs. Guide pairs to tie inside legs together with a scarf or fabric strip (see sketch). Allow students time to experiment walking around an open playing area in your classroom or outdoors. **What makes it hard to move quickly? What can you do to make it easier?**

> *Helping others is something we can do to show God's love to others. Let's play a game in which you have to help your partner.*

2. Pairs stand on one side of open playing area in your classroom or outdoors. At your signal, pairs race to the other side of the playing area. Repeat race several times or as time and interest permit.

Discussion Questions

1. What are some other games in which the players need to help their teammates? (Soccer. Volleyball.) *How do players in these games help each other?*

2. What are some ways in which others have helped you?

3. What are some ways in which you can help someone younger than you? older than you?

Art Center: Foil Scenes

Student Materials
Aluminum foil, scissors, paper, glue, markers.

Prepare the Activity
Cut 1-inch (2.5-cm) strips of aluminum foil into approximately 8-inch (20-cm) and 5-inch (12.5-cm) lengths; prepare several of each length for each student.

Lead the Activity
1. Demonstrate how to roll, twist and fold aluminum strips to create a human figure (see sketch a).

One way people learn about God's love for them is by our caring and helping actions. Make a scene with some foil people to show a way you can show God's love to someone.

2. Students shape figures from aluminum foil strips, tearing or cutting foil as needed to make arms and legs even. Each student makes a figure representing him- or herself and a figure representing a person for whom he or she cares.

3. Students glue their figures to paper, arranging them in poses to show ways of caring for others (show sketch b). To complete scenes, students may draw objects with markers.

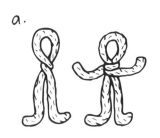

a.

b.

Options
1. Use chenille wire instead of aluminum foil to shape figures.

2. Use play dough or modeling clay to sculpt figures.

3. Older students may pose figures and draw objects to show scenes in which people are showing God's love by helping others.

Discussion Questions

1. *How do we know that God loves us?*

2. *What are some ways a person can show God's love to someone else?*

3. *Because God loves all people, He wants to help them. If a kid wants God's help, what should he or she do?*

Worship Center

Big Picture Verse

"We love because he first loved us." 1 John 4:19

Teacher Materials

Bible, *God's Big Picture* cassette/CD or music video and player, "Picture This!" word chart (p. 473 in this book), large sheet of paper on which you have printed 1 John 4:19, masking tape.

Let's thank God that He loves and cares about everyone— even people who don't care about Him.

Sing to God

Play "Picture This!" encouraging students to sing along with the music and do the actions shown on the word chart or music video. **What words in this song remind us that God cares for people who do not care for Him?** (God creates a world that's good. Jesus loves everyone.)

Hear and Say God's Word

Display paper on which you have printed 1 John 4:19. Have a volunteer read the verse aloud. **Why does this verse say that we can love God and others?** (Because God loved us first!) Volunteers suggest and demonstrate motions for the words. Do the motions and say the words to the verse several times. **One way God showed His love for us was by sending Jesus to take the punishment for our sin.** Talk with students about becoming Christians, following the guidelines in the "Leading a Child to Christ" article on page 30.

Pray to God

Invite volunteers to name people for whom they would like to pray. Lead students in prayer, allowing students to complete the sentence: **Thank You, God, that You care about....**

Options

1. Students sing and do actions for "Love and Power" and/or "People of Courage."
2. During each session invite students to tell prayer requests and things for which they wish to thank God. Record requests and praise items in a prayer journal.

 **Lesson 19**

 **Bible Story Coloring Center**  FOR YOUNGER CHILDREN

Materials

Crayons or markers, a copy of "Elisha helps a widow" picture and story (pp. 103-104 from *Bible Story Coloring Pages*) for each student.

Lead the Activity

Students color page 103; read or tell the story on page 104. **How many children does this widow have? Elisha helped this widow. What are some ways you can help others?**

Option

Cut out several large pot shapes from butcher paper. Students color shapes to look like pots and then tape shapes to classroom walls for decoration.

Skit Center FOR OLDER CHILDREN

Materials

A copy of "Mad About Elisha" skit (pp. 153-156 from *The Big Book of Bible Skits*) for each student; optional—highlighter pens.

Lead the Activity

Students form pairs and read the skit, which tells the story of Elisha's merciful treatment of enemy soldiers. (Optional: Students highlight their parts.) Ask the discussion questions on page 153.

Bible Skills Center FOR OLDER CHILDREN

Materials

Materials needed for "Love and Obey Verses" and/or "Key Word Code" (p. 52 and/or p. 137 from *The Big Book of Bible Skills*).

Lead the Activity

Students complete activities as directed in *The Big Book of Bible Skills*.

Isaiah's Willing Attitude

Big Picture Verse

"I will hasten and not delay to obey your commands." Psalm 119:60

THE BIG PICTURE

Be ready to trust and follow God's good commands.

Scripture Background
Isaiah 6:1-8; 9:1-7

The prophets were people whom God raised up during the dark days of Israel's history. Prophets not only spoke of judgment that would come to pass on the people because of their sin but also were foretellers of future events. God put a telescope before the eyes of the prophets and let them look far into the future. We especially find this spirit of expectation in Isaiah.

Isaiah was a prophet of royal blood. He was a young aristocrat from a princely line. He was brought up in the court and had high standing with the people of Jerusalem.

This great statesman was the prophet of the southern kingdom of Judah. He lived at the time that the northern kingdom of Israel was destroyed by Assyria. Isaiah was the one whose voice saved the kingdom of Judah during these trying hours, telling of the judgment that must fall on Judah because she would not fulfill her mission in the world. In that time, Judah was morally and politically rotten, and danger threatened from the surrounding Gentile nations. Assyria was strong and aggressive, striving for world power. Egypt was on the south, and Palestine was the road between these two enemies. Both Assyria and Egypt aimed at a world empire. Therefore, Palestine became the battleground of the ages. Isaiah did not fail in his ministry. He laid bare the sins of this people and called them to repent and turn to God. "Come back to God," he cried.

Isaiah was also a man of vision. He certainly spoke boldly to his own time, but as a prophet he spoke of the future as well; hence he is the prophet for all times. Through the whole book we find the ultimate triumph of God's plan through His appointed Servant, the Lord Jesus Christ, who would bring final victory through suffering and death (see Isaiah 53). Isaiah's chief theme was the coming One—Jesus. Isaiah saw Christ's near coming and His faraway second coming, but in all he saw Christ. We, too, can see the Word shining clearly and begin to see what the prophet saw: the world's Redeemer, coming first in humiliation and then again in power and great glory.

Adapted from *What the Bible Is All About* by Henrietta C. Mears.

Lesson 20 • Isaiah 6:1-8; 9:1-7

Big Picture Story Center

Teacher Materials

Bible Time Line, drawing materials/equipment.

Student Materials

Drawing materials.

Tell the Story

Move the *Bible Time Line* frame to highlight Picture 20. As you tell each part of the story, draw each sketch. Students copy your sketches.

> *What's the last thing you remember a grown-up telling you to do?*
> *Today we'll write some words that begin with W and we'll hear about a time God gave a man a special job to do.*

1. Israel was now divided in half. The northern half was called Israel, and the southern part was called Judah. For about 300 years in both countries many different kings (and a few queens) ruled. Most of these rulers disobeyed God, doing evil again and again.

1. Draw a stop sign. Add "Wicked."

2. But God never gave up on His people! God wanted His people to stop cheating each other, stop hurting each other and stop worshiping idols, gods who weren't real. God sent many prophets to give His messages and warnings to the people of Israel and Judah, as well as to the other countries around them. Elijah and Elisha were prophets who told God's messages. Another prophet, named Isaiah, lived in Judah, about 100 years after Elisha.

2. "Warning" on a yield sign.

3. God chose Isaiah to be a prophet in a special way. Isaiah had a vision—like a dream. Isaiah could see that he was in heaven! WOW! Isaiah saw God on a throne, sitting very high up with fiery angels on either side of Him. These angels called out, "Holy! Holy! Holy! is the Lord Almighty. The whole earth is full of His glory!"

3. "Wow!" in a thought balloon.

4. When these angels spoke with their powerful voices, everything shook. Smoke filled the throne room! Isaiah thought he was going to die because he had seen God. Isaiah knew he had disobeyed God and was not good enough to be in God's presence. One of the fiery angels brought a glowing coal and touched Isaiah's lips. The angel explained that now Isaiah would be clean and ready for the job God had for him. *Whew!* Isaiah thought.

4. "Whew!" on a piece of coal.

5. THEN, Isaiah heard a voice. It was the voice of GOD! God asked, "Whom shall I send?" Isaiah was amazed. God wanted someone to tell people how great God is! Isaiah had seen how great God is. He knew God had prepared him for this job. So Isaiah was ready and willing to do whatever God wanted! Isaiah said to God, "Here I am. Send me!"

5. "Who" inside a question mark.

6. And God DID. He gave Isaiah many, many messages to tell to kings, to ordinary people and even to people in other countries! Some of these amazing messages were about things that would happen in the future. Many of Isaiah's messages told about Jesus hundreds of years before Jesus was born! One message was that Jesus was going to be the great King! Isaiah also told that Jesus would die to defeat sin. He told many things about how Jesus would take the punishment for our sins.

6. Draw a crown and a cross. Write "Won!"

7. Isaiah told about many other events that were going to happen. Many of them have already happened, like the things Isaiah told about Jesus' birth and death. Some of the things God told Isaiah to write and tell haven't happened yet. But because Isaiah was ready to follow God's commands, God gave him an amazing and very important job.

7. Draw arrows for past and future. Add "Write!"

Get the Big Picture
Whose voice did Isaiah hear? What was Isaiah's job going to be? Why do you think Isaiah wanted to tell God's message? (He knew how great God is. He wanted to obey God.)

Knowing how great God is makes us want to trust Him and obey His commands—right away!

Bible Verse Object Talk: Timed Tasks

Big Picture Verse

"I will hasten and not delay to obey your commands."
Psalm 119:60

Teacher Materials

Bible with bookmark at Psalm 119:60, stopwatch or watch with second hand.

When someone tells us what to do, sometimes we obey right away and sometimes we put off obeying. God wants us to be ready and quick to obey Him. Let's see how quickly you can do what I say.

Present the Object Talk

1. Hold up your watch. **What are some of the things we use watches for? How do watches help us?** Volunteers respond (tell what time it is, get to places on time, bake a cake, play the right number of minutes in a game, etc.).

2. **Sometimes people use watches to find out how fast they can do things.** Invite volunteers to take turns completing one or more of the following tasks while you time them: say the letters of the alphabet, do 10 jumping jacks, say his or her name five times, shake the hands of six people in the room, touch all four corners of the room, etc. Add new tasks or repeat tasks as needed. Older students may take turns giving commands to rest of group. (Optional: Students repeat Psalm 119:60 before doing tasks.)

Conclude

We had fun trying to do these things in a hurry. **What does Psalm 119:60 say we should hurry to do?** Read verse aloud. **Whose commands are we to obey? When we hurry, or hasten, to obey God's commands, it means that we don't try to put off doing what God wants. Because God's commands help us know the best way to live, we are ready and glad to obey them.** Pray, thanking God for His commands and asking His help in following them.

Discussion Questions

1. What are some other things you can do quickly?

2. What kinds of things do you like to take your time to do?

3. Why do you think God wants us to hurry to obey His commands?

4. God tells us to treat others honestly and fairly. How can you be ready to quickly obey this command during the week?

Active Game Center: Connect the Part

Materials
Index cards, marker.

Prepare the Game
Print the following words on index cards, one word per card: "elbow," "foot," "hand," "shoulder," "knee," "back," "wrist," "toe," "head," "finger." Make one set of cards for every six students.

God wants us to be ready to follow His good commands. Let's play a game in which we follow some funny commands to connect groups of people together.

Lead the Game
1. Group students into teams of six. Distribute a set of cards to each team.

2. One student on each team acts as the cardholder. This student mixes up the cards and then holds cards so that the other students cannot see words. Another student from the team picks a card and reads it aloud. Everyone on the team quickly connects the body part written on the card (for example, group stands in a circle with elbows connected in the middle). Cardholder mixes up cards and allows a different student to pick a card while group stays in position. Group tries to connect new body part as well as keeping command from the first card. When the group falls or can no longer stay connected, begin a new round with a new cardholder.

Option
If you have a small class, make one set of cards. Students form pairs. Choose two cards and read them aloud. Students in each pair connect the named body parts (such as wrist to ear). Mix up the cards and choose two new cards.

Discussion Questions
1. What made it hard to stay connected? What made it hard to follow the commands?

2. In what ways can we learn about God's commands? What are some of God's commands you remember? (Treat others fairly. Be patient.)

3. When might a kid your age find it hard to obey one of God's commands?

4. Who helps us get ready to obey? (God. Parents. Teachers.)

Art Center: Chalk Pictures

Student Materials
Colored construction paper, colored chalk, cotton swabs.

Lead the Activity
1. Invite students to suggest Bible commands with which they are familiar or read these commands to students: "Be kind to each other" (1 Thessalonians 5:15), "Be quick to listen" (James 1:19), "Live in peace with each other" (1 Thessalonians 5:13). Encourage students to tell ways in which they may obey one or more of the commands suggested.

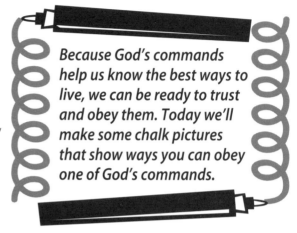

Because God's commands help us know the best ways to live, we can be ready to trust and obey them. Today we'll make some chalk pictures that show ways you can obey one of God's commands.

2. Each student draws a chalk picture of a situation in which he or she may obey one of the discussed commands. After drawing the picture, students rub their chalk marks with cotton swabs to create a blended effect.

Option
Provide small plastic containers filled with a small amount of water or buttermilk. Students dip chalk in the liquid before drawing so that colors are brighter.

Discussion Questions
1. **Who gives you directions that help you do good things?** (Music teacher. Basketball coach. Parents.)

2. **Proverbs 15:1 tells us to use kind words to stop an argument. How can you obey this command?**

3. **What are some other commands you can be ready to obey?** (Be patient. Think about others' needs.)

Lesson 20

Worship Center

Let's thank God that we can trust His good commands and that His commands help us know the best way to live.

Big Picture Verse

"I will hasten and not delay to obey your commands." Psalm 119:60

Teacher Materials

Bible, *God's Big Picture* cassette/CD or music video and player, "Love and Power" word chart (p. 469 in this book), large sheet of paper on which you have printed Psalm 119:60, masking tape.

Sing to God

Play "Love and Power," encouraging students to sing along with the music and do the actions shown on the word chart or music video. **How does knowing God loves us and gives us His power help us to follow His good commands?** (Because God loves us, He will give us only good commands to follow—commands that will help us. Because God is so powerful, He can help us trust Him and obey His commands.)

Hear and Say God's Word

Display paper on which you have printed Psalm 119:60. **The words "hasten" and "not delay" are ways to say "hurry." The person who wrote this psalm says he will quickly follow God's commands and not waste any time by disobeying God's commands. What are some ways we might feel about following God's good commands?** Replace "hasten" and "not delay" with words that students suggest and repeat verse by inserting words. (For example, "I will be happy and excited to obey your commands." "I will be thankful and glad to obey your commands.")

Pray to God

What are some of God's good commands that He tells us to follow? (Tell the truth. Say kind words. Look for ways to do good.) Lead students in prayer, thanking God for the commands mentioned and asking for His help in following and trusting His commands every day.

Options

1. Designate different groups of students to say Psalm 119:60 each time it is repeated. For example, students who have pets say verse one time, then students who are wearing blue, etc.
2. On a large sheet of paper, list the commands that students name at the beginning of the prayer activity. Students refer to paper as they pray.
3. Older students may find and read the following Bible verse commands: Exodus 20:12,15; Galatians 5:13; 6:2; Ephesians 4:29,32; 5:4; 6:1.

 Lesson 20

Bible Story Coloring Center
 FOR YOUNGER CHILDREN

Materials
Crayons or markers, a copy of "Jesus is born" picture and story (pp. 135-136 from *Bible Story Coloring Pages*) for each student.

Lead the Activity
Students color page 135; read or tell the story on page 136. Explain that Isaiah, the prophet, told that God would send His Son, Jesus, to be born on earth. Many years later, God kept His promise and Jesus was born. **If Jesus were born today, how might this picture be different?**

Option
Ask a student to lie down on a large sheet of butcher paper while you trace around him or her. Other students color the body outline to look like the prophet Isaiah, referring to Picture 20 on the *Bible Time Line*. (Make one body outline for each group of four students.)

Skit Center
 FOR OLDER CHILDREN

Materials
A copy of "Trust and Obey" skit (pp. 157-160 from *The Big Book of Bible Skits*) for each student; optional—highlighter pens.

Lead the Activity
Students form trios and read the skit, which tells the story of Uzziah who was king just prior to Isaiah's call to be a prophet. (Optional: Students highlight their parts.) Ask the discussion questions on page 157.

Bible Skills Center
 FOR OLDER CHILDREN

Materials
Materials needed for "Rapid Pass" and/or "Maze of Scrolls" (p. 34 and/or p. 135 from *The Big Book of Bible Skills*).

Lead the Activity
Students complete activities as directed in *The Big Book of Bible Skills*.

Hezekiah Turns Away from Sin

Big Picture Verse

"I have considered my ways and have turned my steps to your statutes." Psalm 119:59

THE BIG PICTURE

Admit when you've done wrong, and ask God's forgiveness and His help to change your actions.

Scripture Background
2 Kings 20:12-19; 2 Chronicles 29—31:1; 32:1-6,20-33

The reign of Hezekiah occupied one of the most important periods in all of Israel's history. The Assyrian armies, like a dark storm cloud, were threatening the northern frontiers. The critical year in Hezekiah's reign was the fourteenth. It was then the Assyrians invaded and the king became mortally sick and then recovered.

During the years of Assyrian attack, King Hezekiah stripped the Temple of its treasures and took the gold from its doors and pillars in order that he might send the Assyrians gold to buy them off. In desperation, help from Egypt was sought. But nothing availed in the face of the fury of the Assyrians. Eventually, during the succeeding idolatrous reign of Hezekiah's son, Manasseh, the kingdom ended and her people were carried into captivity.

Throughout the turbulent time in which Hezekiah reigned, however, Hezekiah was a godly king. In fact, he is reckoned as one of the three most godly kings (the other two being David and Josiah). Hezekiah was one of the noblest princes who ever adorned David's throne. His reign of 29 years offers an almost unmarred picture of persevering warfare against the most intricate and most difficult circumstances—and of glorious victory. Although ready for war when necessary, and brave and skillful in its conduct, Hezekiah gave his heart to the promotion of the internal welfare of his kingdom. He took Isaiah the prophet for his counselor (the rabbis say Isaiah was his tutor). Hezekiah had the good sense to see the effect of his father's evil courses upon the kingdom.

In Hezekiah's life, we see illustrated that the times do not make us good or bad; it is our own choice. It is said of Hezekiah that he repeatedly did what was right in the eyes of the Lord. Despite his past accomplishments, in the one recorded instance of his sin, Hezekiah was not too proud to confess his wrongdoing and seek the Lord's forgiveness.

Adapted from *What the Bible Is All About* by Henrietta C. Mears.

Big Picture Story Center

Teacher Materials

Bible Time Line, drawing materials/equipment.

Student Materials

Drawing materials.

Tell the Story

Move the *Bible Time Line* frame to highlight Picture 21. As you tell each part of the story, draw each sketch. Students copy your sketches.

When is a time you had to admit to doing wrong? Today we're going to hear about a king who had to admit he was wrong.

1. Hezekiah was one of the kings of Judah. His father, Ahaz, had been a very evil king; he disobeyed God all of his life and worshiped the false gods and idols of the countries around him. Hezekiah did not want to be like his father. As soon as he became king, he repaired the doors of God's Temple and opened the Temple again. He called all the men whose families had served in the Temple and told them to get ready to serve God again. They cleaned the Temple and got it ready for people to worship God again.

1. Draw Temple with broken doors. Blacken in and draw new open doors.

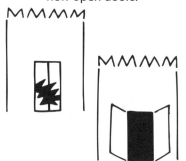

2. When the Temple was ready, Hezekiah sent letters and messengers to everyone in Judah and in Israel, too. He invited everyone to come to Jerusalem to celebrate the Passover. People began to get excited as they heard the news. On the day the Passover began, there was a large crowd of people in Jerusalem. For the first time in a LONG time, people from Israel and Judah worshiped God together in the way He told them to. Everyone was happy; they enjoyed celebrating God's goodness so much that they celebrated for another whole week!

2. Sideways "C"s for crowd.

3. Then a wonderful thing happened. After this great celebration, the people of Israel and Judah decided to get rid of the idols and false gods they had been worshiping. They cleaned up the places where people worshiped false gods. The people were going to worship ONLY the one true God!

3. Draw idol; add "no" slash.

4. Because Hezekiah led his people in doing what was right, God made life peaceful and good for the people of Judah. The Bible tells that King Hezekiah rebuilt many walls and towers in Jerusalem. He built a long tunnel system to bring water into the city and built buildings for storing the extra food from the good harvests.

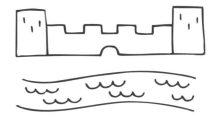
4. Draw walls, towers from rectangles. Add canal with water.

5. Even when the powerful king of Assyria and his army tried to destroy Judah and Jerusalem, Hezekiah told his men to be brave because God would help them. He and the prophet Isaiah prayed to God. And God sent an angel that got rid of the Assyrian army for them—they didn't even have to fight them!

5. Praying face: 3 "7"s, 4 "U"s.

6. Hezekiah obeyed God—most of his life. But even a good king like Hezekiah can do something wrong. Hezekiah became proud of all the good things he had. He enjoyed showing visitors all the fine things he owned. Hezekiah began to depend on his riches instead of trusting God.

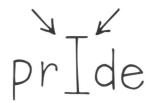
6. Write a large "I." Add letters for "pride." Add arrows.

7. God's prophet Isaiah warned Hezekiah that all his riches would one day be taken away. That got Hezekiah's attention! He realized he had been proud—and he asked God to forgive him. He turned away from being proud and all the people of Judah and Jerusalem asked God to forgive them, too. God brought peaceful, happy times again for the rest of the years of Hezekiah's rule.

7. Draw U-turn sign.

Get the Big Picture

How did Hezekiah show he wanted to obey God? (Repaired the Temple doors. Fixed the Temple. Invited people to come and worship God.) **How did the people show they wanted to obey God?** (Got rid of the idols.) **When Hezekiah became proud, how did God show Hezekiah that his actions were wrong?** (Warned of trouble.)

God wants us to always admit it and ask forgiveness when we've done wrong. It never helps to keep doing wrong. It will only cause us more trouble!

Bible Verse Object Talk: Road Signs

Big Picture Verse

"I have considered my ways and have turned my steps to your statutes." Psalm 119:59

Teacher Materials

Bible with bookmark at Psalm 119:59, separate sheets of paper on which you have drawn road signs (see sketch).

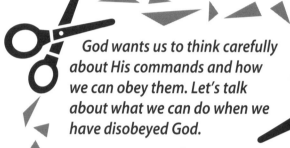

God wants us to think carefully about His commands and how we can obey them. Let's talk about what we can do when we have disobeyed God.

Present the Object Talk

1. One at a time, show each of the road signs you drew. **What would the driver of a car need to do to obey this sign?** Volunteers answer. Explain road signs as needed.

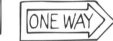

2. **Which of these signs help us know what to do when we realize we have disobeyed God?** Students tell ideas. **The stop sign reminds us that we should stop doing what's wrong. The U-turn sign tells us we should turn away from doing wrong and start doing what God says is right.**

Conclude

Read Psalm 119:59 aloud. **What word in this verse means the same as "commands"?** ("Statutes.") **Psalm 119:59 reminds us to choose to obey God's commands. None of us is perfect; but when we disobey God, we can tell God we're sorry and ask His help in making a U-turn—turning away from our wrong actions and doing what's right.** Pray, asking God for help in obeying Him and thanking Him for forgiving us when we sin.

Discussion Questions

1. What other signs have you seen on the road?

2. What's an example of a time a kid your age might choose to stop doing something wrong and start doing something right?

3. When are times you are tempted to disobey God?

4. Who can help you obey God instead of disobeying Him? (God promises to help us obey. God gives us parents, teachers and friends to help us obey.)

Active Game Center: Turn and Run

Materials
None.

Lead the Game
Students stand shoulder-to-shoulder on one side of a playing area at least 40 feet (12 m) long. Stand at the other end of the playing area and call "run." Students run toward you. Call "freeze." Students must freeze. Shout, "turn around." Students must turn away from you. Call "run." Students run in the opposite direction from you. Continue shouting any variation of these commands (slow motion, crawl, hop, etc.). When the first student reaches you, student becomes caller and a new round begins.

When we do wrong things, it is like turning away from God. But God always forgives us and wants us to turn back toward Him. Let's play a game that reminds us of turning around to move in a new direction.

Options
1. Blow a whistle before you call each command, so students know to prepare for a change and you don't have to call as loudly.
2. If you have a smaller playing area than suggested, students may walk, crawl or hop rather than run.

Discussion Questions

1. When are some times kids your age might want to disobey God?

2. What does God promise to do when we ask His forgiveness?

3. When was a time you decided you wanted to stop doing wrong things and asked God for forgiveness and help to obey His commands instead? Give an age-appropriate example from your own life.

Lesson 21

Art Center: Footprints

Student Materials
Play dough.

Lead the Activity

1. Students form play dough into circles.

2. Demonstrate how to create a "footprint" by pressing the heel of your hand onto the play dough circle and then forming toes by pressing finger into play dough (see sketch). Students create "footprints" using hands.

3. As time permits, students may make other shapes with the play dough.

Because none of us is perfect, there are times when we will disobey God. It's like what happens when we walk down the wrong trail and then have to turn around to get back to the right trail. The play dough footprints we make today will remind us to turn away from wrong actions and obey God.

Options

1. Students form pairs. Give each pair a large sheet of paper. Students remove shoes and socks and trace around their feet, making a path that changes direction.

2. Make actual footprints in play dough.

Discussion Questions

1. *When have you been in a car going the wrong direction?* (On the way to a new place.) *How did you find out you were going the wrong way? What did you do then?*

2. *What are some ways God can help us learn to recognize when we've disobeyed Him?*

3. *How does God help us when we've done wrong?* (Forgives us. Always loves us. Helps us do right.)

4. *How do we know God forgives us?* (He sent Jesus to take the punishment for our sin. God promises to forgive us.) Talk with students about becoming members of God's family, following the guidelines in the "Leading a Child to Christ" article on page 30.

Lesson 21

Worship Center

It is good to know that God always loves and forgives us. He helps us stop doing wrong and start doing right!

Big Picture Verse

"I have considered my ways and have turned my steps to your statutes." Psalm 119:59

Teacher Materials

Bible, *God's Big Picture* cassette/CD or music video and player, "People of Courage" word chart (p. 471 in this book), large sheet of paper on which you have printed Psalm 119:59, masking tape.

Sing to God

Play "People of Courage," encouraging students to sing along with the music and do the actions shown on the word chart or music video. **How does knowing God will always forgive us give us courage to admit the wrong things we have done?**

Hear and Say God's Word

Display paper on which you have printed Psalm 119:59. Ask a volunteer to read the verse aloud. **Other words for "statutes" are "commands," "laws" or "instructions"—God's ways. What did the person who wrote this verse say that he did?** (Thought about the wrong things he was doing. Decided to stop doing wrong things and started following God's ways instead.) Lead the students in repeating the verse a few times in this manner: Say the verse very quietly the first time. Each time you repeat the verse, speak a little louder, shouting the the verse the last time (if possible in your location).

Pray to God

The writer of the Bible verse said he spent some time considering, or thinking about, the ways in which he had disobeyed God. We need to do that, too. Think about something you have done wrong this week and tell God you are sorry. Allow a brief time for students to pray silently. Lead students in prayer, thanking God for His forgiveness and asking Him to help you and your students turn away from wrong actions and follow God's commands. After the prayer, declare to the students that they are completely forgiven.

Options

1. Students sing "Love and Power" (p. 469 in this book). Encourage students to do the actions shown on the word chart or music video.
2. All students line up behind a volunteer. Volunteer leads students to walk around the room while saying "I have considered my ways and have." When the word "turned" is said, students turn around and begin walking in the other direction while saying "my steps to your statutes."

 **Lesson 21**

Bible Story Coloring Center

Materials

Crayons or markers, a copy of "Hezekiah praises God" picture and story (pp. 111-112 from *Bible Story Coloring Pages*) for each student.

Lead the Activity

Students color page 111; read or tell the story on page 112. **What are these people doing to show their love for God? What do you want to thank God for?**

Option

Each student begins coloring his or her own page. After several minutes, each student signs name on page and trades page with another student. Repeat trading several times until all pages are colored.

Skit Center

Materials

A copy of "Heckling Hezekiah" skit (pp. 161-165 from *The Big Book of Bible Skits*) for each student; optional—highlighter pens.

Lead the Activity

Ask eight volunteers to read the skit, which tells the story of the ways in which Hezekiah obeyed God. (Optional: Students highlight their parts.) Ask the discussion questions on page 161.

Bible Skills Center

Materials

Materials needed for "Line Up the Books" and/or "Domino Definition" (p. 31 and/or p. 111 from *The Big Book of Bible Skills*).

Lead the Activity

Students complete activities as directed in *The Big Book of Bible Skills*.

 **Lesson 22**

Josiah, the Child King

Big Picture Verse

"Do what is right and good in the Lord's sight, so that it may go well with you."
Deuteronomy 6:18

THE BIG PICTURE

Look for good leaders who will help you do what's right in God's eyes.

Scripture Background
2 Chronicles 34; 35

Josiah was only eight years old when he was crowned king after his father was assassinated. While he was still young, Josiah turned his attention to seek the God of David (see 2 Chronicles 34).

Although Josiah did not yet know about the law of God at this early stage of his reign, he had a heart full of zeal to make things right in the sight of God. No doubt the ministry of the prophet Jeremiah and that of the prophet Zephaniah were among the influences that led to the reforms under the young King Josiah. From a young age, Josiah looked toward the godly leaders around him for help in knowing how to lead God's people.

During his reign Josiah not only removed all Baal worship in Judah but also went personally to the northern areas of Israel, even into the ruins around them, to destroy the Asherah poles and crush the idols to powder. He acted fully on everything he knew to do.

Perhaps the highlight of Josiah's reign, however, occurred during the repairing of the Temple. During the work, the Book of the Law was found. When Josiah heard the laws God gave to Moses, he tore his clothes and humbled himself. Here was more revealed from God! Instead of thinking he had done enough already, he called his people together to hear God's laws and to promise with their king that they would obey what they had heard. Josiah is a wonderful example of what one person can do when he or she sets out to please God. The results are seen not only in the life of that person but also in the lives of the people who are then encouraged and led to obey God. Unfortunately, the people of Judah did not continue the godly ways in which Josiah led them. Soon after Josiah's death the kingdom of Judah hastened to its end. Judah was reduced to slavery to Egypt.

Adapted from *What the Bible Is All About* by Henrietta C. Mears.

Big Picture Story Center

Teacher Materials
Bible Time Line, drawing materials/equipment.

Student Materials
Drawing materials.

Tell the Story
Move the *Bible Time Line* frame to highlight Picture 22. As you tell each part of the story, draw each sketch. Students copy your sketches.

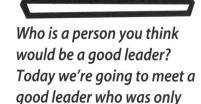

Who is a person you think would be a good leader? Today we're going to meet a good leader who was only eight years old!

1. It had been many years since God's people had gone to the Temple to worship God. The Temple was empty and dirty. But when King Amon was killed, his son, Josiah, was crowned king. Now, Josiah was only eight years old! But Josiah learned quickly that his father's evil ways weren't what he wanted to follow. He began to pray to the God of Israel, whom his ancestor David loved. Josiah tore down the altars to the false gods.

1. Write "8." Add person details and crown.

2. Josiah also wanted to see God's Temple made beautiful again. He sent men to repair the Temple. They brought workers together to fix broken walls, clean the floors, shine the candlesticks and sew new curtains.

2. Temple from rectangles.

3. While the workers were busy, Hilkiah, the high priest, saw something lying in a corner, covered with dust. He picked it up and blew off the dust. It was a scroll, a book written on one long piece of paper made from plants or animal skins and rolled up. Hilkiah unrolled the scroll and began to read. It was a scroll of God's Law! Hilkiah took the scroll to King Josiah's servant. He said, "Look! I found a scroll of God's Law! This is IMPORTANT. Show it to King Josiah!"

3. Scroll from "O"s and "I"s.

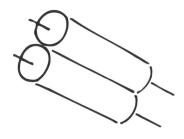

4. King Josiah's servant didn't waste any time. He ran to show King Josiah the scroll of God's Law! King Josiah saw that this scroll had not been read in a long, long time. Josiah asked his servant to please read it aloud.

4. Draw open scroll.

5. As the servant read, Josiah listened carefully. When Josiah heard the laws God gave to Moses, he felt so sad he tore his clothes. He realized that he and his people had not obeyed God! They had not even known what God had asked them to do, because they had not read God's Word. Josiah declared, "We must read God's words to all the people. Then EVERYONE will know how to obey God."

5. Face from "U," "7" for nose. Add details and crown.

6. King Josiah sent messengers to tell everyone to come to the Temple. Mothers, fathers, grandmothers, grandfathers, boys and girls came to hear God's words. King Josiah unrolled the Bible scroll and read it ALL. And all the people LISTENED! When King Josiah finished reading, he said, "I am going to follow the Lord and obey His words. And I want all of you to promise God that we ALL will obey His words." The people did. They promised to obey the God of Israel, the same Lord that Abraham, Moses and David had loved and worshiped.

6. Add open mouth and raised hand from "U"s.

Draw "C"s for crowd listening to king. Add faces.

7. After Josiah destroyed the idols, read God's Word and promised to obey God, THEN he was ready to open the Temple. It was time to celebrate the Passover, to celebrate and remember the time when God brought them out of slavery in Egypt. The people were glad to come and celebrate. King Josiah had everything prepared: the animals, the musicians, the priests—the Bible says there hadn't been such a big celebration of Passover since the days of Samuel! King Josiah was a good leader because he did EVERYTHING he knew how to do to obey God.

7. Music notes from "d"s and "p"s.

Get the Big Picture

What did Hilkiah, the high priest, find in the Temple? (Scroll of God's Law.) **What did Josiah do when he knew his people had not been obeying God's Law?** (Tore his clothes. Called people together to read the Law to them.) **Why do you think Josiah was a good leader?** (He helped others learn and obey God's Law.)

   Good leaders aren't always the strongest or biggest or smartest people. Josiah was only an eight-year-old when he became king! Good leaders do all they can to obey God and help others do what is right, too.

 **Lesson 22**

Bible Verse Object Talk: Magnetic Leaders

Big Picture Verse

"Do what is right and good in the Lord's sight, so that it may go well with you." Deuteronomy 6:18

Teacher Materials

Bible with bookmark at Deuteronomy 6:18, sheet of paper or cardstock, magnet (toy or refrigerator magnet), several iron or steel items (paper clips, nails, pins, washers, etc.).

Present the Object Talk

Hold paper or cardstock horizontally. Invite a volunteer to experiment with the magnet and the items you have collected by placing an item on top of the paper and then moving the magnet under the paper to lead the item around on the paper. Repeat activity with other volunteers and items.

The Bible talks about leaders, people who help others think and act in certain ways. God wants us to look for leaders who will help us do what's right in God's eyes. Look at the way in which these objects follow their leader.

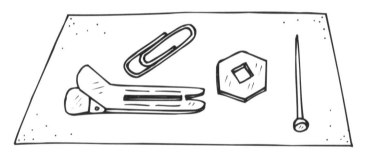

Conclude

These metallic items followed their leader—the magnet. We can choose the kind of people or leaders we want to follow. God gives us people who can lead us to obey Him. Read Deuteronomy 6:18 aloud. **What kind of person does this verse say we should be?** Student answers. **We all need leaders who will help us do what's right in God's eyes and obey Him.** Pray, thanking God for people who help us obey Him.

Discussion Questions

1. What kind of people do we often think of as leaders? (Teachers. Parents. Coaches.)

2. What kind of people make the best leaders? (People who will help us do what's right in God's eyes.)

3. Who has helped you obey God?

4. Who is someone you can help obey God? What is a way you can help that person obey God?

Lesson 22

Active Game Center: Loud Leaders

Materials
Blindfolds.

Lead the Game

1. Designate a playing area. Students form pairs. Three pairs play each round.

2. One student in each of the first three pairs puts on a blindfold. The partner of each blindfolded student takes off a shoe and places it somewhere in the playing area.

3. Shoeless partner and blindfolded partner stand at the edge of the playing area. At your signal, shoeless partner sends blindfolded partner to find his or her shoe, giving directions such as, "Walk three small steps forward" or "Turn to your right and bend down." Student giving directions remains in place.

Good leaders do all they can to obey God and help others do what is right. God gives us people who will be good leaders for us. Let's play a game to practice being good leaders for each other.

4. Once the blindfolded partner finds the correct shoe, the shoeless partner directs him or her back toward his or her partner. (Optional: The blindfolded partner must also put the shoe on the partner's foot.) Repeat play until all students have had a turn to be blindfolded.

Option
Make a separate playing area for each group of three pairs. Mark off playing areas with masking tape, rope or yarn.

Discussion Questions

1. How did your partner act as a good leader? What would happen if you didn't follow your partner's directions?

2. Would you rather be a leader and help people know what to do or be a follower and do what a good leader says to do? Why?

3. How can people who love God be both good followers and good leaders? (Follow and obey God. Help others learn to obey Him, too.)

4. Who are some people you know who can be good leaders for you? How can they lead you in doing what is right in God's eyes?

 Lesson 22

Art Center: Follow the Leader

Student Materials

One 12x18-inch (30x45-cm) sheet of white construction paper for each student, one or more of these drawing materials: crayons, markers, chalk, colored pencils.

Lead the Activity

1. Each student folds a sheet of construction paper in half three times and then opens up the paper.

2. One at a time, say each of the drawing instructions below to lead students in drawing.

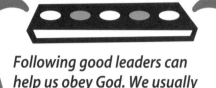

Following good leaders can help us obey God. We usually think of Follow the Leader as a game. Today we're going to play Follow the Leader by drawing in lots of different ways.

Pause after each instruction to allow students time to follow your instruction. Students may choose any of the drawing materials you have provided, drawing in any section of their papers and varying the colors with which they choose to draw. **Draw an object that reminds you of an ocean (a forest, the sky, your backyard). Draw a line that reminds you of being excited (tired, sad, happy).**

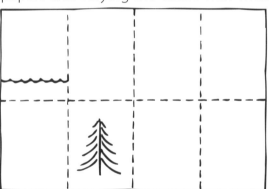

3. Students compare papers with partners, trying to identify the sections in which each drawing instruction was followed.

Options

1. If time permits repeat the activity, inviting older students to be the leaders and give art instructions.

2. Instead of drawing on individual sheets of paper, students draw on a large sheet of butcher paper. Place butcher paper on floor (one paper for each group of eight students). Place drawing materials in the center of the paper. Play music as students walk around the paper. When the music stops, each student stops in place and follows your art instruction. Continue this process until all instructions have been completed.

Discussion Questions

1. Who are some of the leaders you follow? (Coaches. Teachers. Parents.)

2. How do good leaders act?

3. How can you tell a good leader from a not-so-good leader?

4. In what way has a leader helped you learn to obey God? (Reading the Bible. Taking turns with friends.)

Worship Center

Big Picture Verse

"Do what is right and good in the Lord's sight,
so that it may go well with you." Deuteronomy 6:18

Let's thank God that He gives us people who act as good leaders to help us do what is right in God's eyes.

Teacher Materials

Bible, *God's Big Picture* cassette/CD or music video and player, "I Know the King" word chart (p. 463 in this book), large sheet of paper on which you have printed Deuteronomy 6:18, masking tape.

Sing to God

Play "I Know the King," encouraging students to sing along with the music and do the actions shown on the word chart or music video. **If you chose King David as a good leader, what actions of his does this song tell us about that we could follow to do right in God's eyes?** (Trust God with everything. Be kind to others.)

Hear and Say God's Word

Display paper on which you have printed Deuteronomy 6:18. Have a volunteer read the verse aloud. **What does it mean to "do what is right and good in the Lord's sight"?** (To obey the things that God tells us are good. To follow God's commands. To love God and our neighbors.) Divide the students into two groups. Group number one says the first half of the verse and group number two says the second half of the verse. Say "one's" or "two's" to signal to each group when to recite their part. After two times saying the verse in order, mix up when you say "one's" or "two's."

Pray to God

God wants us to look for good leaders who will teach us to follow God and do what is right in His eyes. Who might be a good leader you can follow? Volunteers respond. Lead students in prayer, thanking God for the good leaders He gives us and asking for His help in doing what God says is right.

Options

1. Students sing and do actions for "People of Courage." Play song more than once so that students can listen for and name leaders whose lives and examples the students can follow.
2. Ask an older student to pray during the prayer time.

 **Lesson 22**

Bible Story Coloring Center

Materials

Crayons or markers, a copy of "Josiah hears God's Word" picture and story (pp. 117-118 from *Bible Story Coloring Pages*) for each student.

Lead the Activity

Students color page 117; read or tell the story on page 118. **What is the man doing to help the king learn about God? Who helps you learn about God?**

Option

Students glue completed pictures onto cardstock. Help students cut apart pictures into five or six puzzle pieces. Students put puzzles together. Provide plastic bags in which puzzles may be stored.

Skit Center

Materials

A copy of "This Is the Law" skit (pp. 166-169 from *The Big Book of Bible Skits*) for each student; optional—highlighter pens.

Lead the Activity

Ask six students to read the skit, which tells the story of the discovery and reading of God's Word in the Temple during the time of King Josiah. (Optional: Students highlight their parts.) Ask the discussion questions on page 166.

Bible Skills Center

Materials

Materials needed for "Name that Letter!" and/or "Walking with the Israelites" (p. 48 and/or p. 133 from *The Big Book of Bible Skills*).

Lead the Activity

Students complete activities as directed in *The Big Book of Bible Skills*.

Jeremiah Writes the Word

Big Picture Verse

"I love your commands more than gold, more than pure gold." Psalm 119:127

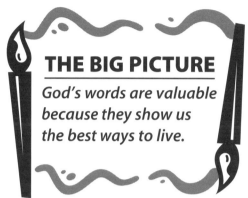

THE BIG PICTURE
God's words are valuable because they show us the best ways to live.

Scripture Background
Jeremiah 1:4-10; 36—40

In Jeremiah is the story of a lad who was called from the obscurity of his native town to assume, at a critical hour in the nation's life, the overwhelming responsibilities of a prophet. Jeremiah came from the village of Anathoth, some three miles (4.8 km) from Jerusalem. Living in this location gave him the advantages of the Holy City. His father, Hilkiah, was a priest, so Jeremiah inherited the traditions of an illustrious ancestry. His early life was, no doubt, influenced by strong religious leaders. God had something even better for Jeremiah than to spend his life as a priest serving at the altar. God appointed this young man to be a prophet of the Lord in this most trying hour in the history of the chosen people.

God often chooses unlikely instruments to do His work and to spread His Word. He chose the sensitive, shrinking Jeremiah for what seemed a hopeless mission, with the words: "Do not say, 'I am only a child.'... Do not be afraid of them, for I am with you and will rescue you" (Jeremiah 1:7,8).

Jeremiah delivered the messages from the Lord to the people by speaking to them as they thronged to the feasts. Often Jeremiah did symbolic things to attract their attention. When he was shut up in prison, he dictated his messages to Baruch, the scribe, who wrote them down and read them to the people. The scroll of Jeremiah that Jehoiakim burned no doubt took Jeremiah and Baruch about one and one-half years to prepare. It was a long and laborious task.

The whole book of Jeremiah is a series of such messages, each of which was spoken to fit the need of the moment. These messages are like gold; and when we apply them to ourselves, we discover that they meet our needs just as they met the needs of Jehovah's wandering people.

Adapted from *What the Bible Is All About* by Henrietta C. Mears.

Big Picture Story Center

Teacher Materials
Bible Time Line, drawing materials/equipment.

Student Materials
Drawing materials.

Tell the Story
Move the *Bible Time Line* frame to highlight Picture 23. As you tell each part of the story, draw each sketch. Students copy your sketches.

What's the most valuable thing you own? Today we're going to talk about one of the most valuable things in the world.

1. The time of the kings ruling over Israel and Judah was almost over. Because most of the kings had led the people away from obeying God, God had warned that their nation would be destroyed. God called a man named Jeremiah to be a prophet like Isaiah, Elijah and Elisha. God told him exactly what messages to tell the people. Jeremiah warned the people to love and obey only God and to stop worshiping idols. But the people of Jerusalem did NOT listen. They no longer cared about loving and obeying God.

1. Draw stop sign.

2. But God still loved the people! He wanted to warn them of the terrible things that would happen to them, so they would stop doing what was wrong. God told Jeremiah, "Take a scroll. Write My words on it." Jeremiah sent for his helper, Baruch (BER-uhk). As Jeremiah spoke God's message, Baruch wrote the words on a scroll.

2. Draw scroll from "O"s and "I"s.

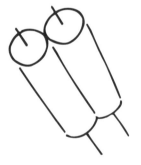

3. When the scroll was finally finished, Jeremiah told Baruch to take it to the Temple and read it to the people. Baruch went to the Temple and read God's words in a loud, clear voice. And this time, some people listened VERY carefully to God's messages.

3. Draw ears from "C"s, add face.

4. One person who listened was a man who went and told the king all about this scroll! The king ordered one of his leaders to bring it to him. The leader read God's words to the king. The king did not like what he heard. In fact, he was so angry that he grabbed a KNIFE.

4. Angry king: "3"s for beard, "C" for ear, "7" for nose.

5. Every time the leader finished reading part of the scroll, the king took the scroll from his hand. He took his knife and sliced off that part of the scroll and threw it into the FIRE! The king didn't care AT ALL about what God said! He wanted to forget about it and didn't want anyone else to read God's message!

5. Knife from 2 "D"s and scroll from "O" and "I"s.

6. But God's words are important and valuable. God loved these people. They needed to know that trouble was coming unless they changed! So God told Jeremiah to write out the same scroll again. The new scroll was to have all the words that were on the first scroll and more besides. Jeremiah and Baruch followed God's instructions and wrote another scroll. But the king and his people still did not listen.

6. Draw larger closed scroll.

7. Then there was a new king. Did he listen? NO! First, Jeremiah was put in jail. THEN the king's officials had Jeremiah thrown into a cistern—a hole deep in the ground where rain water is stored. No one was listening to what God told Jeremiah to say.

7. Write "Jail"; add face and details.

8. The sad part of this story is that all the terrible things that Jeremiah had told the people would happen DID happen, just like God said they would. Their country was destroyed. Soon, an enemy army attacked them and their city burned, just as God had said. The enemies took most of the people away as slaves. The trouble that God said would come DID come. God's words are true and valuable.

8. Draw sad faces.

Get the Big Picture

What does a prophet do? (Tells God's messages to people.) **What did the king do with the scroll of God's words?** (Sliced it into pieces; burned the pieces.) **What did God tell Jeremiah to do next?** (Write the scroll again. Keep warning the people.) **What happened because the people did not listen to God's important words?** (Trouble did come. People were taken as slaves. The city was burned.)

God's words are still just as important today as they were in Jeremiah's day. They are always true, and they are more valuable than anything in the world. God's words show us the best way to live.

Bible Verse Object Talk: Action Words

Big Picture Verse

"I love your commands more than gold, more than pure gold." Psalm 119:127

Teacher Materials

Bible with Psalm 119:127 marked with a bookmark.

Present the Object Talk

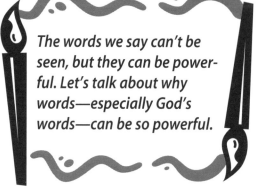

The words we say can't be seen, but they can be powerful. Let's talk about why words—especially God's words—can be so powerful.

1. Whisper "fire!" to a volunteer who then acts out his or her response to the word. Other students in the group try to identify the word. Give clues as needed to help students guess. After the word is guessed ask, **Why is the word "fire" powerful?** (Gives us important information. Knowing about a fire can save our lives.)

2. Repeat activity with other volunteers and these words or phrases: "stop," "free candy," "home run," "goal," "I'm not it," "dinner's ready," "on your mark, get set, go," "foul ball."

Conclude

Why do you think God's words or commands are so powerful? (They help us know the best way to live. They tell us how to obey God instead of sinning.) **Because God's commands help us in so many ways, the Bible says they are very valuable.** Read Psalm 119:127 aloud. **If this verse was written today, what words might be substituted for the word "gold"?** Pray, thanking God for His commands and asking His help to obey them.

Discussion Questions

1. What are some other powerful things that can't be seen? (Wind. Thunder.)

2. What are some ways kids your age can show they think God's commands are valuable?

3. How has one of God's commands helped you know what to do or say? Tell students about a time one of God's commands has helped you.

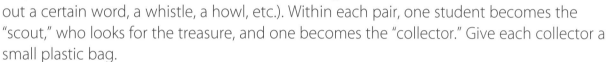

Active Game Center: Treasure Hunt

Materials

Pennies, small plastic bags

Prepare the Game

Around the playing area, hide at least two pennies for each student.

Lead the Game

God's words are valuable because they tell us the best way to live. Let's go on a treasure hunt to remind us that God's Word is like a treasure.

1. Students pair off. Each pair determines a signal they will use to call each other (three claps, calling out a certain word, a whistle, a howl, etc.). Within each pair, one student becomes the "scout," who looks for the treasure, and one becomes the "collector." Give each collector a small plastic bag.

2. At your signal, the scouts move around the playing area to begin searching for the "treasure" (pennies). When a scout finds a penny, he or she cannot touch it but instead must use the pair's pre-determined signal to call the collector. When the collector hears the signal, he or she must go and pick up the treasure and put it in his or her plastic bag. Continue game until each pair has located a penny.

3. Begin a new round of the game with students trading roles. Hide additional pennies if needed.

Options

1. Have students count their "treasure" to determine the winning pair; then invite the winning pair to read Psalm 119:127 aloud.
2. Substitute gold-wrapped chocolate coins for pennies.

Discussion Questions

1. How do God's words help us more than pennies or gold? (They show us the best way to live. They tell us about God's love.)

2. How can we show our love for God's Word? (Pay attention to what it says. Try to obey it.)

3. Who helps you learn about God's Word?

4. One way to obey God's Word is by helping someone in need. How can you obey that command?

Art Center: Better Than Gold

Student Materials

Card stock cut to bookmark size, scissors, glue sticks, one or more of the following gold decorating materials: foil wrapping paper, confetti, metallic pens, glitter pens, crayons.

Lead the Activity

Students decorate their bookmarks with the materials you have provided.

Gold is something we think of as very valuable. A long time ago, a man in Bible times said he loved God's Word more than gold. God's Word gives us the best news in the world. Today you can make a bookmark and decorate it with gold. Use it when you read the Bible!

Options

1. Students may print Psalm 119:127 on their bookmarks before decorating them.

2. Provide clear ConTact paper, so students may cover their bookmarks.

Discussion Questions

1. Why do you think that God's Word is better than gold?

2. In what ways can God's Word help us?

3. What can a person do to show he or she values God's Word? (Read it. Think about it. Memorize it.)

4. How can we use these bookmarks to learn more about God's Word?

 **Lesson 23**

Worship Center

Big Picture Verse

"I love your commands more than gold, more than pure gold." Psalm 119:127

Let's thank God for His words that show us the best way to live!

Teacher Materials

Bible, *God's Big Picture* cassette/CD or music video and player, "God's Holy Book" word chart (p. 459 in this book), paper, marker, large sheet of paper on which you have printed Psalm 119:127, masking tape.

Prepare the Activity

Scramble the letters of four to five words in the verse; write each scrambled word on a sheet of paper.

Sing to God

Play "God's Holy Book," encouraging students to sing along with the music and do the actions shown on the word chart or music video. **What does this song say we can find out by reading God's Word?**

Hear and Say God's Word

Display paper on which you have printed Psalm 119:127. Have a volunteer read the verse aloud. **How did the writer of this verse feel about God's words and commands?** (He thought they were very valuable! More valuable than money!) Lead the group in reciting the verse together. Show paper on which you have printed the scrambled letters of one of the words of the verse. Students identify the scrambled word. Recite the verse together again; then hold up another scrambled word. Repeat until all words have been unscrambled.

Pray to God

What are some of the good things we learn from God's Word? (What God has done. The good news about Jesus. How to get along with others, etc.) Lead students in prayer, thanking God for His words in the Bible that show us the best way to live and asking for His help to understand and follow those words.

Options

1. Ask students for ideas about things to substitute for the word "gold" and then say Psalm 119:127 using the suggested words. (For example: "I love your commands more than ice cream, more than chocolate ice cream.")

2. During the prayer activity, older students find these verses in their Bibles and read them aloud as examples of God's valuable words which tell us how to live: Micah 6:8; Mark 12:30,31; Romans 12:10; Ephesians 5:19,20; Philippians 2:4; James 1:19; James 5:13.

Bible Story Coloring Center

Materials
Crayons or markers, a copy of "The king destroys the scroll of God's Words " picture and story (pp. 119-120 from *Bible Story Coloring Pages*) for each student.

Lead the Activity
Students color page 119; read or tell the story on page 120. **This angry king did not want to obey God's Word. What does God's Word look like today? What can you do to show how important it is?**

Option
Use a paper cutter to cut construction paper into small squares and triangles. Students use glue sticks to glue paper squares and triangles to fill in the picture instead of coloring.

Skit Center

Materials
A copy of "Prophets' Round Table" skit (pp. 170-174 from *The Big Book of Bible Skits*) for each student; optional—highlighter pens.

Lead the Activity
Ask eight students to read the skit, which tells the story of how Jeremiah and other prophets told God's Word. (Optional: Students highlight their parts.) Ask the discussion questions on page 170.

Bible Skills Center

Materials
Materials needed for "Prophet Talk" and/or "Prophets' Wall" (p. 42 and/or p. 143 from *The Big Book of Bible Skills*).

Lead the Activity
Students complete activities as directed in *The Big Book of Bible Skills*.

Daniel Takes a Risk

Big Picture Verse

"Pray continually; give thanks in all circumstances." 1 Thessalonians 5:17,18

THE BIG PICTURE

Pray to God every day.

Scripture Background
Daniel 1; 6

Daniel stands in God's Word as the man who dared to keep a clean heart and body and the man, therefore, whom God chose to tell His message to the Gentile nations of the world. A large part of the book of Daniel is concerned with the thrilling personal life of this peerless captive prince of Judah.

The scene opens upon a little company of four men: Daniel, Hananiah, Mishael and Azariah. They had been taken captive by Nebuchadnezzar and carried away from Jerusalem to his palace in Babylon. Daniel was only about 16 years old.

Daniel and his friends lived in an atmosphere of loose morals and low standards even though they were in a palace. Yet we read that they kept themselves apart from the evil of that court—true to God in a day when everything was against them. We are told that God gave these young men knowledge and skill in all learning and wisdom. When facing a crisis, Daniel was not afraid. He called his prayer partners, and they presented their problem before God. God never disappoints faith in Him.

Later, when the kingdom was taken over by a new ruler, Darius the Mede, Daniel again showed his faith in God. Daniel's conduct in the face of danger was quite deliberate. He knew he had to either deny his religion or be prepared to die for it. His choice was to continue in the same lifestyle of obedience to God. His actions remained unchanged. He prayed as was his custom, knowing that his example would influence the other Jews. Daniel's perseverance during this ordeal was glorious and just what we would expect from a man ripened in years with God. As a result of his faithful actions, Daniel was thrown into the den of lions, but he fell into the hands of the living God. The world cannot breed a lion that God cannot tame! Notice that in these circumstances, Daniel prayed with thanksgiving (see Daniel 6:10); he did not fall down in terror and agony, but he praised God. What an example for us to follow!

Adapted from *What the Bible Is All About* by Henrietta C. Mears.

Big Picture Story Center

Teacher Materials
Bible Time Line, drawing materials/equipment.

Student Materials
Drawing materials.

Tell the Story
Move the *Bible Time Line* frame to highlight Picture 24. As you tell each part of the story, draw each sketch. Students copy your sketches.

What's something you like to do every day?
Today we're going to talk about a man who prayed to God every day, no matter what happened!

1. The King of Babylon had attacked Jerusalem. He took many people to Babylon as captives, just as the prophets had warned. Daniel was a young man who was taken to the king's palace to serve the king. Daniel served so well that he worked as an official for several kings. He was very honest; he loved and obeyed God; and every day, three times a day, Daniel knelt in front of his open window and prayed to God.

2. Darius (duh-RI-uhs), the king of Babylon, was very pleased with Daniel's work. He decided to put Daniel in charge over EVERYONE in the government. When some other government officials heard about the king's plan, they were very jealous that the king liked Daniel so much.

3. These jealous officials spied on Daniel day and night, trying to think of a way to get rid of him or make the king not like him. But they found nothing wrong! When they saw that Daniel knelt in front of his window and prayed to God three times every day, they got an idea.

4. The officials tricked King Darius into making a new law. The law said that for 30 days, nobody could pray to ANYONE except to King Darius. Whoever disobeyed would be thrown to hungry lions! And no one lived through that! The jealous officials were sure Daniel would be eaten by lions, or would Daniel stop praying?

1. Draw a "3." Add details for praying Daniel and window.

2. Draw jealous faces.

3. Add light bulbs over heads.

4. Scroll from "S"s.

5. Daniel soon heard about the new law! Now, Daniel COULD have hidden in the dark and prayed to God. He could have NOT prayed for 30 days. But praying to God was SO important to Daniel that he kept on praying in front of the window three times every day, just as he had always done. The minute the jealous officials saw Daniel praying, they ran to the king to tell him Daniel had broken the law!

5. Draw second praying Daniel figure. Add surprised face.

6. King Darius was very upset—not because Daniel had disobeyed his law but because he realized the leaders had tricked him into making this silly law to get rid of Daniel. In Babylon, once a king made a law, he could never change it. King Darius knew the silly law had to be obeyed. He sadly walked with Daniel—to the LIONS' DEN.

6. Lion from "5," "C"s, "3"s. Teeth from "V"s.

7. King Darius sighed. "You have been very faithful to your God. I hope He can save you from the hungry lions," he said. And with that, Daniel was put into a pit filled with hungry lions. A stone was rolled over the opening to the pit and King Darius had it sealed, so NO ONE could move it.

   That night King Darius worried about Daniel. He walked back and forth, wondering if Daniel's God would save him. Early next morning, the king ran to the lion's den. He called, "Daniel! Did your God save you?"

7. Draw worried face. Add details for king.

8. Daniel called back, "Yes, God saved me from the lions. He sent an angel who shut the lions' mouths. God knew I had done nothing wrong." The king ordered his soldiers to pull Daniel out of the den. He sent a message to EVERYONE in his country that Daniel's God was the REAL God. And the jealous leaders were punished.

8. Lion with closed mouth from "E," "C"s and "3"s.

Get the Big Picture

Why did the officials get the king to make the law? (They were jealous of Daniel.) **What did Daniel do?** (Prayed anyway.) **What did God do when Daniel was with the lions?** (Protected Daniel. Sent an angel.)

God wants us to pray to Him every day. If things are happy or sad, good or bad, He wants us to come to Him and talk with Him! When we pray, we get to know God better. He always wants to hear us pray to Him!

 **Lesson 24**

Bible Verse Object Talk: What Do You Need?

Big Picture Verse

"Pray continually; give thanks in all circumstances."
1 Thessalonians 5:17,18

Teacher Materials

Bible with bookmark at 1 Thessalonians 5:17,18, flashlight with batteries, plant, votive candle, match, large wide-mouthed jar, snack for each student.

If we want to get to know God and obey Him, we need to talk to Him every day. Let's look at these objects and talk about what they need in order to work.

Present the Object Talk

1. Show flashlight and ask students to tell what it needs to work (batteries). **What are some other items which need batteries in order to work?** (CD player, handheld video games, toys, etc.)

2. Show plant and ask students to tell what it needs to grow (water, sunlight). **What are some other things which need water and sunlight to grow?** (Trees, flowers, etc.)

3. Light candle. **What does this candle need to burn?** (Oxygen.) Cover candle with jar and watch to see the candle flame go out. Repeat experiment, inviting students to count how long it takes for the flame to go out.

4. **What do you need to do every day to live and grow?** (Eat food. Drink water. Breathe air.) Serve snack to each student.

Conclude

We've talked about what all these items need. What does 1 Thessalonians 5:17,18 say we need to do? Read verse aloud. **Sometimes we only think about praying to God when we have a problem or need something. But when does 1 Thessalonians 5:17,18 say we should pray? Talking to God every day about what we are doing and the choices we are making helps us love and obey Him.** Lead students in prayer, thanking Him that we can talk to Him.

Discussion Questions

1. When can you talk to God?

2. What are some things a kid your age could tell God about school?

3. Who might help you remember to pray?

4. What's something you'd like to thank God for right now?

Active Game Center: Practice Makes Perfect

Materials

Masking tape, materials for one or more of the activities below.

Prepare the Game

Set up one or more of the activities below.

Lead the Game

Explain activities to the students. Students move around to the different activities as time allows. Make sure students try the chosen activity more than once so that they get to practice it.

Talking to God is so important that He wants us to pray every day so that praying becomes a habit. The more we pray, the more we get to know God and the ways in which we can love and obey Him. Let's practice doing something several times to see if we get better at doing it.

Beanbag Toss

Set a large plastic bowl or tub about 5 feet (1.5 m) from a masking-tape line. Students stand behind line, face away from tub and toss beanbag over shoulder back toward the tub.

Ball Bounce

Place a trash can about 8 feet (2.4 m) away from a masking-tape line. Students stand behind line and throw the ball to bounce it into the trash can. The ball must bounce at least once before it enters the trash can.

Marshmallow Move

Set an open bag of marshmallows and a pair of chopsticks 4 feet (1.2 m) from a plastic bowl. Students use chopsticks to pick up a marshmallow and carry it to the plastic bowl without touching marshmallow with their hands.

Options

1. Let first student in line choose a new way to throw the ball or toss the beanbag. Other students imitate.

2. Create your own stations according to your students' abilities and interests.

Discussion Questions

1. Which activity was the hardest? the easiest?

2. How did the activities become easier the more you practiced them?

3. What other activities do you practice?

4. What would help you remember to pray every day? (A reminder from your parents. Making a sign to help you remember. An alarm clock ringing at the time you want to pray.)

 **Lesson 24**

Art Center: Prayer Journal

Student Materials

12x18-inch (30x45-cm) white construction paper, masking tape, markers, white paper, stapler.

Lead the Activity

1. Each student lightly and randomly places three or four strips of masking tape on a sheet of white construction paper (see sketch a).

2. Students lightly draw designs or pictures on the papers, drawing over the masking tape. Students carefully peel off the masking tape and then fold papers in half, design side out (see sketch b).

One way to help us remember to talk to God is to write our prayers—things we are thankful for, things we need, things we want to talk to God about—in a book. Today we can make prayer books (journals) and decorate special covers for them.

a. 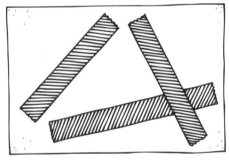   b.

3. Students insert four or five sheets of white paper inside the construction paper cover.

4. Staple each book several times along the folded edge.

Options

1. Students use watercolor paints to paint over masking-tape designs. Allow paint to dry before removing tape.

2. Students write prayer requests or prayers in their journals. Ask students to tell times they can write in their journals during the week.

3. Students may either leave blank the spaces created from masking-tape strips or letter their names and/or "My Prayer Journal" in the spaces.

Discussion Questions

1. Why do you think God wants us to pray?

2. When are some times you or your family pray? When is a new time you might want to pray?

3. What things can we talk to God about? Tell students what you like to talk to God about.

Worship Center

> I'm glad God hears and answers our prayers. Let's thank God that He hears our prayers.

Big Picture Verse

"Pray continually; give thanks in all circumstances."
1 Thessalonians 5:17,18

Teacher Materials

Bible, *God's Big Picture* cassette/CD or music video and player, "People of Courage" word chart (p. 471 in this book), large sheet of paper on which you have printed 1 Thessalonians 5:17,18; masking tape.

Sing to God

Play "People of Courage," encouraging students to sing along with the music and do the actions shown on the word chart or music video. **In this song, who prayed to God for help?** (Daniel. Esther when she fasted.)

Hear and Say God's Word

Display paper on which you have printed 1 Thessalonians 5:17,18. Have a volunteer read the verse aloud. Lead the students in saying the verse, with the boys saying the first word, girls saying the second, etc., alternating on every word. Have students repeat the verse in this manner several times, alternating which group says the first word. **What does it mean to "pray continually"?** (To talk to God about the things that are happening in your day, thanking Him for the good things and asking for his help with the problems. To pray for people often.)

Pray to God

What are some things that we could pray for? List students' praises and requests on the back of the large sheet of paper on which the verse was printed. Encourage students to pray aloud, completing the sentence, **God, I pray for...** and praying for the needs on the list. End prayer by thanking God that He hears our prayers and asking for His help in remembering to pray continually.

Options

1. Older students write new verses to "People of Courage," telling about times other people in the Bible prayed for things. (For example, Moses asking for God's help while he was leading the Israelites; Hannah praying for a baby and having Samuel; Paul praying in prison.)
2. If students made prayer journals in the Art Center, they may write prayer requests and items for which they wish to thank God in their journals.

 **Lesson 24**

Bible Story Coloring Center

Materials

Crayons or markers, a copy of "God protects Daniel in a den of lions" picture and story (pp. 125-126 from *Bible Story Coloring Pages*) for each student.

Lead the Activity

Students color page 125; read or tell the story on page 126. **How does Daniel look even though he is in a den of lions? Why? Daniel must have thanked God for keeping Him safe. What can you thank God for?**

Option

Students draw pictures of things for which they want to thank God.

Skit Center

Materials

A copy of "The Writing on the Wall" skit (pp. 190-194 from *The Big Book of Bible Skits*) for each student; optional—highlighter pens.

Lead the Activity

Students read the skit, which tells the story of another incident in Daniel's life when he obeyed God: when Daniel was called to interpret God's warning to Belshazzar given in the handwriting on the wall. (Optional: Students highlight their parts.) Ask the discussion questions on page 190.

Bible Skills Center

Materials

Materials needed for "Match Up" and/or "Prophet's Message" (p. 47 and/or p. 141 from *The Big Book of Bible Skills*).

Lead the Activity

Students complete activities as directed in *The Big Book of Bible Skills*.

Esther Saves God's People

Big Picture Verse

"It is God who works in you to will and to act according to his good purpose." Philippians 2:13

THE BIG PICTURE

God gets us ready to do good things for Him.

Scripture Background
Esther

At the time of Esther, great Xerxes (Ahasuerus) was ruler of Persia. His tremendous fleet had just been defeated by the Greeks at the battle of Salamis in 480 B.C. In the midst of this famous chapter in world history occurs the beautiful and charming Bible story of Esther. Although God's name is not mentioned in the book of Esther, every page is full of God, who hides Himself behind every word. God has a part in all the events of human life.

Esther is like Joseph and David. God had each one hidden away for His purpose. When the day came, He brought them into prominence to work out His plan. God always has someone ready to fulfill His purposes.

Esther stands out as God's chosen one. She is a sweet and winsome person. The beauty of Esther was that she was not spoiled by her great position. Though she became queen of a great king, she did not forget the kindness of Mordecai who had brought her up from childhood. Esther was faced with the opportunity of a lifetime: to rescue the lives of her oppressed people, the Jews. When she once accepted her dreaded task, she proceeded to carry it out with courage. It was a daring act for her to enter unsummoned into the presence of the king. Yet she knew she must choose the right course at terrible danger to herself.

There is one thing to do always: Do what is right and leave the rest to God. God prepares us for emergencies. He meets the emergencies with human lives which He has redeemed and prepared. There is a time to act. Esther was prepared and brought to the kingdom for just such a time of emergency.

It would do well for each one of us to pause and ask, "Why has God allowed me to live at this particular hour?" To do what is right may mean that we must jeopardize our lives. Then we must face the issue and answer with this young queen, "If I perish, I perish" (Esther 4:16).

Adapted from *What the Bible Is All About* by Henrietta C. Mears.

Big Picture Story Center

Teacher Materials
Bible Time Line, drawing materials/equipment.

Student Materials
Drawing materials.

Tell the Story
Move the *Bible Time Line* frame to highlight Picture 25. As you tell each part of the story, draw each sketch. Students copy your sketches.

What's one thing you did today to get ready to come here? Today we're going to meet a young woman God got ready for a very important job!

1. Many Jews had returned to Israel; but many Jews still lived in Persia, too. One was a man named Mordecai (MAWRD-i-KI). His cousin, Esther, was an orphan, so he raised Esther like his own daughter. Mordecai taught her to trust the one true God, not the idols of Persia.

1. Draw Esther from 3 "7s." Add hair.

2. When Esther was grown, the king of Persia wanted a new queen. He sent officers through the land to find beautiful young women who were taken to the palace. The king would choose one of them as his new queen. Esther was one of the girls chosen. When Esther was brought before the king, he liked her the best! Esther was crowned the new queen. God was preparing Esther to take part in some very big plans!

2. Draw elaborate crown from "O"s, "V"s and "C"s.

3. A man named Haman was the chief official of Persia, next to the king in power. And everyone in Persia BOWED before him—everyone except Mordecai, Esther's cousin! Mordecai bowed only before God. This made Haman ANGRY. He hated Mordecai and all the Jews. Haman told the king how much trouble all the Jews were. He asked the king to make a law that the Jews should all be KILLED!

3. Bowing person from 2 "L"s. Add details.

4. It doesn't seem that the king knew Esther was a Jew. He AGREED to let Haman write the law! And he gave Haman his signet ring to seal it. Haman's law ordered that all the Jews be killed on a certain day. With the king's seal on it, the law could never be changed. What an uproar! The Jews asked each other, "What have WE ever done to deserve THIS?"

4. Signet ring from "O"s and "C"s. Add crown.

5. Mordecai was VERY sad. When Esther heard that he was upset, she sent servants to find out why. Mordecai told Esther about the law. Esther would not escape being killed just because she was queen. Mordecai told her she HAD to talk to the king about this terrible law!

5. Draw teardrops and make into eyes. "U"s for facial features and hair.

6. BUT there was a problem: If a person went into the throne room without being invited and the king didn't hold out his scepter to that person, it meant DEATH! This made Esther afraid to go to the king at first. But Mordecai was sure she had become queen for this very reason! Only someone the king liked more than Haman could plead for the Jews!

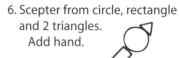

6. Scepter from circle, rectangle and 2 triangles. Add hand.

7. Esther was willing to trust God even if it meant she had to die. Esther fasted for three days—instead of eating she spent time praying to God. Then Esther dressed up—maybe for the last time. She slipped into the throne room, her heart pounding. Would the king hold out his scepter to her? Her life and the lives of her people depended on his next move!!

7. Draw a beating heart.

8. The king held out his scepter! She touched it and invited the king and Haman to two feasts. At the second feast, Esther told the king that an enemy wanted to kill her and her people. The king wanted to know who this enemy was. Esther pointed to Haman and said, "The enemy is Haman!" So the king got rid of Haman and put Mordecai in his place. The king made a new law saying that on the day the Jews were to be killed, they could defend themselves! The Jews' enemies were quickly defeated, and the Jews living in Persia were saved because Esther was ready to obey God!

8. Add hand with finger touching the scepter .

Draw happy faces.

Get the Big Picture

What did Esther do? (Saved her people.) **How did God prepare her for this event?** (Made her queen.)

Queen Esther was ready because she knew how to rely on God. God used her to save all the Jewish people living in Persia. God gets us ready to do good things, too. We may not do the same job Esther did, but God has important work for each of us to do. He will get us ready as we trust Him and obey Him.

Bible Verse Object Talk: Get Ready!

Big Picture Verse

"It is God who works in you to will and to act according to his good purpose." Philippians 2:13

Teacher Materials

Bible with bookmark at Philippians 2:13, one or more of the following diagrams or maps: blueprints, highway map, city street map, topographical or trail map, ocean depth chart, map of school, museum or mall.

We've all done things to get ready for an important event like a birthday party or a Christmas celebration. God wants us to get ready to do the good things He wants us to do, too. Look at these maps and diagrams and think about how they help you prepare for something.

Present the Object Talk

One at a time, show each kind of map or diagram you have brought. **What would this (map) help you get ready for? What kind of information do you learn from this (diagram)? Why is the information on here important? What might happen if you didn't have this map or diagram?** (Might get lost. Wouldn't know how long trip would take. Couldn't plan how to get to the place we're going.)

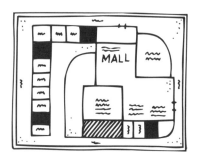

Conclude

Before we take a trip or build a building, it's important to get ready so that we can do a good job. Who helps us get ready to do the good things God wants us to do? Read Philippians 2:13 aloud. **This verse tells us that we don't have to try to obey God by ourselves. He promises to help us love and obey Him.** Pray, thanking God that He is with us to help us do good.

Discussion Questions

1. *What are some other things kids your age need to get ready for?* (Spelling test. Piano recital. Basketball game.) *How do you get ready for them?* (Practice. Ask God's help.)

2. *What are some of the ways we can get ready to do the good things God wants us to do?* (Learn about God. Read the Bible. Talk to God.)

3. *What's something good you think God might want you to do?* (Be honest. Treat others fairly.)

Active Game Center: Ready Or Not!

Materials
Masking tape, rope or yarn.

Prepare the Game
Mark out a playing area with masking tape, rope or yarn (playing area should only allow minimal movement).

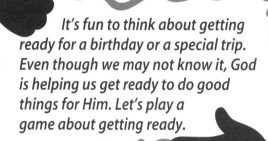

It's fun to think about getting ready for a birthday or a special trip. Even though we may not know it, God is helping us get ready to do good things for Him. Let's play a game about getting ready.

Lead the Game
Students move around the playing area randomly. Call out "Get ready" so that students know to listen; then immediately clap your hands a certain number of times. For example, if you clap your hands three times, students form groups of three and sit down. Repeat play, clapping a different number of times each time. Continue play as time permits.

Options
1. Instead of saying "Get ready," blow a whistle to get students' attention and then bang on a metal pot with a metal spoon to communicate the number of students needed to form a group.
2. An older student may lead this game.

Discussion Questions
1. What did you have to do to get ready in this game? (Stop and listen for the claps.)

2. What kinds of things do you do to get ready for school? for a trip?

3. How can we get ready for the good things God wants us to do? (Pray every day. Read and think about God's Word. Follow the example of people who love God.)

Art Center: When I'm a Grown-Up

Student Materials

A variety of recyclable and/or craft materials (soda cans, craft sticks, cardboard tubes, toothpicks, aluminum foil, egg cartons, Styrofoam pieces, straws, string, paper), scissors, glue, masking tape, markers.

Lead the Activity

1. **What's something you might want to be or do when you're a grown-up? What kind of job do you think you'd like?** As volunteers tell answers (mechanic, teacher, astronaut, fire fighter, computer worker, doctor, etc.), ask, **What kind of object would remind you of that job?**

God wants us to get ready to do good things. We can do good things to help others now and in the future. Today we're going to build objects which remind us of things we might want to do in the future when we're grown-ups.

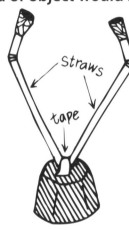
Straws
tape

2. Each student chooses one occupation (more than one student may choose the same occupation) and uses the materials you have provided to construct an object used in that occupation (car, book, rocket, fire engine, computer, stethoscope, etc.). Students may use markers to add details to objects.

Options

1. If craft and recyclable materials are not available, students may draw pictures of objects used in a variety of occupations.

2. Participate in this activity along with students, making an object you use in your occupation.

Discussion Questions

1. What are some ways to get ready for Christmas? a soccer game? a test? a recital?

2. What are some ways in which God gets us ready to do good things? (Gives us the Bible to read. Gives us teachers and parents to help us learn how to obey Him.)

3. What are some good things God wants people in any job to do? (Worship Him. Help others learn about Him.)

Lesson 25

Worship Center

Big Picture Verse

"It is God who works in you to will and to act according to his good purpose."
Philippians 2:13

God wants us to do good things. But He doesn't expect us to do these good things by ourselves. He promises to help us get ready to love and obey Him. Let's praise Him for His love and care.

Teacher Materials

Bible, *God's Big Picture* cassette/CD or music video and player, "People of Courage" word chart (p. 471 in this book), large sheet of paper on which you have printed Philippians 2:13, masking tape.

Sing to God

Play "People of Courage," encouraging students to sing along with the music and do the actions shown on the word chart or music video. **What does the chorus of this song say we should do to be ready for the good things God is preparing us to do?**

Hear and Say God's Word

Display paper on which you have printed Philippians 2:13. Have a volunteer read the verse aloud. **How does God work in us to prepare us to do His good plans?** (He helps us learn how to treat others when we read the Bible. He helps us do the things we learn at church.) Lead students in reciting the verse in this manner: Students take turns calling out one word each to complete the verse. Repeat verse as many times as needed so that every student gets a chance to say a word.

Pray to God

Let's thank God that He gets us ready to do good things. Lead students in prayer: **Thank You, God, for helping us learn how to love and obey You.**

Options

1. Sing "God's Holy Book" (p. 459 in this book), encouraging students to sing along with the music and do the actions shown on the word chart or music video.

2. If your students have already heard the Bible story, listen to the stanza about Queen Esther in "People of Courage" song more than once. Students name actions that prepared her to tell the truth to King Xerxes.

3. Invite a guest to briefly tell students about a way in which God prepared him or her to do good things for Him. Another option is to tell students about an example from your own life.

 **Lesson 25**

Bible Story Coloring Center

Materials
Crayons or markers, a copy of "Queen Esther saves her people" picture and story (pp. 129-130 from *Bible Story Coloring Pages*) for each student.

Lead the Activity
Students color page 129; read or tell the story on page 130. **What is Esther doing? Why? How did God help Esther?**

Option
After coloring page, students cut page apart in six to eight sections, making puzzles. Students trade puzzles and put them together. Students glue completed puzzles to blank paper, so they may take pictures home (or provide envelopes in which student may store puzzle pieces).

Skit Center

Materials
A copy of "Risky Business" skit (pp. 181-185 from *The Big Book of Bible Skits*) for each student; optional—highlighter pens.

Lead the Activity
Students form trios and read the skit, which tells the story of Esther's opportunity to save her people. (Optional: Students highlight parts.) Ask the discussion questions on page 181.

Bible Skills Center

Materials
Materials needed for "What's Next?" and/or "Name that Maze" (p. 36 and/or p. 95 from *The Big Book of Bible Skills*).

Lead the Activity
Students complete activities as directed in *The Big Book of Bible Skills*.

Nehemiah's Big Project

Big Picture Verse

"Whatever you do, work at it with all your heart, as working for the Lord, not for men." Colossians 3:23

THE BIG PICTURE

When we show love for God by working together, good things can be accomplished.

Scripture Background
Nehemiah 1—4; 8; 9

Nehemiah was the cupbearer at the court of King Artaxerxes. This position was one of high honor. But in Nehemiah's position of familiarity with the king, he had not forgotten about his people. The Jews had been back home for almost a hundred years, but they had made no attempt to build Jerusalem beyond the restoration of the Temple because their enemies had made it almost impossible. This news that was brought to him about Jerusalem made Nehemiah very sad. This sadness could not be wholly hidden, and the king detected it.

Nehemiah was loyal enough to his people to ask permission to leave the luxury of the king's court and go back to rebuild Jerusalem, the capital of his homeland. When Nehemiah reached Jerusalem, Ezra had been there for 13 years. Ezra was a priest and had been teaching the people the Word of God. But Nehemiah was a civil governor. He had come with the authority of the king of Persia to build the walls of Jerusalem. After he had been there only three days, he went up and viewed the walls at night. When he saw their dilapidated condition, he encouraged the people to begin building immediately.

The building was not without its difficulties, however. First the Samaritans, the enemies of the Jews, derided them. They hindered their work so that the Jews had to keep watch night and day. Their derision turned to anger, and Nehemiah divided the men into two groups, one keeping watch while the other worked. Again and again, Nehemiah's enemies tried to bring Nehemiah and the people away from the building, but Nehemiah prayed and the enemy was turned back.

Despite their troubles, the work was accomplished in 52 days! Each family was assigned a portion of the wall on which to work. Nehemiah was quite an engineer! Undergirding their efforts and their prayers was the incredible attitude of the people expressed in the sentence, "the people worked with all their heart" (Nehemiah 4:6).

Adapted from *What the Bible Is All About* by Henrietta C. Mears.

Big Picture Story Center

Teacher Materials
Bible Time Line, drawing materials/equipment.

Student Materials
Drawing materials.

Tell the Story
Move the *Bible Time Line* frame to highlight Picture 26. As you tell each part of the story, draw each sketch. Students copy your sketches.

What's a job you need someone else's help to do?
Today we're going to meet a man who showed his love for God by helping people work together to do great things!

1. Nehemiah lived in the country of Babylon, far from his real home in Jerusalem. Like Daniel, Nehemiah had been taken away from Jerusalem many years before. Nehemiah lived in the king's palace and worked for the king.

1. Draw Nehemiah from "N."

2. One day Nehemiah's brother came to visit him. His brother had been left behind when the Babylonians took so many people away. The brothers talked and talked, and Nehemiah wanted to know how things were in Jerusalem. Nehemiah's brother sadly told him that the walls around Jerusalem were broken down and the houses were falling down, too.

2. Falling walls from rectangles.

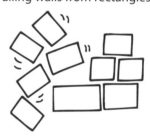

3. When Nehemiah heard this bad news, he was very sad for days and DAYS. He didn't even eat. But he did do something VERY important. He prayed! He asked God to help him find a way to get the king's permission to go and help rebuild the walls and the houses in Jerusalem.

3. Draw "U"s and "3" to make praying hands.

4. Nehemiah's sad face told the king that something was very wrong. The king asked, "Why are you so sad?" Before Nehemiah answered, he silently asked God to help him say the right words. "O King," Nehemiah said, "my brother has told me that the city where our family lived is ruined. The walls are broken down. I want VERY much to go and help the people rebuild the city."

4. Write "sad." Add "U"s for face and ears; "S"s for hair.

5. The king thought about Nehemiah's request. He told Nehemiah not only could he go, but also the king himself would help with supplies and people to do the job! Nehemiah must have been so excited! He thanked the king and soon he was on his way to Jerusalem with people and supplies to help do the job.

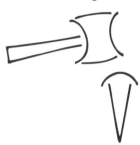

5. Write "help"; add facial details, "M"s for crown and "3"s for beard.

6. Nehemiah called all the people together. He announced that the king had sent him to help rebuild the city walls. Soon people were volunteering to repair a section of the wall. People were talking together about ways to help each other. Many families built the walls near their houses. Everyone worked together. There were people hammering and holding chisels to cut stone and people sawing wood to make gates. Every person worked hard.

6. Hammer from "I"s and "C"s; chisel from a long "V" and "C."

7. But there were enemies of the Jews who didn't want ANYONE to repair Jerusalem. They were angry that Jerusalem would be strong and safe again. They wanted to stop the workers. So they made fun of them. They tried to scare them. They said they would kill them! THEN they tried to make the king of Babylon angry at the workers!

7. Angry face from "U"s, "V."

8. But Nehemiah told the workers not to be afraid. The workers took turns guarding each other. Since they had to spend half their time guarding each other, it took a long time! But finally, the wall was finished. The heavy gates were hung in place. Everyone was glad to see the wall high and strong around the city.

8. Wall from straight lines; gate from "U."

9. The people came together to celebrate the rebuilt walls. Ezra, the priest, read the scroll of God's Law aloud. The people listened. They were very sad that they had not known God's commands earlier, but Nehemiah told them not to be sad—to celebrate. Now they had a city. Now they had heard God's laws and had worshiped God. Now they had worked together and a great thing had been done!

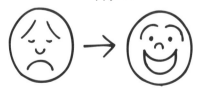

9. Draw sad face. Add arrow and happy face.

Get the Big Picture

What did Nehemiah do first about the wall? (Prayed.) **How did God help the people?** (Made them brave. Gave help from king.) **When we work together, we show love for God like Nehemiah did. And great things are done!**

Lesson 26

Bible Verse Object Talk: Helicopter Project

Big Picture Verse

"Whatever you do, work at it with all your heart, as working for the Lord, not for men." Colossians 3:23

Teacher Materials

Bible with bookmark at Colossians 3:23, ¾x6-in (1.9x15-cm) paper strips, paper clips, scissors, rulers.

Present the Object Talk

1. Students form groups of four. Give each group a paper strip and clip for each student in the group, a scissors and a ruler.

2. First student in each group cuts a 2-inch (5-cm) slit in the top of each paper strip (see sketch a). Second student in each each group folds the lower corners of each strip to a point (see sketch b). Third student in each group attaches a paper clip to the folded part of the strip (see sketch c). Fourth student in each group folds one half of the cut portion of the strips in one direction and the other half in the opposite direction (see sketch d).

3. Students fly helicopters by holding the paper clip and tossing the helicopters up in the air.

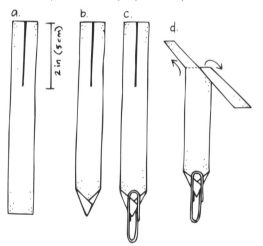

Whenever there is a big or small project to be done, it helps to have more than one good worker. God wants us to do good work to show our love for Him. Today we'll work together to make paper helicopters. Each of you will have a part to do.

Conclude

Because each person did his or her part, we were able to make helicopters. Why does Colossians 3:23 say it's important to do our best work? Read verse aloud. **A good way to show love for God is by working together with other people.** Ask God's help in working with others to do the good things God wants us to do.

Discussion Questions

1. What might have happened if someone didn't do careful work in making the helicopter?

2. What are some times kids need to do their best job when working with others to complete a project? (School projects. Sports teams.)

3. What are some examples of ways in which people who live together need to work together?

4. What's one way you can help someone else by doing your best work?

Active Game Center: Teamwork Run-Around

Materials
Chair for each student, plus one; sealed bag filled with individually wrapped candies for each team.

Prepare the Game
Arrange chairs so that teams face each other with at least 12 feet (3.6 m) between teams. Place extra chair in the middle (see sketch a).

Working together to complete a job usually makes the job easier, and it's more fun. Let's play a fun game in which we need to work together so that we can each have a piece of candy.

Lead the Game
Group students into two equal teams. Students sit in chairs. Give the sealed bag of candy to the first student at the left end of each team. At your signal, the first student from each

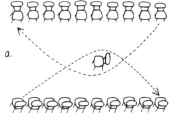

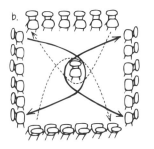

team runs around the center chair to the end of his or her team's chairs. While the student is running, the other students move up one seat to fill the runner's chair, leaving the chair at the right end empty for the runner. Runner sits in empty chair and passes the bag of candy up the line toward the first chair. When student sitting in the first chair receives the candy bag, he or she gets up, runs around the center chair and goes back to the end of the line where the chair is again vacant because the students have moved up one chair. Runner passes the bag of candy up the line again. The team whose players are sitting in original chairs first is the winner. Students eat candy.

Option
If you have twenty or more students, have students form four equal teams and arrange the chairs in a square shape (see sketch b). All teams compete at the same time so that students won't have long to wait before running.

Discussion Questions
1. Was it hard or easy to help each other in this game? Why? Could you have played this game by yourself?

2. What are some other times you work with people? (On a project at school. On a soccer team. To clean up our classroom or homes.)

3. How can you show love for God when you work with other people? (By treating each other patiently and kindly.)

Art Center: Our Church

Student Materials
Masking tape, large sheet of butcher paper, markers, small slips of paper, small paper bag.

Prepare the Activity
Tape butcher paper to a wall. Write a different age group (grandparent, teenager, parent, child your age) on each small slip of paper. Make one paper for each student, repeating categories if needed. Place the strips of paper in the paper bag.

People in a church family often work together to get a job done. Today we're going to draw a mural showing how people of different ages might work together to complete a project.

Lead the Activity
1. Ask students to think of a project that people at church could work together on (Make pizza for a community dinner. Build a preschool playground. Plant a garden at the church, etc.). **We're going to draw a mural showing how people of all ages can work together to complete this project.**

2. Each student chooses a paper from the bag. Students work together to draw mural. Each student draws people of the age group written on slip of paper he or she chose. Give help to students by asking questions such as, **What part of the project do you want to draw? What jobs should the people you draw be doing?** (For example, to plant a garden, mural scenes may show people digging up dirt; planting seeds, trees or flowers; watering; weeding.)

Options
1. Bring fabric or yarn for students to use in decorating the people they draw.

2. Bring magazines, scissors and glue. Students cut out eyes, noses, mouths and ears to glue to the faces of the people they have drawn.

Discussion Questions
1. When are some times that people work together at our church?

2. What are some times that we work together in our class?

3. Why is it important to learn to work together?

Worship Center

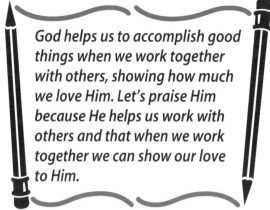

God helps us to accomplish good things when we work together with others, showing how much we love Him. Let's praise Him because He helps us work with others and that when we work together we can show our love to Him.

Big Picture Verse

"Whatever you do, work at it with all your heart, as working for the Lord, not for men." Colossians 3:23

Teacher Materials

Bible, *God's Big Picture* cassette/CD or music video and player, "Picture This!" word chart (p. 473 in this book), large sheet of paper on which you have printed Colossians 3:23 (leave a blank space for the words "work," "heart," "Lord" and "men"), masking tape.

Sing to God

Play "Picture This!" encouraging students to sing along with the music and do the actions shown on the word chart or music video. **What are some good things people in the Bible have done to work together and show God they love Him?** (Nehemiah and the people rebuilding the wall. All the Israelites building the ark of the covenant and the place to worship out in the desert. The disciples working together to spread the news about Jesus and His teachings.) **What are some things people at our church could do together for others to show God we love Him?** (Feed homeless people. Give clothes to people who need them.)

Hear and Say God's Word

Display paper on which you have printed Colossians 3:23. Have a volunteer read the verse aloud, skipping over the blank spaces. Help students guess the missing words by pointing to the first blank and saying something like, "This is a word that means the same as job," or "This is a place your mom or dad may go every weekday." When students guess the word "work," print it in the blank space. Repeat for the other three words. Students recite completed verse together. **How can you do something with all your heart?** (Try to do your best work. Work hard. Do the job cheerfully.)

Pray to God

When are times that kids your age work with others? Volunteers respond. Write the following prayer on the back of the Bible verse paper: "God, please help us to show love to You by working well with others. In Jesus' name, amen." Lead students in saying the prayer in unison.

Options

1. Students sing and do actions for "I Know the King" and/or "Love and Power" (p. 463 and/or p. 469 in this book).

2. Invite an older student to read Psalm 9:1,2 as a prayer to God.

 **Lesson 26**

Bible Story Coloring Center

 FOR YOUNGER CHILDREN

Materials

Crayons or markers, a copy of "Nehemiah rebuilds the walls" picture and story (pp. 131-132 from *Bible Story Coloring Pages*) for each student.

Lead the Activity

Students color page 131; read or tell the story on page 132. **Which part of building this wall would you like to do? Who has helped you do a big job?**

Option

Students build walls from a variety of materials: wooden or cardboard blocks, play dough, marshmallows and toothpicks, pretzels and cheese cubes. (Edible walls may be eaten!)

Skit Center

 FOR OLDER CHILDREN

Materials

A copy of "Keep On Keeping On" skit (pp. 178-180 from *The Big Book of Bible Skits*) for each student; optional—highlighter pens.

Lead the Activity

Students form pairs and read the skit, which tells the story of Nehemiah discussing work to be done with a friend. (Optional: Students highlight parts.) Ask the discussion questions on page 178.

Bible Skills Center

 FOR OLDER CHILDREN

Materials

Materials needed for "Praise Puzzles" and/or "Back-to-Back Attack" (p. 54 and/or p. 64 from *The Big Book of Bible Skills*).

Lead the Activity

Students complete activities as directed in *The Big Book of Bible Skills*.

Celebrate His Birth

Big Picture Verse

"Today in the town of David a Savior has been born to you; he is Christ the Lord." Luke 2:11

THE BIG PICTURE

With people all over the world, we can celebrate the birth of God's Son, the Savior.

Scripture Background
Matthew 1:18—2:23; Luke 1:26-56; 2

He is here! The promised One has come! The One whom all the prophets have foretold: Jesus Christ, the Lord.

Prophets in the Old Testament assured God's chosen people again and again that a Messiah would come who would be the King of the Jews. The Jews, therefore, looked forward with passionate longing and patriotism to the coming of that King in pomp and power.

Expect to find in the Gospels "the one Moses wrote about in the Law, and about whom the prophets also wrote—Jesus of Nazareth" (John 1:45). Think of God coming down to live with humanity! The Gospels are the center of the whole Bible. All that the prophets have said leads us to our Lord's earthly life and work, and all that follows proceeds from them.

In the third Gospel, the evangelist Luke notices that "in those days Caesar Augustus issued a decree that a census should be taken. And everyone went to his own town to register" (Luke 2:1,3). Then Luke brings to our attention the fact that Joseph and Mary went to register and be taxed with the rest. God brings to pass what the prophets had spoken. Micah said that Bethlehem was to be the birthplace of Jesus (see Micah 5:2-5), for He was of the family of David. But Mary lived in Nazareth, a town some distance away. God saw to it that Imperial Rome sent forth a decree to compel Mary and Joseph to go to Bethlehem just as the child was to be born. Isn't it wonderful how God uses the decree of a pagan monarch to bring to pass His prophecies!

The story of the birth of Jesus in Matthew differs from the record in Luke. They complement each other. While there is much untold, God has told us all we need to know. Jesus came as a helpless babe. How human was our Lord! But Jesus was heralded by an archangel, welcomed by an angelic choir and worshiped by earth's wisest philosophers! How divine is our Lord!

Adapted from *What the Bible Is All About* by Henrietta C. Mears.

Big Picture Story Center

Teacher Materials
Bible Time Line, drawing materials/equipment.

Student Materials
Drawing materials.

Tell the Story
Move the *Bible Time Line* frame to highlight Picture 27. As you tell each part of the story, draw each sketch. Students copy your sketches.

> *What have you heard about the time when you were born? In our Bible story today we'll hear about what it was like when Jesus was born and grew into a boy.*

1. Hundreds of years had passed since any prophet in Israel told God's words to the people. But the people still read the scrolls written by the prophets many years earlier. These scrolls told of God's promise to send a great King.

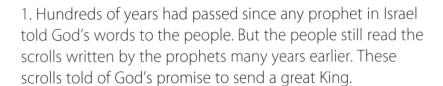

1. Draw open scroll from "O"s and "I"s.

2. One day, a young lady named Mary ESPECIALLY remembered God's promise. She was visited by an ANGEL! The angel told her that she was going to be the mother of God's very special Son, the King whom God had promised. An angel also came to Joseph, the man Mary was going to marry. The angel told Joseph about this special child who was to be born.

2. Angel from "A." Add wings and head.

3. Not long after the angels' visits, the ruler of all the countries in that part of the world wanted to count everyone to keep track of the people he could tax. All the men had to return to the towns where their families were from. Joseph and Mary went to Bethlehem because he belonged to the family of David, the famous king of long, long ago.

3. Draw Bethlehem from squares and "C"s.

4. It was terribly crowded in Bethlehem and Mary's baby was about to be born. The only place Mary and Joseph could find to stay was a stable for animals. It wasn't very fancy, but it was warm and better than being outside.

4. Stable from "C." Add animals from "C"s, "U"s, "V"s and "I"s.

5. That night God's special Son was born. Joseph and Mary named Him Jesus, just as the angels had told them. Baby Jesus slept on hay in an animal feedbox, called a manger.

5. Manger from "V"s and lines. Baby from "C"s.

6. That very same night, some shepherds were nearby with their sheep in the fields. SUDDENLY an angel came to them and the glory of God came shining all around! The shepherds were afraid. But the angel said not to be afraid. There was good news: the Savior, Christ the Lord, was born! A crowd of angels sang in the sky, praising God!

6. Sheep from curly lines. Add face from "U" and ears from "D"s. Add angel as in #2.

7. After the angels went back to heaven, the shepherds hurried off to find the baby Jesus. After they had seen the baby, the shepherds were so excited, they told everyone they met about the wonderful baby! At last the shepherds returned to their sheep in the fields, praising God for everything that they had seen and heard that night.

7. Running shepherd from "O" and "N." Add staff and conversation balloon.

8. Jesus grew and grew. Soon He was sitting up and crawling and then walking. When He was still little, some wise men traveled from far away to worship Him, bringing Him wonderful gifts. When King Herod heard that these men had come to see a child who was to become a great king, Herod wanted to get rid of Jesus. Because of an angel's warning, Joseph took Mary and Jesus and went away one night. They traveled to a country called Egypt and lived there.

8. Draw angry king from "V"s and "C"s.

9. When it was safe to return home, an angel told Joseph he could bring Mary and Jesus back to Nazareth, where they had lived before Jesus was born. Jesus grew up in Nazareth, just as the prophets had said He would. And as Jesus grew, God loved Him and many people did, too!

9. Series of stick figures in larger and larger sizes. Add heart.

Get the Big Picture

Who was glad to know that Jesus was born? (Angels. Shepherds. Wise men.) **What made the birth of Jesus so special? What had God promised that Jesus would do?**

    God had said that Jesus would be born in Bethlehem. He had made this promise through His prophets hundreds of years before. God's promise to send a Savior came true. And more things God had said about Jesus were yet to come true!

    This story of Jesus' birth is so important that now people all over the world celebrate His birthday. They remember the good news about Jesus the Savior.

Bible Verse Object Talk: Worldwide Singing

Big Picture Verse

"Today in the town of David a Savior has been born to you; he is Christ the Lord." Luke 2:11

Teacher Materials

Bible with bookmark at Luke 2:11, world map or globe; optional—a player and recording of "Silent Night" or other carol in a foreign language.

The angels' message about Jesus' birth was such good news that people all over the world celebrate Jesus' birthday. Let's look at some of the places where people believe in Jesus and sing songs about His birth.

Present the Object Talk

1. Show map or globe and point out the area where your church is located. (Optional: Older students may find locations.)

2. Read Luke 2:11. **Another name for the town of David is Bethlehem.** Locate Bethlehem on map or globe. **In the Old Testament part of the Bible, prophets told about God's promise to send His Son to be born in Bethlehem.**

3. **What are the names of some Christmas carols you remember?** Volunteers tell answers. **"Silent Night" is one of the most famous Christmas carols. This carol was first**

written in Germany. Locate Germany on map or globe. **A pastor of a church wrote a poem about Jesus' birth in Bethlehem. He gave the poem as a Christmas gift to his friend Franz Gruber. Later that same night, Mr. Gruber wrote a melody to go with the words. Everyone who heard the carol liked the words so much that the carol spread all over the world.** (Optional: Sing "Silent Night" with students, play recording of the carol in a foreign language or ask someone to sing the carol in another language.)

Conclude

When we sing carols like "Silent Night," we can think about the thousands and thousands of people all over the world who sing this song in their own languages. Let's thank God for sending His Son to be born. Lead students in prayer.

Discussion Questions

1. What are some of the ways that people in our country celebrate Jesus' birth?

2. What are the ways that people in other countries remember Jesus' birth? (People in Mexico act out the story of Joseph and Mary looking for a place to stay. Christians in Israel plant seeds in front of nativity scenes; the growing seeds remind people of new life.)

3. What is your favorite song to sing about Jesus' birth?

Active Game Center: Surpriseball

Materials

Flat bed sheet, two chairs, masking tape, inflated and tied balloon.

Prepare the Game

In the middle of the playing area, spread a bed sheet between two chairs, taping it so that it is hanging vertically (see sketch a). Prepare one playing area for each group of up to 20 students.

> *God's people were expecting God to keep His promise to send the Savior. They waited and waited for the promise to be kept. We're going to play a game in which we wait for something we expect to happen!*

Lead the Game

1. Divide group into two teams of no more than ten students each, sending teams to opposite sides of the sheet. Students sit on the floor, spacing themselves evenly around the playing area and sitting so that they cannot see over the sheet (see sketch b).

2. Students play a game like volleyball, but they remain seated during the game and do not

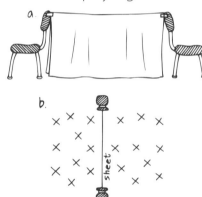

rotate positions. Give one team a balloon. With no advance warning, student from the team with the balloon hits the balloon over the sheet from anywhere in the playing area. Students on the receiving team, who are waiting for the balloon to come over at any time, catch the balloon and tap it twice to teammates before hitting it back over the sheet to the other team. Teams see how many times they can hit the balloon over the sheet without the balloon hitting the ground.

Options

1. To divide the group into teams, instruct each student to find a partner. Then one partner joins the team on one side of the sheet while the other partner joins the opposite team.

2. Make a masking-tape outline around the playing area.

3. If you have mostly younger students, play game without the sheet.

Discussion Questions

1. What did you wait for in this game? What did you expect would happen? (The balloon would come.)

2. What other kinds of things do kids your age wait for, expecting that they will happen? (For things ordered in the mail. For dinner to be ready to eat. For birthdays to come.)

3. Why is waiting for and expecting the birth of Jesus more important than waiting for all these things? (He came to save people from their sins. He is God's Son.)

Art Center: Nativity Scenes

Student Materials

Toilet tissue tubes, scissors, various colors of construction paper including white and/or fabric scraps, glue, markers, pencils.

Prepare the Activity

Cut some tubes in half, providing two full-sized tubes and one half tube for each student. Cut construction paper and/or fabric scraps into rectangles sized to fit around tubes.

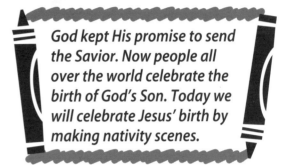

God kept His promise to send the Savior. Now people all over the world celebrate the birth of God's Son. Today we will celebrate Jesus' birth by making nativity scenes.

Lead the Activity

1. Give two full-sized tubes and one half tube to each student. (Optional: If you do not have enough tubes, students work together to make nativity scenes.) Students glue construction paper or fabric rectangles around cardboard tubes to dress nativity scene characters (see

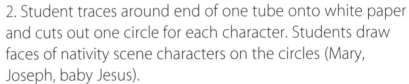

sketch a). If using construction paper, students draw clothing details on the paper.

2. Student traces around end of one tube onto white paper and cuts out one circle for each character. Students draw faces of nativity scene characters on the circles (Mary, Joseph, baby Jesus).

3. Students glue faces to cardboard tubes (see sketch b).

Options

1. Bring one or more nativity scenes (from other countries, if possible) to show students.

2. Provide additional supplies such as yarn for hair and plastic wiggle eyes.

3. Make several different colors of play dough (white, yellow, brown, blue). Students mold nativity scene characters from play dough.

4. Display scenes in various locations around your church.

Discussion Questions

1. How does your family celebrate birthdays? What are some ways we celebrate Jesus' birth at our church?

2. How does your family celebrate Christmas?

3. What promise did God keep on the first Christmas?

4. How did God announce Jesus' birthday? (Sent angels.)

 **Lesson 27**

Worship Center

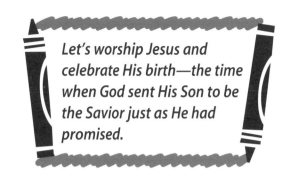

Let's worship Jesus and celebrate His birth—the time when God sent His Son to be the Savior just as He had promised.

Big Picture Verse

"Today in the town of David a Savior has been born to you; he is Christ the Lord." Luke 2:11

Teacher Materials

Bible, *God's Big Picture* cassette/CD or music video and player, "Picture This!" word chart (p. 473 in this book), large sheet of paper on which you have printed Luke 2:11 on one side and "thank you" in different languages on the other (see below for examples), masking tape.

Sing to God

Play "Picture This!" encouraging students to sing along with the music and do the actions shown on the word chart or the music video. **How does this song describe Jesus?** ("God's only Son.") **Jesus has been a part of God's big picture since the beginning! What are some other names for Jesus or words that describe Him?** (Savior. Prince of Peace. Loving.)

Hear and Say God's Word

Display paper on which you have printed Luke 2:11. Have a volunteer read the verse aloud. **What is another name for "the town of David"?** (Bethlehem.) **The angels said these words to the shepherds, but the good news of Jesus' birth is for everyone—even us!** Divide class into three groups. Assign each group a phrase of Luke 2:11: "Today in the town of David," "a Savior has been born to you," "he is Christ the Lord." Repeat verse several times with each group saying their assigned phrases.

Pray to God

Let's thank God that He sent His Son Jesus to keep His promise of a Savior for all people in the world. Show paper you prepared with "thank you" written in several different languages—Spanish: *Gracias* (GRAH-see-ahs); German: *Danke* (DAHN-kuh); French: *Merci* (mayr-SEE); Russian: *Spasibo* (spah-SEE-boh); Chinese: *Xie xie* (shay shay). **This is how people say "Thank you" in (Spanish).** Help students pronounce the phrase in Spanish. Repeat with other languages. Close in prayer, inviting students to tell God "Thank You" for Jesus in any of the languages written.

Options

1. If students give an offering during this worship time, explain that giving money to God is one way we can show our love and thanks to Him. Describe several ways your church uses the offering to help others learn about God and His love.

2. Ask two older students to read aloud these Old Testament prophecies about Jesus' birth: Isaiah 9:6,7; Micah 5:2.

 **Lesson 27**

Bible Story Coloring Center

Materials

Crayons or markers, a copy of "Angels tell the good news of Jesus' birth to shepherds" picture and story (pp. 137-138 from *Bible Story Coloring Pages*) for each student.

Lead the Activity

Students color page 137; read or tell the story on page 138. **What did the angels tell the shepherds? What did the shepherds do once they heard the angels' good news?**

Options

1. Students glue cotton balls to sheep for wool and glue glitter to angels and stars.

2. Provide a copy of "Jesus is born" picture and story (pp. 135-136 from *Bible Story Coloring Pages*). Students color page 135; read or tell the story on page 136.

Skit Center

Materials

A copy of "Herod" skit (pp. 203-206 from *The Big Book of Bible Skits*) for each student; optional—highlighter pens.

Lead the Activity

Students choose parts and read the skit, which tells the story of Herod hearing of the wise men and the birth of Jesus. (Optional: Students highlight their parts.) Ask the discussion questions on page 203.

Bible Skills Center

Materials

Materials needed for "People Scrabble" and/or "Bubble Gum" (p. 62 and/or p. 125 from *The Big Book of Bible Skills*).

Lead the Activity

Students complete activities as directed in *The Big Book of Bible Skills*.

Lesson 28

Announcing the Savior

Big Picture Verse

"John saw Jesus coming toward him and said, 'Look, the Lamb of God, who takes away the sin of the world!'" John 1:29

THE BIG PICTURE

Jesus' baptism and John's announcement help everyone know that Jesus is the Savior.

Scripture Background
Matthew 3; John 1:19-34

John the Baptist's coming was in fulfillment of a messianic prophecy (see Isaiah 40:3 and Malachi 3:1). We see this strange man who appears on the scene in an almost sensational way, wearing clothing made from camel's hair. His food, too, was strange, for locusts and wild honey were his diet.

John's message was as startling as his appearance. He went before his monarch as any Roman officer would go before his king, demanding that the road be repaired and the highway reconstructed. Although he was graduated from no outstanding school, of humble birth, little known and dressed like a desert hermit, John the Baptist was approved of God.

John and Jesus met one day. John recognized immediately that this man was not a subject for the baptism of repentance that he was preaching. There was in His face a purity and majesty that struck John's heart with a sense of his own unworthiness. This man was the Son of God. Jesus was baptized by John in obedience to an appointed ordinance. Jesus set a seal of approval on John's message and work and acknowledged him as the true forerunner of Christ.

After the baptism, the Spirit descended in the bodily shape of a dove. This was a symbol. The coming of the Spirit Himself was a reality. Every event in Jesus' life had significance. Because Jesus went down in the baptismal water of obedience to God, He could come up under an opened sky with the Holy Spirit descending upon Him and hear the voice of His Father declaring Him to be His beloved Son.

Jesus came up out of that water a new man into a new world. His relationship to His Father and His mission were proclaimed.

Adapted from *What the Bible Is All About* by Henrietta C. Mears.

Big Picture Story Center

Teacher Materials
Bible Time Line, drawing materials/equipment.

Student Materials
Drawing materials.

Tell the Story
Move the *Bible Time Line* frame to highlight Picture 28. As you tell each part of the story, draw each sketch. Students copy your sketches.

What words would you use to describe Jesus to someone? Today we'll find out how a man named John described Jesus.

1. Jesus grew up in a small town called Nazareth. Mary and Joseph took good care of Jesus as He grew. As soon as Jesus was old enough, Joseph taught Him how to build things with wood. Jesus probably often helped Joseph in his carpentry shop.

1. Draw saw and hammer from "C"s, "V"s and lines.

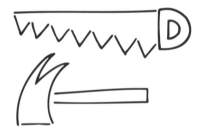

2. The years passed, and Jesus grew up. Now Jesus was 30 years old. He knew it was time to begin His work as God's Son. So Jesus went to find a preacher named John. John had been preaching to many people, telling them that God's kingdom was coming. He was telling people to stop doing wrong and start obeying God. Jesus knew that John was helping people get ready for the time when Jesus would come.

2. "Wrong" with "no" slash.

3. John spent most days in the desert by a river, talking to crowds of people. He warned the people to turn away from all the wrong things they had done. Many of the people who listened believed what John told them. They wanted to show God they were sorry for doing wrong. They wanted to live the way God wanted them to live. John took them into the river where he baptized them with water to show that God had forgiven them, making them clean from the wrong things they had done. John also told the people that someone great would come to show God's great power.

3. River from "S"s. Add stick figures by river.

4. One day, who should come to John but Jesus! Jesus told John, "I want you to baptize Me." John was surprised. He said, "But Jesus, YOU haven't done ANY wrong things. YOU should baptize ME!"

Jesus told John that God wanted Him to be baptized by John. Jesus wanted to show He would always do what God wanted. John wanted to obey God, so he baptized Jesus.

4. Two faces from "7"s, "C"s. Add names.

5. As Jesus was coming up out of the water, something happened that had NEVER happened before! A dove flew down from the sky and rested on Jesus. And God spoke from heaven saying, "This is My Son, whom I love. I am pleased with Him."

5. Dove from "7"s, "V" and "C"s.

6. After Jesus was baptized, He went alone to the desert while John stayed by the river and kept telling people to obey God. Some people asked John if HE was God's Son.

"No," John answered. "I am helping people get ready for His coming. He is so great that I am not even good enough to untie His sandals."

6. Foot and sandal from 2 "L"s, 5 "C"s and 1 "X." Add sole and ties.

7. The next day Jesus came to where John was talking. John stopped and turned to point at Jesus. He said, "Look, there is the One who will take away the sin of the world! This is the One I told you about!" John wanted the people to know that Jesus is God's Son. Because of what John said about Jesus, many people believed that Jesus is God's Son and started following Jesus and listening to Him. John had done his job well.

7. Write "Look" and add eyes.

Get the Big Picture

What was the message John wanted everyone to know? (Stop doing wrong things. Jesus is God's Son who will take away our sins—the wrong things we do.) **How did God show that Jesus was His Son, the promised Savior?** (Sent dove. Said Jesus was His Son.)

As we read in the Bible what John said about Jesus and what happened as Jesus was baptized, we discover that Jesus is truly the Savior! Talk with interested students about salvation. (See "Leading a Child to Christ" on p. 30.)

Bible Verse Object Talk: Here's Jesus!

Big Picture Verse

"John saw Jesus coming toward him and said, 'Look, the Lamb of God, who takes away the sin of the world!'" John 1:29

Teacher Materials

Bible with bookmark at John 1:29, a variety of newspaper and/or magazine ads and announcements (classified ad, product advertisement, notice of sale at a store, announcement of a coming event, etc.).

Present the Object Talk

In the Bible, the good news about Jesus was announced by John the Baptist. Today we hear about good news in lots of different ways. Look at these announcements to find what news is being told.

1. One at a time show the ads and announcements you collected. Ask a volunteer to describe the message of each ad or announcement. **What are some other ways in which announcements are made?** (Birth or graduation announcements. Billboards. TV or radio commercials.)

2. **All of these announcements tell things that will soon happen. But after a few weeks—after the sale is over or after the event has happened—we don't really need to remember the announcement any more. The announcement John made about Jesus, however, is something people have needed to know about and will remember for a long time! The words John said about Jesus are so important that EVERYONE still needs to hear them.** Read John 1:29 aloud.

Conclude

What kind of ad or billboard would you make to announce this good news about Jesus? Volunteers tell ideas. Lead students in prayer, thanking God for the good news that Jesus is His Son.

Discussion Questions

1. Why was Jesus called the "Lamb of God"? ("Lamb of God" is a name for Jesus that tells us that He died to take away our sins. Jewish people used to offer a lamb as a sacrifice to God for their sins; Jesus became like one of those lambs when He died.)

2. What other news about Jesus would you like to announce to others?

3. How would you announce the good news about Jesus?

 **Lesson 28**

Active Game Center: Fast Phrase

Materials
None.

Lead the Game
Choose a volunteer to be the "announcer." At your signal, students begin walking around the room at random. When the announcer says "Hear ye! Hear ye!" students stop walking, spin around where they stand and sit down on the floor as quickly as they can. The first student to sit down tells something he or she knows about Jesus or answers one of the questions below and becomes the new announcer. Repeat play as time and interest allow. (If the first student to be seated has already been the announcer, he or she chooses someone who hasn't yet had a turn to be the announcer.)

John the Baptist's announcement about Jesus helped everyone know—even people today—that Jesus is the Savior. We're going to play a game to announce that great news, too!

Options
1. For each round, name a new action that students need to do when the announcement is made (do a jumping jack before sitting down, place hands on head while spinning before sitting down, hop on one foot twice before sitting down, run to touch the nearest wall, etc.).

2. If it is difficult to determine who is the first student seated, call out another criteria (student wearing the most blue, whose birthday is closest, most letters in last name, etc.).

3. Invite the announcer to say "Hear ye! Hear ye!" in an attention-grabbing way: loudly, clapping on each syllable, etc.

Discussion Questions
1. *Some people learned that Jesus is the Savior by hearing John's announcement or by seeing Jesus being baptized. What are some ways you have learned that Jesus is God's Son, the Savior?*

2. *What does it mean to say that Jesus is the Savior?* (Jesus saves us from the punishment we deserve for our sins.)

3. *How might a kid announce that Jesus is God's Son, the Savior?* (Tell a friend what he or she knows about Jesus. Ask a friend to come to church.)

Art Center: Riverscape

Student Materials

Large sheet of butcher paper, blue crayons and markers, glue, sand, leaves, small flat stones, brown and gray construction paper or tissue paper; optional—newspapers or plastic tablecloth.

Lead the Activity

1. Place butcher paper on table or floor. (Optional: Cover work surface with newspapers or tablecloth.) Students work together to draw a large river outline on the butcher paper, coloring the river with crayons and markers.

2. Students glue sand, leaves and small stones along the edge of the river to represent the riverbanks. Students may also crumple up small pieces of brown or gray paper to look like stones and glue them to the river picture (see sketch a).

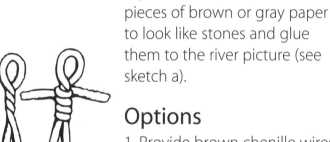

God wanted everyone to hear the great announcement that Jesus is the Savior. Today we can make a big river picture to remember Jesus' baptism and the time when John the Baptist announced Jesus' coming.

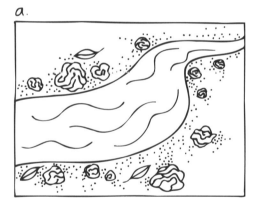

a.

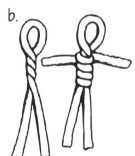

b.

Options

1. Provide brown chenille wires for students to make figures to represent John the Baptist and Jesus (see sketch b).

2. Students make individual river scenes on Styrofoam trays or small pieces of poster board. Mix blue food coloring into white glue. Each student squeezes a glue "river" onto tray or poster board and then glues other items as suggested above along the edge of river. Brown chenille wires can be used to shape figures representing John the Baptist and Jesus.

3. If you have more than 10 students, make more than one river picture.

Discussion Questions

1. What are some ways that people hear the good news about Jesus announced today? How have you heard the good news about Jesus? (Parents. Teachers. Bible stories. Videos.)

2. What have you learned about Jesus?

3. How can kids help other kids hear about Jesus?

Lesson 28

Worship Center

Big Picture Verse

"John saw Jesus coming toward him and said, 'Look, the Lamb of God, who takes away the sin of the world!'" John 1:29

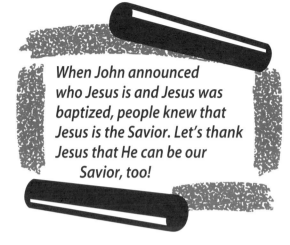

When John announced who Jesus is and Jesus was baptized, people knew that Jesus is the Savior. Let's thank Jesus that He can be our Savior, too!

Teacher Materials

Bible, *God's Big Picture* cassette/CD or music video and player, "I Want to Follow Jesus" word chart (p. 465 in this book), large sheet of paper on which you have printed John 1:29, masking tape, foam ball.

Sing to God

Play "I Want to Follow Jesus," encouraging students to sing along with the music and do the actions shown on the word chart or the music video. **What are some ways kids your age can show they believe that Jesus is the Savior and follow Him?**

Hear and Say God's Word

Display paper on which you have printed John 1:29. Have a volunteer read the verse aloud. Explain to students that "Lamb of God" is a name for Jesus that tells us that He died to take away our sins. **Jewish people used to offer a lamb as a sacrifice to God for their sins. Jesus became like one of those lambs when He died.**

Students sit in a circle. Throw (or roll) the ball to a student, saying the first word of the verse as you throw it. Student who catches the ball says the first and second word of the verse as he or she throws the ball to another student who then says the first, second and third words of the verse. Continue until the entire verse has been said several times or until all students have had at least two turns. **What words did John use to announce Jesus? What words might you use to announce the good news you know about Jesus?**

Pray to God

In John 1:29, John announced that Jesus is the One who takes away our sins. Invite students to repeat this prayer after you: **We're sorry, Jesus, when we do wrong things. Thank You that You are our Savior and will take away our sins. In Your name, amen.**

Options

1. Students sing and do actions for "Jesus' Love" and/or "Picture This!" (p. 467 and/or p. 473 in this book).

2. Instead of asking students to repeat the words of the prayer, invite volunteers to suggest their own words, asking forgiveness for sin and thanking Jesus for being our Savior. Print students' suggestions on a large sheet of paper and read together as a prayer.

 **Lesson 28**

Bible Story Coloring Center

Materials

Crayons or markers, a copy of "John the Baptist preaches about the coming Savior" picture and story (pp. 145-146 from *Bible Story Coloring Pages*) for each student.

Lead the Activity

Students color page 145; read or tell the story on page 146. **Where did John the Baptist live? What did he tell others about Jesus?**

Option

Also provide "John baptizes Jesus" picture and story (pp. 147-148 from *Bible Story Coloring Pages*). Students may choose which picture they color or color both pictures if time permits.

Skit Center

Materials

A copy of "The Birth of John" skit (pp. 195-198 from *The Big Book of Bible Skits*) for each student; optional—highlighter pens.

Lead the Activity

Students choose parts and read the skit, which tells the story of the angel visiting Zechariah and Mary to tell them about the coming births of John and Jesus. (Optional: Students highlight their parts.) Ask the discussion questions on page 195.

Bible Skills Center

Materials

Materials needed for "Good News Fill-In" and/or "Sticky Verses" (p. 58 and/or p. 86 from *The Big Book of Bible Skills*).

Lead the Activity

Students complete activities as directed in *The Big Book of Bible Skills*.

No Temptation Strong Enough

Big Picture Verse

"I have hidden your word in my heart that I might not sin against you."
Psalm 119:11

THE BIG PICTURE
Knowing God's Word will help us do right when we are tempted to do wrong.

Scripture Background
Matthew 4:1-11; Luke 4:1-13

At Jesus' baptism, God endorsed Jesus and His mission and showed to the Jewish nation that Jesus was the Messiah. Hardly had the voice from heaven died away, however, than we hear a whisper from hell. Out of the baptismal benediction of the Father, Jesus stepped into a desperate struggle with the devil.

The crowding together of these two events shows that temptation was as much a part of the preparation of the Servant for His work as His baptism. Suffering and trial are as much God's plan as thrills and triumphs. Jesus was "led" to be tempted. It was no accident or evil fate, but a divine appointment. Temptation has its place in this world. We could never develop without it. There is nothing wrong in being tempted. The wrong begins when we begin to consent to it. We are not to seek temptation of our own accord. We will find that the path of duty often takes us through temptations, but God is faithful and He always makes a way of escape (see 1 Corinthians 10:13). This subject is of great importance. Be sure you understand it.

Notice that in this, the first major conflict of Jesus' public ministry, Satan offered Jesus a shortcut to that universal Kingdom that He had come to gain through the long and painful way of the cross; but Christ came to be a Savior first, then a King. How strong is the temptation to take a shortcut to our ambitions! But through the strength of the Word of God, Jesus stood victorious, His shield undented and untarnished. He went forth to conquer all other temptations until His final victory and ascension to heaven as Lord of all.

Adapted from *What the Bible Is All About* by Henrietta C. Mears.

Big Picture Story Center

Teacher Materials

Bible Time Line, drawing materials/equipment.

Student Materials

Drawing materials.

Tell the Story

Move the *Bible Time Line* frame to highlight Picture 29. As you tell each part of the story, draw each sketch. Students copy your sketches.

When is a time you have had to say no to something you wanted to do? Today we're going to find out how Jesus was able to say no to the devil.

1. After John baptized Jesus in the Jordan River, Jesus went to the desert where He could be alone. Jesus spent 40 days in the desert, praying to God. This time was part of God's plan to prepare Jesus for teaching and healing people.

1. Draw number 40 and add details for praying figure.

2. While Jesus was in the desert, He didn't eat anything. After 40 days without any food, Jesus was very hungry! He was probably tired as well. That's when Satan, God's enemy, came to Jesus. Satan said, "Since You are the Son of God, why don't You make some of these stones into bread?" Satan wanted to see if Jesus would do a miracle just to get Himself something He wanted very badly—food!

2. Stones from "D"s.

3. But Jesus was not going to take any suggestions from Satan! Jesus knew God's Word. And Jesus used God's Word to answer the devil. He said, "It is written: 'Man does not live on bread alone, but on every word that comes from the mouth of God.'" Jesus meant that knowing and obeying what God said was far more important to Him than eating, even when He was very hungry.

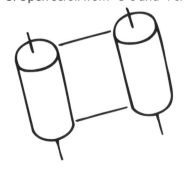

3. Open scroll from "O"s and "I"s.

4. Satan had another idea. He took Jesus up to the highest point of the Temple in Jerusalem. He said, "Since You are the Son of God, why don't You throw Yourself off this high place?" The devil even quoted a Bible verse to make his idea sound good! He said a verse about God sending angels to protect people. But Jesus also answered Satan from God's Word. He said, "It is also written: 'Do not put the Lord your God to the test.'" Jesus meant that He wouldn't do a miracle just to show off or prove He was from God. He didn't come to earth to entertain or impress people. He came to teach them about God and bring forgiveness for their sins!

4. Temple from "7"s. Add 2 small stick figures.

5. Satan couldn't argue with Jesus' words, so he just tried again to get Jesus to disobey God. Satan took Jesus up to a very high mountain. Looking out from there, Satan showed all the beautiful kingdoms of the world. Satan said to Jesus, "I will give you all of this—everything in the world!—if you will bow down and worship me!"

5. Draw mountain and add 2 figures.

6. Jesus knew that Satan would do ANYTHING to get Him to do wrong! He would give Jesus ANYTHING if it meant he could get Jesus to sin. And once more, Jesus answered Satan with God's Word. He said, "Get away, Satan! For it is written: 'Worship the Lord your God and serve him ONLY.'" Jesus knew He had not come to earth to show off or do tricks or get things for Himself. He had come to obey God. And God's Word helped Jesus escape from Satan's temptations!

6. Write "ONLY"; add "GOD" to make acrostic.

Get the Big Picture

What did Jesus say was the most important thing to do? (Obey God.) **What helped Jesus obey God when Satan wanted Him to do wrong?** (Knowing and remembering God's Word.)

When the devil tried to tempt Him into doing wrong, Jesus knew what to say because He knew God's Word. He was able to use God's Word to send Satan away. Knowing God's Word will help us know what to do when we are tempted to disobey God.

Bible Verse Object Talk: Stronger than Sin

Big Picture Verse

"I have hidden your word in my heart that I might not sin against you." Psalm 119:11

Teacher Materials

Bible with bookmark at Psalm 119:11, one or more bottles of vitamins.

Present the Object Talk

One of the best times God's Word helps us is when we're tempted to sin—to disobey God. God's Word helps us be strong and obey God. Let's talk about some things that can help us grow stronger.

1. Show bottle(s) of vitamins. Invite volunteers to read aloud the name(s) of the vitamins. **Why do people take vitamins? How might taking vitamins or eating foods with lots of vitamins help us?** (Helps us stay healthy. Helps our bodies grow strong.)

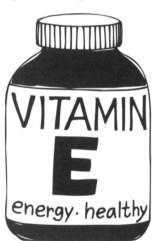

2. One at a time, pantomime (or ask an older student to pantomime) these actions: lifting weights, jogging, getting enough rest, drinking water. Students guess each action. **All these actions can help us become healthier and stronger.**

Conclude

The Bible tells us about something we can do to help us be strong in our desire to obey God when we feel like doing wrong. Read Psalm 119:11 aloud. **What does this verse say we should do to keep from sinning? What do you think it means to hide God's Word in our hearts?** (Read and think about God's Word. Memorize it.) Lead students in prayer, thanking God for His Word and asking His help in obeying it.

Discussion Questions

1. When are some times kids your age might be tempted to do something wrong?

2. What can we do when we feel like disobeying God? (Remember the right things God's Word says to do. Ask God for help in obeying Him.)

3. What are some other ways God helps us obey Him? (Gives us parents and teachers to help us learn about Him. Promises to answer our prayers. Promises to always be with us. Helps us remember verses from His Word.)

Active Game Center: On Your Guard

Materials
Masking tape, one paper cup for each student, at least two soccer balls, volleyballs or foam balls.

Prepare the Game
Divide the playing area in half with a masking-tape line.

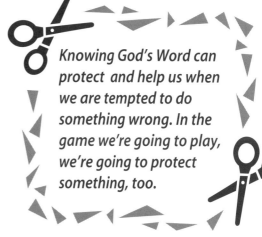

Knowing God's Word can protect and help us when we are tempted to do something wrong. In the game we're going to play, we're going to protect something, too.

Lead the Game
1. Group students into two equal teams, one group on each side of the dividing line. Give each student a paper cup. Each student places the cup somewhere in his or her team's playing area, no more than 20 feet (6 m) from the dividing line. Student then stands about halfway between his or her cup and the dividing line.

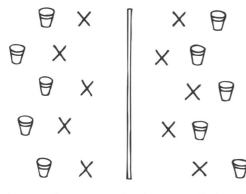

2. Give a ball to one of the teams. A volunteer from that team rolls the ball across the dividing line, trying to knock down the other team's cups. Students standing in front of the cups attempt to protect cups, blocking balls with their hands or feet. Student who catches ball rolls it back across the center line toward the opposite team's cups. Each time a cup is knocked over, the student protecting that cup moves to the side of the playing area. If no cups are knocked down after several minutes of play, add another ball or two so that more than one ball is in play at the same time. Call time after three or four minutes. Ask one or more of the discussion questions. Set up cups again and begin a new round of play.

Option
Use more cups than students so that students have to protect more than one cup at a time.

Discussion Questions

1. What did you do to protect your cup? What does the Bible tell us we can do to protect ourselves from doing wrong, or sinning? (Read and learn God's Word.)

2. What wrong things are kids your age tempted to do? How can God's Word help and protect you when you are tempted? (Help me know what is right.)

3. In His Word, God promises to never leave His children. How can knowing this promise help you when you are tempted to do something wrong?

Art Center: Bible Collages

Student Materials

Large sheets of paper, markers, glue, scissors, a variety of collage materials (yarn, toothpicks, straws, pasta, twigs, chenille wires, rick rack, ribbon, Styrofoam peanuts, etc.).

God's Word can help us know what to do when we are tempted. Today we'll make reminders that the Bible can help us!

Lead the Activity

1. Lead students to suggest things the Bible tells us that help us: "tell the truth" (see Zechariah 8:16), "love others" (see John 15:12), "be kind" (see Ephesians 4;32), "forgive others" (see Ephesians 4:32) and "be patient" (see 1 Thessalonians 5:14). Print suggestions on large sheet of paper.

2. Each student chooses one of the suggestions from the list and writes it on a large sheet of paper.

3. Students glue various materials to their papers to make collages around the words. Invite students to tell where they might display their collages at home to help them remember ways the Bible helps them.

Options

1. Display completed collages on a bulletin board.

2. Invite older students to write Psalm 119:11 on their papers, replacing as many words as possible with pictures or symbols.

Discussion Questions

1. *What are some ways kids can learn things from the Bible?*

2. *Why do we call the Bible God's Word?*

3. *Who has helped you learn what God's Word says?*

4. *When are some times you can read and think about God's Word?*

Worship Center

Big Picture Verse

"I have hidden your word in my heart that I might not sin against you." Psalm 119:11

Teacher Materials

Bible, *God's Big Picture* cassette/CD or music video and player, "Follow the Leader" word chart (p. 453 in this book), large sheet of paper divided in half on which you have printed Psalm 119:11 with one phrase at the top of each half, masking tape.

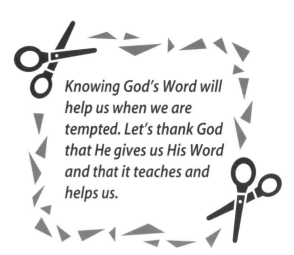

Knowing God's Word will help us when we are tempted. Let's thank God that He gives us His Word and that it teaches and helps us.

Sing to God

Play "Follow the Leader," encouraging students to sing along with the music and do the actions shown on the word chart or the music video. **What did Jesus do when He was tempted? How can we follow His example?**

Hear and Say God's Word

Display paper on which you have printed Psalm 119:11. Have a volunteer read the verse aloud. **How would you say the first part of Psalm 119:11 in a way that your friends would understand? the second part?** ("I will remember Your Word"/"so I won't disobey You." "I will keep thinking about Your words"/"so it will be easier to obey them.") Write students' suggestions under both parts of the verse on the large sheet of paper. Repeat the verse several times, alternating between saying Psalm 119:11 and one of the paraphrases the students suggested.

Pray to God

Briefly tell students about a Bible verse that has helped you when you have been tempted to disobey God. Invite volunteers to tell times they have remembered to obey God's Word when tempted to sin. Lead students in prayer, thanking God for His Word and His help when we are tempted, and asking for His help in remembering His Word.

Options

1. Students find Psalm 96:1-3 in their Bibles and read these verses aloud as a prayer of praise to God.
2. Mark these verses in your Bible for two students to read aloud as reminders of ways the Bible can help them remember to obey God: Joshua 1:9; 1 Corinthians 16:13.

 **Lesson 29**

Bible Story Coloring Center

Materials

Crayons or markers, a copy of "When Jesus is tempted, He obeys God's Word" picture and story (pp. 149-150 from *Bible Story Coloring Pages*) for each student.

Lead the Activity

Students color page 149; read or tell the story on page 150. **Where did Jesus go for 40 days? What did Jesus do when Satan tempted Him to disobey God? How can you obey God's Word?**

Option

Students glue sand on the hills of the desert.

Skit Center

Materials

A copy of "Temptation in the Wilderness" skit (pp. 207-209 from *The Big Book of Bible Skits*) for each student; optional—highlighter pens.

Lead the Activity

Students form pairs and read the skit, which tells the story of Satan trying to tempt Jesus. (Optional: Students highlight their parts.) Ask the discussion questions on page 207.

Bible Skills Center

Materials

Materials needed for "Mixed-Up Books" and/or "Cookie Search" (p. 43 and/or p. 151 from *The Big Book of Bible Skills*).

Lead the Activity

Students complete activities as directed in *The Big Book of Bible Skills*.

Disciples Follow Jesus

Big Picture Verse

"I am the Lord your God, who teaches you what is best for you, who directs you in the way you should go." Isaiah 48:17

THE BIG PICTURE

God chooses all kinds of people to learn from Him.

Scripture Background
Matthew 4:18-22; Mark 2:13,14; 3:13-19; 6:7-13; John 1:35-51

In the Gospels we read of the circumstances in which Jesus called His disciples. We see Jesus preaching by the seashore and selecting four of the fishermen to become His first disciples to learn under His guidance how to become "fishers of men" (Matthew 4:19). They were to turn all the practical knowledge and skill they exercised in the art of catching fish into the work of bringing people into God's kingdom.

It is interesting to note Jesus' call to some of His disciples. Simon and Andrew were virtually in the middle of their work, casting a net into the lake, perhaps thinking about drying the fish that had been caught or nets that needed repair. But as the net flew out over the water, they heard someone calling their names. It was Jesus! He called busy and successful people to follow Him. How was Christ's call received? "At once they left their nets and followed him" (Mark 1:18). The One who called them was worthy of their eager obedience! Jesus called them to know Him, to make Him the core of their daily lives and to live as He lived. Too often there is lost time between our call and our coming; our doing lags far behind our privilege of service.

We find the account of the choosing of the 12 disciples in Mark 3:13-19. Notice verse 14. It tells why Jesus chose these men: "that they might be with him." Mark this verse in your Bible. This is what Jesus wants of His disciples today—that they will take time to be in His presence and commune with Him. In John 15:15, Jesus says, "I no longer call you servants. Instead, I have called you friends." What a wonderful teacher and friend is Jesus!

Adapted from *What the Bible Is All About* by Henrietta C. Mears.

Big Picture Story Center

Teacher Materials

Bible Time Line, drawing materials/equipment.

Student Materials

Drawing materials.

Tell the Story

Move the *Bible Time Line* frame to highlight Picture 30. As you tell each part of the story, draw each sketch. Students copy your sketches.

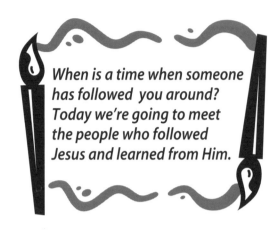

When is a time when someone has followed you around? Today we're going to meet the people who followed Jesus and learned from Him.

1. One day, John the Baptist was talking with two of his friends. Suddenly, John stopped. He pointed at Jesus, who was walking by. "Look," he said, "the Lamb of God!" John was saying that Jesus was the special person God had sent to take the punishment for the wrong things people do. John's friends wanted to know more about Jesus! So they walked quickly after Him. "Where are You staying?" they asked Jesus. Jesus invited them to come along with Him and see.

2. One of John's friends, named Andrew, grew more and more excited as he listened to Jesus! He decided, *I must go and tell my brother about Jesus!* Andrew hurried to find his brother, Peter. He told Peter, "We have found the special person God has sent!" Peter hurried back with Andrew to meet Jesus.

3. The next day, Jesus asked a man named Philip to come along with Him, too. As Philip listened to Jesus, he could hardly WAIT to tell his friend Nathanael! Philip looked for Nathanael and found him under a fig tree. Philip called, "We have found the promised One, Jesus! Come and see!"

4. Nathanael was surprised, but he went with Philip. As Nathanael walked up, Jesus said, "Here is a truthful man! I saw you sitting under the fig tree!" Jesus knew where Nathanael had been! Now Nathanael realized that Jesus truly was the special person God had sent!

1. Draw a walking stick figure, followed by two others.

2. Running figures with legs from "Z"s.

3. Tree from "I"s, "3"s.

4. Surprised face and hair from "U"s and "C"s.

5. Later, Jesus was walking along the edge of the Sea of Galilee, watching fishermen throw their big fishing nets out into the water and pull them in again. Jesus saw Peter and Andrew there and called to them. They looked up, pulled in their nets and hurried to see what Jesus wanted. Jesus invited them to follow Him. Jesus said they would help Him tell people about God and bring people into God's family instead of bringing in fish! Peter and Andrew were glad to leave their boats and go with Jesus right away.

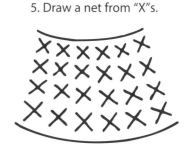
5. Draw a net from "X"s.

6. As Jesus, Peter and Andrew walked along, they saw two other fishermen in a boat, helping their father prepare the fishing nets. Jesus called to them, too. He invited them to follow Him. And so James and John put down their nets and went with Jesus, too.

6. Boat from "C" and upside-down "T."

7. On another day, Jesus saw a man named Matthew sitting at his tax collector's table. "Come with Me, Matthew," said Jesus. Matthew looked up at Jesus, got right up and left his money box and all his work! Now Jesus had fishermen and a tax collector to help Him.

7. Money box from rectangles. Add coins.
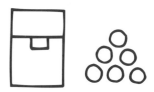

8. Jesus invited more people to be His helpers until He had 12 friends to help Him. Each one was different, but they were all the same in one way: they loved Jesus and wanted to learn from Him. Jesus told His friends many wonderful things about God and about Himself. Then Jesus sent His helpers to cities and towns all around to tell other people what Jesus had taught them.

8. Draw 12 "O"s for helpers. Add details to make different faces.

Get the Big Picture

What kinds of people decided to follow Jesus? What do you think Jesus' disciples learned about Jesus? (How to tell people about God. How to help others learn about Jesus. Who Jesus is.)

Jesus wanted all kinds of people to know Him and learn from Him. Then they could help all kinds of other people know Jesus! Even today, God chooses all kinds of people to learn from Him. God wants us all to be part of His family because He loves us all.

Bible Verse Object Talk: Shoe Talk

Big Picture Verse

"I am the Lord your God, who teaches you what is best for you, who directs you in the way you should go." Isaiah 48:17

Teacher Materials

Bible with bookmark at Isaiah 48:17, a variety of shoes (tennis, dress, sandal, slipper, boot, cleats, etc.) in a bag.

Present the Object Talk

Even though God has made each person different, He wants each of us to learn about Him. Look at the things in this bag that remind us of the different ways in which God has made us and what He wants us to do.

1. Invite volunteers to take turns removing shoes, one at a time, from the bag. As each shoe is shown ask, **What kind of shoe is this? How is it different from other kinds of shoes? How is it the same? When might someone wear this shoe? What makes this shoe useful?**

2. When all the shoes have been shown and discussed say, **Even though these are all shoes, they are all different from each other. In the same way, we're all people made**

by God, but we are different from each other, too. All these different kinds of shoes remind me that God has chosen many different kinds of people to learn from Him.

Conclude

These shoes also remind me of walking down a path or a street. **Listen to Isaiah 48:17 to find out who will help us know the right ways to act.** Read Isaiah 48:17 aloud. **Who does this verse say will teach us and help us learn the best way to live?** Lead students in prayer, thanking God for inviting each of us to learn from Him and for teaching us about Him.

Discussion Questions

1. What are some other kinds of shoes you wear?

2. Wow did God make people alike? How did He make them different?

3. What are some of the ways people today can learn more about God? (Hear Bible stories. Talk to others who love and obey God.)

4. What can you do this week to learn about God?

Active Game Center: Switcheroo

Materials
Masking tape.

Prepare the Game
On the floor, use masking tape to form at least three shapes large enough to fit the number of students in your class. (For example, if you have 20 students, make four shapes large enough for five students to stand in each shape.)

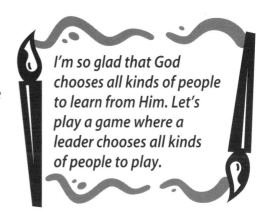

I'm so glad that God chooses all kinds of people to learn from Him. Let's play a game where a leader chooses all kinds of people to play.

Lead the Game
1. Ask a volunteer to be "It." Form three groups from remaining students. Each group stands in a separate shape marked on the floor.

2. One at a time call out such descriptions as "kids wearing blue" or "kids wearing tennis shoes." Students who fit each description run to new shapes while "It" tries to tag them before they are inside their new shapes. Any student who is tagged becomes "It" also. Continue play, periodically calling out "Switcheroo" at which all students must run to new shapes. When only a few students have not been tagged, begin a new round of the game. Begin the new round with a new "It."

It →

Options
1. If you have a large group, choose more than one student to be "It."

2. If space is limited, students jump, hop or tiptoe instead of running between shapes.

3. Play this game outside on a paved area. Draw the shapes with chalk.

Discussion Questions
1. In this game, how did we choose the people who had to switch places?

2. What kinds of people did Jesus choose to be His disciples? What did they do to learn about Jesus? (Traveled with Him. Listened to Him teach.)

3. What are some ways we can learn what God wants to teach us? (Read our Bibles. Listen to teachers and parents. Ask God to help us learn about Him.)

4. What have you already learned about God and how to love and obey Him?

Art Center: Fishers of Men Mobile

Student Materials

Scissors, measuring stick, spool of wire (available at craft or hardware stores), construction paper in a variety of colors, chenille wires, seashells and other sea items (various dried seaweeds, starfish, bits of coral, etc.).

Prepare the Activity

For each student, cut a 36-inch (90-cm) length of wire and five or six lengths of wire that vary from 2 to 4 inches (5 to 10 cm) long.

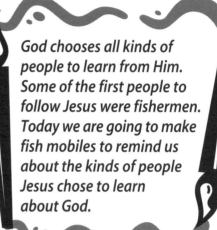

God chooses all kinds of people to learn from Him. Some of the first people to follow Jesus were fishermen. Today we are going to make fish mobiles to remind us about the kinds of people Jesus chose to learn about God.

Lead the Activity

1. Each student creates fish shape from 36-inch (90-cm) length of wire (see sketch a).

2. Students cut out small fish shapes from paper and/or form small fish shapes with chenille wires.

3. Students attach "fish," shells and other items to their fish mobiles with short wire pieces, wrapping one end of wire to fish shape (see sketch b).

4. Students form hangers from remaining lengths of wire and attach to fish shapes. Hang mobiles in classroom, or allow students to take home their mobiles.

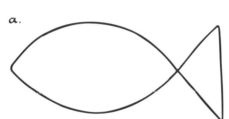

Option

Students write key words or phrases from Isaiah 48:17 on paper fish shapes before attaching them to their mobiles.

Discussion Questions

1. What are some ways kids can learn about God? What are some things you have already learned about God?

2. What would you like to learn about God?

3. Jesus told His disciples they would become fishers of men—they would help others learn about Jesus. What are some ways kids your age can help others learn about Jesus?

Worship Center

> Let's tell God how glad we are that He chooses all kinds of people to learn from Him—even us!

Big Picture Verse

"I am the Lord your God, who teaches you what is best for you, who directs you in the way you should go." Isaiah 48:17

Teacher Materials

Bible, *God's Big Picture* cassette/CD or music video and player, "Jesus' Love" word chart (p. 467 in this book), large sheet of paper on which you have printed Isaiah 48:17, masking tape.

Sing to God

Play "Jesus' Love," encouraging students to sing along with the music and do the actions shown on the word chart or the music video. **What did Jesus say when He invited people to be His disciples? How did Jesus show His love when He asked the disciples to follow Him?**

Hear and Say God's Word

Display paper on which you have printed Isaiah 48:17. Have a volunteer read the verse aloud. **What does Isaiah 48:17 say that God teaches us?** (What is best for us.) **Where does He direct us?** (In the way we should go.) **This verse tells us that as we learn about Him, God will teach us the best way to live.** Point out how the verse is divided into three phrases separated by commas. Then lead students to repeat the verse several times with girls, boys and teacher(s) saying phrases alternately, standing as they say their phrases.

Pray to God

Students sit in a circle. Ask each student to make sure he or she knows the name of the student to his or her right. Then lead students in prayer: **Dear God, thank You for inviting us to learn from You. Thank You for...."** Students say names of students to their right to complete the prayer.

Options

1. Sing "I Want to Follow Jesus" (p. 465 in this book).
2. During the Bible verse activity, lead students to make up a rhythmic pattern (such as three claps and a snap) to use when saying Isaiah 48:17.

 Lesson 30

Bible Story Coloring Center

 FOR YOUNGER CHILDREN

Materials
Crayons or markers, a copy of "Jesus says, 'Follow me'" picture and story (pp. 151-152 from *Bible Story Coloring Pages*) for each student.

Lead the Activity
Students color page 151; read or tell the story on page 152. **What are these men doing? How many fish do you see? What do you think Jesus is telling the men to do? Why might these men want to follow Jesus and learn about Him?**

Option
Students draw other kinds of fish in the water.

Skit Center

 FOR OLDER CHILDREN

Materials
A copy of "Going Fishing" skit (pp. 259-262 from *The Big Book of Bible Skits*) for each student; optional—highlighter pens.

Lead the Activity
Students choose parts and read the skit, which tells about what three of the disciples learned from Jesus by following Him. (Optional: Students highlight their parts.) Discuss the skit by asking, **What did these disciples learn about Jesus by following Him? What are some ways people today can follow Jesus? What have you learned about Jesus?**

Bible Skills Center

 FOR OLDER CHILDREN

Materials
Materials needed for "Name That Disciple" and/or "Scrambled Sea Scene" (p. 61 and/or p. 99 from *The Big Book of Bible Skills*).

Lead the Activity
Students complete activities as directed in *The Big Book of Bible Skills*.

The Paralyzed Man

Big Picture Verse

"My God will meet all your needs according to his glorious riches in Christ Jesus." Philippians 4:19

THE BIG PICTURE

No matter what we need, God helps and cares for us.

Scripture Background
Mark 2:1-12; Luke 5:17-26

It was remarkable how rapidly news spread in the East, without newspapers, televisions, telephones or radios. But in Capernaum a paralyzed man had heard of this new prophet, Jesus, and His gospel of healing. The man's four friends brought him to the house where Jesus was teaching and lowered him into the presence of the Master.

We find in this healing the test and proof of Jesus' power not only as a physician of the body but also as a healer of the soul. "Who can forgive sins but God alone?" (Mark 2:7). Sins are against God and, therefore, He only can forgive. Jesus said, "That you may know that the Son of Man has authority on earth to forgive sins....I tell you, get up, take your mat and go home" (Mark 2:10,11).

The man arose, took up his bed and went forth before them all, a living witness to Jesus' power over sin, a visible illustration of the work which Jesus came to do. Jesus came to give His life as a ransom for many that He might forgive their sins.

God endorsed Jesus' claim to be the Messiah in this miracle. This and the other miracles of Jesus recorded in the Gospels were proofs of His mission from God. They showed that He was the promised Redeemer and King, the One that we all need. Because Jesus is God, miracles were as natural to Him as acts of will are to us! Through His miracles Jesus inspired faith in many of those who saw and heard Him. Even today, as we study the records of Jesus' miracles, we can be confident in Jesus' ability to supply our needs—physical and spiritual.

Adapted from *What the Bible Is All About* by Henrietta C. Mears.

Big Picture Story Center

Teacher Materials
Bible Time Line, drawing materials/equipment.

Student Materials
Drawing materials.

Tell the Story
Move the *Bible Time Line* frame to highlight Picture 31. As you tell each part of the story, draw each sketch. Students copy your sketches.

What do people who can't walk use to get from place to place? In our Bible story today, we'll meet a man who couldn't walk and who was carried to a very strange place!

1. When Jesus lived on earth, He went from town to town, teaching people about God. Besides teaching, He also healed people. If they were sick, He made them well again. If they couldn't walk or hear or see, He made their feet or ears or eyes work the way they should. One day, Jesus was in the town of Capernaum. Crowds of people gathered around Him. They filled the house where He was, and they filled the front yard and the backyard, too! People stood in the door-ways, leaned through the windows and sat or stood on every inch of the floor! People were everywhere!

1. Draw house from rectangles and stairs from "L"s. Add "C"s for people.

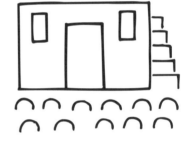

2. Nearby, there lived a man who was paralyzed. In this case, that means his legs didn't work at all. But this man had some wonderful friends. His friends decided, "We'll take our paralyzed friend to Jesus. Jesus can make his legs well!"

2. Lying man from "C"s, "7"s. Add face.

3. Each of four of the friends took a corner of the man's sleeping mat. They lifted the paralyzed man and his mat right up off the ground and started walking. It didn't matter how heavy he seemed or how tired they got. They were going to make SURE that their paralyzed friend got to Jesus! They knew Jesus could help their friend!

3. Add long "C" for mat under lying man. Add "U"s to corners for handles.

4. Finally, they came to the house where Jesus was. Well, they were ALMOST to the house! There were so many people, it was even hard to see the house! How could they carry their friend on his mat through ALL these PEOPLE?

4. Add 4 "C"s and rectangle to drawing of crowded house.

5. They looked at each other. *How could they get their friend to Jesus?!* One of them had an idea! Carefully, the friends carried the man on his mat up the outside steps to the roof. They gently laid their friend down.

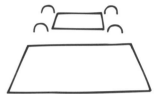
5. Draw roof. Add 4 "C"s and mat.

6. The roof was made of mats of woven branches, plastered with clay. And what do you think those friends did? They pulled up some of these mats and laid them aside. Soon, they had made a HOLE in the roof! They made the hole bigger and BIGGER, until it was SO big they could lower their friend's mat right down through it!

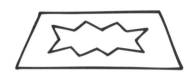
6. Draw roof with hole.

7. The friends slid ropes under the mat and lowered the paralyzed man down through that hole until he was right in front of Jesus! Jesus looked down at the paralyzed man. He knew the man needed two things: to have his sins forgiven and to be healed. So Jesus said to him, "Your sins are forgiven. And so that everyone will know I have the power to forgive sins, pick up your mat. You can walk!"

7. Add long "U" beneath hole. Add man and stick figure for Jesus.

8. Right there, in the middle of that crowd, the man stood. He picked up his mat. And he walked right out of that crowded house! His friends must have been VERY happy! They had known Jesus would be able to make their friend able to walk. And Jesus did! Even better, because He is God's Son, Jesus forgave the man's sins!

8. Draw "A"; add face, arms, feet and rolled mat.

Get the Big Picture
What did the paralyzed man need? (Healing. Forgiveness.) **Why were his friends so determined to bring him to Jesus?**

When the paralyzed man's friends wanted to help their friend, they took him to Jesus. No matter what people need, Jesus is always able to help. He loves us and wants us to tell Him what we need. That's God's big picture of how to take care of our problems!

Bible Verse Object Talk: Ask God!

Big Picture Verse

"My God will meet all your needs according to his glorious riches in Christ Jesus." Philippians 4:19

Teacher Materials

Bible with bookmark at Philippians 4:19, picture or photo of a baby (or a baby doll), sharp object, apple.

Present the Object Talk

1. Show picture or photo of baby, or pass around doll, letting students pantomime ways of caring for a baby. **What are some of the ways people care for babies? How do babies get the things they need?**

No matter how young or old we are and no matter what we need, God says He will give us what we need. Sometimes it seems like we don't get the things we need. Let's talk about why we might feel that way and discover if it's really true.

Someone who cares for a baby will make sure to give the baby things like food, water, milk, hugs and toys to play with.

2. **Listen to this verse about the things we need.** Read Philippians 4:19 aloud. **What does this verse say God does?** (God gives us the good things we need.)

3. **The Bible tells us to ask God for the things we need. But sometimes we ask God for something and we don't get it. Because God loves us so much, He might say no to our request because He knows that what we've asked for isn't good for us.** Show sharp object. **If a baby wants to play with a (knife), how do people protect the baby?**

4. **Other times when we ask God for something, His answer is to wait.** Show apple. **Why is an apple good for you to eat? Why is an apple not good for a baby to eat?** (Baby might choke on apple pieces.) **Just as babies have to wait until they are older to eat apples, God knows we have to wait for some things.**

Conclude

When we pray and ask God to give us the things we need, we know that His answers are always best. Lead students in prayer, thanking God for meeting our needs.

Discussion Questions

1. What are some of the things God provides for us? (People to care for us. Food to eat. Friends.)

2. How do people show that they are depending on God to give them what they need? (Ask God for needs. Don't complain about things they want but don't have.)

3. What's something you are thankful God has given to you?

Active Game Center: Numbered Needs

Materials

Sock (or eraser), chalkboard, chalk.

Lead the Game

1. Play a game like Steal the Bacon. Divide class into two equal teams. Each team stands in a straight line facing the other team, leaving about 10 feet (3 m) between the teams. One team numbers off from one end of the line, while the other team numbers off from the opposite end (see sketch).

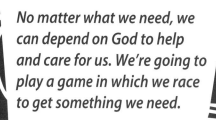

No matter what we need, we can depend on God to help and care for us. We're going to play a game in which we race to get something we need.

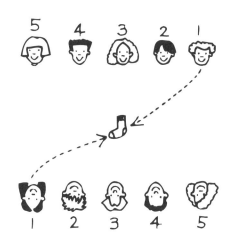

2. Hold up sock (or eraser). **We're going to pretend this is something we need. What is something we need that this (sock) could represent?** (Water, food, air, warm clothes, shelter, etc.) Place the sock in the center of the playing area, reminding students of what it represents.

3. Call a number. Students on both teams with that number run to grab the item in the center. Student who gets the item runs back to his or her team. Student who does not get the item tells a new need that the item could represent for the next round. Print each suggested need on the chalkboard. Call a new number each round.

Options

1. To divide students into two teams, students who have birthdays during the first six months of the year become one team and students who have birthdays during the last six months of the year become the other team. Even the number of players on the two teams after students have grouped themselves according to birthdays.

2. If you have a wide variety of ages in the group, assign numbers so that students compete against students of similar ages.

3. Play this game using objects which more closely represent needs students may have: water bottle, jacket, apple, book, photo of family or friends, etc.

Discussion Questions

1. How do you get most of the things you need every day?

2. How is something you need different from something you want?

3. How does God help and care for our needs? In what way might God use you to meet another's need?

4. How does God care for some of our wants?

 **Lesson 31**

Art Center: Friendly Boxes

Student Materials
Cardboard, pencils, ruler, scissors, construction paper, markers, crayons, stickers, small individually wrapped candies, hole punch, ribbon.

Prepare the Activity
On cardboard draw and cut out several patterns of a triangle, with 9-inch (22.5-cm) sides. Make a sample triangle box, following directions below.

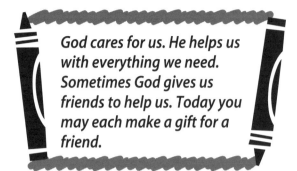

God cares for us. He helps us with everything we need. Sometimes God gives us friends to help us. Today you may each make a gift for a friend.

Lead the Activity
1. Students take turns tracing triangle cardboard patterns onto construction paper. Students cut out construction paper triangles.

2. Each student thinks of a friend to whom he or she would like to give a gift, and something for which to thank the friend. Student writes a short note of thanks (or other greeting) on one side of the paper triangle and decorates the other side. (Optional: Ask Discussion Questions while students are decorating boxes.)

3. Students fold their triangles so that each point meets above the written message and the decorated side is facing out (see sketch a).

4. Students place candies and stickers inside their triangle boxes and punch holes in the three top points of their triangle boxes. Students insert ribbons through the holes and tie to close the boxes (see sketch b).

Option
Provide large sugar cookies and decorating items such as frosting, raisins, small candies, thin licorice, etc. Students decorate cookies and package in resealable plastic bags to give to friends.

Discussion Questions

1. What are some things kids need?

2. What are some ways that God provides kids with what they need?

3. What are some good things friends have done for you?

4. How have friends shown God's care and help to you?

Lesson 31

Worship Center

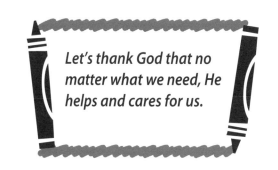

Let's thank God that no matter what we need, He helps and cares for us.

Big Picture Verse

"My God will meet all your needs according to his glorious riches in Christ Jesus." Philippians 4:19

Teacher Materials

Bible, *God's Big Picture* cassette/CD or music video and player, "Follow the Leader" word chart (p. 453 in this book), large sheet of paper on which you have printed Philippians 4:19 in mixed-up order and with space around each word, 15 Post-It Notes numbered 1-15, masking tape.

Sing to God

Play "Follow the Leader," encouraging students to sing along with the music and do the actions shown on the word chart or the music video. **What does this song tell us about the ways in which Jesus helps and cares for us?** (He shows us what to do. He died so that we can be a part of God's family. He tells us what to do in His Word. He helps us know how to pray. He shows us how we can love people everywhere.)

Hear and Say God's Word

Display paper on which you have printed Philippians 4:19. **The words of this verse aren't in the right order. I'm going to give some of you sticky notes with a number written on them. As I read the verse from the Bible, stick your number on the paper to show the correct order of the words.** Give numbered Post-It Notes to students. Slowly read Philippians 4:19 so that the student with "1" on his or her Post-It Note can stick the note by the word "My," the student with "2" can stick his or her note by the word "God," and so on. Read the verse as slowly or as many times as needed for students to correctly number the words. When all the numbers are on the paper, lead students in saying the words in the correct order a few times. **How does God meet our needs at home? at school?** Tell a way in which God meets your needs.

Pray to God

Ask students for any prayer requests or situations in which they or people they know need God's help and care. Lead students in prayer, encouraging volunteers to pray for the requests mentioned. End the prayer time by thanking God that He always helps and cares for us.

Options

1. Students sing and do actions for "Jesus' Love" and/or "He Looked" (p. 467 and/or p. 461 in this book).

2. Before the prayer, lead students on a walk outdoors. Ask students to look for ways in which God shows His care to them (sun, plants, flowers, etc.). If possible, lead both the prayer and Bible verse activities outside.

 **Lesson 31**

 FOR YOUNGER CHILDREN

Bible Story Coloring Center

Materials

Crayons or markers, a copy of "Jesus heals a paralyzed man" picture and story (pp. 161-162 from *Bible Story Coloring Pages*) for each student.

Lead the Activity

Students color page 161; read or tell the story on page 162. **How do you think the paralyzed man felt when he was lowered through the roof? How do you think he felt when he saw Jesus? What happened next?**

Option

Students draw conversation balloons near Jesus and several other people in the picture and write what might have been said.

 FOR OLDER CHILDREN

Skit Center

Materials

A copy of "Pray, Tell Me" skit (pp. 385-388 from *The Big Book of Bible Skits*) for each student; optional—highlighter pens.

Lead the Activity

Students form pairs and read the skit, which tells about what two kids think of prayer and God's help and care for all people, even if prayers aren't answered in expected ways. (Optional: Students highlight their parts.) **What do you learn about God's help and care from the Bible examples in the skit? What's an example of something you need? something you want? How does God show His care for you?**

 FOR OLDER CHILDREN

Bible Skills Center

Materials

Materials needed for "Walk and Talk" and/or "Rearranged Verse" (p. 44 and/or p. 82 from *The Big Book of Bible Skills*).

Lead the Activity

Students complete activities as directed in *The Big Book of Bible Skills*.

 **Lesson 32**

Sermon on the Mount

Big Picture Verse

"Live a life worthy of the calling you have received." Ephesians 4:1

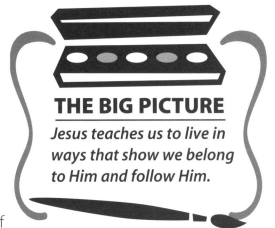

THE BIG PICTURE

Jesus teaches us to live in ways that show we belong to Him and follow Him.

Scripture Background
Matthew 5—7; Luke 6

From the lofty pulpit of a mountain, Jesus preached the sermon that contains the laws of His kingdom (see Matthew 5—7). Read through these chapters and refresh your memory about this most wonderful of Jesus' discourses.

After nearly 2,000 years this Sermon on the Mount has lost none of its majesty or power. The teachings of this sermon surpass all human teachings. The world has not yet caught up with this sermon's simple ideals and requirements.

Many a person who is not a Christian claims that the Sermon on the Mount is his or her religion. How little that person understands the depth of this sermon's meaning. It is important that we do not simply praise this rule as a wonderful theory but that we actually practice it in our own lives, recognizing the source from which it comes. If we let Jesus' teachings operate in our lives, it will change all of our personal relations, heal our social wounds, solve every dispute between nations and, yes, set the whole world in order. The root of this law is kindness. It is true that if human society would acknowledge Jesus as Lord and Savior and claim the standards of the Sermon on the Mount as its own, the world would be set in order. One day filled with kindness would be a bit of heaven. Love would reign instead of lawlessness.

Jesus defines the nature and limit of the Kingdom, the condition for entrance, its laws, its privileges and its rewards. The Sermon on the Mount sets forth the constitution of God's kingdom. Here, the King contrasts the new rule of His kingdom with the old wineskins of the Mosaic Law. The order of His kingdom is a completely new one, where heart attitude must precede outward act and where the law is kept out of love, not fear or duty. Fourteen times the King says, "I tell you," revealing His authority as He expands the law of Moses. The King has spoken: We must not only keep the law outwardly but in spirit as well.

Adapted from *What the Bible Is All About* by Henrietta C. Mears.

Big Picture Story Center

Teacher Materials
Bible Time Line, drawing materials/equipment.

Student Materials
Drawing materials.

Tell the Story
Move the *Bible Time Line* frame to highlight Picture 32. As you tell each part of the story, draw each sketch. Students copy your sketches.

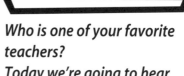

Who is one of your favorite teachers?
Today we're going to hear some of the best teaching from the world's best teacher!

1. One day, Jesus saw a huge crowd of people coming toward Him. They wanted to listen to His teaching. Jesus had many important things to teach the people, so He went up on a mountainside and sat down to teach from there. Now, everyone could see and hear Him!

2. First, Jesus told the people how to be happy the way God wanted them to be. He said, "Happy are those who know they need God. Happy are those who desire to do right. Happy are those who show kindness and make peace." Jesus told the people to show by their actions that they belonged to God, just like bright lights that shine in dark places.

3. Jesus went on to tell the people to obey God's law. "You have heard people say, 'Love your neighbor and hate your enemy.' But I tell you to forgive and love EVERYONE, even those who are enemies." That was a surprise!

4. Jesus also said, "Don't worry about having enough food or clothes." He said that God takes care of the flowers and gives them beautiful clothes to wear. God takes care of the birds and makes sure they are fed. And to God, we are much more important than flowers or birds! So God's children don't need to worry. Instead, we can trust God and do what He wants; He will give us what we need!

1. Draw mountain from upside-down "C." Add "C"s for crowd below.

2. Happy face. Add light rays around face.

3. Two faces: love and hate. Add "no" slash over "hate" face.

4. Draw flower, bird from "Y"s, "V"s and "C"s.

5. Jesus also told the people that if they wanted to obey everything God had said about how to treat other people, there was a simple rule to follow: Treat other people the way you would like to be treated. Sometimes people call that teaching the Golden Rule.

5. Draw two faces smiling at each other.

6. As Jesus finished His long talk with the people, He told a story to help them learn to listen well to what He said and then DO what He taught them.

6. Draw face with big listening ears.

7. Jesus said, "A wise man always builds his house on a strong rock." A person who listens to Jesus' words and obeys them is like this wise builder.

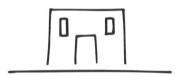
7. Draw house on rock.

8. Jesus went on to say that anyone who hears Jesus' words and does NOT do what Jesus taught is like a man who built his house on sand. Jesus said this kind of person was foolish. Let's find out why.

8. House on sand.

9. Jesus explained that when a storm came, the water rose and the winds blew and the house built on sand fell down! But the house built on the rock stood firmly because it had a strong foundation. When the crowd of people heard all these teachings of Jesus, the Bible says they were amazed! They realized that Jesus' words were really true!

9. Add rain and wind; clouds from "C"s. Scribble over house on sand.

Get the Big Picture

What are some of the things Jesus said we should do in order to build our lives on Him? (Show kindness. Make peace. Love enemies. Treat other people the way we want to be treated.) **When we live in a way that shows we belong to and follow Jesus, we are like the man whose house was built on a rock. Our lives can handle troubles when they come, because we have built our lives on Jesus by trusting in Him and obeying Him every day.**

Jesus wants us to live in ways that show we belong to Him and follow Him. When we are members of God's family, He will help us live in ways that show our love for Him and others.

 **Lesson 32**

Bible Verse Object Talk: Who Am I?

Big Picture Verse

"Live a life worthy of the calling you have received."
Ephesians 4:1

Teacher Materials

Bible with bookmark at Ephesians 4:1, a variety of objects that represent occupations or hobbies (computer disk, gardening glove, book, wrench, basketball, paintbrush, guitar); optional—blindfold.

Present the Object Talk

1. Show one of the objects you collected. (Optional: Blindfold a volunteer who feels the object and then identifies it.) Students tell what

Our friends and families can learn from our words and actions whether or not we have chosen to belong to Jesus and follow Him. The things we do and say every day help people learn about us. See if you can learn what these people are like.

they learn about a person who uses the object. For example, if the object is a gardening glove, students might say "likes to be outdoors," "grows lots of plants" and "works hard."

2. **We can tell what a person is like by the things they do and say. Jesus talks about the words and actions of people whose job it is to follow Him—people who are called Christians. What might Christians do to show that they belong to Jesus?** (Be honest. Help others. Forgive others. Depend on God to give them what is needed. Say kind words to enemies. Don't put bad things into their bodies.) **Christians do these good things to show their love for God.**

Conclude

Reading the Bible helps us learn ways of showing we belong to Jesus. And we learn that God promises to help us obey Him. Pray, asking God's help in following Him.

Discussion Questions

1. Who is someone you know whose actions show they belong to Jesus? What does that person say and do?

2. When is a time a kid your age can show they follow Jesus? How?

3. When might it be hard to follow Jesus? What can we do when we need help loving and obeying Jesus?

Lesson 32

Active Game Center: Color Your Actions

Materials

Balloons in two colors, plastic garbage bag, two large boxes or garbage cans.

Prepare the Game

Inflate and tie balloons, an equal number of each color. (Prepare one balloon for each student. If you have a small group, prepare more than one balloon for each student.) Place balloons in garbage bag for storage.

Lead the Game

1. Play a game similar to soccer, using multiple balloons. Place balloons on the floor in the middle of a large playing area.

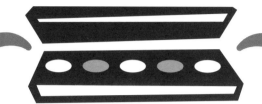

Jesus teaches us to live in ways that show we belong to Him and follow Him. In the game we're going to play your actions will show which team you're on. Let's also see if your attitude when you play can show you belong to Jesus.

2. Students form two teams. Teams line up at opposite ends of the playing area. Assign each team a balloon color and choose a student from each team to be a scorer. Scorer stands behind opposing team, in front of a large box or garbage can (see sketch).

3. At your signal, all team members run to the middle of the playing area and try to kick balloons of their team's color to their scorer. (Optional: Students remove shoes.) Scorer grabs his or her team's balloons and puts them into the box or can. At your signal, scorer counts balloons in box or can. Team with most balloons in the box or can wins. Repeat as time permits, blowing up additional balloons to replace any popped balloons.

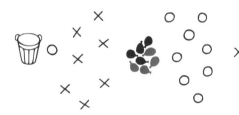

Options

1. When forming teams, assign each team a mix of ages so that teams are of similar strength.

2. Vary the game by asking members of one team to use only right feet and members of the other team to use only left feet while playing the game.

3. If you have limited space, students remain seated on floor and bat balloons rather than kicking them.

Discussion Questions

1. How did you show which team you belonged to in this game? (Kicked balloons of only one color.)

2. What are some actions you can do every day to show that you belong to and follow Jesus? (Read the Bible. Say kind words. Forgive others. Share with others. Be honest. Pray.)

3. Why is it important to live in ways that show we belong to Jesus and want to follow Him? (Because we love God. So that others can learn about God through our actions.)

 **Lesson 32**

Art Center: Look at the Lilies

Student Materials
Pencils, poster board, ruler, scissors, tissue paper in green and a variety of other bright colors, green chenille wires.

Prepare the Activity
Trace and cut out from poster board several 7-inch (17.5-cm) circles and several 4-inch (10-cm) circles to use as patterns (one pattern for every four students). Make a sample flower following directions below.

When Jesus taught how to follow Him, He said that because God cares for us even more than He cares for beautiful flowers, we can depend on Him for what we need. Make some flowers today to help you remember to depend on God's loving care.

Lead the Activity
1. Students take turns using circle patterns to trace larger circle on several bright colors of tissue paper and smaller circle on green tissue paper.

2. Students cut out circles they have traced and place them as shown in Sketch a. Students

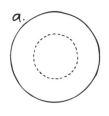 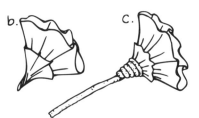

then pinch the middle of the circles and twist to form flower (see sketch b).

3. Twist a chenille wire around the base of the flower to create a stem (see sketch c). Each student may create several flowers.

Options
1. Instead of colored tissue paper, use wrapping paper with floral designs. Students cut out two large circles from the wrapping paper and place the paper circles together so that the printed sides face out. Then students cut one small circle from green tissue paper. Finish the flower as described in Steps 2 and 3.

2. Some students may enjoy drawing a garden scene on a large sheet of butcher paper. Students glue completed flowers to the scene.

Discussion Questions
1. What kinds of flowers have you seen growing in your yard or neighborhood?

2. When we depend on God's loving care for us, we show that we want to follow Jesus. What are some ways people show that they want to follow Him? (Talk to God. Don't use bad words.)

3. Why is it important for people who love Jesus to show that they depend on God's loving care and want to follow Him? (So others can learn about Jesus and the best way to live.)

Lesson 32

Worship Center

Let's show Jesus how glad we are that He teaches us and helps us to live in ways that show we belong to Him and follow Him.

Big Picture Verse

"Live a life worthy of the calling you have received."
Ephesians 4:1

Teacher Materials

Bible, *God's Big Picture* cassette/CD or music video and player, "I Want to Follow Jesus" word chart (p. 465 in this book), large sheet of paper on which you have printed Ephesians 4:1, masking tape.

Sing to God

Play "I Want to Follow Jesus," encouraging students to sing along with the music and do the actions shown on the word chart or the music video. **What are some ways you can show that you want to follow Jesus and belong to Him?** (Choose to be a member of God's family. Express love to God. Show God's love to others.)

Hear and Say God's Word

Display paper on which you have printed Ephesians 4:1. Have a volunteer read the verse aloud. **This verse talks about what we should be like because Jesus has called, or asked, us to follow Him. When we follow Jesus, it means we talk and act in ways that show we have chosen to love and obey God.** Lead students in saying Ephesians 4:1 together. Then have different groups of students say the verse together. **Stand up and say the verse if you (like bananas, are nine or older, have a brother or sister, are younger than nine, play soccer).** Repeat as time allows.

Pray to God

Tell students about a time when someone you know has shown by words or actions that he or she belongs to Jesus. Lead students in prayer, thanking God we can belong to Him and asking His help to follow Him. Talk with students about becoming members of His family. (See "Leading a Child to Christ" on p. 30.)

Options

1. Provide rhythm instruments for students to use as they sing "I Want to Follow Jesus" and other songs on the cassette/CD or music video.

2. Ask two older students to read Matthew 5:3-10 (the Beatitudes) aloud, with one student reading the first phrase of each verse and the second student reading the second phrase.

 **Lesson 32**

Bible Story Coloring Center

Materials

Crayons or markers, a copy of "Jesus loves the children" picture and story (pp. 175-176 from *Bible Story Coloring Pages*) for each student.

Lead the Activity

Students color page 175; read or tell the story on page 176. **How is Jesus showing His love to the children in this picture? How does Jesus show His love to you?**

Option

Students glue finished pictures to 9x12-inch (22.5x30-cm) colored construction paper, centering pictures so that the construction paper creates a border. Display pictures in classroom.

Skit Center

Materials

A copy of "Don't Worry" skit (pp. 217-219 from *The Big Book of Bible Skits*) for each student; optional—highlighter pens.

Lead the Activity

Students choose parts and read the skit, which tells about what Jesus taught some of the disciples. (Optional: Students highlight their parts.) Discuss the skit by asking, **How did these disciples show they belonged to Jesus and wanted to follow Him? How can you put Jesus' words into practice?**

Bible Skills Center

Materials

Materials needed for "Pick and Choose" and/or "Star Maze" (p. 33 and/or p. 159 from *The Big Book of Bible Skills*).

Lead the Activity

Students complete activities as directed in *The Big Book of Bible Skills*.

Lesson 33

Parable of the Sower

Big Picture Verse

"Your word is a lamp to my feet and a light for my path." Psalm 119:105

THE BIG PICTURE

We can learn the very best way to live from God's Word.

Scripture Background
Mark 4:1-20

Everyone can learn from the parables told by Jesus. They were a special teaching instrument of Christ. Jesus used this method of instruction because of the growing hostility toward Him and His message. He was surrounded by enemies who tried to catch Him in His words, but no one could object to a simple story. Besides, stories are remembered by hearers of all ages.

A parable is an analogy. It assumes a likeness between higher and lower things. The word "parable" comes from the Greek word meaning both beside and to throw. A parable, then, is a form of teaching in which one thing is thrown down beside another for comparison and understanding.

The parable of the sower describes first the hard soil that is hostile to the penetration and growth of a seed. Through this parable we are warned not to develop hearts and attitudes hardened to God and His Word. We must never let our familiarity with the things of Christianity make us hard or jaded to the fresh seed God wants to sow in our lives. The shallow soil warns us that while we may look back to an experience of dramatic new life springing up, such life must continue. Many a Christian has pointed back to the time when he or she had an experience with God as proof of life in Him. But initial experience is not enough. God waits for fruit.

The parable also describes soil in which rocks and thorns choke the plant as it attempts to grow. This, too, is a warning: God wants to clear out the obstacles that prevent His truth from growing and flourishing.

When we put God first, distractions don't stifle His work in our lives; we give the distractions to Him and go on to maturity. That is the glorious picture of the fourth soil—soil that supports maturity and the fruit which God so desires to see in us. Soil that is ready for the deep planting of God yields wonderful fruit: healthy, productive lives that exhibit the fruit of His Spirit (see Galatians 5:22,23).

Adapted from *What the Bible Is All About* by Henrietta C. Mears.

Big Picture Story Center

Teacher Materials

Bible Time Line, drawing materials/equipment.

Student Materials

Drawing materials.

Tell the Story

Move the *Bible Time Line* frame to highlight Picture 33. As you tell each part of the story, draw each sketch. Students copy your sketches.

What kinds of seeds have you planted or watched grow? Today we'll hear a story Jesus told about seeds and plants to help us learn that the very best way to live is found in God's Word.

1. One day, Jesus began to tell a crowd this story: "A farmer went out to his field to plant some seeds. As the farmer walked up and down the field, he scattered seeds on the ground. Some of the seeds fell on a hard dirt path. The dirt was too hard for the seeds to put down any roots and grow. So the seeds just lay there on the path. Then birds swooped down and snatched up the seeds."

1. Draw straight line for hard soil; add seeds; add bird from "C"s and "V"s.

2. "Other seeds fell on rocky ground," Jesus said. "The plants sprang up quickly and grew for a little while. But then their roots couldn't get enough water and the plants died."

2. Rocky ground. Add plants; then cross them out.

3. Jesus continued, "As the farmer scattered more seeds, some of the seeds fell among thorny weeds." Jesus shook His head sadly. "The thorny weeds and the plants grew up together. But the thorny weeds grew stronger than the young plants. The weeds CHOKED the life out of the plants and they died."

3. Thorny weeds from lines. Add plants; then cross them out.

4. Some people must have wondered if that farmer was going to have any crop at all! But Jesus wasn't finished. He said, "Some of the seeds fell on good soil. They grew and became a huge crop! In fact, some plants produced 100 times MORE seeds than the farmer had planted."

4. Draw good soil and add growing plants from "V"s. Add "100."

5. Then Jesus ended His parable by saying, "He who has ears to hear, let him hear." The disciples looked at each other with puzzled faces. *What did Jesus mean?* they thought.

5. Question mark.

6. Jesus began to explain to His disciples. "The seeds are like God's Word. When someone hears God's Word, he or she may act in several different ways. People who hear God's Word but never believe it are like the hard dirt on the path where the seeds got eaten by birds." The disciples could tell Jesus felt very sad about these people who never let God's Word into their hearts and minds.

6. Next to the hard ground, add face from "U", "C"s and "V"s. Add "C"s and "I"s for hands over ears.

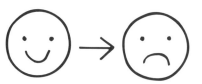

7. "Some other people hear the Word of God and gladly believe it," Jesus said. "But then, later, when it's too much trouble to do what God wants, they stop believing God's Word. They are like the shallow, rocky soil," Jesus said.

7. Next to rocky ground, draw happy face, arrow and sad face.

8. "What about the ground full of thorny weeds?" a disciple asked. "What kind of people are like that?"

Jesus explained, "The thorny, weed-filled ground is like people who have heard God's Word and believe it. They begin to grow, but then they let worries and their desires for other things keep them from growing. Soon they forget all about God. They're too busy with everything else." The disciples must have looked at each other uncomfortably. They knew what it was like to forget about God's Word.

8. Next to thorny weeds, draw worried face from "U"s, "C"s, "M"s; add thought balloon; then cross out "GOD."

9. Then Jesus finished His story by saying, "The good soil is like people who hear and believe the Word of God. They grow and their lives show that they've learned the way God wants them to live." The disciples knew they wanted to be people who were like the good ground, always ready to hear and believe God's Word.

9. Next to good soil, draw plant with happy face on top.

Get the Big Picture

What were the four kinds of soil Jesus told about? What do the different kinds of soil remind us of? (The soil reminds us of four ways people act when they hear God's Word.)
How do the people who are like the good soil act? (They hear God's Word and obey it.)
We want to be like the good soil, ready to hear how we can love and obey God. God's Word shows us the very best way to live!

Bible Verse Object Talk: Follow the Light

Big Picture Verse

"Your word is a lamp to my feet and a light for my path."
Psalm 119:105

Teacher Materials

Bible with bookmark at Psalm 119:105, flashlight, index card on which you have written Psalm 119:105; optional—laser penlight.

God's Word helps us learn to live in the very best way. Because God's Word is so important, it is sometimes compared to a light. Let's use this flashlight to find out how light helps us.

Present the Object Talk

1. While a volunteer covers his or her eyes, hide index card in classroom. Volunteer uncovers eyes.

2. Use flashlight to slowly trace on the classroom floor a path which the volunteer follows, eventually leading the volunteer to the location of the hidden card. (Optional: Use laser penlight instead of flashlight.) Volunteer reads verse aloud.

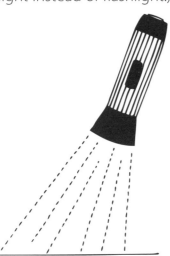

3. Repeat activity with other volunteers as time permits, inviting students to take turns hiding card and using the flashlight. (If you have a large group, use the flashlight to direct student's attention around the room, stopping the light on the location where the card is hidden. One volunteer comes forward to find the card and read it aloud.)

4. Discuss the activity by asking, **How did the flashlight help you? Where did the flashlight lead you?**

Conclude

God's Word, the Bible, is like a light because it shows us the path to follow and the very best way to live. The things we learn in the Bible help us know how to love and obey God. Lead students in prayer, thanking God for His Word.

Discussion Questions

1. When might you need a flashlight or other kind of light to help you find your way?

2. When do kids your age need help to know how to love and obey God? (When someone wants to start an argument. When someone is being unkind.) *How can God's Word help in those situations?* (Helps to know what to say and do. Gives commands to follow.)

 **Lesson 33**

Active Game Center: Best-Way Relay

Materials
Styrofoam peanuts, paper plates.

Lead the Game

1. What do you think is the best way to move this peanut across the room without touching it? Demonstrate (or invite volunteers to experiment with) different ways of using a paper plate as a fan to move the peanut (small quick movements, big sweeping movements, etc.).

Every day we make choices about the best things to do and say. God promises us that His Word will help us make those important choices. Today we're going to find out the best way to complete a relay.

2. Group students in teams of no more than four to six students each. Teams line up single file at one side of the playing area. Give the first student in each line a paper plate and a Styrofoam peanut.

3. At your signal, the first student on each team fans the paper plate to move the peanut across the playing area. Once the peanut reaches the other side of the playing area, student picks up the peanut and brings it back with the paper plate to the next person in line.

Option
If you have mostly younger students, invite them to experiment with moving the peanut, but do not have a competitive relay. Another option for younger students is to shorten the distance the peanut must be moved.

Discussion Questions

1. What was the best way you found to move the peanut?

2. What are some other things you've learned the best way to do? (How to tie shoelaces, so they do not come untied. How to hold the leash when walking the dog. How to brush teeth every day.)

3. What is one thing you have learned from God's Word about the best way to live? (Treat others with kindness. Be patient.)

4. God's Word tells us we should love all people. Why is following this command the best way to live? (It helps us get along with others. Helps us show God's love.)

Art Center: Seed Mosaics

Student Materials

Pencils, paper plates, various types of seeds and beans (unpopped popcorn, sunflower seeds, dill seeds, kidney beans, split peas, etc.), glue.

Lead the Activity

1. Each student draws a design containing several sections on paper plates.

2. Students glue seeds onto their designs, filling in each section with a different kind of seed or bean to make mosaics.

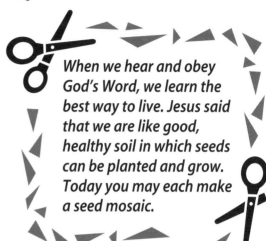

When we hear and obey God's Word, we learn the best way to live. Jesus said that we are like good, healthy soil in which seeds can be planted and grow. Today you may each make a seed mosaic.

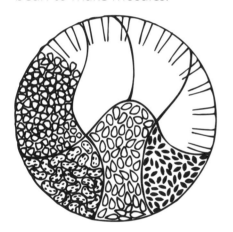

Options

1. Bring small clay or plastic pots, potting soil, potting utensils, seeds and water. Students plant seeds in pots. Students may take home their pots.

2. Bring clay pots, paint or collage items (buttons, fabric pieces, trim, etc.) and glue. Students decorate pots by painting them or gluing collage materials onto them.

3. Students write words such as "grow," "obey" or "Bible" in large bubble letters and glue seeds to fill in the letters.

Discussion Questions

1. *When have you planted something or watched a plant or tree grow? What happened as the plant or tree grew?*

2. *What does a seed need to grow?*

3. *When we hear and obey God's Word, we are like healthy soil. What's something you've learned from God's Word?* (How to obey God. How to treat others.)

Lesson 33

Worship Center

Big Picture Verse

"Your word is a lamp to my feet and a light for my path."
Psalm 119:105

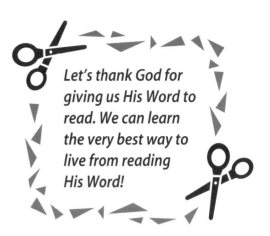

Let's thank God for giving us His Word to read. We can learn the very best way to live from reading His Word!

Teacher Materials

Bible, *God's Big Picture* cassette/CD or music video and player, "Follow the Leader" word chart (p. 453 in this book), large sheet of paper on which you have printed Psalm 119:105, masking tape.

Sing to God

Play "Follow the Leader," encouraging students to sing along with the music and do the actions shown on the word chart or the music video. **Where can we read about what Jesus tells us to do? In God's Word it tells us that we should be kind to everyone. What are some ways we can do that?**

Hear and Say God's Word

Display paper on which you have printed Psalm 119:105. Point out the words "word," "lamp" and "light." **Psalm 119:105 tells us that God's Word is like a lamp and a light. What do a lamp and a light do for us?** (Help us see where to walk. Help us see so that we can do things without hurting ourselves.) **How is God's Word like a light and a lamp for us?** (Helps us know what to do. Tells us the best way to act.). Lead students in saying verse, standing up and then sitting back down each time they say "word," "lamp" or "light." Repeat several times.

Pray to God

Invite students to repeat this prayer after you, one phrase at a time: **God, help us to understand Your Word so that we can live the very best way. In Jesus' name, amen.**

Options

1. Invite older students to find in their Bibles and read these verses which describe God's Word and how it helps us learn the best way to live: Psalm 19:7,8,10; 119:103.

2. Lead students to think of motions or actions that illustrate the words of Psalm 119:105.

 **Lesson 33**

Bible Story Coloring Center FOR YOUNGER CHILDREN

Materials

Crayons or markers, paper.

Lead the Activity

Students draw pictures of plants growing in good soil. **What do plants need in order to grow? Jesus said that people who hear and obey God's Word are like good soil. Their lives show that they've learned the very best way to live.**

Option

Students print the word "Bible" in large letters on their papers and then glue a variety of seeds, grains and dry beans (sunflower seeds, rice, kidney beans, pinto beans, etc.) on top of the letters.

Skit Center  FOR OLDER CHILDREN

Materials

A copy of "The Robot" skit (pp. 400-402 from *The Big Book of Bible Skits*) for each student; optional—highlighter pens.

Lead the Activity

Students form pairs and read the skit, which tells the story of someone trying to assemble a robot without following the instructions. (Optional: Students highlight their parts.) Ask the discussion questions on page 400.

Bible Skills Center FOR OLDER CHILDREN

Materials

Materials needed for "Discover a Story" and/or "Hidden Art" (p. 56 and/or p. 155 from *The Big Book of Bible Skills*).

Lead the Activity

Students complete activities as directed in *The Big Book of Bible Skills*.

Rescued at Sea

Big Picture Verse

"Blessed is the man who trusts in the Lord, whose confidence is in him." Jeremiah 17:7

THE BIG PICTURE

No matter how bad things look, depend on God because He is in control.

Scripture Background
Mark 4:35-41

To those who spend their lives on land, sailors seem to be a special breed—fearless, able to act in terrifying situations. For most of us, hitting small swells in a sailboat sends us back to dry land! But there are times when even those who are experienced on the water stand in terrified awe of a powerful storm.

In this story we read of Jesus asleep on a storm-rocked fishing boat with His disciples bailing water frantically, trying to stay afloat. Imagine their panic as all their efforts seemed to have no effect. Waves continued to crash over their little vessel faster than they could bail—they were doomed, for all they could see! Yet when they called to Jesus in their panic, He simply stood up and said, "Quiet! Be still!" (verse 39). And the terrifying, death-dealing waves turned to calm. "What kind of man is this," they asked each other, "that even the wind and the waves obey Him?" (see verse 41). They were astonished at His power.

We're so like those friends of Jesus! We too often wait until a situation is critical before we call on Him. We're sure we can handle it ourselves—until we begin to sink! Yet Jesus is always there to still the storm, stop the terror. His power has never diminished. He "is the same yesterday and today and forever" (Hebrews 13:8). All we have to do is ask!

Big Picture Story Center

Teacher Materials

Bible Time Line, drawing materials/equipment.

Student Materials

Drawing materials.

Tell the Story

Move the *Bible Time Line* frame to highlight Picture 34. As you tell each part of the story, draw each sketch. Students copy your sketches.

What would your face look like if you were in a boat being rocked by big waves? Today we'll hear how Jesus' friends felt when they were in a storm.

1. When Jesus lived on earth, He could often be found teaching and healing people near the Sea of Galilee. One day, Jesus had been teaching and healing for a VERY long time. Jesus got VERY tired, but so many people who needed His help had come from all over that He and His disciples just stayed and stayed. As the sun set, Jesus and His friends got into a small boat and set out for the other side of the sea, so they could be alone and rest.

1. Draw boat from "C" and lines.

2. While His friends sailed the boat, Jesus lay down on a bench at the back of the boat and fell fast asleep. Suddenly, the wind began to blow. The wind began to knock the boat back and forth. And then, the waves came whooshing up! They slapped the boat so hard, it almost tipped over!

2. Add wind lines and then waves.

3. Jesus' friends began to be very afraid. Some of them rowed as hard as they could, fighting to keep the boat steady. Others began bailing out buckets of water as fast as their arms would go! But even those big, strong fishermen weren't fast enough or strong enough to beat this storm. As the boat began to fill with water, Jesus' friends became even MORE afraid. They knew that if the boat went down, they might all DROWN!

3. Draw bucket from "O" and "U"; add water.

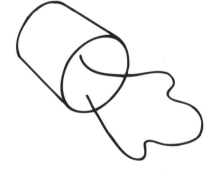

4. And guess who was sleeping through all of this! JESUS! Even with all the rocking and noise from the wind and the waves, He just kept on sleeping soundly! The storm didn't bother Him AT ALL! Finally Jesus' friends yelled, "Teacher, don't you care if we DROWN?!" They were scared and worried and wondered why Jesus didn't do something to HELP!

4. Draw scared face.

5. Maybe Jesus' friends expected Him to help bail the water or row the boat, but what do you think Jesus did? He got up and looked out over the wild, stormy water. Then He said, "Quiet! Be still!" And suddenly, the wind STOPPED! The waves went as flat as if there had never been a wind at all! Jesus' friends stood dripping wet, with buckets and oars in their hands, staring at Jesus. They were AMAZED!

5. "No" slash over stormy scene in #2. Draw new calm sea and boat.

6. Jesus looked from one amazed face to the next and said, "Why are you so afraid? Don't you have faith in Me yet? Don't you know you can trust Me to take care of you?" Jesus' friends had been very afraid of the storm. But what Jesus did to STOP it made them even MORE scared! They said to each other, "Just who IS Jesus? Even the wind and the waves obey Him!"

6. Draw amazed faces.

7. Jesus' friends didn't understand yet that Jesus is God's Son! They didn't know what great power He has and that they could depend on Him to help them in ANY situation, no matter how scary things looked! He is always in control, and we can always go to Him for help.

7. Add conversation balloon to one amazed face.

Get the Big Picture
What did Jesus' friends do at first when they were afraid of the storm? (Rowed hard. Bailed water.) **When they finally asked Jesus for help, what did they discover?**

Jesus' friends learned that no matter how bad things looked, Jesus could always be trusted to help. He was never surprised by even the worst problem! We can always depend on Him, too.

Lesson 34

Bible Verse Object Talk: What's Dependable?

Big Picture Verse

"Blessed is the man who trusts in the Lord, whose confidence is in him." Jeremiah 17:7

Teacher Materials

Bible with bookmark at Jeremiah 17:7, a variety of familiar objects (alarm clock, ruler, pen, flashlight, dictionary, measuring cup, TV remote, etc.).

Present the Object Talk

Show each object one at a time. Invite volunteers to answer these questions about each object:

What is this object used for? When have you used this object? How did this object help you? Why can you depend on this item to help you? When can't you depend on this item to help you?

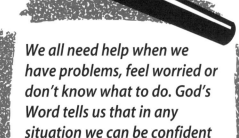

We all need help when we have problems, feel worried or don't know what to do. God's Word tells us that in any situation we can be confident that God will help us. Let's find out why we can depend on God more than any object or person.

Conclude

Even though these items can help us and give us true information in many situations, sometimes they can't help us. Listen to this Bible verse to find out who we can depend on in ANY situation, no matter how bad things look. Read Jeremiah 17:7 aloud. **Why can we be confident in God's help?** (He is more powerful than anything in the world. He loves us and promises to be with us.) Lead students in prayer, thanking God for His help and that He is always with us.

Discussion Questions

1. *What are some other objects that you depend on?* (Car. Bike. Computer.) *Why might these items not always be dependable?* (Cars break down. Bikes get flat tires. Computers "crash.")

2. *What are some times when kids your age need to depend on God's help? people older than you? younger than you?*

3. *What can you do when you need to remember God's help?* (Pray to Him. Remember a Bible verse about His power and help.)

Active Game Center: Balloon Bat

Materials
Masking tape, ruler, inflated and tied balloon, chair or cone.

Prepare the Game
Tear off 3-inch (7.5-cm) strips of tape, two for each student.

Lead the Game
1. Students stand evenly scattered around the playing area. Each student tapes a masking-tape *X* where he or she is standing.

2. Place a chair or cone representing the goal at one end of the playing area.

3. Bat the balloon into the playing area at the

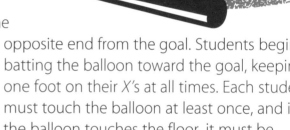

No matter how bad things look or how stuck we feel in a certain situation, we can depend on God because He is in control and promises to help us. We're going to play a game in which we're stuck in one place, but we can still help each other.

opposite end from the goal. Students begin batting the balloon toward the goal, keeping one foot on their *X*'s at all times. Each student must touch the balloon at least once, and if the balloon touches the floor, it must be restarted. After the balloon goes past the goal, begin a new round by batting the balloon into the playing area again.

Options
1. At the start of each new round, students may change places.

2. Adjust size of playing area according to number of students, making sure that students stand at least an arm's distance away from each other. If playing in a small area, students must keep both feet on their *X*'s at all times.

3. Play this game outside on a paved area. Students use chalk to draw *X*'s.

Discussion Questions
1. Even if in our lives we feel stuck in certain situations that make us feel worried, we can be sure God is able to help us in that situation. What can you do to depend on God's help during hard times?
(Pray and ask for His help. Believe God will help. Ask other people who love God for their help.)

2. What are some reasons to depend on God for help? What is He like?

3. How has God helped you or your family in the past? How do you need God's help today?

Art Center: Stormy Seas

Student Materials

White or dark blue construction paper, tissue paper in various shades of blue, purple and gray, glue, crayons or markers, toothpicks.

Lead the Activity

1. Give each student a sheet of white or dark blue construction paper.

2. Students tear tissue paper into small pieces and glue them to construction paper. Encourage students to cover the entire sheet of paper to create stormy sea pictures. **How can you show that there are big waves in your picture? many small waves? What color tissue paper do you think best shows a stormy sea?** Students draw details of waves.

3. Students experiment with arranging toothpicks in boat shapes and then glue the toothpicks onto their pictures.

No matter how bad things look, God is in control and will help us! We're going to make stormy sea pictures to remind us that God is in control of even the sea.

Options

1. If time permits, students create calm sea pictures. Provide white construction paper and light blue, turquoise and yellow tissue paper.

2. Students paint pictures with watercolor paints.

3. Students form boats with yarn lengths instead of toothpicks.

Discussion Questions

1. *What would it be like to be in a boat during a storm? How might you feel?*

2. *Jesus helped His friends when they were afraid of a big storm. When might a kid your age feel afraid?* (Nightmares. Lost in store. Home alone.)

3. *What are some ways that God helps us when we are scared?* (Helps us know what to do. Listens and answers our prayers.)

Lesson 34

Worship Center

Big Picture Verse

"Blessed is the man who trusts in the Lord, whose confidence is in Him." Jeremiah 17:7

Let's thank God that He is always in control, no matter how worried or afraid we feel. I'm glad God promises to help us.

Teacher Materials

Bible, *God's Big Picture* cassette/CD or music video and player, "He Looked" word chart (p. 461 in this book), large sheet of paper on which you have printed Jeremiah 17:7, masking tape.

Sing to God

Play "He Looked," encouraging students to sing along with the music and do the actions shown on the word chart or the music video. **What does this song say God does for us? Why is God able to help us when things look bad? Why can you confidently trust in God?**

Hear and Say God's Word

Display paper on which you have printed Jeremiah 17:7. Have a volunteer read the verse aloud. **To be blessed means to receive God's kindness and to enjoy the good things He wants to give His followers. Who does this verse say is blessed?** (The person who trusts in God. The person who has confidence in God.) Volunteer holds up a number of fingers on one hand. Students repeat the verse in unison as many times as the number of fingers held up. Repeat activity several times, having different volunteers show a different number of fingers each time. **What is one way we can show we have confidence in and trust God?** (Talk to God about our worries.)

Pray to God

Invite volunteers to tell situations in which kids their age need to depend on God's help and remember that He is in control. **Let's tell God we are thankful that we can trust in Him and know that He is always in control.** Lead students in prayer, thanking God that He deserves our trust and asking Him to help us in the situations volunteers mentioned.

Options

1. Ask an older student to lead the Bible verse activity.
2. If students give an offering during this worship time, explain that giving money to God is one way we can show our love and thanks to Him. Describe several ways in which your church uses the offering to help others learn about God and His love.

 **Lesson 34**

Bible Story Coloring Center

Materials

Crayons or markers, a copy of "Jesus calms a storm" picture and story (pp. 159 and 160 from *Bible Story Coloring Pages*) for each student.

Lead the Activity

Students color page 159; read or tell the story on page 160. **How do the disciples look in this picture? Why? How did Jesus help them? When do we need to ask Jesus for help?**

Option

Students color clouds with black chalk or glue aluminum foil to clouds. Students may also cut lightning streaks from foil to glue to the picture and then glue gold glitter to lightning.

Skit Center

Materials

A copy of "Farewell" skit (pp. 311-314 from *The Big Book of Bible Skits*) for each student; optional—highlighter pens.

Lead the Activity

Students choose parts and read the skit, which tells about a time when the apostle Paul and other believers needed to depend on God's care and power. (Optional: Students highlight their parts.) Discuss the skit: **When are kids your age worried or afraid? When might kids your age need to depend on God's power?**

Bible Skills Center

Materials

Materials needed for "Speed Order" and/or "Simon Says Verse" (p. 35 and/or p. 85 from *The Big Book of Bible Skills*).

Lead the Activity

Students complete activities as directed in *The Big Book of Bible Skills.*

A Boy's Lunch

Big Picture Verse

"Command them to do good, to be rich in good deeds, and to be generous and willing to share."
1 Timothy 6:18

THE BIG PICTURE

God can do great things with our gifts to Him.

Scripture Background
Mark 6:30-44; John 6:1-15

Advertising directs us to notice what is newest, brightest, biggest or most expensive. In the light of such seeming grandeur, many smaller things appear less attractive or no longer worthy of our attention. Even in Christian circles, we are encouraged to admire the large church, applaud the grand building or attend the ministry that displays the most striking results. That which seems humble or insignificant is often overlooked.

However, this is not the way of God, for God delights in using the foolish things of the world to confound the wise and using the weak things to overcome the strong. Just as surely as the disciples were completely unable to feed the crowd, so we need to realize that in everything, God not only has the answer, He IS the answer. Jesus not only gave the hungry bread, He IS the Bread of Life. It delights Him when we finally realize that we are completely unable to remedy a situation by our wealth, our education or our power. Only then do our hearts grow ready to give up our own ideas, turn to the all-sufficient One and humbly receive His help!

The other side of this coin is that no one person or act—no matter how poor, unsightly or insignificant that person or act may seem to us—is insignificant to God. When we give to God all that we are and all that we have, whether we think it is significant or not, He is able to take what we give to Him and make it into something completely beyond what we could have imagined! He is infinitely creative! There is no end to what He can do with what is truly given into His hand.

Lesson 35 • Mark 6:30-44; John 6:1-15

Big Picture Story Center

Teacher Materials

Bible Time Line, drawing materials/equipment.

Student Materials

Drawing materials.

Tell the Story

Move the *Bible Time Line* frame to highlight Picture 35. As you tell each part of the story, draw each sketch. Students copy your sketches.

When you are hungry, where do you get food? Today we'll find out where a lot of hungry people got their lunch!

1. Jesus was a VERY famous teacher. Many people wanted to see Him. One day a big crowd gathered to see Jesus. Men and women stopped working and children stopped playing. They heard where Jesus was going to be and RAN to see Him. As Jesus started teaching about God, more and MORE people gathered. Soon hundreds and THOUSANDS of people sat around Jesus, quietly listening. They wanted to hear everything He had to say.

1. Draw stick figure Jesus and many "C"s for crowd.

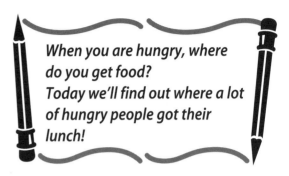

2. As it got late in the day, Jesus' helpers were getting hungry! They knew the people who were listening to Jesus were probably hungry, too. One disciple said to Jesus, "Teacher, we are far from town. It is getting late. Send the people away, so they can go find something to eat." But Jesus just looked at the disciple and said, "YOU feed them!"

2. Draw setting sun.

3. Well, the disciple was very surprised. *Jesus must be joking*, he thought. "There are 5,000 people here!" said the disciple. "We'd have to work for eight months to earn enough money to buy food for all these people! We couldn't POSSIBLY buy enough bread for all these people!"

"Then go and see how much bread you can find," Jesus answered.

3. Disciple from "L"s and "O"s and "C"s.

304

4. The disciples searched and searched and searched through the crowd. Hadn't ANYONE brought food along? Finally Andrew found a young boy who had five loaves of bread and two fish for his lunch. Andrew took the boy to Jesus.

"This boy has five loaves of bread and two fish," said Andrew. "But what good will that do us? This little bit of food would not even feed a few of us. There is not enough here to feed all these people!" Jesus turned to the boy. We don't know what Jesus said to the boy, but we do know that the boy gave his small lunch to Jesus.

4. Basket from "O," "U" and "X"s. Add fish and bread.

5. Jesus asked everyone to sit down in groups. He took the bread in His hands, thanked God for it and divided the bread among the disciples. He told them to go and share it. The disciples gave the pieces to the groups of people. The people shared those pieces of bread, and where there had been five loaves of bread, now there was enough bread for EVERYONE to eat all they wanted!

5. Draw pieces of bread from "C"s and "V"s.

6. Jesus also took the two fish and divided them, giving pieces to the disciples. The disciples took the pieces of fish and shared them with every group of people. And everyone ate and ate and ate, until they were happy and full!

6. Draw happy face.

7. Jesus told His disciples, "Now go and pick up the leftovers and put them in baskets." How could there be LEFTOVERS from just five loaves of bread and two fish? But when they had gathered up the pieces, there were 12 baskets FULL of leftovers! Jesus had been able to feed more than 5,000 people from one little boy's lunch!

7. Twelve baskets from "U"s and "X"s. Add "3"s for leftovers.

Get the Big Picture

What happened as a result of the little boy's gift to Jesus? (Jesus made the lunch into enough food to feed over 5,000 people!) **Why do you think the little boy was willing to give his lunch to Jesus?**

When we are willing to give what we have to God, God can do great things with our gifts to Him!

Bible Verse Object Talk: Gifts to Grow By

Big Picture Verse

"Command them to do good, to be rich in good deeds, and to be generous and willing to share." 1 Timothy 6:18

Teacher Materials

Bible with bookmark at 1 Timothy 6:18, popcorn kernels, measuring cup, popcorn maker, two bowls, napkins; optional—salt.

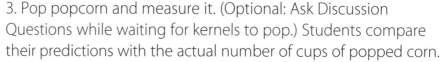

Our gifts to God can be used by Him in many ways. Even small gifts of love and time can make a big difference. Let's look at something that starts out small and grows to be big!

Present the Object Talk

1. Pour popcorn kernels into measuring cup until they measure ½ cup (or the measurement appropriate for your popcorn maker). Ask a volunteer to look at the measuring cup and tell how much corn is in the cup.

2. **What happens to these popcorn kernels when they are heated?** (They pop. They get

bigger.) Invite students to tell how much corn they think will be popped from the ½ cup of kernels.

3. Pop popcorn and measure it. (Optional: Ask Discussion Questions while waiting for kernels to pop.) Students compare their predictions with the actual number of cups of popped corn.

4. Serve popcorn to students. (Optional: Students sprinkle salt on popcorn.)

Conclude

Sometimes we think our gifts to God are small and won't make much of a difference. But even our small gifts can be used by God in great ways. Listen to 1 Timothy 6:18 to find out some ways we can give to God. Read verse aloud. **What does this verse say we can give to others? How are our right actions a gift to God?** (Our right actions show love for God and help others learn about Him.)

Discussion Questions

1. What are some other things that start out small and get bigger? (Cookies, until they're baked. Babies, until they grow to be adults. Plant and tree seeds, until they're planted and watered.)

2. In what ways might kids your age give to God? (Give time to help others. Donate possessions that are needed by others.) Tell students about ways the people in your church give to others to show love for God.

3. What is one way you can give to God?

Active Game Center: Bread, Basket, Fish

Materials

Large sheet of paper, marker.

Lead the Game

1. Students form two teams and stand in the center of a large playing area. Designate a safe zone (wall, door, etc.) for each team, one on each end of the playing area.

2. Play a large-group version of Rock, Paper, Scissors using the words "bread," "basket" and "fish" and these signs: bread—fist, basket—two hands cupped together, fish—two palms pressed together moving like a fish. **Bread defeats fish because bread is wrapped around fish for eating. Basket defeats bread because bread is put into the basket. Fish defeats basket because live fish can flop out of the basket.** Write signs and scoring system on large sheet of paper to which students can refer.

> *When we give to God, He can do great things with our gifts to Him. A boy once gave his lunch to Jesus. Jesus used this small lunch to feed a huge crowd. Let's play a game to remind us of the gifts given by this boy.*

bread

basket

fish

3. Each team huddles near its safe zone and chooses one sign. Then, after moving to the center of the playing area, all members of each team say "Bread, basket, fish" aloud in unison and show their team's chosen sign. Winning team chases the losing team back toward the losing team's safe zone. Any student who is tagged joins the winning team. If both teams show the same sign, teams rehuddle and play again. Repeat game as time permits, with team members taking turns choosing their team's sign.

Options

1. Play game outdoors if possible, using more than one playing area if you have more than 30 students.

2. Play game in pairs. After the first round, each winner plays another winner and each loser plays another loser. Game is over when one student has won five rounds. Play as many games as time and interest allow.

Discussion Questions

1. What did Jesus do with the boy's bread and fish?

2. What can we give to God to show love for Him? (Actions that show obedience to God. Time praying to Him or reading His Word. Money to help others.)

3. How might God use gifts like these? (Kind action might help someone who is sad and remind the person of God's love.)

Lesson 35

Art Center: Fish Prints

Student Materials
Styrofoam cup and pencil for each student, markers, white paper.

Lead the Activity
1. Each student tears off several pieces of Styrofoam from a cup, making each piece approximately 2 to 3 inches (5 to 7.5 cm) in size.
2. Student uses a pencil to etch fish shapes and details into Styrofoam pieces (see sketch a).

Our gifts to God can make a big difference. God can do great things with our gifts to Him. We're going to make fish prints to remember the small gift a boy gave to God and that God used in an amazing way!

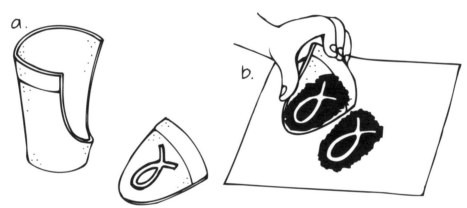

3. Students color over their etchings with markers and quickly press colored side of Styrofoam onto white paper to make prints (see sketch b). Encourage students to draw and print as many fish as time permits.

Option
In addition to cups, you may also provide Styrofoam meat trays for students to use.

Discussion Questions

1. *What are some ways that kids can give to God?* (Show love to others. Help others who have problems. Share with others. Tell others about God.)

2. *In what ways have you seen people in our church give to God?* (People play instruments or sing songs. People give money. People pray for others.)

3. *What are some of the ways our church uses the money people give to God?* (To pay for items the church uses to help others learn about God. To support missionaries who tell others.)

Lesson 35

Worship Center

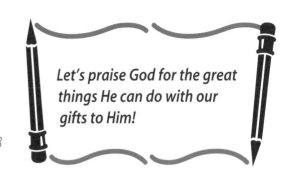

Let's praise God for the great things He can do with our gifts to Him!

Big Picture Verse

"Command them to do good, to be rich in good deeds, and to be generous and willing to share." 1 Timothy 6:18

Teacher Materials

Bible, *God's Big Picture* cassette/CD or music video and player, "Follow the Leader" word chart (p. 453 in this book), large sheet of paper on which you have printed 1 Timothy 6:18, masking tape.

Sing to God

Play "Follow the Leader," encouraging students to sing along with the music and do the actions shown on the word chart or the music video. **Why is sharing with others a way of giving to God?** (God tells us to care for each other. When we obey God, we show our love for Him.) **How does God use a gift of sharing?** (Other people learn about Him. God provides for others' needs through our gifts.)

Hear and Say God's Word

Display paper on which you have printed 1 Timothy 6:18. Have a volunteer read the verse aloud. Say the verse in unison with students. **Who are some people with whom you can share or for whom you can do good things? What are some ways you can treat others that will show love for God?** Then ask students to form a single-file line that curves around the room. Stand at the front of the line and say the first word of the verse. Student standing behind you says the second word. Continue saying words of the verse in this manner until each student has had a turn to say a word of the verse or the verse has been repeated several times.

Pray to God

Praying for someone can be like giving a gift to them. Who are some people you would like to pray for? Students tell prayer requests. Lead students in prayer, encouraging students to pray for the requests they mentioned. End prayer by thanking God for the great things He can do for those people.

Options

1. Students sing and do actions for "I Want to Follow Jesus," "Picture This!" and/or "Jesus' Love," following the actions shown on the word charts (see p. 465, p. 473 and/or p. 467 in this book) or the music video.

2. Lead students in choral speaking with the words of the song "Follow the Leader." Divide the group into two or more groups and assign each group parts of the song to speak.

 **Lesson 35**

Bible Story Coloring Center

Materials
Crayons or markers, a copy of "Jesus uses a boy's lunch to feed 5,000 people" picture and story (pp. 167-168 from *Bible Story Coloring Pages*) for each student.

Lead the Activity
Students color page 167; read or tell the story on page 168. **How many fish and pieces of bread are in the boy's lunch? How did Jesus use the boy's gift to help others?**

Option
Students glue short pieces of green yarn as grass in the picture.

Skit Center

Materials
A copy of "The Talents" skit (pp. 230-233 from *The Big Book of Bible Skits*) for each student; optional—highlighter pens.

Lead the Activity
Students choose parts or form groups of four and read the skit, which tells the story of three servants who chose different ways to use their talents. (Optional: Students highlight their parts.) Ask the discussion questions on page 230.

Bible Skills Center

Materials
Materials needed for "Book Guess" and/or "Map of Miracles" (p. 25 and/or p. 163 from *The Big Book of Bible Skills*).

Lead the Activity
Students complete activities as directed in *The Big Book of Bible Skills*.

A Blind Man Sees the Truth

Big Picture Verse

"Come, let us bow down in worship, let us kneel before the Lord our Maker; for he is our God."
Psalm 95:6,7

THE BIG PICTURE

Believing in God and His power makes us want to worship Him.

Scripture Background
John 9

Every miracle is a parable from which we may learn Christ's ways, and Jesus' healing of the blind man, described by John in chapter 9, is an example of this. When the disciples asked if sin had caused the man's blindness, Christ denied that sin was the cause of the malady and then called attention to God's intention that new sight might be given to him and greater glory might be given to God.

Christ bequeathed to this man not only physical sight, but also an opportunity for faith and an experience for certainty! There was no inherent value in the mud or the water of the Pool of Siloam. Rather, Christ created an opportunity for the man to exercise his faith and literally see the result. When he had obeyed, his experience confirmed his faith—he could see! Regardless of the doubt of the neighbors or the opposition of the Pharisees, the man insisted, "One thing I do know. I was blind but now I see!" (verse 25).

The greatest gift of this healing, however, was the man's admission into fellowship with Christ Himself. Although his insistence that Jesus must be a righteous person caused the man to be cast out of the synagogue, Christ sought out the excommunicated one and brought him into sweet fellowship. He was no longer an outcast, no longer blind; and now, the realm of spiritual sight and fellowship with God was his as well. Is it any wonder that he worshiped Jesus? Jesus has done the same for us. Let us worship such a Savior!

Based on the notes of Henrietta C. Mears.

 **Lesson 36** • John 9

Big Picture Story Center

Teacher Materials
Bible Time Line, drawing materials/equipment.

Student Materials
Drawing materials.

Tell the Story

Move the *Bible Time Line* frame to highlight Picture 36. As you tell each part of the story, draw each sketch. Students copy your sketches.

How would you help a person who cannot see? Today we'll hear how Jesus helped a man who couldn't see.

1. One day a blind man moved slowly through the streets of Jerusalem. When he reached a familiar place, he sat down with his little bowl to beg for the coins people would drop in. In those days, all that most blind people did was wait for people who passed by to give them food or money.

1. Draw beggar's bowl from "U," "O". Add coins.

2. Suddenly the man heard a voice ask, "Teacher, why is that man blind? Did he do something wrong—or did his parents?"

That man is talking about me! the blind man thought. He strained to hear the answer. Jesus was the Teacher! He said, "This man did not sin, nor did his parents. He is blind, and now God's work can be shown in his life."

2. Draw face of blind man from "U," "C"s, "V"s and "7."

3. *What does Jesus mean?* the blind man wondered. He heard Jesus spit on the ground. Then he heard sounds of someone stirring up the dirt. Then the blind man felt gentle, wet hands touching his eyes as Jesus patted damp mud over them! Then Jesus said, "Go wash off the mud in the Pool of Siloam." The blind man slowly made his way to the pool.

3. Draw question mark; add details to make a face.

4. As he splashed cool water on his face, the man realized he could SEE his hands. He could SEE the water! He jumped up, eager to see his friends' faces as he told how Jesus had healed his eyes! He couldn't wait!

4. Draw two hands from "U"s, happy face and water drops.

5. But when the man told his story, not everyone believed him. Some people said he wasn't the same man who had been blind. But he insisted, "I AM the man!" "Then tell us again how your blindness was cured!" they said. "The One called Jesus healed me—and now I can SEE!" the man answered.

5. Suspicious face from "U" and "V"s.

6. The people took the man to the synagogue, the place where people met to pray. When he told the leaders how Jesus had healed him, an argument started! Some shouted that Jesus could not be from God because He had healed the man on the Sabbath (the holy day of rest). Healing on the Sabbath was against God's rules! But others wondered how someone not from God could do such amazing things!

6. Arguing face from "U"s and "V"s. Add fist from "U"s and lines.

7. "All I know is that I was blind, but now I see!" the man replied. When the leaders asked AGAIN how Jesus opened his eyes, the man answered, "I've told you over and over! Do you want to follow Him, too?"

7. Draw face with closed eyes; then change to open eyes.

8. That made the leaders FURIOUS! "WE don't follow Jesus!" they shouted. The man said, "If Jesus were not from God, He could not have healed me." That was IT! The leaders threw the man out of the synagogue!

8. Shut doors from rectangles and lines. Add stick figure.

9. Jesus soon found the man. "Do you believe in the Son of God?" Jesus asked. "Who is He?" the man wanted to know. Jesus said, "You have seen Him. He is talking to you!" The man looked up at Jesus. He knew that voice!! The man said, "Lord, I believe in You!" And he worshiped Jesus, whose power had changed the man's life!

9. Draw smiling face.

Get the Big Picture

What did Jesus do to show how powerful and great He is? What did the blind man learn about Jesus? (That Jesus is God's Son.) **How did the man feel about Jesus?**
Jesus still does wonderful things today! He can do anything and He is always ready to hear our prayers. When we see how great Jesus' power is, it makes us want to worship Him, just as the man did whose blindness had been healed! Worshiping Jesus means we show how much we love and respect Him.

Bible Verse Object Talk: Thumb Wrap!

Big Picture Verse

"Come, let us bow down in worship, let us kneel before the Lord our Maker; for he is our God." Psalm 95:6,7

Teacher Materials

Bible with bookmark at Psalm 95:6,7; masking tape, a variety of classroom objects (pencil, paper, book, cup of water, marker, paper clip).

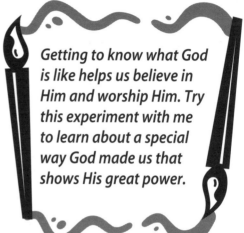

Getting to know what God is like helps us believe in Him and worship Him. Try this experiment with me to learn about a special way God made us that shows His great power.

Present the Object Talk

1. With masking tape, wrap together the thumb and first finger of a volunteer's writing hand. Then ask the volunteer to try to write his or her name on a piece of paper.

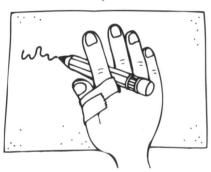

2. Repeat with other volunteers and these tasks: turn pages of a book, drink cup of water, pick up a paper clip, open a door, button or unbutton a coat or sweater, etc.

3. Discuss the activity by asking, **What made your task so hard to do? What would happen if you didn't have a thumb? What would happen if you only had thumbs on your hands?** Volunteers tell ideas.

Conclude

God made our fingers and thumbs to work just right. Listen to these verses that talk about God as the One who made us. Read Psalm 95:6,7 aloud. **One way to worship God for making us is by thanking Him.** Lead students in prayer, thanking God for making us in such special ways.

Discussion Questions

1. *What are some other special ways that God has made us?* (We can taste different flavors. Our arms and legs have joints, so they can bend.)

2. *What's something about the way you're made for which you want to thank God?* Tell students something you're glad God has made you able to do.

3. *What are some of the ways people in our church thank and worship God?* (Sing songs of praise. Pray. Tell others about God's greatness.)

Active Game Center: X Marks the Spot

Materials

Large sheets of paper, markers, masking tape, index cards, scissors, one blindfold for every eight students.

Prepare the Game

Draw several circles inside of each other on a large sheet of paper (see sketch), making one paper target for every eight students. Tape target(s) onto wall at eye level of students. Cut index cards in half.

We want to worship God when we see His great power. In today's Bible story, a blind man saw Jesus' power and realized Jesus is God. Let's play a game to find out what it might be like to be blind.

Lead the Game

1. Give each student half of an index card. Student draws a large *X* on the card and writes initials in one corner. Students make masking-tape loops to put on the backs of their cards.

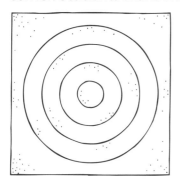

2. Play a game similar to Pin the Tail on the Donkey. Students stand in single-file lines of no more than eight students each, approximately 5 feet (1.5 m) away from a target. Blindfold the first student in each line. Each blindfolded student walks to the target and tries to stick his or her *X* onto the center of the target. Then student takes off blindfold and returns to the end of the line. Next student in line is blindfolded and takes a turn. Repeat activity until all students have had a turn.

Options

1. If you are unable to use blindfolds, put a large paper bag over students' heads or simply ask students to close their eyes while playing the game.

2. Assign points to each section of the target. Students take several turns each to see who can accumulate the most points.

Discussion Questions

1. What are some other things it would be hard to do if you were blind?

2. What are some other ways God has made our bodies in special ways?

3. What are some ways we see God's power? What has God made that shows His power?

4. In what ways can we worship Jesus for His power? (Sing songs about how great He is. Tell Him what we love about Him when we pray to Him. Thank Him for being our God.)

Art Center: Drawing Blind

Student Materials

Markers, paper, kitchen towels.

Lead the Activity

1. Group students in pairs. Tell students that they are going to follow your directions to draw outdoor scenes.

2. Give each student a marker and a sheet of paper. Also give one student in each pair a towel to place over his or her hand and paper while drawing (see sketch).

3. Instruct students to draw things such as these: a tree, a mountain, a path, a bird, a person on the path, a flower, etc. Pause after giving each instruction, giving students time to draw the item. One student in each pair draws with hand covered while the other student draws with hand uncovered.

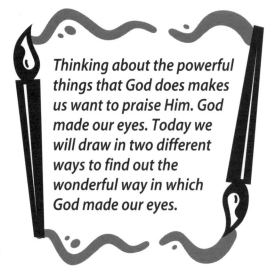

Thinking about the powerful things that God does makes us want to praise Him. God made our eyes. Today we will draw in two different ways to find out the wonderful way in which God made our eyes.

4. After completing the first scene, students turn papers over and repeat the activity with students trading tasks. After completing both scenes, students compare their pictures.

Options

1. Students cover hand and paper with large paper towels or, instead of using towels, students take turns to be blindfolded while they draw.

2. Ask each student to place a sheet of paper on top of his or her head and follow your drawing instructions.

Discussion Questions

1. What made it hard to draw with your hand covered?

2. What are some other things it would be hard or impossible to do if you couldn't see?

3. What are some of your favorite things to look at?

4. What are some other ways in which we learn about God's power? (When we see other wonderful ways in which He has made us. When He gives us what we need. When He helps us know what to do.)

Lesson 36

Worship Center

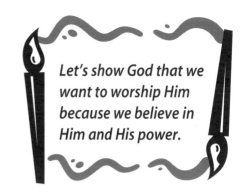

Let's show God that we want to worship Him because we believe in Him and His power.

Big Picture Verses

"Come, let us bow down in worship, let us kneel before the Lord our Maker; for he is our God." Psalm 95:6,7

Teacher Materials

Bible, *God's Big Picture* cassette/CD or music video and player, "He Looked" word chart (p. 461 in this book), large sheet of paper on which you have printed Psalm 95:6,7, masking tape.

Sing to God

Play "He Looked," encouraging students to sing along with the music and do the actions shown on the word chart or the music video. **What are some reasons this song gives us for wanting to worship God?** (He looks for us. He loves us. He won't leave us. He's like the perfect parent. He helps us.)

Hear and Say God's Word

Display paper on which you have printed Psalm 95:6,7. Have a volunteer read the verse aloud. **What does this verse say we should do when we worship?** (Kneel down or bow down before God.) **How does kneeling or bowing show we are worshiping God?** (It shows we are giving respect to someone who is important or powerful, just like people bow to kings and queens.) Divide students into three groups. Assign each group one of the phrases of the verses. Students stand together. Lead groups in saying phrases in order, each group bowing or kneeling as they say the phrases. All groups say verse reference together.

Pray to God

One way we can worship God is by telling Him why we think He is so great. What are some things God has done that we are thankful for? (Forgives our sins. Always loves us. Created the world. Sent Jesus to take the punishment for our sins.) List students' ideas on the back of the Bible verse paper. Lead students in prayer, volunteers completing the sentence **God, I worship You because You....** Students refer to ideas listed on paper.

Options

1. Ask an older student to find the definition of "worship" in a Bible dictionary. Student reads definition aloud during the verse activity.
2. After singing "He Looked," lead students in a silent prayer time. Suggest one thing for everyone to pray about silently (reasons to worship God) and then allow 15 to 20 seconds of silence. End the prayer time with a concluding sentence of prayer.

 **Lesson 36**

Bible Story Coloring Center

Materials

Crayons or markers, a copy of "Jesus helps a blind man see" picture and story (pp. 177-178 from *Bible Story Coloring Pages*) for each student.

Lead the Activity

Students color page 177; read or tell the story on page 178. **Who needed help in this picture? How did Jesus use His power to help the man?**

Option

When students are finished coloring pictures, allow students to cut the pictures into five or six puzzle pieces. Students trade pieces with a partner and put puzzles together.

Skit Center

Materials

A copy of "It's a Miracle" skit (pp. 234-239 from *The Big Book of Bible Skits*) for each student; optional—highlighter pens.

Lead the Activity

Students choose parts and read the skit, which tells about what the religious leaders thought of Jesus' miracles and His claim to forgive sins. (Optional: Students highlight their parts.) Ask the discussion questions on page 234.

Bible Skills Center

Materials

Materials needed for "Ball Toss" and/or "Rolling Words" (p. 28 and/or p. 83 from *The Big Book of Bible Skills*).

Lead the Activity

Students complete activities as directed in *The Big Book of Bible Skills*.

 **Lesson 37**

Parable of the Good Samaritan

Big Picture Verse

"Be completely humble and gentle; be patient, bearing with one another in love." Ephesians 4:2

THE BIG PICTURE

Loving God means loving all kinds of people.

Scripture Background
Luke 10:25-37

The story about the good Samaritan is an ironic parable. Consider the priest and the Levite who passed the beaten man. They may have been returning from Temple duties (teaching and singing about God's law of love, of course), or they were on their way to the Temple to do the same. If they chose to stop and help the beaten man and he died, they would become unclean, unable to serve in the Temple. If they helped the beaten man and he lived, they would be delayed and unable to serve in the Temple! In any case, showing love for this injured brother of their own race was out of the question. Their priority was to worship God in the Temple, not to act on His law of love! Following their rules to show their love for God was more important to them than God's law of love that demanded they help the wounded man.

Another irony is that prejudice against Samaritans ran high in Israel—they were considered unclean half-breeds. The Samaritan who helped the man out of compassion would have been avoided (or even hated) by many Jews. Yet he did not take into account the wounded man's ethnic or religious background; he simply helped him! God's law of love moved him to compassion. Unlike the priest and the Levite, the Samaritan considered the beaten man's needs ahead of possible consequences to himself.

Who is your neighbor, by Jesus' definition? Think for a moment. Your neighbor's race, position or even prejudice toward you may need to be ignored. Like the Samaritan did, we need to demonstrate our love for God by loving every person He places in our paths. Such love may not easily be given, but by His Spirit, God will make us able to act out of compassion and be a neighbor to all those we meet.

Big Picture Story Center

Teacher Materials
Bible Time Line, drawing materials/equipment.

Student Materials
Drawing materials.

Tell the Story
Move the *Bible Time Line* frame to highlight Picture 37. As you tell each part of the story, draw each sketch. Students copy your sketches.

Who has helped you when you have been hurt?
Today we'll hear about someone who was hurt and needed help.

1. One day Jesus was talking to a man about God's command to love your neighbor as yourself. The man asked Jesus, "Well, then, who is my neighbor?" Jesus answered the man's question by telling a story.

1. Draw a question mark.

2. Jesus' story happened on the road to Jericho. This road went up and down and around many hills. People who traveled the road had to be very careful of robbers hiding in the hills. These robbers hurt people and took their money! Jesus said, "There was a man traveling from Jerusalem to Jericho. He hurried past one hill and another hill and another hill. And then it happened!

2. Draw a curvy road; add hills from "C"s.

3. "Some robbers jumped out and grabbed him. They tore off his clothes and beat him and took all his money. Then they left the man lying beside the road. The poor man was so badly hurt, he couldn't get up. All he could do was hope that someone would come by and help him.

3. Draw wounded man from "3" and "7"s.

4. "And THEN—he heard footsteps! Someone was coming! The man turned his head and saw a priest. *Oh good,* thought the man. He knew a priest taught the people about God. He was sure the priest would help him. But the priest looked at the hurt man, crossed to the other side of the road and WALKED AWAY.

4. Add "U"s for footprints walking away.

5. "The poor hurt man was all alone again. And THEN—he heard more footsteps. Someone else was coming! The man turned his head and saw a Levite! *Oh good!* the poor hurt man thought. He knew a Levite taught the people God's laws. He was sure the Levite would help him. But the Levite crossed to the other side of the road and WALKED AWAY! The poor hurt man was sad and all alone again. He must have wondered if ANYONE would ever help him!

5. Add another set of footprints beside the first.

6. "And THEN—he heard the clippety-clop of a donkey! The hoofbeats were getting closer. Someone was coming! *Maybe this person will help me,* thought the poor hurt man.

6. Draw donkey from 2 "U"s and 2 "V"s; add details.

7. "The man on the donkey stopped. He got off his donkey, and he knelt down beside the hurt man. Now the amazing thing about THIS was that the man who stopped to help was a Samaritan. For hundreds of years, Jews had been ENE-MIES of the Samaritans. Jews and Samaritans didn't like each other at all! But this did not stop the Samaritan from helping the hurt man—even though the hurt man was a Jew.

7. Write "ENEMY"; add "no" slash.

8. "The Samaritan put soothing medicine on the man's wounds. He bandaged all the hurts and gently helped the hurt man onto the donkey. At last they came to an inn, a place where travelers could stay. The Samaritan put the man to bed and tried to make the man comfortable. He even paid the owner of the inn to take care of the hurt man!"

8. Bottle from 2 "O"s and lines.

9. When Jesus finished the story He asked, "Which of the men was a neighbor to the hurt man?" Of course, it was the man who HELPED him! Then Jesus said, "Go and do the same. Be a good neighbor to ANYONE who needs your help!"

9. Draw heart.

Get the Big Picture

Who showed God's love in this story? What would most people have expected the Samaritan to do? (To walk away from the man who was his enemy.)

The Samaritan acted as if the hurt man were his neighbor. Jesus told this story to help us understand that if we love God, we should show it by loving all kinds of people!

Bible Verse Object Talk: Balloon Drop

Big Picture Verse

"Be completely humble and gentle; be patient, bearing with one another in love." Ephesians 4:2

Teacher Materials

Bible with bookmark at Ephesians 4:2, balloons; optional—balls.

Present the Object Talk

1. Invite a volunteer to stand next to you. **Let's see how many balloons (Kaitlyn) can hold.** Ask other volunteers to blow up balloons and give them to volunteer to hold. (Optional: Use balls instead of balloons.)

The Bible is full of stories about what it means to love God. One way to love God is to show His love to all kinds of people by caring about their needs. Let's watch someone in our class try to help another person.

2. When volunteer cannot hold any more balloons, ask him or her to help you with a classroom task (open or shut a door, find verse in Bible, etc.). After volunteer expresses difficulty in helping you while still holding onto the balloons, ask, **What would you have to do in order to help me?** (Drop the balloons.) **When others need our help, sometimes we need to drop what we're doing or put aside until later something we're doing so that we can help them.**

3. **Listen to Ephesians 4:2 to find the word that describes someone who thinks about what others need instead of always thinking about him- or herself.** Read Ephesians 4:2 aloud. **Someone who is humble cares about other people and wants to help them. What else does this verse say we should do?** (Be patient with others as a way of showing love.) **Ephesians 4:2 doesn't say to care only about people we like or who like us. When we say we love God, it means we want to show His love to all kinds of people.**

Conclude

Lead students in prayer, asking God's help in showing love for Him by caring for others.

Discussion Questions

1. In what way has someone been patient with you? helped you with something you needed?

2. When might you need to stop doing something in order to help someone who needs help? (Stop watching TV when parent needs help setting the table. Stop playing a game at recess when a friend gets hurt.)

3. How many different ways of helping someone can you think of?

Active Game Center: Relay Fun

Materials
Index cards, marker.

Prepare the Game
Print each of these kinds of people on separate index cards: baby, old person, basketball player, soccer player, toddler, movie star, teenager, race-car driver, juggler.

Loving God means loving all kinds of people. We're going to play a game in which we need different kinds of people to play.

Lead the Game
1. Group students into two equal teams. Teams line up on one side of an open area in your classroom. Stand between the two teams.

2. At your signal, the first student in each team runs to you. Show him or her one of the cards you prepared. Student returns to his or her team and then moves across the room and back as though he or she is a (basketball player). Students continue taking turns until all students on the team have had a turn. Play as many rounds of the game as time permits.

Options
1. Make additional cards to use in the relay: tiptoe, walk backwards, jump, hop, slide, etc.

2. Place a chair or cone on the opposite side of the room from each team. Students must move around the chair or cone to complete the relay.

Discussion Questions

1. What kinds of people were needed to play this game? (Toddler. Basketball player.)

2. One way to love God is to show His love to all kinds of people. How can you show love to people who are different from you? (Play with or talk to kids you don't usually play with. Ask a new person to sit with you and your friends at lunch. Don't join in with others who are making fun of someone else.)

3. Why does God want us to love others? (Because God made and loves all people. Each person is important to God.)

Lesson 37

Art Center: Give It Away!

Student Materials

A cleaned empty can (coffee, juice, potato chip, soup, etc.) for each student, scissors, wrapping paper, tape, collage materials (fabric pieces, buttons, trim, beads, etc.), glue, markers.

Lead the Activity

1. Students cut and tape wrapping paper to fit around their cans.

2. Students decorate cans by gluing collage materials onto the cans and drawing designs or pictures with markers.

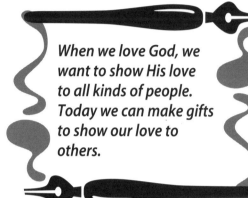

When we love God, we want to show His love to all kinds of people. Today we can make gifts to show our love to others.

3. As students are decorating cans, ask volunteers to tell to whom they wish to give their cans. **When will you give this person the can? What do you think he or she might use it for?**

Options

1. Provide one or more school supply items (crayons, small paper tablets, pencils, erasers, markers, stickers, etc.). Students place items into decorated cans. Give cans to a charitable organization for distribution to needy children.

2. If you have mostly younger students, precut wrapping paper to fit around cans.

3. If you are unable to provide enough cans, students may decorate lunch bags for use by a shelter that distributes food to children.

Discussion Questions

1. What are some other gifts you have given to people? What are some gifts people have given to you?

2. What are some other ways in which we can show God's love to others? What kinds of gifts can we give them that we don't make or buy? (Patience. Listening. Help to complete a task.)

3. When might it be hard for a kid to show love to someone?

Lesson 37

Worship Center

Big Picture Verse

"Be completely humble and gentle; be patient, bearing with one another in love." Ephesians 4:2

Let's thank God that He loves us and helps us show His love to all kinds of people.

Teacher Materials

Bible, *God's Big Picture* cassette/CD or music video and player, "Jesus' Love" word chart (p. 467 in this book), large sheet of paper on which you have printed all but four words of Ephesians 4:2 (leave blanks for "humble," "gentle," "patient" and "love"), masking tape.

Sing to God

Play "Jesus' Love," encouraging students to sing along with the music and do the actions shown on the word chart or the music video. **In what ways does this song say Jesus showed love for others?** (Healed the sick and sad people. Called His disciples to follow Him. Made blind people able to see.) **How can we show love for others?**

Hear and Say God's Word

Display paper on which you have printed Ephesians 4:2. Help students guess the missing words by pointing to the first blank and giving a clue such as, "This is a word that means the opposite of proud." When students guess the word "humble," print it in the blank space. Repeat for the other three words. Students recite completed verse together. **What does "bearing with one another in love" mean?** (Caring about people even when they are mean to us or are different from us.)

Pray to God

It's not always easy to care for other people. Let's ask God for help by saying the words of Ephesians 4:2 as a prayer. Ask students to repeat the words of this prayer after you, one phrase at a time: **Dear God, please help us be completely humble and gentle and patient, bearing with one another in love. In Jesus' name, amen.**

Options

1. Invite older students to think of motions illustrating the words of Ephesians 4:2.

2. Ask students to read from a dictionary the definitions for the words "humble," "gentle" and "patient." As each definition is read aloud, invite volunteers to tell ways to demonstrate these words in the way they treat others.

Bible Story Coloring Center

Materials

Crayons or markers, a copy of "Jesus tells about a good Samaritan" picture and story (pp. 179-180 from *Bible Story Coloring Pages*) for each student.

Lead the Activity

Students color page 179; read or tell the story on page 180. **Who needs help in this picture? Why? Who helped the man? Who has helped you when you were hurt? How?**

Option

Students draw pictures of ways in which they can help others. Cut around completed pictures and glue them to a large sheet of butcher paper. Print "Loving God means loving all kinds of people" on the paper and display it in a well-traveled area of your church.

Skit Center

Materials

A copy of "Mine, Mine, Mine" skit (pp. 377-380 from *The Big Book of Bible Skits*) for each student; optional—highlighter pens.

Lead the Activity

Students form pairs and read the skit, which tells about what two kids think of showing God's love to others. (Optional: Students highlight their parts.) Ask the questions on page 377 and invite volunteers to tell ways they can care for others.

Bible Skills Center

Materials

Materials needed for "Get a Clue!" and/or "Missing Halves" (p. 46 and/or p. 145 from *The Big Book of Bible Skills*).

Lead the Activity

Students complete activities as directed in *The Big Book of Bible Skills*.

The Welcoming Father

Big Picture Verse

"The Lord is gracious and compassionate, slow to anger and rich in love." Psalm 145:8

THE BIG PICTURE

God is eager to love and forgive us.

Scripture Background
Luke 15:1,2,11-32

The parable of the prodigal son is probably more preached-about than any other parable, but the story remains fresh, for this young man's tale is full of lessons. First, he did not deliberately set out to wreck himself or hurt his father. He simply chose to please himself, thinking this would bring joy. However, pleasing ourselves is the essence of sin, making us thoughtless of the pain to others or the damage to ourselves. The young man meant no harm, but he caused a great deal of it. Second, he paid a terrible price for his self-pleasing: it cost him the fellowship of his father, all the joys of home and, ultimately, his freedom; for when his money was gone, he was sent to feed swine—not something he chose to do!

But when the young man dared to face the facts, he didn't say "I will reform" or "I will work harder"; he said, "I will go to my father!" No other plan would suffice. And when his father saw him coming, he did not stand waiting for a confession of guilt or a request to live with the servants. He ran to meet his son, to hug him and to smother him with kisses! The son's very act of coming home was confession enough! So is our Father with us. He longs for us to come to the place where we face our need of Him. He looks longingly for us to come home. And He knows it is easier for us to confess our wrongs when our heads are pillowed on His shoulder.

Big Picture Story Center

Teacher Materials
Bible Time Line, drawing materials/equipment.

Student Materials
Drawing materials.

Tell the Story
Move the *Bible Time Line* frame to highlight Picture 38. As you tell each part of the story, draw each sketch. Students copy your sketches.

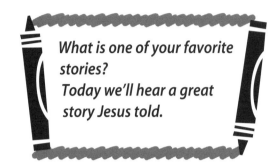

What is one of your favorite stories?
Today we'll hear a great story Jesus told.

1. Once Jesus went to a dinner where there were many people who were proud of the way they obeyed God. Some of them said Jesus was wrong to care about people who didn't follow God's laws as well as they did. They thought God only loved people who obeyed God. So after dinner, Jesus told a story to teach what God's love is really like.

2. The story went something like this: A man had two sons and owned a big farm. He loved both his sons very much and planned to divide his money between them when they were older. But the younger son didn't want to WAIT for his share of the money. He wanted it NOW! He was eager to leave home and do what he wanted, even if it was wrong.

3. So the father sadly gave the younger son his part of the money. The younger son said good-bye and headed to a faraway city. There, he started spending his money VERY foolishly—on wild parties and anything he thought would make him happy. He had lots of friends who enjoyed the parties he paid for!

4. But one day the younger son looked in his money bag. It was completely EMPTY! All of a sudden, people he thought were his friends didn't come to see him anymore. He was all alone. And he was in big TROUBLE. He had no money to buy food or to pay for a place to live. This was awful!

1. Draw table; add "C"s for people.

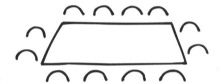

2. Three "U"s; add details to make faces of father and sons.

3. Full money bag from "U" and "C"s.

4. Empty money bag. Add details to make sad face.

5. At last he found a job taking care of pigs! And he was so HUNGRY all of the time, he started thinking about eating the pigs' food!

5. Pigs from "O"s, "C"s and "V"s.

6. One morning the younger son thought, *I am starving to death while the people who work for my father have plenty of food to eat. I'm going to go back home. I'll tell my father I was wrong. I'll tell him I don't deserve to be treated like his son anymore. But I'll ask him if I can please be his servant.*

6. Print word "DAD" in thought balloon.

7. Meanwhile, back on the farm, the father missed his younger son VERY much. Every day he looked down the road, just hoping his son might be coming home again. One day, he looked and someone was walking down the road! Could it be? YES! It was his son! The father was SO excited, he RAN to meet his son! He hugged him and kissed him. He couldn't hug him enough, even though his boy was smelly and dirty and ragged and didn't DESERVE to be kissed at all!

7. Draw 2 faces from "7"s and "C"s; add arms from "C"s and legs from lines.

8. The father told his servants to bring his son new clothes and sandals and a ring of his own. Then the father had a BIG party to celebrate! Even though the younger son had been foolish and selfish and wrong, his father still loved him and forgave him! But the older brother didn't think the father should welcome his foolish brother at all!

8. Ring from "O"s and triangle.

9. The people at the dinner who thought they were better than others were like that older brother. Jesus told this story because He wanted them to know that God is like that patient, loving father. God is so full of love for us, He wants us with Him and wants to forgive us when we do wrong!

9. Open-armed father from "L"s and "U"s; add details.

Get the Big Picture

How would you describe the father? the younger son? What did the father do to show his love? (Welcomed his son. Celebrated his return.)

No matter what wrong things we do, God is patient and loving. He is eager to love and forgive us. That's a good reason to celebrate!

Bible Verse Object Talk: Fast and Slow

Big Picture Verse

"The Lord is gracious and compassionate, slow to anger and rich in love." Psalm 145:8

Teacher Materials

Bible with bookmark at Psalm 145:8, scratch paper, pencil, coin, crackers; optional—stopwatch or watch with second hand.

God's love and forgiveness are so amazing that the Bible talks about them in many different ways. Let's do some actions that help us understand the ways in which God treats us.

Present the Object Talk

1. Invite volunteers to take turns seeing how slowly and then how quickly they can complete a variety of tasks: do three jumping jacks, write his or her name, crumple up four pieces of paper, flip a coin five times, eat a cracker. (Optional: Time students using watch, limiting the slow actions to about 30 seconds.) If you have a small class, students complete tasks individually. If you have a large class, ask more than one volunteer to complete tasks at the same time.

2. **Your actions were good examples of what it means to do things slowly and what it means to do things quickly. Psalm 145:8 tells us something God is slow to do and something God is quick to do.** Read verse aloud. **What does this verse say God is slow to do?** (Be angry.) **What does this verse say God is eager to give us a lot of?** (His love.) **God cares for each of us so much that He is eager and glad to show His love to us. He is quick to forgive us when we've done wrong things.**

Conclude

Lead students in prayer, thanking God for His love and forgiveness.

Discussion Questions

1. What are some ways in which God has shown His love to us? (Hears and answers prayer. Gives us courage. Gives what we need every day. Provided a way for us to become members of His family.)

2. When might kids your age feel as though God doesn't love them? (When they've done wrong. When they have problems. When prayers aren't answered right away.)

3. How many different words can you think of that describe God's love and forgiveness?

Active Game Center: Favorite Things

Materials
None.

Lead the Game
Students stand in the middle of the room. As you ask the questions below, point to opposite walls of the room as you say each answer. Each student runs and touches the wall that indicates his or her answer.

> *The Bible teaches us that God is eager and glad to love and forgive us. Let's play a game to show some things that we are eager about.*

Ask questions such as "What's your favorite thing to eat—ice cream or cookies?" "What's your favorite game to play—baseball or soccer?" "What's your favorite thing to do—watch TV or play with a friend?" "What's your favorite thing to ride—a skateboard or a bike?" "What's your favorite thing to do with your family—go to a park or go out to eat?" "What's your favorite pet—a cat or a dog?"

Ask additional questions as needed, playing as many rounds as time allows. (Note: Students with answers other than the two given with the question sit down in the middle of the room. Invite these students to say their answers aloud.)

Options
1. Ask an older student to ask the questions or suggest additional questions.

2. Alternate the way in which students move during this game. Instead of running to the wall, students may hop, skip, walk backwards, tiptoe, etc.

Discussion Questions
1. What does it mean to be eager? (To be so excited about something you want to do it right away. To look forward to something so much you can hardly stand waiting for it to happen.)

2. What are some things you are eager to do?

3. What is God eager to do for us? (Love and forgive us.)

4. How does it make you feel to know God is eager to love and forgive you? Since God forgives us, how should we treat others?

Art Center: Prodigal Son Puppets

Student Materials

One lunch bag and two tongue depressors for each student, crayons, markers; optional—Bible.

Lead the Activity

1. Each student colors a house scene on one side of an upside-down bag and an outdoor scene of a road on the other side.

2. Students draw faces and clothing on tongue depressors to represent characters in the story—father and younger son.

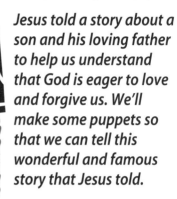

Jesus told a story about a son and his loving father to help us understand that God is eager to love and forgive us. We'll make some puppets so that we can tell this wonderful and famous story that Jesus told.

3. Students use the bag and puppets to act out the story. (Optional: Read Luke 15:11-24 aloud as students act out the story.) Repeat story as time permits.

Options

1. Bring fabric, scissors and glue. Students use these materials to clothe their tongue-depressor puppets.

2. Older students may make additional puppets representing the older son, servants, friends of the younger son and pigs. Read verses 25-32 in addition to the verses listed above.

3. Older students may enjoy telling the story while others act it out.

Discussion Questions

1. *How would you describe the actions of the father in this story?* (Patient. Loving.) *What was the son like?* (Selfish and then sad.)

2. *What did the younger son do that was wrong? How did the father feel about the son's actions?*

3. *How did the father show that he was glad and eager to forgive the son?*

4. *How does God show that He is eager to love and forgive us?* (Promises to always be with us and help us. Helps us do what's right.)

 Lesson 38

Worship Center

Big Picture Verse

"The Lord is gracious and compassionate, slow to anger and rich in love." Psalm 145:8

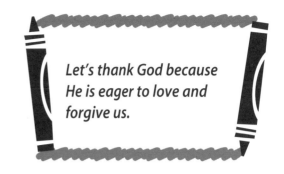

Let's thank God because He is eager to love and forgive us.

Teacher Materials

Bible, *God's Big Picture* cassette/CD or music video and player, "He Looked" word chart (p. 461 in this book), large sheet of paper on which you have printed Psalm 145:8, four index cards on which you have printed the following words or phrases, one word or phrase per card: "gracious," "compassionate," "slow to anger," "rich in love."

Sing to God

Play "He Looked," encouraging students to sing along with the music and do the actions shown on the word chart or the music video. **What words of this song remind us that God is eager to love and forgive us?** (God looked for us until He found us because He loves us each so much.)

Hear and Say God's Word

Display paper on which you have printed Psalm 145:8. Give index cards to volunteers. Say the word or phrase on the card as you hand it to each volunteer. **As I read Psalm 145:8, listen for the word or words on your card. When you hear them, stand up and hold up your card. The rest of us will echo the word or words as you hold up your card.** Say verse, pausing for volunteers to hold up cards and students to echo the word or words. Collect cards and give to different volunteers. Say Psalm 145:8 aloud, allowing students with cards to pop up and say words. Repeat as time allows, with different students holding the cards each time. **What does Psalm 145:8 say about God? What are some other things you know about God?**

Pray to God

Lead students in prayer, inviting volunteers to complete this sentence prayer: **Dear God, Your love makes me feel....** End the prayer time by thanking God for His love and forgiveness.

Options

1. Students sing "Picture This!" and/or "Jesus' Love" (p. 473 and/or p. 467 in this book) and do the actions shown on the word chart or the music video.

2. Invite a musician from your church to play one or more of the suggested songs for this lesson on a guitar, flute, trumpet, etc.

 **Lesson 38**

Bible Story Coloring Center  FOR YOUNGER CHILDREN

Materials
Crayons or markers, a copy of "Jesus tells about a patient father" picture and story (pp. 183-184 from *Bible Story Coloring Pages*) for each student.

Lead the Activity
Students color page 183; read or tell the story on page 184. **How does the father appear to feel? How do you think the son feels? What did the father do to show he loved his son?**

Option
Students glue completed pictures onto large sheets of construction paper and then draw conversations balloons for the father and son. Students write what they think the father and son are saying.

Skit Center FOR OLDER CHILDREN

Materials
A copy of "Forgive and Forget" skit (pp. 226-229 from *The Big Book of Bible Skits*) for each student; optional—highlighter pens.

Lead the Activity
Students form groups of four and read the skit, which tells the parable Jesus told about the forgiving master and the unforgiving servant. (Optional: Students highlight their parts.) Ask the discussion questions on page 226.

Bible Skills Center FOR OLDER CHILDREN

Materials
Materials needed for "Spell It!" and/or "Picture Parables" (p. 26 and/or p. 157 from *The Big Book of Bible Skills*).

Lead the Activity
Students complete activities as directed in *The Big Book of Bible Skills*.

 **Lesson 39**

A Widow's Small Gift

Big Picture Verse

"Freely you have received, freely give."
Matthew 10:8

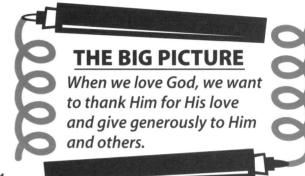

THE BIG PICTURE
When we love God, we want to thank Him for His love and give generously to Him and others.

Scripture Background
Mark 12:41-44; Luke 20:45-47; 21:1-4

The Court of Women, large enough to hold 15,000 people, was where one could find the Temple treasury. This treasury consisted of a row of large closed boxes with funnel-shaped metal tops into which one put money offerings. In full view of the crowd, every-one could present his or her coins. But imagine the attention a wealthy person would draw as he or she poured a bagful of coins down a metal funnel! Even amid milling throngs of people, such a noise would call attention to the fact that here was a wealthy person!

At the edge of this noisy, milling crowd, Jesus and His disciples stood people-watching one day. But as they gazed at that crowd, Jesus pointed out only one person for His friends to watch. The widow Jesus pointed out came quietly to the offering box and slipped in two *lepta*—the smallest, thinnest coins made. Together, the widow's two coins were worth about half a cent. Yet out of all that throng, rich and poor, she was the only one whom Jesus thought important enough to point out. The reason? She had given more than anyone else: she had given all she had.

God still is not impressed with the amount we give. His measure of generosity focuses not on how much we give but on why we give. He is looking to see if our hearts are open and willing to give all to Him, because what He calls us to give today is the same as it was then—everything! And in Him, we can give generously with perfect confidence in God's care for us. Like the widow, we can freely give that last half-cent, because we know He will care for us.

Big Picture Story Center

Teacher Materials

Bible Time Line, drawing materials/equipment.

Student Materials

Drawing materials.

Tell the Story

Move the *Bible Time Line* frame to highlight Picture 39. As you tell each part of the story, draw each sketch. Students copy your sketches.

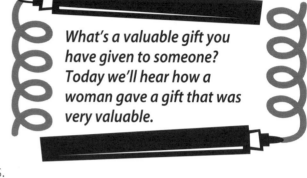

What's a valuable gift you have given to someone? Today we'll hear how a woman gave a gift that was very valuable.

1. In Bible times many people worshiped God at the Temple in Jerusalem. Jesus worshiped there, too. Often when Jesus was at the Temple, people crowded around Him to hear everything He said. One thing Jesus said on this day was to watch out for people who do good things just to impress others.

1. Letter "WATCH OUT"; turn "O" and "U" into eyes.

2. After teaching all day, Jesus and His friends sat down near a row of big offering boxes. People brought gifts of money to the Temple and put the money in these boxes. Some of the people were very rich, throwing in handfuls of gold coins from their big money bags. Sometimes the rich people looked around to smile and nod when others noticed how much money they were giving. The sound of many big, valuable coins made it obvious when a rich person had given a lot of money.

2. Offering box from rectangle, "O", "V." Add coins, smiling face.

3. Jesus and His friends watched person after person put money in the boxes. Jesus' friends may have been amazed at how much money some people gave! Perhaps they wondered why Jesus had warned them to be careful of people who do good things to impress others! *Weren't these rich people doing a good thing by giving God so much money?*

3. Add more coins and a question mark.

4. Then Jesus and His friends saw a very poor woman walk to an offering box. She didn't have to carry a big bag. She had only two little coins in her hand. They were so TINY that both of them together were worth less than one of our smallest coins. The poor woman quietly dropped those two tiny coins into the offering box and then walked away. If the two little coins made any sound, no one seemed to notice.

4. Add two tiny coins to others.

5. Of course, Jesus knew all about the poor woman. He knew that she had to work very hard to get money for food. He knew that those two little coins were ALL the money she had in the world!

5. Circle two coins; add "ALL."

6. Jesus told His friends, "This poor woman has given MORE than all the others." *What on earth could Jesus mean by that? How could the poor woman's two tiny coins be worth MORE than all the gold coins the others put in?* Jesus explained, "After they have given to God, those other people still have plenty of money left for themselves. But THIS woman has no more. She gave ALL she had."

6. Draw two empty hands from "U"s and lines.

7. As the disciples thought about what Jesus said, they must have begun to understand. The poor woman didn't give her two little coins because she HAD to. She certainly wasn't trying to IMPRESS anyone by what she gave. She gave her gift to God ONLY because she loved God VERY much. She trusted Him, too. She knew that God loved and cared for her. And she wanted to show her thankfulness to Him. Jesus' explanation helped His friends understand that the poor woman's gift really was the biggest gift of all!

7. Draw gift box. Add heart around gift.

Get the Big Picture

How did the woman show her love for God? How were the other people who gave money different from the woman?

It's good to give money to God, but what's most important to God is that we love Him first and most of all! When we love God most, we give generously. We may think we don't have much to give to God. But how much we give is less important than whether or not we give it gladly and out of love.

Bible Verse Object Talk: It's Free!

Big Picture Verse

"Freely you have received, freely give."
Matthew 10:8

Teacher Materials

Bible with bookmark at Matthew 10:8, marker, one index card and one bite-sized snack item, sticker or small prize for each student.

Prepare the Object Talk

On one card, print the word "FREE." (If you have a large group, prepare several "FREE" cards.) Shuffle "FREE" card in with blank cards.

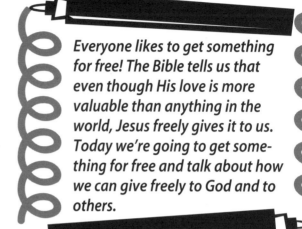

Everyone likes to get something for free! The Bible tells us that even though His love is more valuable than anything in the world, Jesus freely gives it to us. Today we're going to get something for free and talk about how we can give freely to God and to others.

Present the Object Talk

1. Students sit in a circle. Give each student a card, keeping cards facedown.

2. At your signal, students pass cards facedown around the circle. When you signal "stop," each student looks at his or her card. Student holding card marked "FREE" gets a (snack) for him- or herself and gives a (snack) to one other student. Repeat the activity until all students have received a (snack).

Conclude

In this activity we received our (snacks) for free. Matthew 10:8 talks about the way in which Jesus gives us what we need. Read verse aloud. **Jesus said these words when He was telling His followers to help and care for others. Jesus has given His love to us for free! We don't have to do anything to earn it!** Lead students in prayer, thanking God for His free gift of love and asking His help in giving freely in return.

Discussion Questions

1. What are some other things God freely gives us? (Forgiveness of sins. Friends and family.) Talk with students about God's free gift of salvation. (See "Leading a Child to Christ" on p. 30.)

2. What can we give to God that money can't buy? (Our love. Our obedience.)

3. What can we give to others that money can't buy? (Friendship. Honesty. Patience.)

Lesson 39

Active Game Center: Toss 'Em

Materials

One or more of each of the following containers: paper plates, paper cups, coffee cans, plastic bowls; masking tape; two coins for each student.

Prepare the Game

Set out containers and make a masking-tape square as shown in sketch. (If you have more than 16 students, make additional squares with additional containers in them.)

In the Bible we read a story about a poor woman who showed she loved God by generously giving her last two coins. We are going to play a game with coins and think about how we can give generously to God as a way of thanking Him for His love.

Lead the Game

Give each student two coins. Students stand around the square. Students take turns tossing coins, trying to get coins into containers. When a student's coin lands in a container, he

or she tells a way to give to God or to others (donate food to needy people, treat others kindly, pray for others, etc.). After each student has had a turn, collect coins and redistribute. Students trade places around the square and play again. Repeat game as time permits.

Options

1. Set up the containers on one end of a table. Students line up and toss coins from the opposite end of the table.

2. Place candy or stickers on some of the plates and in the bottom of some of the cans, bowls and cups. When a student's coin lands in one of these containers, student gets candy or stickers.

3. Ask one or two older students to distribute and collect coins.

Discussion Questions

1. What does it mean to give generously? (Give more than what is required or expected.)

2. What are some ways you can give generously at school? (Share your lunch. Help others with what you are learning if they don't understand. Help your teachers.) *at home?* (Offer to do chores that you don't usually do. Share toys with your brothers and sisters. Share a computer game.)

3. How can you give generously to God to show your thankfulness for His love? (Give my time by reading the Bible and praying. Care for others to show God's love.)

Art Center: Coin Rubbings

Student Materials

A variety of coins, paper, crayons.

Lead the Activity

Student places a coin under a sheet of paper and carefully rubs a crayon over the coin so that the design of the coin appears on the paper. Encourage students to make rubbings of a variety of coins, placing the rubbings to create an interesting design.

When we love God, we want to thank Him and give generously to Him. Giving money at church and to people who need it is one way to give to God. We are doing coin rubbings today to remind us to give to God.

Options

1. Unwrap crayons so that students may rub the side of each crayon.

2. Provide leaves, bark, cardboard shapes and other textured objects with which students may make rubbings.

3. Provide chalk for students to use in making rubbings.

Discussion Questions

1. **What are some of the things our church does with the money we give?** (Pays the people who work at the church. Sends it to missionaries. Buys paper and crayons. Pays electricity bills.)

2. **What are some other ways to give to God besides giving money?** (Give time helping others. Give love to Him by obeying His commands.)

3. **Who is someone you think is generous? Why?**

Lesson 39

Worship Center

God is so generous in the way He loves us. Let's thank Him for His love and ask His help in giving generously to Him and to others.

Big Picture Verse

"Freely you have received, freely give." Matthew 10:8

Teacher Materials

Bible, *God's Big Picture* cassette/CD or music video and player, "I Want to Follow Jesus" word chart (p. 465 in this book), large sheet of paper on which you have printed Matthew 10:8, masking tape.

Sing to God

Play "I Want to Follow Jesus," encouraging students to sing along with the music and do the actions shown on the word chart or the music video. **When Jesus lived on earth, He gave generously to others. What does this song say that He did?** (Came to bring good news. Took our sins away by dying on the cross.) **How can we follow Jesus' example of giving generously?**

Hear and Say God's Word

Display paper on which you have printed Matthew 10:8. Lead students in repeating the verse. The first time through, clap for each word as you say it. The second time through, say "Freely" and then clap five times for the remaining five words. The third time through, say "Freely you" and then clap four times. Continue process until the whole verse has been said. **The Bible says that we have freely received God's love and forgiveness. We have not had to pay anything or work for it. What can we give freely and generously?** (Our love and care for others. Our possessions. Our friendship.)

Pray to God

Giving generously means to give more than what is required or expected. How can we give generously to others? Volunteers respond. Lead students in prayer, allowing volunteers to ask God for His help in giving generously in one of the ways suggested.

Options

1. Older students may read aloud these verses which describe ways of giving to God and others: Proverbs 25:21; Luke 6:38; Acts 20:35; 2 Corinthians 9:7.

2. Provide a variety of rhythm instruments for students to play while singing "I Want to Follow Jesus."

 **Lesson 39**

Bible Story Coloring Center

Materials

Crayons or markers, a copy of "A poor woman gives all she has" picture and story (pp. 193-194 from *Bible Story Coloring Pages*) for each student.

Lead the Activity

Students color page 193; read or tell the story on page 194. **How was the widow in this picture giving generously to God? What did Jesus say about her gift?**

Option

Provide a copy of "A woman shows love to Jesus" picture and story (pp. 195-196 from *Bible Story Coloring Pages*) for each student. As students color the picture, read or tell the story, which describes the way in which a woman in the Bible gave generously to Jesus.

Skit Center

Materials

A copy of "Sacrifice Until It Kind of Hurts" skit (pp. 242-244 from *The Big Book of Bible Skits*) for each student; optional—highlighter pens.

Lead the Activity

Students choose parts and read the skit, which tells the story of the widow's gift. (Optional: Students highlight their parts.) Ask the discussion questions on page 242.

Bible Skills Center

Materials

Materials needed for "Book Pass" and/or "Tape Time" (p. 29 and/or p. 87 from *The Big Book of Bible Skills*).

Lead the Activity

Students complete activities as directed in *The Big Book of Bible Skills*.

Lesson 40

The Entrance of the King

Big Picture Verse

"Great is the Lord and most worthy of praise; his greatness no one can fathom." Psalm 145:3

THE BIG PICTURE

Jesus is so great that we can't help but praise Him.

Scripture Background
Mark 11:1-10; Luke 19:28-40

On the morning of Palm Sunday there was a stir in Bethany and along the road leading to Jerusalem. It was understood that Jesus was to enter the city that day. The people were gathering in crowds. A colt was procured; the disciples, having thrown their robes over it, placed Jesus upon it, and the procession started. This little parade may have seemed insignificant compared to a procession that celebrated the coronation of a king or the inauguration of a president, but it meant much more for the world. Jesus, for the first time, permitted a public recognition and celebration of who He was—the Messiah, Savior and King of the world. The end was approaching with awful swiftness and He must offer Himself as Messiah, even if it meant being rejected.

In their enthusiasm, the people tore off branches from the palm and olive trees and carpeted the highway, while shouts rang through the air. They believed in Jesus and in all their enthusiasm were not ashamed of their King. In answer to the crowds who asked, "Who is this?" they boldly answered, "This is the prophet, Jesus, from Nazareth of Galilee." It took courage to say that in Jerusalem. Jesus was not entering the city as a triumphant conqueror as the Romans had done. No sword was in His hand. His mission was salvation!

In the evening the crowds dispersed, and Jesus quietly returned to Bethany. It might have seemed like nothing in the way of making Jesus King had been accomplished. But His hour had not yet come. Christ must be Savior first and then come again as King of kings and Lord of lords.

Adapted from *What the Bible Is All About* by Henrietta C. Mears.

Big Picture Story Center

Teacher Materials
Bible Time Line, drawing materials/equipment.

Student Materials
Drawing materials.

Tell the Story
Move the *Bible Time Line* frame to highlight Picture 40. As you tell each part of the story, draw each sketch. Students copy your sketches.

What kinds of parades have you seen?
Today we're going to hear about a very important parade!

1. For three years, Jesus had traveled around the country of Israel, teaching people about God. He had fed hungry people and made sick people well. Wherever Jesus went, people came from all over to see Him!

1. Draw a "3" and details for Jesus. Add "C"s for people.

2. Now Jesus was going to Jerusalem, where God's Temple was. He was going to celebrate the holiday of Passover in Jerusalem. But Jesus wasn't ONLY going to Jerusalem to celebrate Passover. He knew that it was time to show people that He was the Savior (called the Messiah) God had promised to send.

2. Sideways "J"; add lines to make city gate and wall.

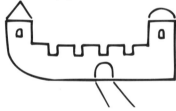

3. As Jesus and His friends walked toward Jerusalem, Jesus sent two of His disciples to bring Him a donkey. Soon the disciples returned with the donkey. They threw their coats over the donkey's back, and Jesus sat on the donkey and rode it up the road to Jerusalem. The world's most important parade had begun!

3. Donkey from "U"s, "I"s and "V"s.

4. As Jesus rode toward Jerusalem, the news spread quickly: "Jesus is coming!" Crowds gathered along the road, shouting, singing and waving palm branches. Some spread their coats and lay palm branches on the roadway like a beautiful carpet! This was the way the people welcomed a great king! They called out, "Hosanna! Hosanna! Blessed is He who comes in the name of the Lord! Hosanna in the highest!"

4. Add road to donkey; palm branches from lines.

5. Some people thought that Jesus the Messiah would be a mighty king—a fierce warrior to save them from the Romans, who had taken over their country. Whatever their reasons, people came from EVERYWHERE to join the shouting, singing crowd!

5. Crown from "O" and "V"s.

6. Soon the people in Jerusalem heard the noise. "What is going on? Who is coming?" they asked. Now many more people ran from their houses into the streets of Jerusalem. Jesus rode through the shouting, singing crowds. It seemed that EVERYONE had come to greet the King!

6. Draw faces over wall in #2.

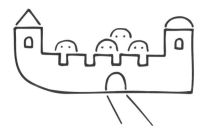

7. When He got to the Temple, Jesus got off the donkey and went into the Temple. Some children walked with Him, waving their palm branches and singing, "Hosanna! Hosanna!" The Temple leaders growled to Jesus, "Do You hear what they are SINGING to You? Make them be quiet!"

Jesus told the leaders, "These children are right to sing praises to Me. In fact, if they were not praising Me, the rocks would shout out praise to Me!"

7. Temple from rectangles and "M"s.

8. Jesus showed the people that He is the Messiah sent from God. But He would not become the kind of king some people expected. Instead, Jesus knew it was almost time for Him to show how very much He loves everyone. Jesus was going to die on a cross to pay for all the wrong things people had done. Then all people could become part of God's family! Jesus knew this was God's good plan. But for now, Jesus waited.

8. Draw a cross.

Get the Big Picture

What are some reasons people had for praising Jesus as He entered Jerusalem? (Jesus had done many miracles. Jesus had helped them.) **What are some reasons we can praise Him?** (He loves us. He forgives our sins.)

Jesus is the great King of all kings. He loves us so much, He was willing to die so that we could be part of God's family. The more we know about Jesus, the more reasons we have to praise Him!

Bible Verse Object Talk: Wave Bottle

Big Picture Verse

"Great is the Lord and most worthy of praise; his greatness no one can fathom." Psalm 145:3

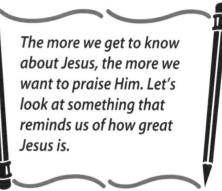

The more we get to know about Jesus, the more we want to praise Him. Let's look at something that reminds us of how great Jesus is.

Teacher Materials

Bible with bookmark at Psalm 145:3, clear plastic bottle, water, blue food coloring, mineral oil; optional—picture of ocean or starry sky.

Prepare the Object Talk

Fill bottle half full with water. Add several drops of blue food coloring. Fill remainder of bottle with mineral oil. Fasten cap tightly. (Note: If you have a large group, prepare more than one bottle.)

Present the Object Talk

1. Show bottle. Ask a volunteer to hold the bottle horizontally and gently tilt the bottle from end to end, creating a wave-like motion. Allow time for students to experiment with the bottle.

2. **The waves in this bottle remind me of the ocean. What words would you use to describe an ocean? How hard do you think it might be to see to the very bottom of**

the ocean or a deep lake? Why? Volunteers tell ideas. (Optional: Show picture of ocean instead of using wave bottle, or show starry sky picture and talk with students about the impossibility of counting all the stars in the sky.)

Conclude

The ocean is so big and so deep we can't understand exactly what it is like. Listen to what the Bible says about the Lord. Read Psalm 145:3 aloud. **The word "fathom" means to understand. This verse tells us that the Lord is so great we can never understand exactly how great He is! Because Jesus is so great, we want to praise Him.** Lead students in prayer, thanking Jesus for His greatness.

Discussion Questions

1. What are some other things that remind us of how great Jesus is? (The miracles He did on earth. His resurrection.)

2. What are some of the ways people praise Jesus for His greatness? (Sing songs about Him. Pray. Tell others about His greatness.)

3. What would you like to praise Jesus for?

Active Game Center: Palm-Branch Pickup

Materials

Green construction paper, scissors or paper cutter, markers.

Prepare the Game

Cut construction paper into small squares, making at least ten squares for each student.

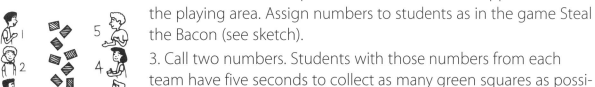

When Jesus was entering Jerusalem, people praised Him by covering the ground with branches from palm trees. We're going to play a game and praise Jesus, too.

Lead the Game

1. Give each student 10 squares of paper and a marker. Students number squares 1 to 10 and then randomly place squares, numbered side down, in center of playing area.

2. Divide students into two teams. Teams line up shoulder-to-shoulder on opposite sides of the playing area. Assign numbers to students as in the game Steal the Bacon (see sketch).

3. Call two numbers. Students with those numbers from each team have five seconds to collect as many green squares as possible. Call "stop" when time is up; students return to teams with the squares they collected. Volunteer(s) from team who collected the square with the highest number tells a reason to praise Jesus.

4. To play another round, volunteers return squares to playing area, numbered side down. Play as many rounds as time allows.

Options

1. If you have fewer than 10 students in your class, make more than 10 squares for each student. Divide students into two teams, but tell all students to collect squares at the same time. Students race to collect squares until there are no more remaining on the ground. Volunteer from team with most total points tells a reason to praise Jesus.

2. Cut the papers into palm-branch pieces.

3. For older students, each team totals the numbers on the squares they collect. Volunteer from team with most points tells a reason to praise Jesus.

Discussion Questions

1. Instead of laying palm branches on the ground, how might we show praise to an important person today? (Putting down a red carpet where that person is going to walk. Clapping for a person.)

2. What are some ways we can give praise to Jesus today? (Sing songs to Him. Pray to Him and tell Him what we praise Him for. Tell other people how great He is.)

3. What are some reasons Jesus is so great?

 **Lesson 40**

Art Center: Palm Sunday Map

Student Materials
Length of butcher paper, crayons, green construction paper, fabric scraps, scissors, glue.

Prepare the Activity
Draw a road on the butcher paper (see sketch). Prepare one length of butcher paper for each group of six to eight students.

The more we learn about Jesus, the more we want to praise Him. When Jesus rode into Jerusalem on a donkey, big crowds of people welcomed Him and praised Him. Let's draw a map of what the road into Jerusalem might have looked like.

Lead the Activity
1. Show butcher paper you prepared. Lead students to suggest items for the map: palm trees by the side of the road, palm branches and coats on the road, gate into Jerusalem and buildings in Jerusalem.

2. Guide students in choosing assignments: draw trees, gate or buildings; cut branches from green construction paper or coats from fabric. More than one student may work on each part of the map. Students glue completed branches and coats onto road. While students are working, talk about the story events with students and ask the Discussion Questions below.

Options
1. An older student may read Mark 1:8-10 aloud after the map is completed.

2. Provide one or more of these materials for students to add to the map: small live palm branches, brown paper bags to cut and crumple for rocks.

3. Students may cut 2x10-inch (5x25-cm) rectangles from white construction paper, fold in half and draw people on them to make stand-up figures.

4. Poster board may be substituted for butcher paper.

Discussion Questions
1. What are some things people do today to praise Jesus?

2. How have we praised Jesus today in our church?

3. What are some reasons you think Jesus deserves our praise?

4. What can you do to praise and show love for Jesus?

 **Lesson 40**

Worship Center

Big Picture Verse

"Great is the Lord and most worthy of praise; his greatness no one can fathom." Psalm 145:3

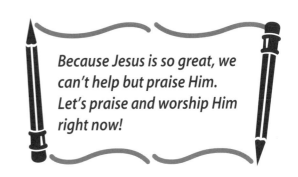

Because Jesus is so great, we can't help but praise Him. Let's praise and worship Him right now!

Teacher Materials

Bible, *God's Big Picture* cassette/CD or music video and player, "Psalm 9:1,2,10" word chart (p. 477 in this book), large sheet of paper on which you have printed Psalm 145:3, masking tape.

Sing to God

Play "Psalm 9:1,2,10," encouraging students to sing along with the music and do the actions shown on the word chart or the music video. **What might it mean to praise the Lord with all of your heart while singing?** (To be thinking about God and what the words of the song say about Him when you are singing.)

Hear and Say God's Word

Display paper on which you have printed Psalm 145:3. Volunteer reads verse aloud. **"Fathom" means understand or measure. What does Psalm 145:3 tell us no one can completely understand or measure?** (The Lord's greatness.) **God is so great that we can never even completely understand how wonderful He is! What are some things you DO know about God's greatness?** Volunteers tell ideas. Lead students in saying Psalm 145:3, clapping in rhythm with the words (for example, clap as you say the words "Great," "Lord," "worthy" and "praise"). Repeat verse several times.

Pray to God

Students tell more ideas about why Jesus is so great. List ideas on back of verse paper. Students use ideas listed on paper as they say prayers of praise to Jesus. End prayer by asking Jesus for His help in understanding more of His greatness and for a reminder to praise Him when we learn new ways He is great.

Options

1. Older student finds definition of "praise" in a Bible dictionary and explains it to the class.

2. Students sing and do actions for "Easter Means..." and/or "Picture This!" (p. 449 and/or p. 473 in this book.)

3. If time permits, invite students to suggest other rhythmic motions (snap fingers, stamp feet, etc.) for the verse. Group says the verse while performing suggested motions.

4. Lead students in writing their own psalm of praise.

 Lesson 40

Bible Story Coloring Center

Materials

Crayons or markers, a copy of "People welcome Jesus to Jerusalem" picture and story (pp. 189-190 from *Bible Story Coloring Pages*) for each student.

Lead the Activity

Students color page 189; read or tell the story on page 190. **How do the people in this picture look? What are they doing to show they are glad to see Jesus?**

Option

Provide green construction paper, scissors and glue. Students cut and fringe small palm branches to glue onto their colored pictures.

Skit Center

Materials

Bibles.

Lead the Activity

Students find Luke 19:28-40 in their Bibles. Assign these parts to volunteers: narrator, Jesus, owners of colt, disciples, crowd, Pharisees. Students read Scripture aloud, acting out the story action. Repeat drama several times with different volunteers.

Bible Skills Center

Materials

Materials needed for "Gospel Puzzles" and/or "Computer Art" (p. 59 and/or p. 127 from *The Big Book of Bible Skills*).

Lead the Activity

Students complete activities as directed in *The Big Book of Bible Skills*.

Jesus on Trial

Big Picture Verse

"Greater love has no one than this, that he lay down his life for his friends." John 15:13

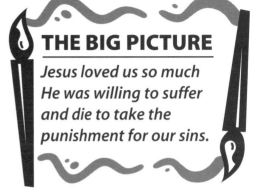

THE BIG PICTURE

Jesus loved us so much He was willing to suffer and die to take the punishment for our sins.

Scripture Background
Luke 22:39-48; John 13:1-30; 18:1-14, 19-24,28—19:16

Take note of the sad record of events in connection with Jesus' death. Most of the Jews had rejected Jesus completely. Jesus gathered His disciples around Him in an upper room. He wanted to comfort His disciples, for He knew how hard it would be for them when He was gone. They would be like sheep without a shepherd.

What a picture we have in the upper room: Jesus, the Son of God, girded with a towel and a basin of water in His blessed hands, is washing His disciples' feet! Jesus' actions showed that there is no loving others without living for others.

Look also into the Garden of Gethsemane. The change from the scene in the upper room is like going from warmth to cold, from light to darkness. Only two hours had passed since Judas left the supper table. Now we see him betraying his best friend. In the shadow of the garden a band of soldiers approached, led by Judas. He stepped up to kiss Jesus. Yes, he was a disciple. But the Scriptures had said that Jesus would be betrayed by a friend and sold for thirty pieces of silver. Remember, Judas did not have to betray his Lord to carry out God's plan. Nothing happens because of a prophecy. The prophecy happens because God's plan was going to take place. No one ever had to sin to carry out any of God's plan.

Worst of all, His friends deserted Him. Peter denied Him, and all forsook Him and fled except for John the beloved. We follow Jesus, bound as a captive, into Pilate's hall and then before Herod. Yet Jesus was the One in command of the situation all through this terrible drama. He went forth as a voluntary sacrifice. He deliberately tasted death for every man. Finally, we follow Him along the Via Dolorosa to the cross.

The hour had come. The mission of our Lord on earth was ended. The greatest work of Christ remained to be done. He was to die that He might glorify the Father and save the sinful world. He came to give His life as a ransom for many. Christ came into the world by the manger and left it by the door of the cross.

Adapted from *What the Bible Is All About* by Henrietta C. Mears.

Big Picture Story Center

Teacher Materials
Bible Time Line, drawing materials/equipment.

Student Materials
Drawing materials.

Tell the Story
Move the *Bible Time Line* frame to highlight Picture 41. As you tell each part of the story, draw each sketch. Students copy your sketches.

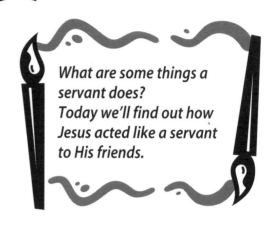

What are some things a servant does? Today we'll find out how Jesus acted like a servant to His friends.

1. Everyone in Jerusalem was looking forward to the Passover celebration and eating a special dinner as well as singing and praying to God. But this Passover time would be different, especially for Jesus and His friends.

1. Draw stick figures; music notes from "d"s and lines.

2. Jesus and His friends gathered for their special meal, but no servant came to wash everyone's feet. So Jesus washed the feet of each of His friends. He talked about the ways He had shown love to them and how He wanted them to show love to each other. Then, while they ate, Jesus said, "One of you will give Me to My enemies. They will kill Me on a cross."

2. Foot from "L"s and "C"s; add bowl and water.

3. *How could this be?* Jesus' friends wondered. When Jesus had ridden into town four days earlier, the people had called Him their KING! But even though many people loved Jesus, some of the leaders HATED Him. They said, "We must STOP Jesus. If we don't get RID of Him soon, WE won't be in charge anymore!" They made a mean plan to KILL Him.

3. Draw crown from "V"s and "O"; add "no" slash.

4. Jesus knew their plan and that His friend Judas had been paid with 30 coins to lead them to Jesus when there weren't many people around. But Jesus also knew that He had come to earth to take the punishment for all the wrong things people had ever done—or ever would do. God was in charge of what was happening. And God was going to use the leaders' evil plan to do something VERY GOOD!

4. Coins; turn into "GOOD."

5. After their meal, Jesus and His friends walked to the near-by Mount of Olives together. He asked His friends to wait for Him while He went off by Himself to pray. Jesus asked God to help Him as He followed this plan to take the punishment for all the wrong things people had done.

5. Ridge from "C"; trees from "3"s and lines.

6. When Jesus finished praying, He woke His sleeping friends. Judas was coming. But Judas wasn't alone. A crowd of men, armed with swords and clubs, had come with Judas to take Jesus away! Judas kissed Jesus to show the men whom they should arrest. Jesus could have stopped the men, but He quietly let them take Him.

6. Crowd from "C"s; add swords and clubs.

7. Many, many years before, the prophets of God had said that Jesus would be as quiet as a sheep when all this happened. They had said Jesus would let people hurt Him and never say anything to defend Himself or hurt them in return. God's prophets had also said that all of Jesus' friends would run away and leave Him alone. And they did!

7. Running stick figure from "N."

8. The men with the swords and clubs took Jesus to the house of the high priest. There the leaders told lies about Him. People slapped Him and hurt Him. And He let them.

Then they took Jesus to the Roman ruler named Pilate. They wanted to get permission to KILL Jesus on a cross. Pilate knew Jesus had not done anything wrong, but he gave permission, just so the other leaders wouldn't cause any trouble for him. The Roman soldiers took Jesus. They hurt Him and put a crown of hard, sharp thorns on His head. They made fun of Him. And Jesus let them. He was willing to do this because He loved us.

8. Draw crown of thorns from circles and "V"s. Draw heart around crown of thorns.

Get the Big Picture

How did Jesus show His love for us? (He died for us.) **What are some ways we can show our love for Him?** (Tell other people about Him. Obey His Word.)

Jesus had come to earth to take the punishment for all the sins people had ever done—or would do. Jesus was willing to do this because He loves us. And Jesus knew that even when He died, He wouldn't STAY dead! God would turn this very BAD event into a very GOOD thing!

Bible Verse Object Talk: Measure Up!

Big Picture Verse

"Greater love has no one than this, that he lay down his life for his friends." John 15:13

Teacher Materials

Bible with bookmark at John 15:13, a variety of items used for measuring—ruler, yard stick, thermometer, rain gauge, measuring cup, tape measure, scale.

Present the Object Talk

One at a time, show each measuring item. Allow students time to experiment with each item. If possible, students measure themselves and/or classroom items. Discuss items used for measuring:

When we want to find out how big something is, we measure it. But there's one thing that is so great it can't be measured. As we measure some things today, be thinking about what this great thing might be.

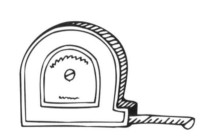

What does this item measure? What's something small this item might measure? What might be the biggest thing this item could measure?

Conclude

It's fun to measure all kinds of different items. Listen to what the Bible says is so great. Read John 15:13 aloud. **Who is this verse talking about?** (Jesus.) **What does this verse say Jesus did? Why did Jesus give up His life?** (To show His love for us.) **Jesus loves us so much He was willing to die, taking the punishment for our sins. His love for us can't be measured.** Lead students in prayer, thanking Jesus for His great love. Talk with interested students about becoming members of God's family. (See "Leading a Child to Christ" on p. 30.)

Discussion Questions

1. What are some other words you would use to describe Jesus' love? Why can't Jesus' love be measured? (It's too big!)

2. How does Jesus show His love for us today? (Forgives our sins. Promises always to be with us and help us. Hears and answers our prayers.)

3. When Jesus lived on earth, what else did He do to show His great love? (Taught people about God. Healed sick people. Cared for many people.)

Active Game Center: Toe Talk

Materials
Bible, index cards, marker.

Prepare the Game
Print the words of John 15:13 on index cards, one word per card. Make one set of verse cards for every 8 to 10 students.

Lead the Game
1. Group students in teams of 8 to 10. Each team lines up single-file on one side of playing area.

Students remove shoes and socks. Place a mixed-up set of verse cards across the playing area from each team.

2. At your signal, the first student from each team skips across playing area to cards, picks up one card and places it in between his or her first two toes. Student walks back to team with card held between toes. If card falls before he or she returns to the team, student must stop to replace card. Next student in line repeats action until all cards have been collected. Students on each team work together to order verse cards. First team finished reads verse aloud. Students check verse in Bible.

One of the ways Jesus showed His love just before He suffered and died to take the punishment for our sins was to wash His disciples' feet. Washing feet was something a servant would usually do. Let's play a game that uses our feet!

Option
If your class has fewer than 16 students, all students act as one team and race against the clock.

Discussion Questions

1. Jesus showed us His love and laid down His life for us by dying on the cross. How might we do what John 15:13 says and show love to our friends? (Help them even when we don't feel like it. Be friendly even if they aren't being very friendly to us. Think of a caring thing you can do and do it.)

2. What can we do to thank Jesus for laying down His life for us? (Accept his offer to take the punishment for our sins and believe in His death and forgiveness.)

Art Center: Nature Pictures

Student Materials

Leaves in a variety of sizes and shapes, small twigs or other nature items (bark, seeds, acorns, etc.), a sheet of cardboard or poster board for each student, glue.

Lead the Activity

1. To remind them of Jesus' love, students form pictures (cross, heart, people who care for them, Bible) by arranging nature materials on sheets of cardboard or poster board. Allow students time to experiment with several pictures before gluing nature materials. If students need help thinking of picture ideas, ask, **What pictures remind you of the word "love"? How have you learned about Jesus' love? What has Jesus done to show His love for you?**

Jesus loved us so much He was willing to die to take the punishment for our sins. Jesus shows His love for us in many ways. Today we'll use these things often found in a garden to make pictures that remind us of Jesus' love.

2. Invite volunteers to show and describe their completed pictures.

Options

1. Suggest students make pictures representing events from this lesson's Bible story (the Last Supper or Jesus' arrest in the Garden of Gethsemane).

2. If nature materials are not available, students may draw with markers or crayons.

Discussion Questions

1. *When Jesus lived on earth, what are some of the ways He showed His love for people?* (Helped them. Healed them. Told them about God.)

2. *What are some of the ways Jesus shows His love for us today?* (Forgives our sins. Hears our prayers. Provides people who care for us. Keeps His promise to always be with us.)

3. *What difference does it make to know about Jesus' love?* (When we know about Jesus' love, then we know that our sins can be forgiven and that we can become members of God's family.)

 **Lesson 41**

Worship Center

Big Picture Verse

"Greater love has no one than this, that he lay down his life for his friends." John 15:13

> The Bible tells us that Jesus loved us so much He was willing to suffer and die to take the punishment for our sins. Let's thank Jesus for that by worshiping Him!

Teacher Materials

Bible, *God's Big Picture* cassette/CD or music video and player, "Easter Means..." word chart (p. 449 in this book), large sheet of paper on which you have printed John 15:13, masking tape.

Sing to God

Play "Easter Means...," encouraging students to sing along with the music and do the actions shown on the word chart or the music video. **What does this song tell us about Jesus' love for us?** (He died on the cross for our sins. He rose again. He sent His Spirit here to stay with us.)

Hear and Say God's Word

Display paper on which you have printed John 15:13. Volunteer reads verse aloud. Lead students in standing up and saying John 15:13, clapping once for each word of the verse. (Variation: Students clap once for each syllable.) Repeat verse several times. **What does John 15:13 tell us is the greatest way to show love?** (Lay down your life for your friends.) **Jesus laid down His life for us by dying on the cross and rising again. What are some of the ways we can show love to our friends?** (Help them even when we don't feel like it. Be patient even when it's hard.)

Pray to God

Let's tell Jesus how thankful we are that He loves us. Lead students in repeating prayer after you, one phrase at a time: **Thank You, Jesus, that You love us so much You were willing to suffer and die for us and take the punishment for our sins. We love You, too. Amen.**

Options

1. During each session, invite students to tell prayer requests and things for which they wish to thank God. Record requests and praises in a prayer journal.

2. Students sing and do actions for "Everywhere I Go." (p. 451 in this book.)

 **Lesson 41**

Bible Story Coloring Center  FOR YOUNGER CHILDREN

Materials

Crayons or markers, a copy of "Jesus washes His friends' feet" picture and story (pp. 197-198 from *Bible Story Coloring Pages*) for each student.

Lead the Activity

Students color page 197; read or tell the story on page 198. **What is Jesus doing in this picture? Why was Jesus willing to do the job of a servant? What are some other ways Jesus shows He loves us?**

Option

After pages are completed, each student cuts his or her picture into four irregular pieces. Several students mix their pieces together and then see how quickly they can find their own pieces and put pages back together again.

Skit Center FOR OLDER CHILDREN

Materials

A copy of "Trials, Trials, Trials" skit (pp. 245-249 from *The Big Book of Bible Skits*) for each student; optional—highlighter pens.

Lead the Activity

Students form groups of eight and read the skit, which tells the story of Jesus' trial before Caiaphas, the high priest, and Pilate. (Optional: Students highlight their parts.) Ask the discussion questions on page 245.

Bible Skills Center FOR OLDER CHILDREN

Materials

Materials needed for "Bible Book Mix-Up" and/or "Balloon Pop" (p. 37 and/or p. 147 from *The Big Book of Bible Skills*).

Lead the Activity

Students complete activities as directed in *The Big Book of Bible Skills*.

Lesson 42

New Life in Jerusalem

Big Picture Verse

"Just as Christ was raised from the dead through the glory of the Father, we too may live a new life." Romans 6:4

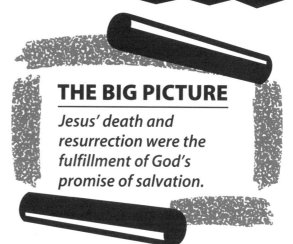

THE BIG PICTURE

Jesus' death and resurrection were the fulfillment of God's promise of salvation.

Scripture Background
Mark 15:21—16:8; Luke 20:10-18

We turn with great relief from the sorrow and death of the cross, the darkness and gloom of the tomb, to the brightness and glory of the resurrection morning. We have a Savior who is victorious over death. On the third day the tomb was empty! The grave clothes were all in order. Jesus had risen from the dead, but not as others had done. When Lazarus came forth, he was bound in his grave clothes. He came out in his natural body. But when Jesus came forth, His natural body was changed to a spiritual body. The changed body came right out of its linen wrappings and left them as empty as the butterfly leaves the chrysalis shell.

At the cross we have hate's record at its worst and love's record at its best. Christ was so hated that He was put to death. God so loved us that He gave us life. There were three crosses on Calvary's hill. On two of them were thieves who were dying for their crimes. But one thief met Jesus that day, and the way he was saved is the way every sinner must be saved. This thief believed on the Lamb of God who died on the cross that day to pay the penalty of sin.

Our faith is one of four letters instead of two. Other religions say, "Do." Our faith says, "Done." Our Savior has done it all on the cross. He bore our sins and when He gave up His life, He said, "It is finished" (John 19:30). This was the shout of a conqueror. He had finished the plan of redemption. Nothing was left for us to do. Has the work been done in your heart?

Adapted from *What the Bible Is All About* by Henrietta C. Mears.

Big Picture Story Center

Teacher Materials

Bible Time Line, drawing materials/equipment.

Student Materials

Drawing materials.

Tell the Story

Move the *Bible Time Line* frame to highlight Picture 42. As you tell each part of the story, draw each sketch. Students copy your sketches.

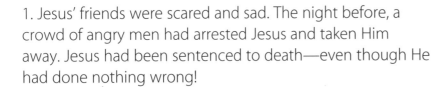

What are some ways people celebrate Easter?
Today we'll talk about why a time that started out so sad became something to celebrate!

1. Jesus' friends were scared and sad. The night before, a crowd of angry men had arrested Jesus and taken Him away. Jesus had been sentenced to death—even though He had done nothing wrong!

1. Draw scared face, moon and star.

2. Late in the morning, Roman soldiers made Jesus carry a heavy cross on His back. Jesus had been so badly beaten that He could hardly walk. So the soldiers made another man help Jesus. When they arrived at the place of crucifixion, the soldiers nailed Jesus to His cross and placed the cross into the ground. People came up to Jesus and spit on Him. They said terrible things to Him. Jesus let them. He could have stopped them, but He loved us so much He was willing to be hurt and killed to take the punishment for our sins.

2. Draw sun and hill; add cross.

3. Soon it got very dark, even though it was the middle of the day! Suddenly there was a huge EARTHQUAKE! And then, Jesus died. It was a horrible, scary time!

3. Color over sun. "W"s for earthquake.

4. After Jesus was dead, two of His friends laid His body in a tomb in a garden. (A tomb is a little room usually made in the side of a hill.) A HUGE rock was rolled in front of the doorway, so no one could get inside. Jesus' friends went home feeling very sad. It looked like EVERYTHING had gone

4. Tomb from "U"s, "O".

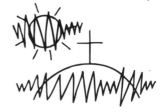

wrong! But what they didn't understand was that this day, as awful and horrible as it was, would turn out to be a BIG part of God's GOOD plan!

5. On the third day after Jesus died, several women who had been Jesus' friends got up very early. They wanted to get to the tomb by the time the sun was rising. But when they got to the garden where the tomb was, they could see that the big rock that had been in front of the tomb doorway had been ROLLED AWAY!

6. One of the women, Mary, didn't know what to think! She ran to get Peter and John, two more of Jesus' friends. Peter and John ran back to the tomb. And when they went inside, they could see that Jesus' body was GONE! Peter and John went home, wondering what was going on!

7. But Mary, who had followed them back to the garden, stayed there, crying. When she looked into the tomb again, it WASN'T empty. Now she saw two ANGELS!

One angel asked, "Why are you sad?"

Mary said, "Because Jesus' body is gone. I don't know where He is!" She turned away from the tomb and almost bumped into someone. *Is this the gardener?* she wondered. But then the person spoke.

8. "Mary!" He said. Mary knew that voice—it was JESUS! Jesus was there in front of her. And He was ALIVE! She was so very HAPPY! Jesus said to her, "Go and tell the others."

And Mary DID! She must have run like the wind! Coming through the door to the house where Jesus' friends were, she said, "Jesus is ALIVE! I've SEEN Him!" Jesus' friends were amazed! What Jesus had said was true! God's plan was GOOD! Soon Jesus came to see His friends. And they began to tell everyone the GOOD NEWS: Jesus is alive! And He is STILL alive!

5. Add rising sun behind tomb. Change rock to open door.

6. Tomb interior from "U"s. Add question mark.

7. Angels from "O"s and triangles.

8. Ears from question marks. Add happy face from "U"s.

Get the Big Picture

How did Jesus' friends feel at the beginning of the story? (Sad. Scared.) **How did they feel at the end?** (Happy. Surprised.)

Jesus died to take the punishment for our sins, as God had promised He would. And because He is alive, all people everywhere can have salvation and eternal life. When we believe that Jesus is God's Son and that He died for us, our sins are forgiven and we can be part of God's family!

 **Lesson 42**

Bible Verse Object Talk: Dead or Alive?

Big Picture Verse

"Just as Christ was raised from the dead through the glory of the Father, we too may live a new life."
Romans 6:4

Teacher Materials

Bible with bookmark at Romans 6:4, two each of several examples of fruits with pits (avocados, peaches, olives, dates, plums), knife.

Prepare the Object Talk

Cut open one of each kind of fruit and remove the pit.

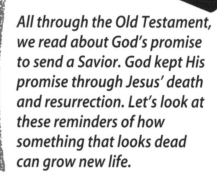

All through the Old Testament, we read about God's promise to send a Savior. God kept His promise through Jesus' death and resurrection. Let's look at these reminders of how something that looks dead can grow new life.

Present the Object Talk

1. One at a time, show each fruit pit. **What fruit do you think this pit is from? Does the pit look dead or alive? Why? What would happen if this pit was planted in good soil and watered?**

2. Show each fruit. Invite students to match fruit with their pits. After each fruit and pit are matched correctly, comment, **Even though the pits, or seeds, look like they are dead, new plants are able to grow from them.**

Conclude

When Jesus died, His friends thought they would never see Him again. But God's power made Jesus come back to life again. Read Romans 6:4 aloud. **What does this verse say we may have because of Jesus' death and resurrection?** (A new life.) **Jesus made it possible for us to become members of God's family.** Thank God in prayer for His gift of salvation.

Discussion Questions

1. Why was Jesus the only One who could take the punishment for our sins? (Jesus is the only person who never sinned. He is the One God promised to send.)

2. When we choose to become members of God's family, what does He give us? (Forgiveness for our sins. Eternal life.)

3. What are some other things in nature that remind us of new life? (Flowers. Baby animals. Butterflies.)

Lesson 42

Active Game Center: Plate Toss

Materials
Paper plates, markers.

Prepare the Game
Print the letters from the sentence "Jesus is alive," printing one letter on each paper plate. Make one set for every 12 students. Use a different color marker each time you print the sentence.

Lead the Game
1. Divide class into teams of no more than 12. Each team lines up single-file at one side of the playing area. Give each student a paper plate written in his or her team's color. (Some students may have more than one paper plate.)

2. Students take turns throwing the paper plates like Frisbees. Then, at your signal, first student in each line runs to collect one of his or her team's paper plates. Next students in line repeat process.

3. When all of the paper plates have been collected, teams put them in order to read "Jesus is alive."

God's promise of salvation came true in Jesus' death and resurrection. Let's play a game where we are reminded of Jesus' resurrection.

Options
1. If you have a smaller playing area, challenge students to skip or hop (or another way of movement) to collect the plates and return to line.
2. Students retrieve the plates in order. The first team to complete the sentence gives an example of how we know Jesus is alive.

Discussion Questions

1. What are some other ways to complete the sentence "Jesus is…"?

2. What are some ways we can show Jesus we are thankful for the wonderful news that He died to take the punishment for our sins and that He is alive today?

3. How does your family celebrate Jesus' resurrection at Eastertime?

Art Center: Cross Reminders

Student Materials
Poster board, pencil, ruler, scissors, toothpicks, glue.

Prepare the Activity
Cut a poster board cross for each student (see sketch a). Make a sample cross reminder following the directions below.

Lead the Activity
Give each student a poster board cross. A section at a time, student covers cross with a thin layer of glue and arranges toothpicks as shown in Sketch b.

We're sad to think that Jesus died, but His death on a cross and His resurrection make it possible for us to become members of God's family and receive God's gift of salvation. Keep the cross you make today as a reminder of Jesus' great love for you.

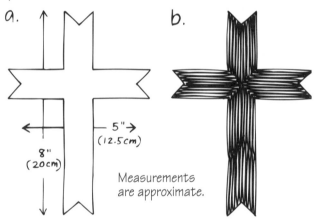

a.

5" (12.5cm)

8" (20cm)

Measurements are approximate.

b.

Options
1. When glue is slightly dry, students paint crosses silver or gold.

2. Provide self-adhesive picture hangers for students to attach to the backs of their crosses.

3. Provide additional items for students to glue onto crosses as reminders of events in the story of Jesus' death and resurrection: small silk flowers representing the garden tomb in which Jesus was buried, scraps of purple fabric representing the Temple veil that was torn when Jesus died, twine glued in a circle shape representing a crown of thorns.

Discussion Questions

1. What are some ways we remember Jesus' death and celebrate His resurrection? (Thank Jesus for His love. Sing special songs. Celebrate Easter with our church families at special worship services.)

2. What do Jesus' death and resurrection help us learn? (Jesus' death helps us learn about His love for us. Jesus' resurrection helps us learn about God's great power.)

3. What can you do or say to show that you are thankful for Jesus' death and resurrection?

 **Lesson 42**

Worship Center

Big Picture Verse

"Just as Christ was raised from the dead through the glory of the Father, we too may live a new life."
Romans 6:4

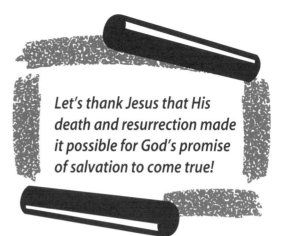

Let's thank Jesus that His death and resurrection made it possible for God's promise of salvation to come true!

Teacher Materials

Bible, *God's Big Picture* cassette/CD or music video and player, "Easter Means..." word chart (p. 449 in this book), large sheet of paper on which you have printed Romans 6:4, masking tape, four index cards on which you have printed the following words or phrases on both sides of cards, one word or phrase on each card: "Christ," "raised," "glory," "live a new life."

Sing to God

Play "Easter Means...," encouraging students to sing along with the music and do the actions shown on the word chart or the music video. **What does this song say "salvation" means?** (Jesus died for our sins. He rose again so that we can live forever with Him!) **We are saved from punishment for our sins because Jesus took the punishment instead!**

Hear and Say God's Word

Display paper on which you have printed Romans 6:4. Give index cards to volunteers. Say the word or phrase on the card as you hand it to each volunteer. **As I read Romans 6:4, listen for the word or words on your card. When you hear them, stand up and hold your card up high. The rest of us will echo the word or words again as you hold up your card.** Say verse, pausing for volunteers to hold up cards and students to echo each word. Repeat as time allows, different students holding the cards each time. **Why does Romans 6:4 say we can live a new life?** (Because Christ was raised from the dead.)

Pray to God

Play "Easter Means..." song again. Students listen to song and silently thank God for Jesus' death and resurrection. Conclude silent prayer time by thanking God aloud for His gift of salvation.

Options

1. Designate different groups of students to say words or phrases from index cards each time the verse is repeated. For example, students who have pets say "Christ," and then students who are wearing blue say "raised," etc.

2. Invite older students to create their own sign-language motions for the words of Romans 6:4. Students demonstrate motions while repeating verse.

 **Lesson 42**

Bible Story Coloring Center

Materials
Crayons or markers, a copy of "Jesus talks to Mary in the garden" picture and story (pp. 205-206 from *Bible Story Coloring Pages*) for each student.

Lead the Activity
Students color page 205; read or tell the story on page 206. **Why was Mary sad? What good news about Jesus did she discover?**

Option
Choosing from pages 189,199-207 in *Coloring Pages,* give each student a different page to color. After pages are colored, guide students to put the pages in order. Mix up the pages and see how fast students can reorder them.

Skit Center

Materials
A copy of "He's Alive!" skit (pp. 254-258 from *The Big Book of Bible Skits*) for each student; optional—highlighter pens.

Lead the Activity
Students read the skit, which tells the story of how some of Jesus' friends discovered He is alive. (Optional: Students highlight their parts.) Ask the discussion questions on page 254.

Bible Skills Center

Materials
Materials needed for "Easter Story Comparison" and/or "Grapevine Lines" (p. 57 and/or p. 153 from *The Big Book of Bible Skills*).

Lead the Activity
Students complete activities as directed in *The Big Book of Bible Skills.*

Lesson 43

Jesus' Farewell Promise

Big Picture Verse

"[Jesus said,] 'Surely I am with you always, to the very end of the age.'"
Matthew 28:20

THE BIG PICTURE

Because Jesus is alive, we know He will keep His promise to be with us now and forever.

Scripture Background
Matthew 28:16-20; Acts 1:1-11

What a wonderful 40 days Jesus' disciples spent with the Lord before His ascension! How anxious they were to hear His last words of instruction! In the first chapter of Acts we read of the great commission, the ascension and the promise of Christ's return.

But the disciples still were not satisfied as to the time when Christ would set up His kingdom on earth. They still expected a kingdom that would give them political independence and establish them in a place of leadership in the world. Jesus' answer was that their power was not to be political but spiritual.

Finally, after leading them out to Bethany, He was received into heaven to sit at the right hand of God. He who had taken upon Himself the form of a servant is now highly exalted. He is in the place of power, ever making intercession for us. He is our advocate.

At the ascension of Christ, our Lord went out of sight but stayed with us in a far more real way. He is no longer an earthly Christ, confined to Jerusalem, but He is a universal Christ. He could say to His disciples who mourned for Him, "I am with you always." How different was the hope and joy of those chosen followers from their despair and shame at the crucifixion! The disciples returned to Jerusalem with great joy to wait for the fulfillment of their Lord's promise.

As He was with the disciples, Christ is with His followers today too, always working in us and through us. We are laborers together with Him. Let us who are redeemed follow Jesus, our example, and go forth to serve, secure in the promise of His presence and our place some day by His side.

Adapted from *What the Bible Is All About* by Henrietta C. Mears.

Big Picture Story Center

Teacher Materials
Bible Time Line, drawing materials/equipment.

Student Materials
Drawing materials.

What's a promise someone has made to you? Today we'll learn a wonderful promise Jesus made to us!

Tell the Story
Move the *Bible Time Line* frame to highlight Picture 43. As you tell each part of the story, draw each sketch. Students copy your sketches.

1. After Jesus died and came back to life, He visited His friends many times. Once, Jesus surprised two of His friends by walking with them along a road. Each time Jesus talked with His friends, He helped them understand more about God's good plans for them.

1. Draw road from two "S"s. Add stick figures.

2. Once when He was eating with His disciples, Jesus said, "Wait in Jerusalem for the gift My Father promised. In a few days, you will receive this IMPORTANT gift." God would send His Holy Spirit to help Jesus' followers know He was with them and to help them live as God wanted them to.

2. Gift box from lines and "3"s.

3. On another day, Jesus gave His friends more important instructions. "I want you to tell all the people in the world about My love for them," Jesus said. "Teach people EVERY-WHERE how to obey My instructions about how to live." Jesus' friends may have thought, *How could we do a big job like that?* But then Jesus promised that He would be with His friends all the time, everywhere they went, always!

3. Megaphone: "O," lines and "C"s. Add "TELL EVERYONE!"

4. When it was time for Jesus to go back to heaven, His friends walked up the Mount of Olives to meet Him. (The Mount of Olives is a hill outside the city of Jerusalem where many olive trees grow.)

4. Ridge from "C"; trees from "3"s and lines.

5. When they were all together, Jesus said, "I want you to be witnesses of Me to people all over the world." Jesus wanted the disciples to tell others all the things they had seen Jesus do and all the words they had heard Him say.

"The Holy Spirit will help you," Jesus said. "Start in the city of Jerusalem. Then tell about Me outside the city. Don't forget the people in Judea and Samaria. Go all over the earth telling about Me!"

5. Draw 4 circles; add labels.

6. After Jesus said this, He began to rise from the ground, higher and higher until a cloud hid Him. The disciples were still looking up into the sky when, suddenly, two angels appeared! "Why do you stand here looking into the sky?" the angels asked. "Jesus has gone to heaven! Someday He will come back the same way He left."

6. Heads from "C"s; cloud from "3"s.

7. Jesus' friends walked back down the hill. They must have been VERY excited to know that Jesus would come back again. They may also have felt a little sad that Jesus was not with them anymore. But then they remembered the promise Jesus made: "I AM with you ALWAYS." Even though they could no longer see Him, He was still with them!

7. Add "I am with you always" to cloud.

8. Those first friends of Jesus obeyed His instructions. They waited in Jerusalem until God sent His Spirit to be with them and help them. Then the disciples went to MANY places, telling people about Him. Soon people EVERYWHERE were talking about the good news about Jesus!

8. Add arrows to circles in #5, beginning at Jerusalem.

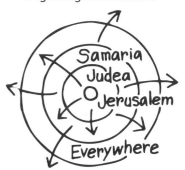

Get the Big Picture

What promise did Jesus make to His disciples? (To always be with them.) **What things do you think the disciples told others about Jesus?** (Jesus is alive. Jesus died for you.)

Jesus came to earth and died on the cross to take the punishment for our sins. That was an important part of God's big plan. But Jesus came back to life! And because He is alive, we know He will keep His promise to be with us, the people in God's family, now and forever!

Bible Verse Object Talk: Balloon Pop

Big Picture Verse

"[Jesus said,] 'Surely I am with you always, to the very end of the age.'" Matthew 28:20

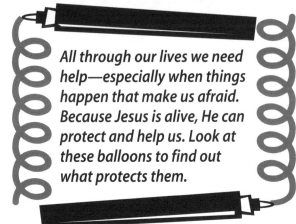

All through our lives we need help—especially when things happen that make us afraid. Because Jesus is alive, He can protect and help us. Look at these balloons to find out what protects them.

Teacher Materials

Bible with bookmark at Matthew 28:20, two large balloons, transparent tape, sewing needle; optional—additional balloons.

Prepare the Object Talk

Inflate (a little less than full) and tie the balloons. Place a 2-inch (5-cm) strip of tape at end of one balloon. Smooth over the tape to remove all air bubbles. Practice Step 2 before class.

Present the Object Talk

1. Hold up the needle and the balloon without the tape. **What will happen when I poke the balloon with the needle? The balloon doesn't have any protection against the sharp needle, so it will pop.** Use the needle to pop the balloon.

2. Hold up the second balloon. Firmly push the needle through the tape, keeping a good grasp on the needle. Then smoothly remove the needle. **Why didn't this balloon pop?** Volunteers tell ideas. **This balloon didn't pop when I poked it with the needle because it had something helping it to stay strong and not pop.** Show students the tape on the balloon. (Optional: Depending on the number of students in your group and their ages, invite students to blow up balloons and attempt to pop them with and without tape.)

Conclude

Jesus promises to help us. Because Jesus is alive, we know He will keep His promises to us. Listen to Jesus' promise. Read Matthew 28:20 aloud. **Jesus promises to be with us now and forever, helping us and caring for us.** Lead students in prayer, thanking Jesus for His promise to be with us.

Discussion Questions

1. When do people need to know of Jesus' help?

2. When are some times kids your age need to remember that Jesus is with them?

3. What are some other promises Jesus makes to His followers? (To hear and answer their prayers. To forgive sins.)

 **Lesson 43**

Active Game Center: Partner Play

Materials
Several tennis balls.

Lead the Game

1. Divide group into equal teams of at least six students each. (Join a team yourself if needed.) Teams line up in single-file lines on one side of the playing area with plenty of space between teams. Students become partners with team member behind or in front of them in line.

Because Jesus is alive, we know He will keep His promise to always be with us, helping us to obey His commands. Let's play a game we can only win if we have a partner helping us.

2. Give the first partners in each line a tennis ball. At your signal, first partners on each team roll ball back and forth to each other while moving to the opposite side of the playing area and then back to line. Next partners in team repeat action. Continue until all partners on each team have had a turn. Switch partners and repeat play.

Options

1. If you have fewer than 12 students, time partners with a stopwatch. Partners race against their own or other partners' times.

2. For a variation during repeat play, have partners bounce or gently kick ball back and forth.

Discussion Questions

1. *What would happen if you had no partner for this game?* (You wouldn't be able to get the ball back quickly or follow the rules of the game.)

2. *What are some of the ways Jesus helps us?* (Helps us remember His Word. Helps us know what to do to obey Him. Forgives us.)

3. *How does it make you feel to know that Jesus promises to always be with you?*

Art Center: Promise Clouds

Student Materials

Large sheets of white construction or butcher paper, scissors, markers, pencils, cotton balls, several staplers and staples, newspapers or scratch paper, ruler, string or white yarn.

Lead the Activity

1. Demonstrate to students how to cut out a large cloud shape from paper (see sketch a). Students cut out free-form cloud shapes.

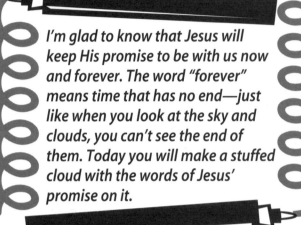

I'm glad to know that Jesus will keep His promise to be with us now and forever. The word "forever" means time that has no end—just like when you look at the sky and clouds, you can't see the end of them. Today you will make a stuffed cloud with the words of Jesus' promise on it.

2. Students use markers to write Jesus' promise, "I am with you always," on their cloud shapes. After writing words, students trace around the shape onto a second sheet of paper, cut second cloud out and staple both clouds together around the edges, leaving an opening large enough to insert stuffing (see sketch b).

a.

c.

b.

I am with you always

I am with you always

3. Students pull apart cotton balls, glue them to both sides of their clouds and then stuff shapes with crumpled newspapers or scratch paper.

4. Each student staples his or her cloud closed and staples a 12-inch (30-cm) length of string or yarn to the top of the cloud (see sketch c). Hang clouds from classroom ceiling or allow students to take clouds home and hang them in their rooms.

Options

1. Provide white or blue puff paint for students to write words.

2. If you have mostly younger students, print "I am with you always" on large sheet of paper or chalkboard for students to copy.

Discussion Questions

1. When are some times kids your age might be glad to remember Jesus' promise to be with them?

2. Where are some places you go? Because Jesus promises to be with you in all places, how can Jesus help you in those places? (He can help us treat others fairly at school or in our neighborhood.)

3. What are some other promises Jesus has made? (To forgive our sins. To hear and answer our prayers. To give us courage to do right.)

Lesson 43

Worship Center

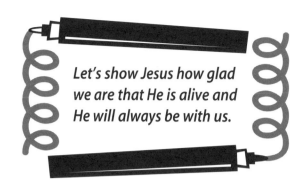

Let's show Jesus how glad we are that He is alive and He will always be with us.

Big Picture Verse

"[Jesus said,] 'Surely I am with you always, to the very end of the age.'" Matthew 28:20

Teacher Materials

Bible, *God's Big Picture* cassette/CD or music video and player, "Everywhere I Go" word chart (p. 451 in this book), large sheet of paper on which you have printed Matthew 28:20, masking tape.

Sing to God

Play "Everywhere I Go," encouraging students to sing along with the music and do the actions shown on the word chart or the music video. **When are some times Jesus is with us?** (At school. In my neighborhood. At home.) **Because Jesus is with us, how does He help us?** (He listens to our prayers. He helps us obey His commands.)

Hear and Say God's Word

Display paper on which you have printed Matthew 28:20. Volunteer reads verse aloud. **When might someone your age be glad to remember Jesus' promise?** Volunteers respond. Lead students in saying the verse. Use a quiet voice at the start, get louder toward the middle and then speak quietly at the end. Raise and lower your hand to show when voices should be raised and lowered. Repeat verse several times, varying when you speak loudly and softly.

Pray to God

Ask students for any prayer requests or situations in which they or people they know need to believe Jesus is always with them. Lead students in prayer, encouraging volunteers to pray for the requests mentioned. End the prayer time by thanking Jesus that He is always with us and will help us to obey His commands.

Options

1. Students sing and do actions for "Easter Means..." and/or "Psalm 9:1,2,10" (p. 449 and/or p. 477 in this book).

2. Have an older student lead the Bible verse activity.

 **Lesson 43**

Bible Story Coloring Center

Materials

Crayons or markers, a copy of "Jesus goes back to heaven" picture and story (pp. 213-214 from *Bible Story Coloring Pages*) for each student.

Lead the Activity

Students color page 213; read or tell the story on page 214. **What happened when Jesus went back to heaven? How do you think the disciples felt when Jesus left?**

Option

Provide cotton balls and glue. Students glue cotton to clouds.

Skit Center

Materials

A copy of "Good News" skit (pp. 263-266 from *The Big Book of Bible Skits*) for each student; optional—highlighter pens.

Lead the Activity

Students form pairs and read the skit, which tells the story of the two disciples, Andrew and Philip, deciding what to do after Jesus returned to heaven. (Optional: Students highlight their parts.) Ask the discussion questions on page 263.

Bible Skills Center

Materials

Materials needed for "Life of Jesus Time Line" and/or "Hidden Words" (p. 60 and/or p. 73 from *The Big Book of Bible Skills*).

Lead the Activity

Students complete activities as directed in *The Big Book of Bible Skills*.

 **Lesson 44**

God's Family Grows

Big Picture Verse

"God has poured out his love into our hearts by the Holy Spirit, whom he has given us."
Romans 5:5

THE BIG PICTURE

God's gift of the Holy Spirit made it possible for the family of believers to grow as they showed God's love and care.

Scripture Background
Acts 2

Next in importance to the coming of the Lord Jesus Christ to this earth is the coming of the Holy Spirit. The Church was born on that day of Pentecost. Become familiar with this account given in Acts 2.

Pentecost was one of the most popular of the feasts, and Jerusalem would be crowded with people from everywhere. It was 50 days after the crucifixion. But this time Pentecost was not to be a Jewish feast but the dawn of a new day, the birthday of Christ's Church.

The scene opened with the disciples assembled together, with their hearts fixed on Christ, waiting for His promise to be fulfilled. The Holy Spirit Himself descended that day and as a result, the disciples were endowed for special service. The wonderful thing about Pentecost was that the disciples were filled with the Holy Spirit so that they might be witnesses.

The power of the Holy Spirit was first shown when Peter, the humble fisherman, rose to speak and 3,000 souls were saved! The only way to account for Peter's boldness as he stood that day to preach before a multitude on the streets of Jerusalem is to look to the source of power, the Holy Spirit.

What glorious days followed, in teaching and fellowship and signs and wonders and, above all, salvation. The daily life of these first believers was so marvelous that it is not surprising that it found favor with all the people and that additions were made day by day. This is the real objective of the Church—then and now!

Adapted from *What the Bible Is All About* by Henrietta C. Mears.

Big Picture Story Center

Teacher Materials
Bible Time Line, drawing materials/equipment.

Student Materials
Drawing materials.

Tell the Story
Move the *Bible Time Line* frame to highlight Picture 44. As you tell each part of the story, draw each sketch. Students copy your sketches.

How many people do you think make a big family?
Today we'll hear about the very first church. It was like a big family!

1. After God raised Jesus from the dead, Jesus talked with His friends many times. But one day, Jesus went back to heaven. *What's going to happen now?* the friends wondered.

1. Draw question mark; add face details.

2. Some of Jesus' friends may have thought about going back to their old jobs as fishermen or tax collectors. But they remembered Jesus' words before He left.

   "Do not leave Jerusalem," Jesus had said. "Wait for the gift My Father promised you—the Holy Spirit. When the Holy Spirit comes, you will receive power and you will tell people everywhere about Me." So Jesus' friends stayed in Jerusalem together. They prayed and waited.

2. Draw fish and coins.

3. Ten days later on a special holiday called Pentecost, the waiting was OVER. While Jesus' friends were all together praying, they heard a sound like a rushing, powerful wind. They looked up from their praying to see what was happening. *What was THIS?* It looked like little flames of fire were burning above each of their heads! And when they began to talk, they were speaking other LANGUAGES! God had sent His Holy Spirit, just as Jesus had said He would!

3. Lines for wind; flame from "C"s.

4. This was too EXCITING to stay indoors! As Jesus' friends came outside, they saw a HUGE crowd of people coming toward them. These people had all heard the sound of the rushing wind, too. They came hurrying up to where Jesus' friends were.

4. House from "U"s, lines. Add "C"s for crowd.

5. As these people came near and listened, they heard the different languages Jesus' friends were speaking. Many of the people in that crowd were visiting Jerusalem from other places in the world. They were amazed to hear Jesus' friends speaking in their own languages!

5. Surprised face from question marks and "3"s. Add details.

6. Then Peter began to explain the amazing things that were happening. Peter told them about Jesus and how He died on a cross. Peter said that Jesus came back to life to show that He truly was from God. The people asked Jesus' friends, "What shall we do?"

6. Exclamation point; draw lines to make cross.

7. Peter told them, "You must stop doing wrong and start obeying God. Believe in Jesus and be baptized. God will give you His gift of the Holy Spirit, too." And that day, about 3,000 people became part of God's family! This big family met every day. They sang and praised God and talked to each other about Jesus.

7. Print "3,000." Add faces.

8. This big family loved each other in a BIG way! They shared all the things they had. People sold things they owned so that they would have money to give to others who needed food or clothes. Their love came from God; His Holy Spirit helped them love each other. And every day, more and more people became part of God's family as the good news about Jesus spread throughout the city of Jerusalem.

8. Add a heart around faces.

Get the Big Picture

What are some things Jesus' friends did to obey Jesus? (They waited for the Holy Spirit. They told others about Him.) **to show God's love to each other?** (They shared with each other. They prayed together.)

God's family still shows lots of love. That's the way Jesus said other people would know who was in His family: by the love we show each other.

Bible Verse Object Talk: Overflowing Love

Big Picture Verse

"God has poured out his love into our hearts by the Holy Spirit, whom he has given us." Romans 5:5

Teacher Materials

Bible with bookmark at Romans 5:5, small or medium-sized glass jar, large baking pan with sides, measuring utensils, baking soda, vinegar, food coloring.

God's gift of the Holy Spirit makes it possible for His followers to show love and care for others. When we accept God's love, it overflows to others. Watch to see what overflows in this experiment.

Present the Object Talk

1. Set the jar in the middle of the baking pan. Pour 1 tablespoon of baking soda into the jar. Measure 1 cup of vinegar and add several drops of food coloring to the cup. Pour vinegar into the jar. The liquid will bubble up and overflow the jar.

2. **When the vinegar and baking soda were mixed together, they formed a gas called carbon dioxide. The gas pushed the liquid out the top of the bottle so that the liquid overflowed.**

Conclude

The Bible talks about how God's love can overflow. Read Romans 5:5 aloud. **God loves us so much He wants each of us to show His love to others. God showed His love to us by sending the Holy Spirit. The Holy Spirit helps us show love to others so that the family of people who believe in God can grow.** Lead students in prayer, thanking God for sending the Holy Spirit and asking His help in showing His love to others.

Discussion Questions

1. What are some other things you have seen that overflow? (A river or lake that overflows its banks. A soda can that has been shaken before opening.)

2. What are some of the other ways God has shown His love to us?

3. What are some ways we can show God's love to others?

4. How has someone shown God's love to you?

Active Game Center: Full Cups

Materials
Two containers (buckets, bowls or plastic tubs), a small plastic cup and water, uncooked rice or uncooked beans for each team of six students.

Prepare the Game
Fill half of the containers with an equal amount of water, rice or beans. For each team, set an empty container and a full container next to each other on one side of the playing area.

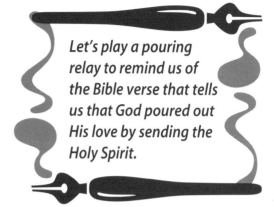

Let's play a pouring relay to remind us of the Bible verse that tells us that God poured out His love by sending the Holy Spirit.

Lead the Game
1. Group students into teams of no more than six. Teams line up in single-file lines across the room from containers. Give a cup to the first student in each line.

2. At your signal, the first student in each line runs to the filled container opposite from his or her team, takes one full scoop with cup and pours contents of cup into empty container. Student returns to line and gives cup to next student who repeats process. Several times

during the game, call out "Full Cups." Each student with a cup in his or her hand when "Full Cups" is called must go to another team's container and transfer a scoop for that team instead. The first team to transfer all its contents wins.

Option
Play game outdoors and fill containers with ½ cup water. Give the first student in each team a straw. Student runs to team's containers, puts straw into water and then places finger over one end of the straw. Student then withdraws straw, positions it over the empty container and takes finger off the top of the straw to release water. Student runs back to line and gives straw to next student in line.

Discussion Questions
1. *God has given us the Holy Spirit because He loves us. What are some other ways God has shown love to us?* (Sent Jesus to take the punishment for our sins. Created a beautiful world for us to enjoy. Answers our prayers.)

2. *The Holy Spirit helps us show God's love and care to others. What are some things we can do for others with the help of the Holy Spirit?*

Art Center: Family of Hands

Student Materials
Paper in a variety of colors, pencils, scissors, tape.

Prepare the Activity
As directed below, trace your hands on a sheet of paper and cut out.

Lead the Activity
1. Show sample cutout of your hands. Give each student a sheet of paper. Student places hands on paper so that thumbs slightly overlap (see sketch a). A classmate traces around the student's hands.

2. Student cuts out the hands, being careful to leave thumbs connected, and writes his or her name on one hand and the name of another church family member on the other hand. Students make as many hands as time permits, writing different names on the hands (friends, family members, church staff, missionaries, etc.). As students write names, talk about the variety of people in your church family.

3. Tape all hands together to make a hand garland (see sketch b). Display garland on classroom wall or on the wall of a well-traveled area in your church.

As the first church family grew bigger and bigger, the people showed God's love and helped each other. Often we use our hands to help each other. Let's see how many hands we can make and connect together, naming some of the people in our church family.

a.
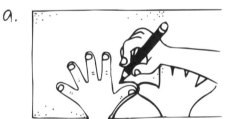

b.

Option
Students draw pictures of people on the handprints near their names.

Discussion Questions

1. Who is someone older than you in our church family? younger than you? the same age as you?

2. How did we help each other make the hand garlands? What are some other ways you can help and show God's love to the people in our church family?

3. How does showing God's love to others help our church family? (People learn about God. People in the church family like being together and worshiping God together.)

Worship Center

Big Picture Verse

"God has poured out his love into our hearts by the Holy Spirit, whom he has given us." Romans 5:5

Let's thank God for giving us the Holy Spirit so that we can show God's love and care to others.

Teacher Materials

Bible, *God's Big Picture* cassette/CD or music video and player, "Psalm 9:1,2,10" word chart (p. 477 in this book), large sheet of paper on which you have printed Romans 5:5, masking tape.

Sing to God

Play "Psalm 9:1,2,10," encouraging students to sing along with the music and do the actions shown on the word chart or the music video. **What are some of the reasons we should sing praises to God?** (He gave us the Holy Spirit. He loves us. He helps us care for others.)

Hear and Say God's Word

Display paper on which you have printed Romans 5:5. Volunteer reads verse aloud. **What are some things we pour?** (Juice. Water. Milk.) **What does Romans 5:5 tell us God has poured into, or given, us?** (His love.) **When we receive His love, we can show that love and care to others!** Lead students in reciting the verse in this manner: Students take turns calling out one word each to complete the verse. Repeat verse as many times as needed so that every student gets a chance to say a word.

Pray to God

What are some ways we can show God's love and care to each other? Students tell ideas. Lead students in prayer, volunteers asking for God's help in showing love and care to others in the ways mentioned. End prayer by thanking God for sending the Holy Spirit.

Options

1. Ask an older student to find the words "Pentecost" and "Holy Spirit" in a children's Bible dictionary and read the definitions to the group.

2. Students sing and do actions for "God's Amazing Power" and/or "Picture This!" (p. 457 and/or p. 473 in this book).

 **Lesson 44**

Bible Story Coloring Center

Materials

Crayons or markers, a copy of "God sends the Holy Spirit" picture and story (pp. 215-216 from *Bible Story Coloring Pages*) for each student.

Lead the Activity

Students color page 215; read or tell the story on page 216. **When the Holy Spirit came, God sent fire to show how powerful His Spirit is. These people are telling about Jesus. What do you think they are saying about Jesus?**

Option

Provide small fabric pieces that students may glue onto the clothing of the people in the picture.

Skit Center

Materials

A copy of "Acts" skit (pp. 267-269 from *The Big Book of Bible Skits*) for each student; optional—highlighter pens.

Lead the Activity

Students form pairs and read the skit, which tells the story of Luke writing about the events of Pentecost. (Optional: Students highlight their parts.) Ask the discussion questions on page 267.

Bible Skills Center

Materials

Materials needed for "Match Up" and/or "Bible Book Basics" (p. 47 and/or p. 117 from *The Big Book of Bible Skills*).

Lead the Activity

Students complete activities as directed in *The Big Book of Bible Skills*.

A Lame Man Walks Again

Big Picture Verse

"Live a life of love, just as Christ loved us."
Ephesians 5:2

THE BIG PICTURE
Giving to others doesn't depend on how rich we are because Jesus helps us give more than money.

Scripture Background
Acts 3:1-16

Acts 3 opens at the Beautiful Gate of the Temple. Peter healed a cripple, lame from birth, who had been carried daily to this place to beg for his living. The miracle attracted the notice of the Jewish leaders and resulted in the first real opposition to the Church.

When a great crowd had gathered around the lame man who had been so miraculously healed, Peter took advantage of the circumstances to preach his second recorded sermon. Again he preached that Christ was the long-promised Messiah. So powerful were the words of Peter and John that a total of 5,000 men now turned to Christ!

We find that this kind of preaching brought unity and a spirit of giving in the Church. The Church became so unselfish that many sold all they had and gave it to the apostles to distribute as each saw a need. No one was compelled to part with personal possessions. The sharing of property was voluntary, not obligatory.

As Christians, we claim to give all to Christ. Complete surrender is the condition He sets down for discipleship. The power in the apostles' story was that their lives fitted in with the life of their risen Christ. "You've got to show me" is the attitude of the world today. Those early Christians did show the world by their lives and their conduct. Thousands of articles have been written about motivating people to give of their time and possessions to others. There will be plenty of service among God's followers when we give place to His Spirit. The Spirit-filled believer will be a serving believer.

Adapted from *What the Bible Is All About* by Henrietta C. Mears.

 **Lesson 45** • Acts 3:1-16

Big Picture Story Center

Teacher Materials
Bible Time Line, drawing materials/equipment.

Student Materials
Drawing materials.

Tell the Story
Move the *Bible Time Line* frame to highlight Picture 45. As you tell each part of the story, draw each sketch. Students copy your sketches.

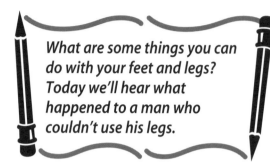

What are some things you can do with your feet and legs? Today we'll hear what happened to a man who couldn't use his legs.

1. Every day, HUNDREDS of people went to worship God in the Temple in Jerusalem. And every day, these people passed through the Temple gate where a man sat, begging. You see, this man was lame. That meant his feet and legs didn't work, so he couldn't walk or run.

1. Draw "X" for legs; add stick figure.

2. In his hands, the lame man held a bowl. Every day, as people went into the Temple, he asked them to give him money. He needed help! But the only help he got was coins in his beggar's bowl.

2. Draw bowl from "O" and "U."

3. One day, when Peter and John were on their way into the Temple, the lame man called, "Do you have some money for a poor lame man?" But Peter knew the lame man needed something else besides money. Peter said, "I have no silver or gold to give you. But I WILL give you what I have."

3. Make faces from "P" and "J."

4. Peter took the lame man by the hand and helped him to his feet, saying, "In the name of Jesus, walk!" And the man DID! His feet and legs were suddenly STRONG! He walked. He leaped!

4. Leaping figure from "N."

5. The man was so excited and happy, he went into the Temple with Peter and John, jumping up and down and praising God!

5. Draw man's face near Peter's and John's.

6. The people in the Temple were amazed. "That's the same man who's been sitting and begging by the Temple gate for years!" someone said. Everyone wondered how this man could be jumping and walking! Soon a crowd had gathered!

6. Add "C"s for crowd around Peter, John and man.

7. Peter said, "Why does it surprise you that this man can walk? WE haven't made this man walk by our own goodness or power! It is the power of God—the power of the same God who sent Jesus to you, even though you killed Him—it is HIS power that has healed this man. By trusting in the name of Jesus, this man is completely well!"

7. Print "GOD"; add burst from "V"s.

8. The people listened as Peter told all about God's power. And THOUSANDS more people believed in Jesus and became part of God's big family, the Church!

8. Add smiling faces to crowd.

Get the Big Picture

What did the lame man usually get when he begged? (Money.) **What did he need most?** (To be able to walk again.) **What did Peter give him to help him?** (He healed Him with God's power.)

When we give to others, we don't have to give money, either. We can give to others by being friendly, kind or patient. Jesus helps us give to other people in more ways than just giving money!

Bible Verse Object Talk: Circle Attraction

Big Picture Verse
"Live a life of love, just as Christ loved us." Ephesians 5:2

Teacher Materials
Bible with bookmark at Ephesians 5:2, hole punch, tissue paper, small round balloon.

Jesus helps us give more than money to others. Our gifts of love can make a big difference. Watch the different actions that take place in this experiment.

Prepare the Object Talk
Use the hole punch to make 20 to 30 tissue-paper circles. Inflate and tie the balloon.

Present the Object Talk
1. Place the tissue-paper circles on a table.

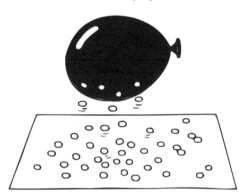

2. Rub the balloon against your hair (or a carpet) at least 10 times. Then hold the rubbed side of the balloon several inches (cm) above the paper circles. The paper circles will be attracted to the balloon and jump off the table onto the balloon.

3. As time permits, invite volunteers to take turns creating the attraction between the balloon and the paper circles. (Optional: Provide additional balloons and circles so that more volunteers can participate at once.) **Rubbing the balloon makes an electric charge that attracts, or pulls, the paper circles.**

Conclude
When we show Jesus' love to others, it attracts them to Jesus and helps them want to learn about Jesus. Read Ephesians 5:2. **How does this verse describe the way Jesus' followers should live? What should we be like?** Volunteers tell ideas. Lead students in prayer, asking His help in giving and showing love to others.

Discussion Questions
1. What other kinds of things attract each other? (Magnets attract many metal items. Flowers attract bees. Gravity attracts, or pulls, falling objects.)

2. How does showing Jesus' love help others learn about Him? (Helps others discover what the people who love Jesus are like. Helps others understand how much Jesus loves them.)

3. How has someone shown Jesus' love to you and your family?

4. How can you show Jesus' love to someone else?

Active Game Center: Secret Pass-Off

Materials
Marbles or other small objects.

Lead the Game

Jesus helps us share what we have to help other people. Let's play a game in which we are secretly trying to give something away.

1. Choose at least one volunteer to become a "watcher." One Watcher for every six or seven students will be needed. Watchers close eyes while you quietly give marbles or other small objects to no more than half of remaining students.

2. Watcher opens eyes. All students put hands behind backs and begin walking around the room, passing objects to each other while keeping hands behind backs. At the same time, Watchers try to detect who are holding the objects. To increase challenge, all students should pretend to pass objects.

3. Call time after 30 seconds or so. Watchers name students they think are holding objects. If their guesses are correct, students holding objects give them to the Watchers. If their guesses are incorrect, begin a new round of play. After the second round, choose new Watchers whether or not all objects have been collected. Play as many rounds as time allows.

Discussion Questions

1. Was it easier to be a watcher or a secret giver?

2. Why does Jesus tell us it is important to give to each other?

3. Besides money, what else does Jesus help us give to others?

Lesson 45

Art Center: Look Who's Walking!

Student Materials

Butcher paper, scissors, measuring stick, tape, pencil, markers or crayons.

Prepare the Activity

Cut a long length of butcher paper in half to make a continuous strip with approximately 2 feet (.6 m) for each student. Tape strip to wall of classroom or hallway, positioning the bottom edge of the paper along the floor. (If needed, cut butcher paper into shorter lengths.)

No matter how much money we have, Jesus helps us give His love to others. Two of Jesus' followers didn't have money to give, but because of Jesus' power they helped a lame man walk. Today we'll make a mural to remind us of this Bible story.

Lead the Activity

1. Students line up along the butcher and take turns tracing each others' legs from just above the knees. As students pose, encourage them to stand in a variety of positions (as if running, jumping, tiptoeing, hopping, etc.).

2. Remove paper from wall and place on table or floor. Students draw shoes and color in their legs and shoes.

3. Attach paper to wall again to display the mural. Print the title "Showing God's Love Everywhere We Go" on mural.

Options

1. Bring a variety of fabric scraps for students to cut and glue to shoe drawings.

2. Students draw additional details on mural: dogs, cats, bouncing basketball, soccer ball, Hopscotch grid, etc.

Discussion Questions

1. *Where are some places you walk? some places you play? In what ways can you give love to others by helping them in those places?*

2. *What are some ways people have helped you?*

3. *What are some gifts that don't require money that we can give to others?* (Time to help. Kindness. Patience. Honesty. Prayer.)

Lesson 45

Worship Center

Big Picture Verse

"Live a life of love, just as Christ loved us." Ephesians 5:2

> *Let's thank Jesus that He helps us give much more than money to other people.*

Teacher Materials

Bible, *God's Big Picture* cassette/CD or music video and player, "Everywhere I Go" word chart (p. 451 in this book), large sheet of paper on which you have printed Ephesians 5:2, masking tape.

Sing to God

Play "Everywhere I Go," encouraging students to sing along with the music and do the actions shown on the word chart or the music video. **Why is it important to know that Jesus is always with us?** (He can always help us when we have problems. He shows us ways to help others.)

Hear and Say God's Word

Display paper on which you have printed Ephesians 5:2. Volunteer reads the verse aloud. Point out that the verse is separated into two parts by the comma. Divide students into two groups. Assign each group one half of the verse. Each group says their part of the verse when you point at them. Repeat, varying when you point at each group. **What can we do to "live a life of love"?** (Show love to others all the time with our actions and our words.)

Pray to God

When are some times it is hard for kids your age to show Jesus' love to others?
Volunteers respond. Add to the Bible verse paper to make it read "God, please help us to live a life of love, just as Christ loved us. Amen." Lead students in reciting the prayer together.

Options

1. Invite a guest to share about a way he or she has given gifts other than money to people (Bibles to other countries, meals for homeless people, yard work for elderly people, etc.).

2. After group says sentence prayer, volunteers pray for God's help in situations mentioned in discussion.

Bible Story Coloring Center  FOR YOUNGER CHILDREN

Materials

Crayons or markers, paper.

Lead the Activity

Invite students to draw pictures of items that they can share with others. **What are some other things we can share to show our love for Jesus? Who can you share with?** Students may also draw pictures of people they want to share with.

Skit Center FOR OLDER CHILDREN

Materials

A copy of "Crippled" skit (pp. 270-273 from *The Big Book of Bible Skits*) for each student; optional—highlighter pens.

Lead the Activity

Students form trios and read the skit, which tells the story of the lame man's healing. (Optional: Students highlight their parts.) Ask the discussion questions on page 270.

Bible Skills Center FOR OLDER CHILDREN

Materials

Materials needed for "Content Concentration" and/or "Puzzling Words" (p. 45 and/or p. 97 from *The Big Book of Bible Skills*).

Lead the Activity

Students complete activities as directed in *The Big Book of Bible Skills*.

 **Lesson 46**

Saul Meets Jesus

Big Picture Verse

"The wages of sin is death, but the gift of God is eternal life in Christ Jesus our Lord." Romans 6:23

THE BIG PICTURE

Becoming a Christian is more than knowing facts about God; God invites each of us to choose to belong to God's family and accept Jesus' love.

Scripture Background
Acts 9:1-31

The story of Saul's conversion is one of the most thrilling accounts in history. Saul was born at Tarsus, of purely Jewish stock. His teacher was Gamaliel, the great teacher of the Pharisees. Like all Hebrew boys, he learned a trade—he was a tentmaker.

First, he was a man "breathing out murderous threats against the Lord's disciples" (Acts 9:1). In fact, Saul made havoc of the Church! Saul's persecution of the believers, however, like the confusion of tongues at the tower of Babel, scattered the Christians throughout the world. Saul had already begun his work of spreading the gospel, but he didn't know it! Saul thought he was stamping out Christianity. Instead, he was spreading it! Persecution always has spread Christianity like wind spreads fire. This has been true down through the centuries since our Lord lived on the earth.

But at the same time he was relentlessly pursuing Jesus' followers, Saul was struggling with his own aroused conscience. He knew he was in the wrong, but he wouldn't give up. This is why Jesus told him in a vision that it was hard for Saul to struggle against the sharp points of the truth (see Acts 26:14).

The vision occurs in the dramatic story of Jesus' confrontation with Saul on the road to Damascus. On the way to Damascus, on a mission of persecution of the Christians, the young Pharisee had a head-on collision with Jesus Christ! In a blinding flash of light Saul was converted and made an apostle by Christ Himself. It was to Saul that Christ gave first-hand revelations of truth, and to him Christ committed the doctrine of the Church. Then we find Saul preaching in the synagogues "that Jesus is the Son of God" (Acts 9:20). There is no doubt that Saul, later called Paul, holds a very important place as a Christian leader in the New Testament.

Adapted from *What the Bible Is All About* by Henrietta C. Mears.

Lesson 46 • Acts 9:1-31

Big Picture Story Center

Teacher Materials

Bible Time Line, drawing materials/equipment.

Student Materials

Drawing materials.

Tell the Story

Move the *Bible Time Line* frame to highlight Picture 46. As you tell each part of the story, draw each sketch. Students copy your sketches.

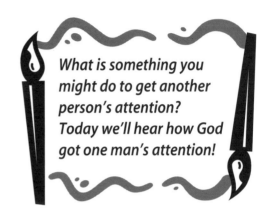

What is something you might do to get another person's attention? Today we'll hear how God got one man's attention!

1. Jesus had gone back to heaven. He had sent His Spirit to help His friends tell others about His love. All over Jerusalem, people were talking about Jesus. And they were believing in Jesus and accepting His love for them so that God's family got bigger every day. That was GOOD NEWS to many people! But to Saul, it was TERRIBLE news.

1. Draw large heart. Print "GOD'S FAMILY" inside.

2. Saul was an important religious leader in Jerusalem. But he didn't believe Jesus was God's Son. And he was angry that so many people DID believe that Jesus was sent from God. He was so angry, he wanted to punish people who loved Jesus!

2. Draw "no" slash over heart

3. First, Saul got permission from the religious leaders to throw the people who loved Jesus into JAIL. Then Saul left for Damascus (duh-MAS-kuhs). People came to Damascus from all over the world. Saul thought that if he could keep people there from telling about Jesus by putting them into jail, maybe he could stop this talk about Jesus from spreading.

3. Write "jail." Add face to "a," bars from other letters.

4. As Saul and the men traveling with him got close to Damascus, a bright light from heaven suddenly flashed like lightning around Saul! WOW! Saul fell to the ground. "Saul, Saul!" a voice said. "Why are you fighting against Me?"

4. Flash of light from "V"s.

5. Saul gasped, "Who...who are You, Lord?"

"I am Jesus, the One you are trying to hurt." UH-OH! Saul had been so certain that Jesus was NOT God's Son. But now he heard Jesus speaking to him! "Go into the city," Jesus told Saul. "You will be told what to do next."

5. Scared face from "O"s, "C" and "3"s.

6. When Saul got up, he couldn't see anything. The people with him took him by the hand and led him to a place to stay. For three days, Saul didn't eat or drink; he prayed.

6. Kneeling figure from circle, line and "V"s.

7. Soon, God sent a man named Ananias to help Saul. Ananias prayed for Saul, and Saul could SEE again! Saul finally understood that Jesus is God's Son and that He is alive. Now Saul himself wanted to be Jesus' friend! Ananias baptized Saul and brought him to meet Jesus' friends in Damascus—the same people Saul had wanted to arrest three days before!

7. River from "S"s; add stick figures.

8. Jesus' friends were afraid of Saul at first. But they soon saw that Saul was truly a changed man. So Jesus' friends helped him and after a few days, Saul began to tell people all over Damascus the good news about Jesus! When people heard Saul (later called Paul), they were AMAZED.

8. Scared face to smiling face.

Get the Big Picture

What was Saul like before he met Jesus on the road to Damascus? (He wanted to hurt people who believed in Jesus.) **What difference did meeting Jesus make in Saul's life?** (He stopped being angry at the people who loved Jesus. He believed that Jesus is God's Son. He told others about Jesus.)

God invites each of us to choose to believe that Jesus is His Son and that He died to take the punishment for our sins. When we accept Jesus' love for us, we become members of God's family.

Bible Verse Object Talk: Paid in Full

Big Picture Verse

"The wages of sin is death, but the gift of God is eternal life in Christ Jesus our Lord." Romans 6:23

Teacher Materials

Bible with bookmark at Romans 6:23, calculator, large sheet of paper, marker, blank check, pen.

Present the Object Talk

God wants us to be part of His family so much that He made it possible for us to receive His love and forgiveness for the wrong things we do. Let's find out how Jesus paid for our sins.

1. **If we were to owe money for the wrong actions we've done, we would probably owe a lot of money.** Ask students to name wrong actions (lying, stealing, cheating, fighting, etc.). As you list each wrong action on paper, have class decide on a dollar amount as penalty, or punishment, for each action (for example, $100 for lying), and write this amount next to the action. Ask a volunteer to add the amounts on the calculator and announce total to class. (Optional: Depending on the age of your group, you may add amounts on the calculator yourself.)

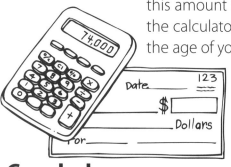

2. **If someone loved you enough, he or she could pay what you owe for your wrong actions by writing a check for the full amount.** Write out a check for the total amount, leaving the "to" and "from" portions blank.

Conclude

The good news we read in the Bible is that the amount or punishment owed for our sin has been completely paid by Jesus, God's Son. Read Romans 6:23 aloud. **When Jesus died on the cross, He made it possible for our sin to be paid in full so that we can be part of God's family. What a great gift He gave us!** Complete the check, making the check out to "God," signing it from "Jesus" and writing "For (your name)'s sin" in the check memo portion. Lead students in prayer, thanking God for His gift of salvation.

Discussion Questions

1. How does doing wrong usually make a person feel?

2. How can asking God to forgive our sins help us? (God promises to give us forgiveness and make us members of His family.)

3. How do we know that God's love is big enough to forgive all the wrong things we and others do? (The Bible tells us so. God always keeps His promises.)

4. How have you learned about God's love for you?

Active Game Center: Who Does God Love?

Materials

Blindfold.

Lead the Game

1. Play a game like Marco Polo. Ask a volunteer to stand on one side of the playing area. Blindfold the volunteer. Students quietly position themselves at random around the playing area. Volunteer begins calling "God loves...." Rest of students answer "me."

2. Blindfolded volunteer moves toward students by listening to their voices. As he or she continues calling "God loves...," students around the room must respond each time. Depending on the size of your playing area, the students who respond to the blindfolded volunteer may stay frozen in one spot or may move around as they respond. (If you have a large playing area or a large number of students, students should stay frozen.)

To become a Christian, we must make a choice to accept Jesus' love and be a part of God's family. The game we're going to play will remind us of God's love for us.

God loves...

3. When the volunteer finds and tags a student, that student (or a student who hasn't had a turn yet) is blindfolded for the next round. Continue game as time permits.

Options

1. Instead of responding "me," students may respond with names of friends or family members.

2. A paper bag may be used instead of a blindfold.

Discussion Questions

1. *What are some choices players made in this game?*

2. *What are some choices kids your age make every day? What are some hard choices? some easy ones?*

3. *What might be one of the most important choices anyone can ever make?* (Whether or not to become a Christian and be a part of God's family.)

4. *How can we choose to become part of God's family?* (By asking Jesus to forgive our sins and to be with us forever.)

Art Center: Personal Mementos

Student Materials

Large sheet of paper, markers, one fist-sized rock for each student.

Lead the Activity

1. Invite volunteers to suggest phrases or short sentences about God's love for all people ("God's love is for you and me!" "God's love is forever!" "God's love never quits!"). Print phrases or sentences on large sheet of paper to which students may refer.

2. Students write their names, today's date and a short phrase or sentence about God's love on their rocks, making mementos about God's love.

God loves us so much that He wants each person to know about Him and to accept His love and become part of His family. Today you can make a memento, or reminder, of God's love for you.

3. Students may also draw additional symbols (stars, sun, hearts, Bibles) on their rocks. Ask students where they will keep their mementos, or reminders, of God's love.

Option

If rocks are not available, provide air-drying clay or play dough. Students form clay or dough into flat shapes (circles, squares, hearts or triangles) and use pencils, nails or toothpicks to etch names, date and phrases or sentences.

Discussion Questions

1. What are some of the ways you have learned about God's love?

2. Who has helped you learn about God's love?

3. What are some things God has made that remind you of His love for you?

4. Why is it important for each person to accept God's love? Talk with interested students about becoming members of God's family. (See "Leading a Child to Christ" on p. 30.)

Lesson 46

Worship Center

Big Picture Verse

"The wages of sin is death, but the gift of God is eternal life in Christ Jesus our Lord." Romans 6:23

> *Let's thank God that He loves each of us and allows us to make the choice to belong to His family by accepting His love and forgiveness.*

Teacher Materials

Bible, *God's Big Picture* cassette/CD or music video and player, "God's Amazing Power" word chart (p. 457 in this book), large sheet of paper on which you have printed Romans 6:23, masking tape.

Sing to God

Play "God's Amazing Power," encouraging students to sing along with the music and do the actions shown on the word chart or the music video. **According to this song, why can we praise God? What are some other reasons God is amazing?** (He loves us all. He wants each of us to be a part of His family. He made the world.)

Hear and Say God's Word

Display paper on which you have printed Romans 6:23. **What are wages?** (What you get for doing something. Parents or older brothers and sisters get wages or money for working.) **What does Romans 6:23 say are the wages of choosing to sin and disobey God?** (Death.) **What is the free gift that God offers us instead?** (Life forever with Him when we make the choice to belong to His family.) Lead students in saying Romans 6:23 by pointing at each word. Students say word in unison as you point at it. Repeat with volunteers pointing at words and leading students through verse.

Pray to God

Let's thank God that He loves each of us and wants us to be in His family. Lead students in prayer, thanking God that we can belong to His family when we accept His love and forgiveness. Talk with interested students about becoming members of God's family.

Options

1. If students give an offering during worship time, explain that giving money to God is one way to thank Him for His love for us and His free gift of eternal life. Describe several ways that your church uses the offering to help others learn about God's love and His gift of eternal life (for example, tell students about a missionary the church supports).
2. Older student leads Bible verse activity.

Bible Story Coloring Center

FOR YOUNGER CHILDREN

Materials
Crayons or markers, a copy of "Jesus talks to Saul" picture and story (pp. 221-222 from *Bible Story Coloring Pages*) for each student.

Lead the Activity
Students color page 221; read or tell the story on page 222. **What was Saul like before Jesus talked to him? What did Saul learn about Jesus?** (That Jesus is God's Son.)

Option
Also provide a copy of "Saul escapes in a basket" picture and story (pp. 223-224 from *Bible Story Coloring Pages*). **This picture shows how Saul got away from the people who didn't want him telling others that he was a member of God's family and had accepted Jesus' love.** Students color page 223 as you read or tell the story page 224.

Skit Center

FOR OLDER CHILDREN

Materials
A copy of "The Bully" skit (pp. 337- 339 from *The Big Book of Bible Skits*) for each student; optional—highlighter pens.

Lead the Activity
Students form groups of four and read the skit, which tells the story of a bully who tries to convince people he has changed. (Optional: Students highlight their parts.) Ask the discussion questions on page 337.

Bible Skills Center

FOR OLDER CHILDREN

Materials
Materials needed for "Rapid Pass" and/or "Dot Definitions" (p. 34 and/or p. 105 from *The Big Book of Bible Skills*).

Lead the Activity
Students complete activities as directed in *The Big Book of Bible Skills*.

God's Message for Peter

Big Picture Verse

"Accept one another, then, just as Christ accepted you, in order to bring praise to God." Romans 15:7

THE BIG PICTURE

God's love is for everyone, not just people like us.

Scripture Background
Acts 10

Peter is an outstanding figure in the first twelve chapters of Acts. His sermon at Pentecost led the early believers into wonderful days of spiritual growth. But what had Peter done since Pentecost? It is not only what a person believes but also what is done about the belief that counts. Christ had told Peter that he was to be a witness. Following Christ's command, Peter helped start the first Church, worked miracles and baptized thousands.

During this time his ministry had been among the Jews. Jewish believers fervently preached the gospel—to other Jews. They kept the traditions of avoiding Gentiles, their homes and their "unclean" foods. This desire to stay pure could have easily turned the Early Church into an isolated Jewish sect.

We find Peter now in the house of Simon the tanner. God was going to show Peter that the gospel was for the Gentiles as well as the Jews. The high wall of religious difference between Jew and Gentile must be broken down. Peter was the man God used to start leveling it. Christ was building a Church and He wanted both Jews and Gentiles to be the living stones of which it was to be formed.

At Pentecost, Peter had used the "keys of the kingdom" (Matthew 16:19) entrusted to him to open the door of the gospel to the Jews. Peter, in the house of Cornelius, put the key into the lock of the door that had barred the Gentiles and opened it. God had opened the door of salvation to everyone. The old traditions were done. Jesus' new law of love for everyone was now the rule.

Jesus gave us this law of love as well. It demands that we ask God to free us from traditional prejudices and help us see others as He does. Rather than encouraging us to isolate ourselves from the world, God propels us into it as He did Peter. God wants us to share His love, a love that goes beyond fear and prejudice.

Adapted from *What the Bible Is All About* by Henrietta C. Mears.

Big Picture Story Center

Teacher Materials
Bible Time Line, drawing materials/equipment.

Student Materials
Drawing materials.

Tell the Story
Move the *Bible Time Line* frame to highlight Picture 47. As you tell each part of the story, draw each sketch. Students copy your sketches.

Who are some kinds of people a kid your age might have trouble accepting? Today we'll hear how Peter learned to accept people different from him.

1. In God's growing family, most of the people were Jews. Jesus was a Jew and so were His disciples. But Peter, one of Jesus' disciples, learned in a very strange way that God's love is for everyone—even for people who aren't Jews. (People who aren't Jews are called Gentiles.) Here's what happened.

1. Draw stick figures; add "Jews" and "Gentiles."

Jews   Gentiles

2. A man who was a Gentile, named Cornelius, loved God. One day while Cornelius was praying, God sent an angel to him. "Cornelius," the angel said, "God hears your prayers. Send for a man named Peter in the city of Joppa."

2. Angel from "V"s and "O"; add details.

3. Right away Cornelius sent three men to Joppa so that they could invite Peter to his house. These three men arrived in Joppa the next day.

3. Print "Joppa" and add 3 faces.

4. When they arrived, Peter was up on the flat roof of the house. Peter was praying while he waited for lunch to be ready. While Peter prayed, God showed him a strange dream: a big sheet with all KINDS of animals in it, from frogs and lizards to pigs and horses!

4. Sheet from "C"; snake from 2 "S"s; pig from "O"s and "V"s; horse from "U", "V"s and lines.

5. God said to Peter, "Peter, you can eat any of these kinds of meat for your lunch!" Well, Peter knew that Jews were not allowed to eat these kinds of meat, so he said to God, "Certainly NOT! Nothing unclean has EVER been in MY mouth."

"Don't call anything unclean that I have made CLEAN!" God said.

5. Add "no" slash.

6. God showed Peter this same strange dream TWO more times! While Peter thought about this dream, God said, "Three men are at your house. Go with them!"

6. Draw thought balloon.

7. Peter went downstairs. Sure enough, three men were at the gate wanting to see him! And they were Gentiles, people that Jews were supposed to stay away from. But God had said to go WITH them. Then Peter must have understood: ALL kinds of people can be part of God's family. So the next day, they all set out for Cornelius's house.

7. Draw "1,2,3" and add details to make 3 different faces.

8. When Peter and his new friends got to Cornelius's house, they found that the house was full of people. Peter said to all the people, "I know now that God loves EVERY person. He has sent me to tell you the good news about Jesus."

8. House from 2 triangles and lines. "C"s for crowd; add faces.

9. The people believed the things Peter said. Right then and there, they became part of God's family! And right then and there, God's Spirit came to them JUST like He had come to Peter. EVERYONE was the same to God. God LOVED them ALL!

9. Add heart around "Jews" and "Gentiles" in #1.

Get the Big Picture

What did Peter learn about God's love? (His love is for everyone—Jews and Gentiles.)
How did Peter show God's love and acceptance? (He told Cornelius, a Gentile, the good news about Jesus.)

God's love is for everyone, not just people who are like us. And just as He loves everyone, He wants us to love and accept every person in His family!

Bible Verse Object Talk: Circle Talk

Big Picture Verse

"Accept one another, then, just as Christ accepted you, in order to bring praise to God." Romans 15:7

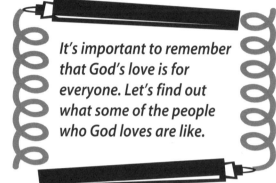

It's important to remember that God's love is for everyone. Let's find out what some of the people who God loves are like.

Teacher Materials

Bible with bookmark at Romans 15:7, large sheets of paper, marker.

Prepare the Object Talk

Draw two large intersecting circles (called a Venn diagram) on several large sheets of paper (see sketch).

Present the Object Talk

Write the names of two volunteers at the top of each circle. Then interview them to find several differences and similarities between them, writing the similarities in the overlapping area of the circles and writing the differences in the remaining areas of the circles. **What do you like to do at school? What is your favorite TV show? favorite color? favorite food?**

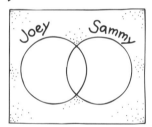

What color are your eyes? As you fill out the diagram, talk about the ways students are the same and different. **God made people alike in some ways and different in others.** Continue activity with other volunteers and new circles. (Optional: Group children into pairs. Give each pair a Venn diagram and invite them to draw pictures or write words to show their differences and similarities.)

Conclude

Listen to Romans 15:7 to find out what God wants us to do for each other whether we are alike or different. Read verse aloud. **When we accept others, it means that we want to show God's love by telling them the good news about Jesus and treating them in kind and fair ways. God's love is for everyone.** Write "Loved by God" in overlapping area of circles. Pray, thanking God for His love and asking His help in showing love to others.

Discussion Questions

1. How are you alike or different from the people in your family? a friend in your neighborhood or class at school?

2. How do you think you might be alike or different from a kid your age who lives in a country far away from here?

3. How might you help someone who is different from you learn about God's love? How might you accept that person and treat him or her fairly?

Active Game Center: All Strung Up

Materials

Ball of yarn or crepe paper roll of the same size for every four to six students.

Lead the Game

1. Students number off to form teams of four to six players. Teams form single-file lines in center of the playing area, leaving plenty of space between teams.

2. Give the first student in each line a ball of yarn or roll of crepe paper. The first student holds the end of the yarn or paper to his or her stomach with one hand and then passes the rest to the next student in line. Students

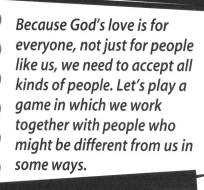

Because God's love is for everyone, not just for people like us, we need to accept all kinds of people. Let's play a game in which we work together with people who might be different from us in some ways.

continue passing yarn or crepe paper to student at end of line who wraps it around his or her back and passes it back to the front of the line. Passing continues until students have wrapped themselves (from the waist down) with the entire ball of yarn or roll of crepe paper. (Note: Students should stand as close together as possible to speed up the wrapping process.) The first team to finish names a way to accept other people who are different from them or a way to share God's love with people who are different.

Discussion Questions

1. *What are some ways the people on your team are different from each other?* (Hair color. Places we live in. Names. Interests. Ages.)

2. *What kinds of things do all people have in common?* (Need air, water, food and shelter. Loved by God. Jesus died for our sins.)

3. *How are we to treat all people, even if they seem different from us?* (Love them in the same way we want to be loved.)

4. *What can we do to help all people learn about God's love?* (Pray for them. Tell them about God's love. Invite them to church.)

Art Center: Multi-Colored Quilt

Student Materials

12-inch (30-cm) construction paper squares in a variety of colors, used magazines, scissors, glue, markers, tape.

Lead the Activity

1. Each student chooses two colors of paper squares.
2. On one square, each student glues pictures of people cut or torn from magazines. Encourage students to include

a variety of people (age, gender, race, occupation) on their squares.

3. On the second square, each student draws or writes ways to accept or show love to the people they pictured. To help students think of ways of accepting others, ask the Discussion Questions at the bottom of this page.
4. Students write their names on their squares. Guide students to tape squares together, forming a quilt-like pattern (see sketch).

When we think of all the different kinds of people in the world, it's good to know that God's love is for everyone, not just people like us. We're going to make a quilt of many colors to show the people God loves and ways we can love and accept them, too.

Options

1. Instead of taping quilt squares together, glue them onto a large sheet of butcher paper or poster board.
2. Provide one or more kinds of trim (rick rack, yarn, lace, ribbon, decorative buttons, braid, etc.) for students to add to their quilt squares.
3. Students may choose to write their names in a decorative fashion (use a variety of colors, write letters with dots, write block letters, etc.).
4. Take instant pictures of students to attach to quilt squares.

Discussion Questions

1. How do we know that God loves all people? (The Bible says so. God made all people. God sent Jesus to die for the sins of all people.)

2. How can you treat others to show you think they are special?

3. How can you treat others in ways that show you want to be friends?

4. What are some ways of accepting others by treating them fairly?

 **Lesson 47**

Worship Center

Big Picture Verse

"Accept one another, then, just as Christ accepted you, in order to bring praise to God." Romans 15:7

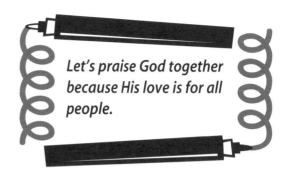

Let's praise God together because His love is for all people.

Teacher Materials

Bible, *God's Big Picture* cassette/CD or music video and player, "Easter Means..." word chart (p. 449 in this book), large sheet of paper on which you have printed Romans 15:7, masking tape.

Sing to God

Play "Easter Means...," encouraging students to sing along with the music and do the actions shown on the word chart or the music video. **Why does Easter remind us of salvation?** (Because at the first Easter, Jesus died on the cross to save us from the punishment for our sins.) **Who can receive the gift of salvation?** (Everyone. Jesus died on the cross for everyone, not just for people like us.)

Hear and Say God's Word

Display paper on which you have printed Romans 15:7. Volunteer reads verse aloud. **What are some ways we can show we accept others?** (Choose them for a game at recess. Sit by them at lunch. Listen to people when they talk to you. Treat all people kindly.) **When we do actions like this, Romans 15:7 says we are praising God.** Divide class into three groups. Assign each group one phrase of the verse ("Accept one another, then," "just as Christ accepted you" and "in order to bring praise to God"). Students from each group move around classroom to find a student from each of the other two groups and repeat phrases together in order. Repeat as time allows.

Pray to God

Don't say any names out loud. Think of someone you have a hard time accepting or being kind to. Pray silently to God, asking Him to help you accept that person in ways that please God. End prayer time by thanking God that He has accepted us and that we can please Him by accepting others.

Options

1. Invite an older student to read Romans 15:5-7 as a closing prayer.

2. During the verse activity, list ways of accepting others on a large sheet of paper. Then, before they pray, students may refer to the list for prayer ideas.

 **Lesson 47**

Bible Story Coloring Center

Materials
Crayons or markers, a copy of "Peter preaches to Cornelius" picture and story (pp. 227-228 from *Bible Story Coloring Pages*) for each student.

Lead the Activity
Students color page 227; read or tell the story on page 228. **Who is Peter talking to? What do you think he is saying about Jesus?**

Option
The Bible tells us that everyone in Cornelius's house listened to Peter tell about Jesus and then believed in Jesus. Encourage students to draw additional people listening to Peter's words.

Skit Center

Materials
A copy of "The Gentiles, Too?" skit (pp. 292-296 from *The Big Book of Bible Skits*) for each student; optional—highlighter pens.

Lead the Activity
Students form trios and read the skit, which tells the story of Peter's vision and his visit to Cornelius's house. (Optional: Students highlight their parts.) Ask the discussion questions on page 292.

Bible Skills Center

Materials
Materials needed for "Who's Got the Beans?" and/or "Code Fill-In" (p. 41 and/or p. 109 from *The Big Book of Bible Skills*).

Lead the Activity
Students complete activities as directed in *The Big Book of Bible Skills*.

Peter's Unexpected Escape

THE BIG PICTURE

God always answers prayer—sometimes in ways we don't expect.

Big Picture Verse

"Devote yourselves to prayer, being watchful and thankful." Colossians 4:2

Scripture Background
Acts 12:1-17

How we pray grows out of the way we perceive God. When we pray as Jesus taught us, we declare that we belong to the holy and powerful Father who loves us. Praying in this way is not a means of getting God to do what we want done—it is our way of saying we desire what He desires.

In the story of Peter's escape from prison, we see the believers gathered together in earnest prayer. Through the long night they asked God to free Peter, and miraculously He did! Peter, once freed, recognized this divine intervention: "Now I know without a doubt that the Lord sent his angel and rescued me" (Acts 12:11).

Knowing that his friends were praying for him, Peter went to the house where they were together in prayer. Their astonishment at this unexpected answer to prayer knew no bounds, even to the point of refusing entrance to Peter. Their anxiety over Peter's welfare had caused them to pray, but their prayers had not caused them to live in a spirit of confidence.

The way to be anxious about nothing is to be prayerful about everything. The prayer of faith must then be a prayer of thanksgiving and confidence in God's response. Put your prayers into God's hands and go off and leave them there. Do not worry about them. Give them completely as the farmer gives the wheat to the soil after the soil has been properly plowed. If you do this, the peace of God will stand guard over your heart and mind.

Adapted from *What the Bible Is All About* by Henrietta C. Mears.

Big Picture Story Center

Teacher Materials
Bible Time Line, drawing materials/equipment.

Student Materials
Drawing materials.

Tell the Story
Move the *Bible Time Line* frame to highlight Picture 48. As you tell each part of the story, draw each sketch. Students copy your sketches.

When is a time you've been afraid? Today we'll hear how God rescued Peter from a very scary situation!

1. It was time for the Passover, usually a joyful time in Jerusalem. But for God's growing family, it was a SCARY time. You see, Herod, the Roman ruler, had sent soldiers to arrest and KILL James, one of Jesus' followers! Everyone in God's family was very sad. And they were wondering what that cruel ruler Herod would do next!

2. It wasn't long before Herod did something else to make them afraid. He sent soldiers to arrest Peter, another one of Jesus' friends. Herod had Peter put into prison. Herod was planning to keep Peter in prison until the Passover holiday was over. Then Herod planned to accuse Peter of doing something wrong and put him on trial, so Herod could kill him, too.

3. Peter's friends knew that Peter might be killed. So guess what they did. They prayed! They met at the house of a woman named Mary and prayed and prayed with all their might, asking God to protect Peter and to help them.

4. The night before Herod was going to have Peter killed, God sent an angel to Peter's prison cell. The angel said, "Quick, get up!" And the chains around Peter's arms just fell off! Then Peter and the angel walked right past the guards!

1. Draw scared faces, sad faces, question marks.

2. Peter from "P" and "3"s; add prison bars.

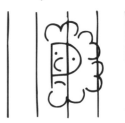

3. Draw praying hands from "U"s and lines; add face.

4. Moon from "C"s; add stars.

5. When Peter and the angel got to the huge iron gate leading to the city, the gate opened as if an invisible hand was pushing it! Peter followed the angel to the end of the street, and then the angel simply DISAPPEARED!

5. Gate from "U"; add open side and stick figures.

6. Peter hurried to the house where his friends were praying. He knocked on the door. A servant girl named Rhoda called out, "Who's there?"

"Peter!" he answered. Rhoda was so overjoyed that she ran to the room full of praying people without even opening the door!

"Peter's at the door! Peter's at the door!" she cried.

"WHAT?" they asked. "You must be crazy! Peter's in prison. He can't be at the door."

6. Knocking hand and door from "U"s; add details.

7. But Peter kept knocking on the door! When Rhoda finally opened it, Peter's friends were amazed and happy to see him!

7. Draw happy, amazed faces.

8. "God heard your prayers for me," Peter said. "God rescued me! God sent an angel in answer to your prayers!"

Everyone was VERY glad that Peter was safe. They knew now that God had heard and answered their prayers! And so they prayed again—to THANK God for sending Peter safely back to them!

8. Make an acrostic of "PRAYER," "ANSWER" and "SURPRISE!"

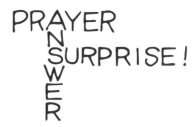

Get the Big Picture

What did Peter expect would happen? What did his friends do? How did God surprise Peter? (Sent an angel to his prison cell.) **When were Peter's friends surprised?** (When Peter came to their house.)

Sometimes when we pray, we may think that God doesn't hear us because He doesn't answer us when we expect He will or in the way we expect He will. But God really DOES hear—and He DOES answer our prayers. Sometimes, He answers them in ways that we don't expect! He loves us and He loves to surprise us!

Bible Verse Object Talk: Watch and Wait

Big Picture Verse

"Devote yourselves to prayer, being watchful and thankful." Colossians 4:2

Teacher Materials

Bible with bookmark at Colossians 4:2, newspapers, paper plate, glue, salt, paintbrush, watercolor paint, container of water.

Sometimes when something takes a long time to happen, we get tired of waiting and watching for it to happen. When we pray to God, we need to wait and watch to see Him answer our prayers. Watch to see what happens in this experiment.

Present the Object Talk

1. Cover table or floor with newspapers. Squeeze glue onto paper plate, creating a design of thick lines that intersect.

2. Immediately pour salt over the lines, making sure to cover the glue completely. Shake excess salt onto glue. Saturate paintbrush with water so that it is very wet. Then dab water-

color paint onto one of the lines, holding the brush at one place. The color will move along the lines as the salt absorbs the water in the paint. Encourage students to keep watching to see what happens to the paint.

3. After the color has stopped spreading, rinse the brush in water and apply another color of paint at a different place. The two paints will mix at the point where they meet. **What did you expect would happen? What did happen?**

Conclude

Just as we watched to see what would happen with the paint, it's up to us to keep watching to find out how God will answer our prayers. We know God will always keep His promise to answer our prayers. Read Colossians 4:2 aloud. **When we devote ourselves to prayer, we never give up praying and looking to see how God will answer our prayers. Sometimes God answers our prayers in ways we don't expect.** Lead students in prayer, thanking God for always hearing and answering our prayers.

Discussion Questions

1. *What are some things kids your age often talk to God about?* (When help is needed to do something. To thank Him for having something good or for something good happening.)

2. *Why might God answer a prayer by saying "no" or "later"?* (God knows what's best for us.)

3. *In what way has God answered a prayer for you or someone in your family?*

4. *What's something you want to talk to God about?*

Lesson 48

Active Game Center: Watch Your Back!

Materials
Large Post-it Notes.

Lead the Game

1. Place a Post-it Note on the back of each student.

2. At your signal, students begin trying to grab Post-it Notes from each other. Students may not hold onto or touch their own Post-it Notes in defense. They must watch out for anyone who is trying to grab their notes as they attempt to grab other students' notes.

God always answers our prayers, though sometimes He does it in ways we don't expect. That's why today's Bible verse tells us we need to be watching for the ways He answers. Let's play a game in which we need to be watchful, too!

When a student's note is grabbed, that student gives his or her note (and all those collected) to the person who grabbed the note. Student then moves to the side of the playing area. Grabbing continues until only one student has his or her note or time is called. Redistribute Post-it Notes and play again as time allows.

Option
Instead of Post-it Notes, play game with long, narrow fabric strips that students tuck into their clothes.

Discussion Questions

1. *What did you watch for while you played this game? What happened if you didn't watch?*

2. *Because we know God always answers prayer, what should we do after we pray for something?* (Be watching for how God is going to answer our prayer. Not worry about things we have prayed about, but trust God to take care of them.)

3. *What kinds of things should we talk to God about when we pray?* (Things we are thankful for. Reasons we love Him. Problems we or other people are having and need His help with.)

Art Center: Banner Parade

Student Materials
Butcher paper, scissors, markers, tape and/or thumbtacks; optional—one or more pairs of edging scissors.

Prepare the Activity
Cut butcher paper in a variety of sizes and shapes (see sketch), one for each student.

Lead the Activity
1. Each student chooses a banner from the ones you have prepared. (Optional: Students may trim banners with edging scissors.)

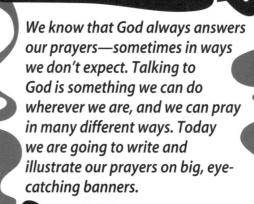

We know that God always answers our prayers—sometimes in ways we don't expect. Talking to God is something we can do wherever we are, and we can pray in many different ways. Today we are going to write and illustrate our prayers on big, eye-catching banners.

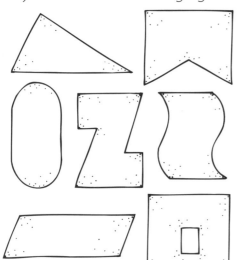

2. Students write and illustrate prayers on their banners. If students need help thinking of prayers, ask the Discussion Questions below.

3. Display banners in your classroom or in a well-traveled location at your church.

Options
1. Allow students to cut their own banner shapes.

2. Provide additional supplies for students to use in making their banners (watercolor paint, puff paint, metallic pens, wrapping paper scraps, etc.).

Discussion Questions
1. *What kinds of things do you often hear people pray about?* Tell students something you have recently prayed about.

2. *What are some things you would like to thank God for?*

3. *When are some times you need God's help?*

4. *Who are some people you would like to pray for?*

Lesson 48

Worship Center

Let's thank God that He always answers prayer, even in ways we don't expect!

Big Picture Verse

"Devote yourselves to prayer, being watchful and thankful." Colossians 4:2

Teacher Materials

Bible, *God's Big Picture* cassette/CD or music video and player, "God's Amazing Power" word chart (p. 457 in this book), large sheet of paper on which you have printed Colossians 4:2 (leave blank spaces for some of the letters in each word), masking tape.

Sing to God

Play "God's Amazing Power," encouraging students to sing along with the music and do the actions shown on the word chart or the music video. **When does this song tell us we can call on (pray to) God and ask for His amazing power?** (When anything is going wrong.) **When else can we pray to God?** (Anytime, even if everything is going well. We can be sure that He will always answer our prayers!)

Hear and Say God's Word

Display paper on which you have printed Colossians 4:2. Volunteers guess letters to fill in blanks and find correct words. When all blanks have been filled in, volunteer finds Colossians 4:2 in Bible and reads verse aloud. **What does it mean to "devote yourselves to prayer"?** (To be dedicated to doing it often.) **How can we be "watchful and thankful" when we pray?** (Watch for God's answers to our prayers and remember to thank Him for those answers, instead of only asking for more things.) Students repeat verse in unison several times.

Pray to God

What are some prayers you want God to answer? Students tell prayer requests. Lead students in prayer, encouraging volunteers to pray for requests mentioned. Thank God that He hears our prayers and will answer them. Ask for His help in watching for and understanding His answers when He gives them.

Options

1. Invite older students to create their own sign-language motions for "God's Amazing Power" and/or Colossians 4:2.

2. During the prayer, have students suggest sentences for a prayer thanking God for His amazing power and that He answers prayer. Print the words on the back of the Bible verse paper. Students read words together as a prayer.

 **Lesson 48**

# Bible Story Coloring Center

FOR YOUNGER CHILDREN

Materials

Crayons or markers, a copy of "An angel frees Peter" picture and story (pp. 229-230 from *Bible Story Coloring Pages*) for each student.

Lead the Activity

Students color page 229; read or tell the story on page 230. **Where had Peter been? Who did God send to rescue Peter from prison?**

Option

Students draw before-and-after pictures, first drawing Peter chained and asleep in a prison cell and then drawing Peter knocking on the door of the house where his friends were praying.

# Skit Center

FOR OLDER CHILDREN

Materials

A copy of "Free!" skit (pp. 297-298 from *The Big Book of Bible Skits*) for each student; optional—highlighter pens.

Lead the Activity

Students form trios and read the skit, which tells the story of Peter's arrival at the home of his friends who were praying for him. (Optional: Students highlight their parts.) Ask the discussion questions on page 297.

# Bible Skills Center

FOR OLDER CHILDREN

Materials

Materials needed for "Order Up!" and/or "True or False?" (p. 32 and/or p. 115 from *The Big Book of Bible Skills*).

Lead the Activity

Students complete activities as directed in *The Big Book of Bible Skills*.

Paul Preaches in Lystra

Big Picture Verse

"Give thanks to the Lord, call on his name; make known among the nations what he has done." Psalm 105:1

THE BIG PICTURE

To help others learn about God, tell about the great and wonderful things He has done.

Scripture Background
Acts 14:8-20

Up through Acts 12 we have seen the beginning of the Church, with Peter as its leader, in Jerusalem. From Acts 13 on we are going to see Paul and the missionary journeys that spread the gospel. Through these journeys Paul changed Christianity from its Jewish tribal confines to a worldwide influence. He tried to break down the barriers between Jew and Gentile and between slave and free.

Paul's purpose in all his travels was to tell the gospel of Jesus Christ. Why was Paul not ashamed of this gospel? Because it reveals what the sinner needs and what may be received on the ground of simple faith. Paul was proud of the gospel because he had proved its power in his own life and in the lives of all who would believe.

God's power was seen in Lystra as the lame man was healed. The watching people knew they were witnesses to miraculous power. But they wrongly attributed the miracle to Paul and Barnabas. A distressed Paul urged them to "turn from...worthless things to the living God, who made heaven and earth and sea and everything in them" (Acts 14:15). Paul took this opportunity to once again tell the good news of the gospel.

Good news! These words will command the attention of anyone. But the real value of good news depends on the source—who said it. That is why the gospel Paul presents is so welcome. The news comes from God. The news is all about God and what He has done to show His love to the world.

Adapted from *What the Bible Is All About* by Henrietta C. Mears.

Big Picture Story Center

Teacher Materials
Bible Time Line, drawing materials/equipment.

Student Materials
Drawing materials.

What's something great you have heard about? Today we'll find out about the great things Paul told!

Tell the Story
Move the *Bible Time Line* frame to highlight Picture 49. As you tell each part of the story, draw each sketch. Students copy your sketches.

1. The good news of Jesus was spreading all over! Paul and his friend Barnabas were telling God's good news from city to city. But some of the religious leaders were FURIOUS at Paul and Barnabas! The leaders wanted Paul and Barnabas to stop teaching about Jesus. The leaders even tried to get people to KILL Paul and Barnabas!

2. But Paul and Barnabas didn't stop telling about Jesus. They knew God is greater than anyone. They trusted God's power to protect them. One day they traveled to the town of Lystra, where there was a big temple to the false god Zeus. The people of Lystra believed Zeus was the most powerful god. They worshiped him at this temple.

3. Paul and Barnabas began to tell the good news about Jesus. A large crowd gathered to hear them. In the crowd, Paul saw one man who was crippled. He had NEVER been able to walk.

4. Paul called out to the lame man, "Stand up on your feet!" The lame man DID. He JUMPED up and started WALKING around! God's power healed the man. The crowd went wild with excitement!

1. Draw 2 cities from rectangles; add walking stick figures.

2. Temple from 2 "Z"s and lines.

3. Crippled man from "O," "V"s and "W".

4. Standing man from "O" and "V"s. Add amazed faces.

5. But the people didn't understand what had happened. They thought that Paul and Barnabas were really their false gods Zeus and Hermes. An old story told that Zeus and Hermes had once come to Lystra dressed as men, but no one had welcomed them except an old man and his wife. So the town had been punished!

5. Print "Zeus" and "Hermes"; add "no" slash.

6. Remembering that story, the people didn't want to make the same mistake again! They rushed off to the temple of Zeus to get the priest! Paul and Barnabas soon realized that the people planned to WORSHIP them!

6. Add "C"s for crowd to temple in #2.

7. "Stop!" yelled Paul and Barnabas. "We are just MEN, people like you! We came to tell you about the only living God, the creator of all things!" Paul told how everything good comes from God, not from idols or men.

7. Print "GOD" and "ONLY' as an acrostic.

8. Just then, the same men who had been trying to kill Paul in other cities came into Lystra. "Paul and Barnabas are troublemakers!" they said. Soon everyone in the city was so ANGRY that they began to throw rocks at Paul. When he fell down, they dragged him out of town and left him, thinking he was dead. But Paul's Christian friends found him and helped him back into town. And the very next day, Paul and Barnabas were traveling again!

8. Draw angry and sad faces; add walking stick figure with happy face.

Get the Big Picture

Who did the people of Lystra think Paul and Barnabas were? (The false gods Zeus and Hermes.) **What did the people in Lystra want to do? What did Paul tell them?** (He told them to worship only the one true God, the One who has done great things.)

We know about the great things God has done, too. We can see the beautiful world God has made. And we can read about God's greatness in the Bible. God wants us to tell others about the great things He has done to help others learn about Him!

 **Lesson 49**

Bible Verse Object Talk: Message Fun

Big Picture Verse

"Give thanks to the Lord, call on his name; make known among the nations what he has done." Psalm 105:1

Teacher Materials

Bible with bookmark at Psalm 105:1, paper, markers.

Prepare the Object Talk

On each sheet of paper, write one of the following personalized license-plate messages: "CR8OR" ("Creator"), "GDLVSU" ("God loves you"), "GDS4EVR" ("God is forever"), "GD4GIVS" ("God forgives") and "GDSGR8" ("God is great").

Because we're glad to know about God and His love for us, we want others to know about Him, too. See what you can discover from these special messages.

Present the Object Talk

1. **When have you seen a personalized license plate?** Volunteers answer. **People get personalized license plates because the plates tell messages the people want others to know.**

2. **Listen to this Bible verse to find out what messages we can tell.** Read Psalm 105:1 aloud. **When we tell about the great and wonderful things God has done, we help others learn about Him.**

3. One at a time, show the license-plate messages you prepared. Allow volunteers time to discover what the message on each plate says. (Optional: Give paper and markers to students for them to create additional messages about the great and wonderful things God has done, limiting messages to seven characters. Display papers in a well-traveled area of your church.)

Conclude

Lead students in prayer, inviting volunteers to name great and wonderful things God has done.

Discussion Questions

1. What are some great and wonderful things God has done?

2. Who has told you about how great God is? When?

3. How did people learn about God in Bible times? How do people learn about God today?

Active Game Center: Hop and Tell

Materials
Markers, butcher paper, masking tape.

Prepare the Game
On butcher paper, draw one large snail-shaped spiral for every five students. Divide each spiral into a dozen spaces, marking the center circle "Rest" (see sketch). Tape each paper spiral to the floor.

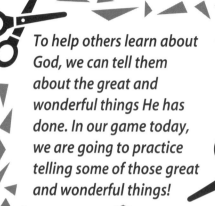

To help others learn about God, we can tell them about the great and wonderful things He has done. In our game today, we are going to practice telling some of those great and wonderful things!

Lead the Game
1. Gather students into groups of five, instructing each group to stand at one of the snail-shaped spirals.

2. The first student in each group hops on one foot all the way around the spiral to the "Rest" circle where he or she can rest on both feet before turning and hopping back on one foot. If he or she hops back and forth without hopping on any lines or putting both feet down (except in the "Rest" circle), student writes in any one of the spaces a great and wonderful thing God has done. Next student repeats action and if he or she is successful, student writes in another space a great and wonderful thing God has done. Continue game until all students have written something or as time allows.

Options
1. Rather than preparing snail-shaped spirals ahead of time, allow groups to create their own game paths in class. Suggest curved or zig-zag path options.

2. Younger students may walk on the spiral rather than hopping. Older students may toss beanbags onto spirals, writing great things God has done in the spaces on which the beanbags land.

Discussion Questions

1. What are some of the great and wonderful things God has done that you wrote down?

2. What are some more great things God has done that you have read about or heard about in the Bible? (Created the world. Saved Noah and the animals from the flood. Sent Jesus to us. Pushed back the waters of the Red Sea, so the Israelites could escape the Pharaoh of Egypt.)

3. What are some great things God has done for you or other people you know? (Took the punishment for sins. Answered prayers. Showed His love to us.)

Lesson 49

Art Center: Chalk Walk

Student Materials
Sidewalk chalk, bucket of soapy water, paper towels.

Lead the Activity

1. Lead students outdoors to a sidewalk or asphalt area. Assign each student a section or area in which to draw. (Optional: Draw lines to designate drawing areas.)

2. Students use chalk to draw pictures of things God has done. Encourage students to include pictures of things God has made and people whom God has helped. Each student may draw one large picture or several smaller pictures in the drawing area.

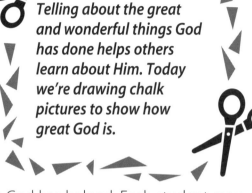

Telling about the great and wonderful things God has done helps others learn about Him. Today we're drawing chalk pictures to show how great God is.

3. When pictures are completed, students wash hands in soapy water and then walk around the chalk drawings to observe them. Invite volunteers to describe their pictures to the group.

Options

1. If sidewalk chalk is not available, spread out a length of butcher paper on sidewalk (or on classroom or hallway floor). Tape edges firmly in place. Students draw with markers.

2. Invite others in your church to walk along and observe the chalk drawings.

Discussion Questions

1. What has God made that shows how great He is?

2. Who are some of the people in the Bible God has helped? How?

3. What are some of the ways that God helps people today?

4. How has God helped you and your family?

Worship Center

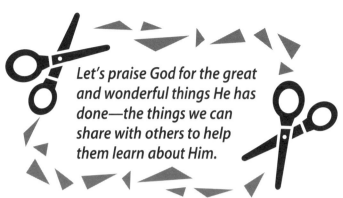

Let's praise God for the great and wonderful things He has done—the things we can share with others to help them learn about Him.

Big Picture Verse

"Give thanks to the Lord, call on his name; make known among the nations what he has done." Psalm 105:1

Teacher Materials

Bible, *God's Big Picture* cassette/CD or music video and player, "Psalm 9:1,2,10" word chart (p. 477 in this book), large sheet of paper on which you have printed Psalm 105:1, masking tape.

Sing to God

Play "Psalm 9:1,2,10," encouraging students to sing along with the music and do the actions shown on the word chart or the music video. **What does it mean to be glad and rejoice in God?** (To be glad and joyful, or happy, for the great things God has done.) **What are some reasons to be glad and rejoice in God?**

Hear and Say God's Word

Display paper on which you have printed Psalm 105:1. Volunteer reads verse aloud. Underline these words and phrases: "thanks," "call," "make known" and "what he has done." Lead students in reciting the verse several times, standing when they say one of the underlined words or phrases. **What are some ways to call on God's name?** (Pray. Sing worship songs to Him.) **What are some things God has done for which you want to thank Him?**

Pray to God

Tell students about one of the great and wonderful things God has done that you like to share with others. Lead students in prayer, inviting volunteers to complete the sentence, **I praise You, God, because of the great and wonderful things you have done, like....**

Options

1. Have older students read Psalms 66:1-4;105:1-5; 145:3-5 aloud as prayers of praise to God.

2. If you are keeping a prayer journal with your students, ask volunteers to read through the past prayer requests and thank God for hearing and answering the prayers.

 **Lesson 49**

Bible Story Coloring Center  FOR YOUNGER CHILDREN

Materials

Crayons or markers, a copy of "Philip tells the good news about Jesus to an Ethiopian man" picture and story (pp. 219-220 from *Bible Story Coloring Pages*) for each student.

Lead the Activity

Students color page 219; read or tell the story on page 220. **Just like Paul, Philip was one of Jesus' followers who told others about Jesus. Where was Philip when he talked to this man? Why do you think Philip wanted to tell others about Jesus?**

Option

Each student begins coloring his or her own page. After several minutes, each student signs name on page and trades page with another student. Repeat trading several times until all pages are colored.

Skit Center  FOR OLDER CHILDREN

Materials

A copy of "Triple P Trial" skit (pp. 285-291 from *The Big Book of Bible Skits*) for each student; optional—highlighter pens.

Lead the Activity

Students read the skit, which tells the story of Philip, Peter and Paul preaching the good news of salvation. (Optional: Students highlight their parts.) Ask the discussion questions on page 285.

Bible Skills Center FOR OLDER CHILDREN

Materials

Materials needed for "Name That Letter!" and/or "Balloon Bop" (p. 48 and/or p. 65 from *The Big Book of Bible Skills*).

Lead the Activity

Students complete activities as directed in *The Big Book of Bible Skills*.

Thankful Songs in Prison

Big Picture Verse

"Sing and make music in your heart to the Lord, always giving thanks to God the Father for everything, in the name of our Lord Jesus Christ." Ephesians 5:19,20

THE BIG PICTURE

We can thank God for all things and in all circumstances because we know He is always with us.

Scripture Background
Acts 16:6-40

Paul and Barnabas were the first missionaries to travel to countries other than their own. The greatest enterprise in the world is missions, and this is the beginning of this great movement. The whole idea began just the way it should, at a prayer meeting (see Acts 13:2,3).

After Luke joined the missionary party, Paul was called to the area of Macedonia by a vision and the cry, "Come over to Macedonia and help us" (Acts 16:9). The first convert in Europe was not a famous scholar or some mighty ruler, but a businesswoman, Lydia, a seller of purple-dyed garments. The second convert in Europe was very different from the first, as were the circumstances. Lydia was converted in a prayer meeting, but it took an earthquake to arouse the next convert—a jailer.

Paul met this jailer while he was in prison. Paul and Silas sang in the jail at Philippi at midnight when their backs were bleeding and sore! Their praise is an example of joy in the midst of trouble and problems. Paul knew that the secret of joyful thankfulness was in Christ.

Later, in writing to the church at Philippi, Paul wrote "Finally, my brothers, rejoice in the Lord!" (Philippians 3:1). Paul seems to laugh out loud for sheer joy in this letter. He is the rejoicing apostle. The words "joy" and "rejoice" occur in this epistle 16 times. "Be glad" is Paul's exhortation. "Joy" and "rejoice" and "all" are the words to underline and take note of. We are commanded to give thanks and rejoice in all circumstances. Sinners (like the jailer) are attracted to Jesus by the joy of Christians. And joy drives out discord. It helps in the midst of trials. Paul's life is the best evidence of a grateful spirit in all circumstances.

Adapted from *What the Bible Is All About* by Henrietta C. Mears.

Big Picture Story Center

Teacher Materials

Bible Time Line, drawing materials/equipment.

Student Materials

Drawing materials.

Tell the Story

Move the *Bible Time Line* frame to highlight Picture 50. As you tell each part of the story, draw each sketch. Students copy your sketches.

How might you feel if someone followed you around all day? Today we'll hear what happened when a slave girl followed Paul and Silas for days and days!

1. Paul and Silas had come to Philippi to tell people about Jesus. Many people had listened and had become members of God's family. A new church had been started there and things were great!

1. Draw city gates from 2 "P"s and lines; add cross.

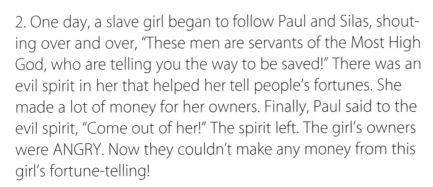

2. One day, a slave girl began to follow Paul and Silas, shouting over and over, "These men are servants of the Most High God, who are telling you the way to be saved!" There was an evil spirit in her that helped her tell people's fortunes. She made a lot of money for her owners. Finally, Paul said to the evil spirit, "Come out of her!" The spirit left. The girl's owners were ANGRY. Now they couldn't make any money from this girl's fortune-telling!

2. Shouting girl's face from "O"s; add hair from "3"s.

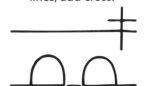

3. The angry men took Paul and Silas to the city leaders. They said, "They are teaching things that we think are wrong!" Other people began to shout, too. The leaders ordered the soldiers to beat Paul and Silas. They tore off Paul's and Silas's clothes and beat them with whips that cut their backs open.

3. Angry face from 2 "V"s and "C."

4. After Paul and Silas were beaten, they were taken to JAIL. The jailer put them in a cell where he was sure they could NEVER get out! Their feet were clamped into stocks—two huge blocks of wood hinged together and locked down, with holes cut for a man's legs to go through. Paul and Silas were locked in a dirty, cold jail!

4. Print "Jail"; add lines and two faces.

5. Now, they could have complained. But what do you think they did instead? They SANG! They PRAYED! They PRAISED GOD! Even though their backs and legs must have been hurting terribly, Paul and Silas knew God was with them. And He would take care of them!

5. Make singing mouths; add music notes to jail.

6. Around midnight, the ground began to tremble and shake. God sent an EARTHQUAKE! The prison doors flew open. The chains fell off. The stocks broke apart! The jailer woke up and RAN to see what had happened. When he saw that the prison doors were open, he was going to kill himself! He was sure his prisoners had escaped. And he'd be KILLED if his prisoners got away! But Paul shouted, "DON'T HURT YOURSELF! WE'RE HERE!"

6. Earthquake from small "W"s that get larger.

7. The jailer got a torch. He ran into Paul and Silas's cell. "What must I do to be saved?" he asked them. The jailer wanted to know what made them sing when they were in jail. Why didn't they run away when they had the chance? And what made them care about their jailer?

Paul and Silas told the jailer, "Believe in the Lord Jesus Christ, and you will be saved—you and all your household!"

7. Torch from "V"s; add hand from "C"s and worried face.

8. The jailer took Paul and Silas to his home and bandaged their wounds. Then he called his family and servants to listen to Paul and Silas tell about Jesus. They learned how Jesus had died to take the punishment for their sins and had come back to life again. EVERYONE in the house believed in Jesus and was baptized.

The very next morning, the city leaders found out they had made a BIG mistake to arrest and beat Paul and Silas. Paul and Silas were free again to tell people the good news about Jesus.

8. "C"s for gathered household; turn "C"s into happy faces as you finish story.

Get the Big Picture

Why were Paul and Silas put into jail? (Angry people told lies about them.) **What did they do in jail?** (Sang. Prayed. Praised God.)

Sometimes we can be scared or have big problems, too. But we can thank God no matter what happens to us because we know He is always with us.

Bible Verse Object Talk: Making Music

Big Picture Verse

"Sing and make music in your heart to the Lord, always giving thanks to God the Father for everything, in the name of our Lord Jesus Christ." Ephesians 5:19,20

Teacher Materials

Bible with bookmark at Ephesians 5:19,20, six identical clear water glasses, pitcher of water, spoon.

We all have times or situations that make us feel sad or happy. Because we know God is good and always with us, we can thank God for all things. Let's try a fun way to give thanks to God.

Prepare the Object Talk

Fill the glasses with water as shown in sketch.

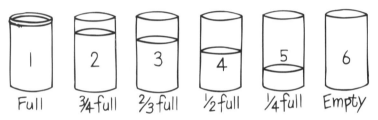

| 1 | 2 | 3 | 4 | 5 | 6 |
| Full | ¾ full | ⅔ full | ½ full | ¼ full | Empty |

Present the Object Talk

1. Demonstrate how to play musical notes by gently tapping the glasses with the spoon. Point out to the students that different amounts of water in glasses cause different notes. (Optional: Invite volunteers to experiment with tapping the glasses.)

2. **It's fun to make up our own music with these glasses. Listen to Ephesians 5:19,20 to see what it says about music.** Read verses aloud. **Making music in our heart means we're so glad and thankful that our prayers to God are like songs. Many of the songs we sing in church are prayers of thankfulness and praise to God.**

3. Choose a phrase from the verses such as "giving thanks to God the Father" or "Sing and make music in your heart" and tap the glasses as you say or sing the words. Invite students to say or sing the words with you. (Optional: Invite several students to tap the glasses for these or other phrases from the verses.)

Conclude

Lead students in a prayer of thanks to God.

Discussion Questions

1. What are some ways of giving thanks to God? (Saying prayers. Writing prayers.)

2. What are some things you are thankful for?

3. When might you and your family give thanks to God at home?

 **Lesson 50**

Active Game Center: Musical Cans

Materials
God's Big Picture cassette/CD and player, empty soda can for each student.

Lead the Game
1. Play a game like Musical Chairs with students. Students form a large circle, standing about 1 foot (30 cm) apart. Give each student a soda

can to place at his or her feet. Ask one volunteer to put his or her can to the side of the playing area, away from the circle.

2. Start the music. Students begin to walk clockwise around the cans. When you stop the music, each student picks up the closest can. The student left without a can answers one of the Discussion Questions. Continue playing as time allows.

Option
Substitute index cards in a variety of colors for soda cans.

> *One of the ways to give thanks to God for all things and in all circumstances is by singing and making music to God. We're going to play music in our game today and answer questions about thanking God.*

Discussion Questions

1. **When are some times it might be hard for a kid your age to thank God?** (When something scary, bad or sad is happening.)

2. **Why should we still give thanks to God in these hard times?** (Because we can trust that God will help us through the hard situations. He will always care for us, no matter what situation we are in.)

3. **What are some good things for which to thank God? How has God shown His goodness to you?**

 **Lesson 50**

Art Center: Thankful Memories

Student Materials
Large sheet of butcher paper, markers, measuring stick, tape or thumbtacks.

Prepare the Activity
Draw lines on butcher paper to outline a memory box, dividing it into sections of various sizes (see sketch). Make at least one section for each student.

Whether something good or something bad is happening to us, we can be thankful to God for all things because we know He is with us. Let's remember things we want to thank God for.

Lead the Activity

1. Explain to students that a memory box is usually a large shallow box divided into small sections. In each section is an object or picture that helps people remember things that

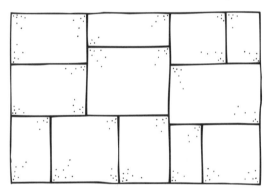

have happened. **Today we're going to make a drawing like a memory box.** Show paper you prepared.

2. Each student chooses a section of the memory box outline. Invite students to draw pictures of items and people for which they are thankful in their sections of the memory box. **Draw your picture large enough to fill the section.** Display with a heading such as "A Memory Box of Thanks."

Options

1. Prepare a memory box outline for each group of four to six students.

2. Students outline items or people on construction paper, cut out shapes and glue them to the memory box.

3. Students write prayers of thankfulness in some sections of the memory box.

4. Students draw pictures on separate sheets of paper and glue pictures to the insides of shallow boxes.

Discussion Questions

1. Who is a person you're thankful for? Why? How can your picture show the reason you are thankful for this person?

2. When have you been thankful to God for helping you or your family in a difficult time?

3. What's something God has made for which you want to thank Him?

Worship Center

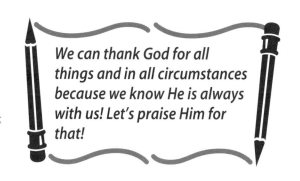

We can thank God for all things and in all circumstances because we know He is always with us! Let's praise Him for that!

Big Picture Verse

"Sing and make music in your heart to the Lord, always giving thanks to God the Father for everything, in the name of our Lord Jesus Christ." Ephesians 5:19,20

Teacher Materials

Bible, *God's Big Picture* cassette/CD or music video and player, "God's Amazing Power" word chart (p. 457 in this book), large sheet of paper on which you have printed Ephesians 5:19,20, masking tape.

Sing to God

Play "God's Amazing Power," encouraging students to sing along with the music and do the actions shown on the word chart or the music video. **What happened when Paul and Silas praised God and gave thanks to Him when they were in jail?** (God sent an earthquake and they were freed. They told the jailer about Jesus.) **Why does this song say we can praise God for Jesus?** (Jesus healed the lame.)

Hear and Say God's Word

Display paper on which you have printed Ephesians 5:19,20. Volunteer reads the verses aloud. **What does Ephesians 5:19,20 command us to do?** (Sing and make music to God. Give thanks for everything.) **Let's do these commands! First we'll sing the words of these verses to a familiar song.** Sing "Silent Night" with students to review the melody. Then sing Ephesians 5:19,20 to the same tune by using the following line substitutions:

Sing and make music, in your heart
To the Lord, always giving thanks,
To God the Father for everything,
In the name of our Lord Jesus Christ,
In the name of the Lord, in the name of the Lord.

Practice singing the new words several times until students are familiar with them.

Pray to God

Now let's give thanks to God for everything! Lead students in prayer, with volunteers completing the sentence: **Thank You, God, for....** Allow as many students to pray as possible before ending prayer time by thanking God that He is always with us

Option

Briefly tell about or invite a guest to tell about a difficult situation when you or the guest thanked God.

 **Lesson 50**

Bible Story Coloring Center

 FOR YOUNGER CHILDREN

Materials

Crayons or markers, a copy of "Paul and Silas sing praise to God in jail" picture and story (pp. 233-234 from *Bible Story Coloring Pages*) for each student.

Lead the Activity

Students color page 233; read or tell the story on page 234. **Where are Paul and Silas? What are they doing? Why are they thanking and praising God?**

Option

Students may draw and color pictures of things for which they are thankful. Display pictures on a bulletin board.

Skit Center

 FOR OLDER CHILDREN

Materials

A copy of "Troublemakers" skit (pp. 305-310 from *The Big Book of Bible Skits*) for each student; optional—highlighter pens.

Lead the Activity

Students read the skit, which tells the story of Paul's visits to Thessalonica, Berea and Athens. (Optional: Students highlight their parts.) **How did Paul's actions show that he was convinced of God's care for him? What do you think Paul thanked God for in Thessalonica, Berea and Athens?**

Bible Skills Center

 FOR OLDER CHILDREN

Materials

Materials needed for "Spelling Race" and/or "Follow the Clues" (p. 40 and/or p. 119 from *The Big Book of Bible Skills*).

Lead the Activity

Students complete activities as directed in *The Big Book of Bible Skills*.

Lesson 51

Paul Speaks Out

Big Picture Verse

"Always be prepared to give an answer to everyone who asks you to give the reason for the hope that you have." 1 Peter 3:15

Scripture Background
Acts 24–28

THE BIG PICTURE

Keep on telling about God your whole life, looking for ways to share God's love with others in every situation.

By the end of his life, Paul was known as the great missionary to the Gentiles. On his three missionary journeys he founded many churches and wrote his epistles. The combination of Roman citizenship, Greek education and Hebrew religion wonderfully qualified him for his great work; but you will find that he trusted only in the grace and apostleship that he received directly from Jesus Christ.

Throughout his travels, Paul had one message—faith in the crucified and risen Lord. He would hear nothing else; he spoke nothing else; he lived nothing else. Even after two years' imprisonment, Paul still eagerly spoke of His Savior to the governor, Festus. Being sent on to Rome, Paul traveled on a ship that was wrecked in a terrific storm off the coast of Malta. Despite the perilous circumstances in which he found himself, he once again spoke out God's message of encouragement and love. Once arriving in Rome, Paul was kept a prisoner in his own rented house for several years. Even in prison the great preacher and evangelist led the servants in Nero's own palace to Christ. Service for the Master can brighten life's darkest hours.

During his imprisonment, Paul wrote many of his epistles—Philemon, Colossians, Ephesians and Philippians. Even while in a dungeon in Rome, expecting at any hour to be beheaded, Paul wrote his second epistle to Timothy. Paul's witness was astounding in its constancy.

Acts is the only unfinished book in the Bible. Notice how abruptly it closes! How else could it close? How could there be a complete account of our Lord's lifework as long as He lives? Our risen and ascended Lord still lives. From the center—Christ—the lines are seen proceeding in every direction, but the uttermost part of the earth is not yet reached. The book is evidently a fragment. The gospel of Christ moves on! You are still living the Acts.

Adapted from *What the Bible Is All About* by Henrietta C. Mears.

Big Picture Story Center

Teacher Materials
Bible Time Line, drawing materials/equipment.

Student Materials
Drawing materials.

Tell the Story
Move the *Bible Time Line* frame to highlight Picture 51. As you tell each part of the story, draw each sketch. Students copy your sketches.

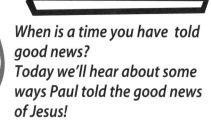

When is a time you have told good news?
Today we'll hear about some ways Paul told the good news of Jesus!

1. Paul was a prisoner now. The leaders in Jerusalem who had wanted to stop him from telling about Jesus had finally gotten him arrested. But because Paul was a Roman citizen, he received permission to sail to Rome to meet with the mighty Roman emperor.

1. Draw hull of ship from "C"s. Add details as shown.

2. At the first stop of their journey, Julius, the centurion who was to take Paul to Rome, let Paul visit friends. When the ship sailed again, the wind nearly blew the small ship off course. At the second stop, Paul and his friends and Julius got on a larger ship sailing for Italy.

2. Add mast from "+" and sails from "7"s to hull.

3. This ship was loaded with cargo and 276 passengers. As they traveled, the weather grew worse and worse! THEN the winds became BIG gusts. Waves tossed the ship from side-to-side! Day after day the storm raged. The sailors threw overboard the cargo and EVERYTHING they didn't need! But the terrible storm kept on. "We're going to die!" cried the sailors.

3. Add lines for wind and "C"s for waves.

4. But Paul had good news! "Don't be afraid," Paul said. "God has promised we'll all be safe." As the ship began to break apart, everyone jumped overboard and swam or floated to land! The ship was gone and the cargo had sunk, but everyone was safe—just as God had promised and Paul had told them.

4. Add stick figures to water.

5. Paul and his shipmates landed on an island. The people of the island kindly built a fire while Paul gathered wood. A very poisonous snake darted out of the pile of wood in Paul's hand and bit him. But the snake's poison didn't hurt Paul at all. Everyone was amazed!

5. Fire from "X" and "V"s. Add snake from "S".

6. While Paul was on the island, he met a man who was sick. Paul prayed for him and God healed him! Soon, every other sick person on the island came to see Paul. Each one went away healed! For three months, Paul helped the people on the island. He taught them about Jesus, too!

6. Praying hands from "U"s and "I"; add face.

7. When spring came, it was time to sail for Rome. After several stops, Paul and his traveling companions arrived in Rome. Even though he was still a prisoner, Paul was not thrown into a dungeon or put into stocks. He was allowed to rent a house and a soldier was left to guard him. Paul must have told that soldier about the Lord Jesus!

7. House from rectangles, "U"s; add soldier.

8. For the next two years, Paul lived in his house and gladly welcomed everyone who came to see him. He preached and taught about Jesus, and many people believed the good news about Jesus. Paul's enemies in Jerusalem thought that by arresting Paul they were going to stop his preaching, but Paul didn't let anything stop him from sharing the good news! Now, in Rome, there were new opportunities to tell even MORE people about Jesus!

8. Add stick figures and conversation balloon to house.

Jesus is God's Son

Get the Big Picture

What were some of the things that happened to Paul? (Shipwrecked. Bit by a snake. Arrested.) **What did Paul do in each of those situations?** (Showed love for God and others. Told others about Jesus.)

No matter what happened to him, Paul kept on telling people about Jesus. We can keep on telling about Jesus our whole lives, too, always looking for ways to share God's love with others.

 **Lesson 51**

Bible Verse Object Talk: Salt Surprise

Big Picture Verse

"Always be prepared to give an answer to everyone who asks you to give the reason for the hope that you have." 1 Peter 3:15

Teacher Materials

Bible with bookmark at 1 Peter 3:15, plastic wrap, bowl, tape, measuring spoon, salt, metal pan with lid.

Prepare the Object Talk

Tightly stretch a piece of plastic wrap over the bowl, taping it securely.

It's important for God's followers to keep telling others about Him, giving reasons why we believe in and love God. See if you can figure out the reason, or explanation, for why something in this experiment moves without our touching it.

Present the Object Talk

1. Sprinkle one teaspoon of salt evenly onto the plastic. Then invite a volunteer to stand several feet (m) from the bowl and bang the lid onto the pan at the level of the top of the bowl. The salt will move on the plastic.

2. As time permits, invite additional volunteers to take a turn banging the pan. Ask students to tell reasons why they think the salt moves. Acknowledge each student's idea.

3. **We've talked about some ideas about why the salt moves. Listen to the reason, or explanation, according to scientists: We can't see sounds, but they are vibrations in the air, so sounds make the air move. These vibrations in the air make the plastic move, or vibrate, so that the salt moves.**

Conclude

Hearing a reason for why something is true helps us understand it better. Listen to 1 Peter 3:15 to find what God wants us to be ready to give a reason for. Read verse aloud. **The hope we have is our belief in God and His love and forgiveness for us. This verse reminds us to tell others about what we believe.** Lead students in prayer, asking His help in telling others about His love.

Discussion Questions

1. What do you know about God that others should know? about Jesus?

2. Who has told you about Jesus and helped you learn about reasons to love and obey Him?

3. What are things kids your age can do to learn about Jesus? (Read the Bible. Listen to stories from the Bible. Ask parents or teachers to help you understand what verses from the Bible mean.)

Lesson 51

Active Game Center: Sprint to Safety

Materials
Masking tape, one spoon for every six to eight students, dry beans.

Prepare the Game
Make a masking-tape line on one side of an open playing area.

Lead the Game
1. Group students into teams of six to eight. Teams line up single file opposite the masking-tape line. Hand a spoon to the first student on each team. Place five or six beans in each spoon.

It is important to keep on telling people about God our whole life, looking for ways to share God's love with others in every situation. In our game today, we are going to discuss different ways to share God's love.

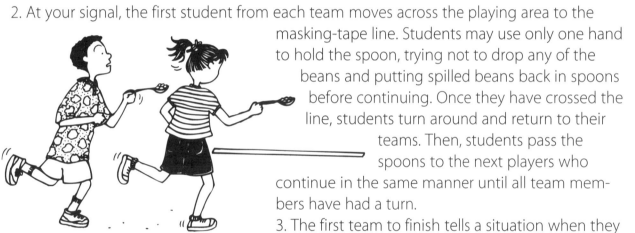

2. At your signal, the first student from each team moves across the playing area to the masking-tape line. Students may use only one hand to hold the spoon, trying not to drop any of the beans and putting spilled beans back in spoons before continuing. Once they have crossed the line, students turn around and return to their teams. Then, students pass the spoons to the next players who continue in the same manner until all team members have had a turn.

3. The first team to finish tells a situation when they could tell others about God and share His love.

Option
Play the game outside. Use chalk or rope to make a line and use eggs instead of beans. If a student drops the egg, he or she starts over with a new one.

Discussion Questions
1. What are some ways to share God's love at home? in your neighborhood?

2. Why is it important that when you tell someone about God's love, you also treat them and other people around them with love and kindness?

3. What are some things you could tell others if they asked you about God?

4. What could be a reminder to watch out for opportunities to share about God? (Write 1 Peter 3:15 on card to display in room at home.)

Art Center: Puppet Talk

Student Materials
Sheets of paper, markers, white construction paper, scissors, glue, craft sticks.

Prepare the Activity
Make a sample stick puppet following directions below.

Lead the Activity
1. On each side of a sheet of paper, student draws a picture of a place he or she goes (school, playground, mall, park, beach, etc.).
2. Student draws and cuts out several construction paper faces representing him- or

Every day in lots of ways we can share God's love with others—by telling about Him and by treating others in loving ways. Let's make stick puppets to show ways of sharing God's love.

herself and family or friends. Students glue faces to ends of craft sticks to make stick puppets.

3. Students use stick puppets and pictures to act out situations in which they can show God's love to others.

4. As time permits, students use puppets to act out situations for each other.

Options
1. Students may draw, cut out and attach clothing onto their stick puppets.
2. Provide paper bags in which students place stick puppets to take home.

Discussion Questions
1. Who do you usually go to the (park) with? How can you share God's love with (her)?

2. When is a time you can share God's love at school? What might happen?

3. Who has shared God's love with you or told you about Him? How? How might you follow (his) example?

4. What can you tell others about God?

 **Lesson 51**

Worship Center

Big Picture Verse

"Always be prepared to give an answer to everyone who asks you to give the reason for the hope that you have." 1 Peter 3:15

Let's praise God for His wonderful love that we can tell others about our whole life long!

Teacher Materials

Bible, *God's Big Picture* cassette/CD or music video and player, "Psalm 9:1,2,10" word chart (p. 477 in this book), large sheet of paper on which you have printed 1 Peter 3:15 (with room to write below the verse), masking tape.

Sing to God

Play "Psalm 9:1,2,10," encouraging students to sing along with the music and do the actions shown on the word chart or the music video. **What are some of the wonders of God's love that you can share with others?** (God's forgiveness of sin. God hears and answers prayer.)

Hear and Say God's Word

Display paper on which you have printed 1 Peter 3:15. Have a volunteer read the verse aloud. **How would you say 1 Peter 3:15 in your own words?** (Be ready to give an answer to anyone who asks about your faith in God. Plan what to say about God and His love so that you can immediately answer people who ask you about Him.) Write students' suggestions below the verse. Repeat the verse several times, alternating between saying 1 Peter 3:15 and one of the paraphrases the students suggested.

Pray to God

The more we find out how wonderful God's love is, the more we want to tell others about Him. Lead students in thanking God for His love and asking for God's help in knowing when and how to tell others about His love for them.

Options

1. Students sing and do actions for "Picture This!" and/or "Everywhere I Go" (p. 473 and/or p. 451 in this book).

2. Write a prayer together with your students, thanking God for His love and asking for His help in telling others about it. Read the prayer together.

 **Lesson 51**

Bible Story Coloring Center

Materials

Crayons or markers, a copy of "Paul tells a king about Jesus" picture and story (pp. 235-236 from *Bible Story Coloring Pages*) for each student.

Lead the Activity

Students color page 235; read or tell the story on page 236. **Who is Paul talking to in this picture? What do you notice about Paul? Why do you think talking about Jesus was so important to Paul?**

Option

Provide a copy of "Paul's ship wrecks in a storm" picture (p. 237 from *Coloring Pages*) for students to color. Tell or read the story on page 238 while students color.

Skit Center

Materials

A copy of "Emergency" skit (pp. 326-329 from *The Big Book of Bible Skits*) for each student; optional—highlighter pens.

Lead the Activity

Students form trios and read the skit, which tells the story of Paul's shipwreck on the way to Rome. (Optional: Students highlight their parts.) **Why was Paul a prisoner? What did Paul do to help his fellow travelers? What did he tell them about God?**

Bible Skills Center

Materials

Materials needed for "Go Fish!" and/or "Lost Letters" (p. 30 and/or p. 149 from *The Big Book of Bible Skills*).

Lead the Activity

Students complete activities as directed in *The Big Book of Bible Skills*.

God's Big Picture and You

Big Picture Verse

"No eye has seen, no ear has heard, no mind has conceived what God has prepared for those who love him." 1 Corinthians 2:9

THE BIG PICTURE

No matter where you are or what happens in your life, you can experience God's forgiveness and goodness and live as God wants you to.

Scripture Background
Selections from the Epistles

The whole Bible is built around the story of Christ and His promise of life everlasting to all people. The Old Testament is an account of a nation (the Jewish nation). The New Testament is an account of a man (the Son of man). The nation was founded and nurtured of God in order to bring the man into the world. His appearance on the earth is the central event of all history. The Old Testament sets the stage for it. The New Testament describes it.

As a man, Christ lived the most perfect life ever known. He was kind, tender, gentle, patient and sympathetic. He loved people. He worked marvelous miracles to feed the hungry. Multitudes—weary, pain-ridden and heartsick—came to Him, and He gave them rest. He died to take away the sin of the world and to become the Savior of all people.

Then He rose from the dead. He is alive today. He is not merely an historical character but a living person—the most important fact of history and the most vital force in the world today. And He promises eternal life to all who come to Him.

The writers of the epistles tell us the kind of life we should live because of Christ's work for us. The secret of Christian living is simply to allow Christ to meet our needs. There is nothing mysterious about faith. It is a simple act of will. Either we will believe God or we won't. We decide. When we decide to believe God absolutely, supernatural life and power enter our lives. A miracle is wrought within us, and the story of God's goodness continues in our lives.

Adapted from *What the Bible Is All About* by Henrietta C. Mears.

Big Picture Story Center

Teacher Materials
Bible Time Line, drawing materials/equipment.

Student Materials
Drawing materials.

Tell the Story
Move the *Bible Time Line* frame to highlight Picture 52. As you tell each part of the story, draw each sketch. Students copy your sketches.

What's your favorite story from the Bible? Today we'll find out how you're part of God's never-ending story!

1. God's never-ending story began with God creating the world and the first people, Adam and Eve. Even though Adam and Eve sinned, God loved them and promised to send a Savior who would take the punishment for people's sins. God gave a special country to a man named Abraham and called him to be the beginning of His people—the people through whom God would send the Savior.

1. Draw earth. Print "SAVIOR."

2. After God's people lived in Egypt for 400 years, God sent Moses to bring them back to their special land. Because God loved them, He sent judges and kings to lead them. He sent prophets to tell them God's messages—messages telling them to obey God, telling them about the future and telling them that God had promised to send a Savior.

2. Crown from "O" and "V"s, scroll from "S"s. Add "PROMISED" to "SAVIOR."

3. And many years later, what happened? The Savior God had promised came to earth! Jesus was born! When Jesus grew up, He taught people about God. He healed sick people and even brought dead people back to life. But some people hated Jesus. Jesus let them kill Him so that He could take the punishment for all the wrong things people do—their sins. And Jesus came back to life! When He went back to heaven, He sent the Holy Spirit to help all the people who believe in Him.

3. Draw cross around "PROMISED" and "SAVIOR." Add "JESUS."

4. This is the good news, or gospel, that the New Testament tells about. All the stories we read about Jesus' life are part of the New Testament books called the Gospels.

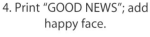

4. Print "GOOD NEWS"; add happy face.

5. The rest of the New Testament books tell about people who listened to this good news and became part of God's family. Many of these books are letters written to the people in the first churches. These letters tell God's family about God's plan and how to live as God wants them to.

5. Envelope and stamp from rectangles; address it "To: God's Family."

6. For instance, one of Paul's letters tells how God's family is like the parts of a person's body—every part is important and all the parts have to work together. "Love each other," Paul wrote. And Paul also wrote that God's plan is so wonderful that no one can imagine what God has prepared for those who love Him!

6. Draw eye, hand, ear. Add heart and face with thought balloon.

7. The last book of the Bible tells about all the things that will happen when Jesus comes back to earth. Everyone will know He is the greatest King!

7. Crown from "O" and "V"s. Add "JESUS."

8. But the story doesn't end there! Because Jesus died to take the punishment for our sins, we can all become part of God's family and live with Him forever. Anyone who asks Jesus to forgive his or her sins will be forgiven. And anyone who asks can become a member of God's family.

That's the best news in the world! If you have asked Jesus to forgive your sins and make you part of God's family, that makes YOU part of God's big picture! The big picture of God's love just keeps getting BIGGER!

8. Frame from rectangle and "3"s. Add happy faces and names of students.

Get the Big Picture

The whole story of God's big picture is about how much He loves us—and everyone in the world! What are some ways God shows He loves us? (Gives us friends and family. Forgives our sins. Hears and answers our prayers. Gives us courage to obey Him.) **What are some ways we can help others learn about God's love?** (Pray for them. Tell them about God's love. Tell them what Jesus did to show love.)

No matter who we are or what happens to us, we can know God's goodness and can live as God wants us to!

Bible Verse Object Talk: Zigzag Pictures

Big Picture Verse

"No eye has seen, no ear has heard, no mind has conceived what God has prepared for those who love him." 1 Corinthians 2:9

Teacher Materials

Bible with bookmark at 1 Corinthians 2:9, two identically sized magazine pictures, sheet of paper that is the same height and twice as wide as one picture, ruler, scissors, glue.

Prepare the Object Talk

At the same time, accordion-fold the paper and both pictures, making each pleat about 1 inch (2.5 cm) wide. Open up the pictures and cut along the folded lines. (Discard any end pieces less than 1 inch [2.5 cm] wide.) Glue alternating strips of the pictures in order to the pleats on the sheet of paper. Refold the paper.

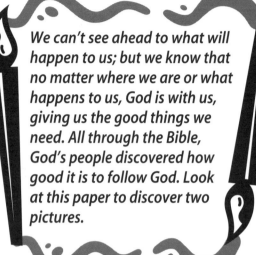

We can't see ahead to what will happen to us; but we know that no matter where we are or what happens to us, God is with us, giving us the good things we need. All through the Bible, God's people discovered how good it is to follow God. Look at this paper to discover two pictures.

Present the Object Talk

1. Open the paper and show it to students, holding it upright but slightly angled so that students look along the paper from one end only. Ask volunteers to describe what they see.

Then show paper from other end.

2. Allow time for students to experiment with holding the paper to see both zigzag pictures.

Conclude

When we looked at the paper, we discovered two pictures. The Bible tells us about something we haven't seen yet, but we'll discover as we grow older. Read 1 Corinthians 2:9 aloud. **This verse helps us remember that we can experience God's love and goodness now and in the future.** Lead students in prayer, thanking Him for His love and for the good things He gives us.

Discussion Questions

1. What are some of the good things God gives the people who love and obey Him? (Courage. Wisdom to make good choices. Answers to prayer.)

2. How has God helped you and your family in the past? What good things has He provided for you?

3. How has God helped our church?

 Lesson 52

Active Game Center: God's Amazing Plan

Materials
Bible, masking tape, blindfold.

Prepare the Game
Use masking tape to divide playing area into four sections (see sketch).

Lead the Game
1. Choose one volunteer to be blindfolded and one to be "It." Blindfolded volunteer stands in the middle of the playing area.

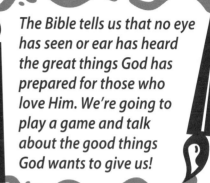

The Bible tells us that no eye has seen or ear has heard the great things God has prepared for those who love Him. We're going to play a game and talk about the good things God wants to give us!

2. At your signal, "It" and remaining students move randomly (but quietly) around the playing area. Blindfolded volunteer counts to twenty and then says "Stop." All students freeze where they are, and volunteer points toward one of the playing-area sections. If "It" is in that section, "It" reads 1 Corinthians 2:9 aloud or answers one of the Discussion Questions below. If "It" is not in that section, all students in that section move to the side of the playing area. Repeat play until blindfolded volunteer finally points to the section where "It" is standing. Play again with new volunteers as time allows.

Option
If you have a large number of students, choose more than one "It" for each round of the game.

Discussion Questions
1. *What are some good things God gives His followers?* (Forgiveness for sins. Courage to do right. People to care for us.)

2. *What are some good things God promises to help you do?* (Treat others fairly. Be patient with brothers and sisters. Love others.)

3. *When are times that it is hard to live as God wants us to? What can you do then? (*Pray and ask for His help. Read the Bible to learn more about how He wants us to live.)

Lesson 52

Art Center: Frame Fun

Student Materials

5x7-inch (12.5x17.5-cm) sheet of colored poster board for each student, hole punch, marker, glue, scissors, a variety of decorating materials (buttons, pasta in different shapes and colors, rickrack, etc.), yarn or ribbon.

Lead the Activity

1. Using hole punch, student makes two holes at center top of a sheet of poster board. Student writes "God loves" underneath the holes (see sketch).

2. Student decorates the frame by gluing decorating materials to edges of poster board, leaving an open area in the center of the poster board for a photo.

3. Students cut and insert a length of yarn or ribbon through holes and tie into a loop for hanging. Students take home frames and glue photos of themselves to open area.

God wants to show His love to you more and more as you grow older and learn new things. As you follow and obey God, you can always experience His goodness. Today you can make a frame for a photo of yourself as a reminder of God's love for you.

Options

1. Use an instant camera to take each student's photo. Student glues photo to center of frame.

2. For older students, provide magazines from which students may cut words that describe themselves or God's love.

3. Ask students ahead of time to bring photos from home.

Discussion Questions

1. In what ways has God shown His love for you already?

2. How have you learned about God's love for you? (From God's Word, the Bible. From teachers and parents.)

3. Why is it good to know about God's love for you?

4. How can you show that you love God?

444

 **Lesson 52**

Worship Center

Big Picture Verse

"No eye has seen, no ear has heard, no mind has conceived what God has prepared for those who love him." 1 Corinthians 2:9

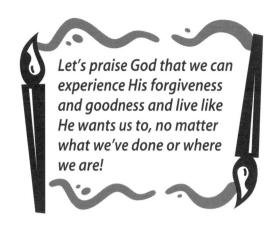

Let's praise God that we can experience His forgiveness and goodness and live like He wants us to, no matter what we've done or where we are!

Teacher Materials

Bible, *God's Big Picture* cassette/CD or music video and player, "Everywhere I Go" word chart (p. 451 in this book), large sheet of paper on which you have printed 1 Corinthians 2:9, masking tape.

Sing to God

Play "Everywhere I Go," encouraging students to sing along with the music and do the actions shown on the word chart or the music video. **How does this song say Jesus helps us because He's always with us?**

Hear and Say God's Word

Display paper on which you have printed 1 Corinthians 2:9. Volunteer reads verse aloud. **The word "conceived" means thought of, or imagined. What does 1 Corinthians 2:9 say no one's mind has imagined?** (The great things God has prepared for people who love Him.) Students form three groups. Lead groups in saying verse, pointing to each group when they should begin. Repeat several times.

Pray to God

Students share prayer requests. Lead students in prayer, encouraging volunteers to pray for requests and pray for other students in the group to be able to live as God wants us to. End prayer by thanking God that He has great plans for us as His children. Talk with interested students about becoming members of God's family. (See "Leading a Child to Christ" on p. 30.)

Options

1. Older students look up these Bible verses about God's plans for us and read them to the class during the Bible verse activity: Psalm 33:11; Psalm 40:5, Proverbs 19:21, Jeremiah 29:11.

2. Have an older student list prayer requests on the back of the Bible verse paper. Volunteers refer to list when praying.

3. Students plan and practice motions for the words of 1 Corinthians 2:9.

Bible Story Coloring Center

Materials
Crayons or markers, drawing paper.

Lead the Activity
Students draw pictures of themselves. Display pictures on classroom walls as in an art gallery.

Options
1. Play "Picture This!" from *God's Big Picture* cassette/CD or music video as students draw pictures.
2. Students cut construction paper frames to fit around their pictures.

Skit Center

Materials
A copy of "I Will Return" skit (pp. 366-369 from *The Big Book of Bible Skits*) for each student; optional—highlighter pens.

Lead the Activity
Students form groups of four and read the skit, which tells the story of a captain's instructions to his soldiers until he returns. (Optional: Students highlight their parts.) Ask the discussion questions on page 366.

Bible Skills Center

Materials
Materials needed for "Book Traders" and/or "Paul's Letters" (p. 38 and/or p. 165 from *The Big Book of Bible Skills*).

Lead the Activity
Students complete activities as directed in *The Big Book of Bible Skills*.

Bible Bookfinder

Old Testament

Genesis and Exodus, Leviticus and Numbers,

Deuteronomy,

Joshua, Judges, Ruth,

First and Second Samuel, First and Second Kings.

First and Second Chronicles, Ezra, Nehemiah too;

Esther, Job, Psalms and Proverbs—

Now we're halfway through!

Ecclesiastes and the Song of Songs,

Isaiah, Jeremiah, Lamentations,

Ezekiel, Daniel, Hosea, Joel,

Amos, Obadiah.

Jonah, Micah, Nahum, Habakkuk too;

Zephaniah, Haggai, Zechariah, Malachi—

Now we're all through!

New Testament

Matthew, Mark, Luke and John,

Acts and Romans too;

First and Second Corinthians, Galatians and Ephesians.

Philippians, Colossians, First and Second Thessalonians,

First and Second Timothy,

Titus and Philemon,

Hebrews, James—now we're almost done.

First and Second Peter, First and Second and Third John,

Jude and Revelation.

That's all the books of the Bible for your memorization!

Bible Bookfinder

```
A                   G                   A            G
Genesis and Exodus, Leviticus and Numbers, Deuteronomy,
A                   G                        A      G    D
Joshua, Judges, Ruth, First and Second Samuel, First and Second Kings.
A                   G         A           G
First and Second Chronicles, Ezra, Nehemiah too;
A         G                   A              G    D
Esther, Job, Psalms and Proverbs—Now we're halfway through!
Bm                F#m             G          A        D
Ecclesiastes and the Song of Songs, Isaiah, Jeremiah, Lamentations,
Bm                F#m     G    A    D
Ezekiel, Daniel, Hosea, Joel, Amos, Obadiah.
A              G       A      G
Jonah, Micah, Nahum, Habakkuk too;
A                   G              A            D
Zephaniah, Haggai, Zechariah, Malachi. (Now we're all through!)


A                   G          A            G
Matthew, Mark, Luke and John, Acts and Romans too;
A                   G    A          D
First and Second Corinthians, Galatians and Ephesians.
   Bm          F#m            G        A   D
Philippians, Colossians, First and Second Thessalonians,
Bm              F#m   G        A   D
First and Second Timothy, Titus and Philemon,
                 G              A      D
Hebrews, James—now we're almost done.
A                   G          A              G
First and Second Peter, First and Second and Third John,
A         G
Jude and Revelation—
A                                         D        A   D
That's all the books of the Bible for your memorization!
```

Music: Mary Gross. © 1998 Gospel Light.
Permission to photocopy granted. • *God's Big Picture Leader's Guide*

Easter Means...

1. People waved palm branches one sunny day;
   People praised Jesus in many ways.
   Some sang songs, some clapped their hands,
   Some shouted words of praise.
   Jesus rode in on a donkey,
   And Easter was on its way.

   Chorus:
   Easter means salvation,
   Salvation means we win!
   Easter means salvation,
   Salvation means Jesus died for our sins,
   He rose again,
   And we'll live forever with Him!

Easter

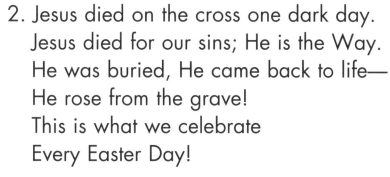

salvation

forever

2. Jesus died on the cross one dark day.
   Jesus died for our sins; He is the Way.
   He was buried, He came back to life—
   He rose from the grave!
   This is what we celebrate
   Every Easter Day!

   Chorus

3. Jesus' friends talked to Him on Easter Day;
   Jesus' friends walked with Him and talked and prayed.
   Jesus went to heaven,
   Sent His Spirit here to stay.
   We remember Jesus' death
   And resurrection when we say:

   Chorus

Easter Means...

Introduction: C   F   G

     C   F   C

1. People waved palm branches one sunny day;

     C   F   G

People praised Jesus in many ways.

           F   G

Some sang songs, some clapped their hands,

           Em   A

Some shouted words of praise.

         F   G   F   G   C   G

Jesus rode in on a donkey, and Easter was on its way.

Chorus:

     C   F   C   G

Easter means salvation, salvation means we win!

     C   F   C   F   G

Easter means salvation, salvation means Jesus died for our sins,

     F   G

He rose again,

         F   G   C   F   C   G

And we'll live forever with Him!

     C   F   C

2. Jesus died on the cross one dark day.

     C   F   G

Jesus died for our sins; He is the Way.

          F   G   Em   A

He was buried, He came back to life—He rose from the grave!

F   G   F   G   C   G

This is what we celebrate every Easter Day!

Chorus

     C   F   C

3. Jesus' friends talked to Him on Easter Day;

     C   F   G

Jesus' friends walked with Him and talked and prayed.

     F   G   Em   A

Jesus went to heaven, sent His Spirit here to stay.

         F   G   F   G   C   G

We remember Jesus' death and resurrection when we say:

Chorus

Note: The recorded arrangement contains a modulation which is not added here.

Words and Music: Gary Pailer. ©1994 Gospel Light.
Permission to photocopy granted. • *God's Big Picture Leader's Guide*

Everywhere I Go

Chorus:
Everywhere I go,
With everyone I know,
Even when my life's not fair,
Even when I think no one cares;
No matter what I grow up to be,
No matter who likes me,
I still have Jesus living in me.

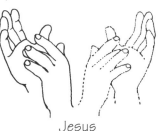

Jesus

1. When I play basketball, He is there with me;
   When I trip and fall, He is there with me;
   No matter what I do, Jesus always is living in me.

Chorus

basketball
(shoot imaginary basket)

2. When I'm late for school, He is there with me;
   When I feel like a fool, He is there with me;
   When I feel His care, He is there with me;
   When I forget He's there, He is there with me;
   No matter where I go, Jesus always is living in me.

fall (fingers "stand,"
then "fall off" hand)

Chorus

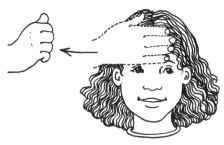

forget

embarrassed (for "like a fool")

school
(two claps)

Words and Music: Marc and Judy Roth, Lynnette Pennings, Mary Gross. ©1994 Gospel Light.
Permission to photocopy granted. • *God's Big Picture Leader's Guide*

Everywhere I Go

```
G         C         G         C              G
```
Everywhere I go, with everyone I know,
```
                    C              D                      G
```
Even when my life's not fair, even when I think no one cares;
```
G                   C         G         C
```
No matter what I grow up to be, no matter who likes me,
```
 F          C    D    G      F    C    G
```
I still have Jesus living in me.

```
            G                   D
```
1. When I play basketball, He is there with me;
```
      G                   D
```
When I trip and fall, He is there with me;
```
         G              F    C         G    F    C    G
```
No matter what I do, Jesus always is living in me.

Chorus

```
            G                   D
```
2. When I'm late for school, He is there with me;
```
         G                   D
```
When I feel like a fool, He is there with me;
```
         G                   D
```
When I feel His care, He is there with me;
```
         G                   D
```
When I forget He's there, He is there with me;
```
         G                   F    C         G    F    C    G
```
No matter where I go, Jesus always is living in me.

Chorus

Follow the Leader

Chorus:
Follow the leader,
He shows us what to do.
Jesus is our Leader;
His love is true.

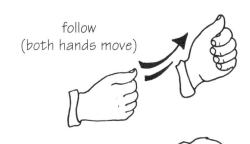

follow
(both hands move)

1. Jesus died; He rose for me,
   To make me part of God's family.
   When I ask Him and believe,
   God's child I can be.

   Chorus

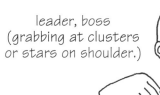

leader, boss
(grabbing at clusters
or stars on shoulder.)

2. Jesus knew what to say
   When the devil got in His way.
   Jesus showed us what to do.
   We'll learn God's Word, too.

   Chorus

Jesus

3. Jesus knew how to pray;
   He talked to God His Father every day.
   We can talk to God the same way;
   He wants us to pray.

4. Jesus showed us how to share;
   He showed God's love to people everywhere.
   We can tell everyone
   Of God's Son.

   Chorus

   His love is true.   *(three times)*

love

true

Words and Music: Judy and Marc Roth, Mary Gross, Lynnette Pennings. © 1994 Gospel Light.
Permission to photocopy granted. • *God's Big Picture Leader's Guide*

Follow the Leader

Chorus:

      D Em D G D   Asus A

Fol-low the Leader, He shows us what to do.

               G   D   Asus   A

Jesus is our Leader; His love is true.

         D   A   G   A

1. Jesus died; He rose for me, to make me part of God's family.

         D   A   D

When I ask Him and believe, God's child I can be.

Chorus

         D   A   G   A

2. Jesus knew what to say when the devil got in His way.

         D   A   D

Jesus showed us what to do. We'll learn God's Word, too.

Chorus

         D   A   G   A

3. Jesus knew how to pray; He talked to God His Father ev'ry day.

         D   A   D

We can talk to God the same way; He wants us to pray.

         D   A

4. Jesus showed us how to share;

      G   A

He showed God's love to people everywhere.

         D   A   D

We can tell everyone of God's Son.

Chorus

Tag:

      G   A   D A   D A   D

His love is true;   His love is true;   His love is true.

Words and Music: J. and M. Roth, M. Gross, L. Pennings. © 1994 Gospel Light.
Permission to photocopy granted. • *God's Big Picture Leader's Guide*

God Is So Strong

1. Stronger than a redwood tree is my God.

   Stronger than earth's gravity is my God.

   Stronger than a hurricane is my God.

   Stronger than a mountain range is my God.

   Chorus:

   He's stronger than you can imagine—
   How can I describe?
   God is so strong, He can make the dead alive!
   He's stronger than you can imagine—
   How can I describe?
   God is so strong, He can make me new inside!

2. When I know I've won the race, He's my God.

   When I know I'm in last place, He's my God.

   When I know that I've done wrong, He's my God.

   When I know I can't be strong, He's my God.

   Chorus

   He's the place where I can hide,

   'Cause His love's so big and wide.

strong

God

Words and Music: Judy and Marc Roth, Lynnette Pennings, Mary Gross. ©1994 Gospel Light.
Permission to photocopy granted. • *God's Big Picture Leader's Guide*

God Is So Strong

Introduction: C   F   C   G   C

        C   F

1. Stronger than a redwood tree is my God.

        C   G

Stronger than earth's gravity is my God,

        C   F

Stronger than a hurricane is my God.

        C   G   C   C7

Stronger than a mountain range is my God.

Chorus:

            F   C

He's stronger than you can imagine—How can I describe?

F   C   G

God is so strong, He can make the dead alive!

            F   C

He's stronger than you can imagine—How can I describe?

F   C   G   C

God is so strong, He can make me new inside!

        C   F

2. When I know I've won the race, He's my God.

        C   G

When I know I'm in last place, He's my God.

        C   F

When I know that I've done wrong, He's my God.

        C   G   C   C7

When I know I can't be strong, He's my God.

Chorus

Tag:

            G   C   G   C

He's the place where I can hide, 'cause His love's so big and wide.

Words and Music: Judy & Marc Roth, L. Pennings, M. Gross. ©1994 Gospel Light.
Permission to photocopy granted. • *God's Big Picture Leader's Guide*

God's Amazing Power

Refrain:

Well, it was there at creation, and it's still going strong:
God's amazing power.
You can call on Him when anything's going wrong:
God's amazing power.

God (ASL)

1. He stopped Saul with a blinding light;
   God's great power gave Saul new sight.
   His power is real; He's always the same;
   And that is why we praise His name!
   God's amazing power,
   God's amazing power.

amazing (ASL)

2. God sent Paul to tell about Jesus,
   About God's love and His life that frees us.
   God's power is real; He healed the lame;
   And that is why we praise His name!
   God's amazing power,
   God's amazing power.

power (ASL)

3. Paul and Silas were jailed for Jesus' sake;
   They praised God and God sent a quake!
   God's power is real; He's always the same;
   And that is why we praise His name!
   God's amazing power,
   God's amazing power.

light (ASL)

Refrain

real (ASL)

lame (ASL)

praise (ASL)

Words: Michael and Jenny Greenberg, Lynnette Pennings, Mary Gross. Music: Michael and Jenny Greenberg. © 1998 Gospel Light.
Permission to photocopy granted. • *God's Big Picture Leader's Guide*

God's Amazing Power

Refrain:

Em   D   Em
Well, it was there at creation, and it's still going strong:

Em   D   Em
God's amazing power.

          Em   D   Em
You can call on Him when anything's going wrong:

Em   D   Em
God's amazing power.

1.

Am   Em
He stopped Saul with a blinding light;

D   Em
God's great power gave Saul new sight.

Am   Em
His power is real, He's always the same;

        D
And that is why we praise His name!

Em   D   Em   D   Em   D   Em
God's amazing power,   God's amazing power.

2.

Am   Em
God sent Paul to tell about Jesus;

D   Em
About God's love and His life that frees us.

Am   Em
God's power is real; He healed the lame;

D
And that is why we praise His name!

Em   D   Em   D   Em   D   Em
God's amazing power,   God's amazing power.

3.

Am   Em
Paul and Silas were jailed for Jesus' sake;

D   Em
They praised God and God sent a quake!

Am   Em
God's power is real; He's always the same;

D
And that is why we praise His name!

Em   D   Em   D   Em   D   Em
God's amazing power,   God's amazing power.

Refrain

Words: Michael and Jenny Greenberg, Lynnette Pennings, Mary Gross. Music: Michael and Jenny Greenberg. © 1998 Gospel Light.
Permission to photocopy granted. • *God's Big Picture Leader's Guide*

God's Holy Book

Chorus:

God's got a plan,

Hold on to His hand,

His Word is true.

God made His plan

Before time began.

God's got a plan for me

And for you.

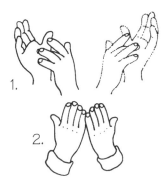

Bible
"Jesus" + "book")

The Bible is God's holy book,

It's God's written Word.

The Bible is God's holy book,

It's the best news ever heard.

The Bible is God's holy book,

It helps us understand.

The Bible is God's holy book,

It tells us about His plan.

Chorus

true

God's Holy Book

Chorus:

    Em   B7   Em   B7
God's got a plan, hold on to His hand, His Word is true.
    Em   B7
God made His plan before time began.
    Em   B7   Em
God's got a plan for me and for you.

      Em   Bm   B7
The Bible is God's holy book, it's God's written Word.
      Em   B7   Em
The Bible is God's holy book, it's the best news ever heard.
      Em   Bm   B7
The Bible is God's holy book, it helps us understand.
      Em   B7   Em
The Bible is God's holy book, it tells us about His plan.

Chorus

Note: The recorded arrangement contains a modulation which is not added here.

He Looked

He looked until He found me
Because He loves me so;
He's always looking out for me;
He won't leave me on my own.

Chorus:

God's the loving Shepherd;
He's the Perfect Dad.
I am important to Him;
He'll help me through when things look bad.

I'm so glad God loves me,
And I'm gonna let it show;
I'm gonna do my best for Him,
'Cause I want everyone to know:

Chorus

Words and Music: Mary Gross. ©1994 Gospel Light.
Permission to photocopy granted. • *God's Big Picture Leader's Guide*

He Looked

C   G

He looked until He found me

                             C

Because He loves me so;

                            G

He's always looking out for me;

                        C   C7

He won't leave me on my own.

Chorus:

                        F

God's the loving Shepherd;

            C

He's the Perfect Dad.

                    G

I am important to Him;

                            C

He'll help me through when things look bad.

                  G

I'm so glad God loves me,

                C

And I'm gonna let it show;

                G

I'm gonna do my best for Him,

                C   C7

'Cause I want everyone to know:

Chorus

Words and Music: Mary Gross. ©1994 Gospel Light.
Permission to photocopy granted. • *God's Big Picture Leader's Guide*

I Know the King

Chorus:
I know the King personally;
I know the King personally!
(boys) **I'm a prince.**
(girls) **I'm a princess.**
We're royal family.
We know Him personally!

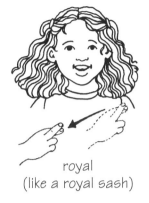

royal
(like a royal sash)

1. God is King over every king.
   He's the Ruler over everything.
   I'm His child, that makes me royalty!
   And royalty is what I'm gonna be!

   Chorus

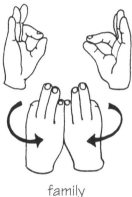

family

2. David had a giant mess!
   How he'd survive was anyone's guess.
   But David trusted God with everything.
   I'll trust God with my problems; He's the King!

   Chorus

Words and Music: Judy and Marc Roth. ©1994 Gospel Light.
Permission to photocopy granted. • *God's Big Picture Leader's Guide*

I Know the King

Chorus:

    E   A   E   B

I know the King personally; I know the King personally!

         E   E7

(boys) I'm a prince, *(girls)* I'm a princess,

        A   E   B   E   E7

We're royal family. We know Him personally!

    A   E

1.   God is King over every king.

    B   E   E7

He's the Ruler over everything.

    A   E

I'm His child, that makes me royalty!

      B7   E   B7

And royalty is what I'm gonna be!

Chorus

    A   E

2.   David had a giant mess!

      B7   E   E7

How he'd survive was anyone's guess.

      A   E

But David trusted God with everything.

      B7   E   B7

I'll trust God with my problems; He's the King!

Chorus

Note: The recorded arrangement contains a modulation which is not added here.

464

Words and Music: Judy and Marc Roth. ©1994 Gospel Light.
Permission to photocopy granted. • *God's Big Picture Leader's Guide*

I Want to Follow Jesus

1. In the days of the Bible,
   Came someone called Jesus.
   Came to bring the good news,
   Take our sins away.

2. John said Jesus was God's Son;
   People followed Jesus.
   Led them on an adventure,
   Changed all of their lives!

Chorus:

Now I,
I want to follow Jesus.
He's the one who takes us on
Adventures every day.
Now I,
I want to follow Jesus,
'Cause He's the one who makes us strong
To follow in His ways.

3. Still He calls us to follow
   On the great adventure.
   Once we hear of God's love,
   How can we stay away?

Chorus

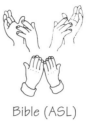

Bible (ASL)

follow (ASL)

strong (ASL)

God (ASL)

love (ASL)

Words and Music: Steve Boschetti, Lynnette Pennings, Mary Gross. © 1998 Gospel Light.
Permission to photocopy granted. • *God's Big Picture Leader's Guide*

I Want to Follow Jesus

Introduction: F   Bb   C7   F :|

F   Bb   C7   F
In the days of the Bible, came someone called Jesus.
F   Bb   C7   F
Came to bring the good news, take our sins away.
F   Bb   C7   F
John said Jesus was God's Son; people followed Jesus.
F   Bb   C7   F
Led them on an adventure, changed all of their lives!

Chorus:
        F   Bb   Gm
Now I, I want to follow Jesus.
C   C7   F
He's the One who takes us on adventures every day.
        F   Bb   Gm
Now I, I want to follow Jesus,
        C   C7
'Cause He's the One who makes us strong

        Gm   C7   F   Bb   C7   F
To follow in His ways.

F   Bb   C7   F
Still He calls us to follow on the great adventure.
F   Bb   C7   F
Once we hear of God's love, how can we stay away?

Chorus

Words and Music: Steve Boschetti, Lynnette Pennings, Mary Gross. © 1998 Gospel Light.
Permission to photocopy granted. • *God's Big Picture Leader's Guide*

Jesus' Love

1. Two thousand years ago,
   Jesus lived in the Middle East.
   His first job was a carpenter;
   Then He did a wonder at a wedding feast!
   Then He called His twelve disciples,
   "Won't you come follow Me?"
   He was teaching crowds about God
   And making blind eyes see.

"carpenter"

two, one thousand (ASL) ("m" for thousand)

wonder (ASL)

"called" ("come" motion)

follow (ASL)

Chorus:

Jesus' love is real; Jesus' love is really real!
It's not a fairy tale.
Jesus' love is true; Jesus' love is truly true!
And if you know Him, you know that He loves you.

blind (ASL)

2. Two thousand years ago,
   Jesus lived in the Middle East.
   He lived His life for God;
   And He gave His life for the very least.
   See, in those days people left you out
   If you were sick or lame.
   But Jesus touched the sick and sad
   And made them whole again.

Chorus

worthless (ASL) (for "very least")

"left you out"

sick (ASL)

whole, well (ASL)

sad (ASL)

lame (ASL)

Words and Music: Marc and Judy Roth. © 1998 Gospel Light.
Permission to photocopy granted. • *God's Big Picture Leader's Guide*

Jesus' Love

1.
   C
Two thousand years ago, Jesus lived in the Middle East.
   C   C7
His first job was a carpenter; then He did a wonder at a wedding feast!
              F   C
Then He called His twelve disciples, "Won't you come follow Me?"
              G   F
He was teaching crowds about God
                          C   C7
And making blind eyes see.

Chorus:
F
Jesus' love is real; Jesus' love is really real!
C   C7
It's not a fairy tale.
F
Jesus' love is true; Jesus' love is truly true!
G   C
And if you know Him, you know that He loves you.

2.
   C
Two thousand years ago, Jesus lived in the Middle East.
   C   C7
He lived His life for God; and He gave His life for the very least.
              F   C
See, in those days people left you out if you were sick or lame.
       G   F
But Jesus touched the sick and sad
                          C
and made them whole again.

Chorus

Note: The recorded arrangement is in a different key; key is changed here for ease of guitar use.

Words and Music: Marc and Judy Roth. © 1998 Gospel Light.
Permission to photocopy granted. • *God's Big Picture Leader's Guide*

Love and Power

1. God's love lives in me;

   God's love lives in me.

   Now I can care for anyone in need,

   'Cause God's love lives in me.

God (ASL)

love (ASL)

2. God's power lives in me;

   God's power lives in me.

   Now I can show God's love in ev'ry deed,

   'Cause God's power lives in me.

lives (ASL)

help (ASL)
for "care for"

3. God's love lives in me;

   God's love lives in me.

   Now I can show love in my family,

   'Cause God's love lives in me.

power (ASL)

4. God's power lives in me;

   God's power lives in me.

   Now I have power to love my enemies,

   'Cause God's love and power live in me.

family (ASL)

Words and Music: Gary Pailer. © 1998 Gospel Light.
Permission to photocopy granted. • *God's Big Picture Leader's Guide*

Love and Power

```
      D           C        D/D/C/D/D        D           C        D/D/C/D/D
1. God's love lives in me;              God's love lives in me.
         A           G        D/D/C/D/D
   Now I can care for anyone in need,
            A        G        D/D/C/D/D
   'Cause God's love lives in me.


      D           C        D/D/C/D/D        D           C        D/D/C/D/D
2. God's power lives in me;             God's power lives in me.
         A           G        D/D/C/D/D
   Now I can show God's love in ev'ry deed,
            A        G        D/D/C/D/D
   'Cause God's power lives in me.


      D           C        D/D/C/D/D        D           C        D/D/C/D/D
3. God's love lives in me;              God's love lives in me.
         A           G        D/D/C/D/D
   Now I can show love in my family,
            A        G        D/D/C/D/D
   'Cause God's love lives in me.


      D           C        D/D/C/D/D        D           C        D/D/C/D/D
4. God's power lives in me;             God's power lives in me.
         A           G        D/D/C/D/D
   Now I have power to love my enemies,
            A        G        D/D/C/D/D
   'Cause God's love and power live in me.
```

Words and Music: Gary Pailer. © 1998 Gospel Light.
Permission to photocopy granted. • *God's Big Picture Leader's Guide*

People of Courage

1. Life gets rough every once in a while,
   Tears come easy and it's hard to smile.
   Tough to think when life's this wild—
   What's a kid to do?

tears (ASL)

think (ASL)
(finger rolls out)

Chorus:

Be on your guard; stand firm in the faith;
Be people of courage; be strong.

2. Daniel was set up by some nasty men;
   Said if he prayed to God instead of the king,
   He'd be thrown in the lions' den—
   What's a guy to do?

guard (ASL)

Chorus

"what?"

3. Pretty Queen Esther had to be strong;
   Her people would be killed and that's an awful wrong.
   She fasted three days; then she told the king the truth—
   She saw what God can do!

Chorus

firm, strong
(ASL)

courage (ASL)

faith (ASL)

see (ASL)

God (ASL)

Words: Marc and Judy Roth, Lynnette Pennings, Mary Gross. Music: Marc and Judy Roth. Chorus from 1 Corinthians 16:13. © 1998 Gospel Light.
Permission to photocopy granted. • *God's Big Picture Leader's Guide*

People of Courage

	E7		A7

1. Life gets rough every once in a while,

E7   A7

Tears come easy and it's hard to smile.

E7

Tough to think when life's this wild—what's a kid to do?

Chorus:

          A7   E7

Be on your guard; stand firm in the faith;

   B7   A7   E7   B7

Be people of courage; be strong.

Chorus

E7   A7

2. Daniel was set up by some nasty men;

                 E7   A7

Said if he prayed to God instead of the king,

E7

He'd be thrown in the lions' den—what's a guy to do?

Chorus

E7   A7

3. Pretty Queen Esther had to be strong;

E7   A7

Her people would be killed and that's an awful wrong.

E7   A7

She fasted three days; then she told the king the truth—

E7

She saw what God can do!

Chorus

Note: The recorded arrangement is in a different key; key is changed here for ease of guitar use.

Words: Marc and Judy Roth, Lynnette Pennings, Mary Gross. Music: Marc and Judy Roth. Chorus from 1 Corinthians 16:13. © 1998 Gospel Light.
Permission to photocopy granted. • *God's Big Picture Leader's Guide*

Picture This!

Hey, hey, hey, now—God's big picture! (three times)

Chorus:

Welcome to the gallery of God's creation; *(echo)*
All through time it's caused a big sensation. *(echo)*
Unpack your sketchbook, pull out your pen,
Get water and paints and we're ready to begin—

Picture this—God creates a world that's good;
Picture this—People don't do what they should.
Picture this—God calls people for His own;
Picture this—God's way to live made known.

Picture this—A gallery of judges and kings;
Picture this—The promises the prophets bring.
Picture this—God's people leave their land;
Picture this—They return to build again.

Chorus

Picture this—God sends His only Son;
Picture this—Jesus loving everyone.
Picture this—Jesus died and now He lives;
Picture this—Eternal life He gives!

Picture this—People learn why Jesus died;
Picture this—God's family grows world-wide!
Picture this—Jesus' friends do what they should;
Picture this—The world is changed for good!

Welcome to the gallery of God's creation; *(echo)*
All through time it's been a big sensation. *(echo)*
The gallery is growing; where are you?
Ooh—You're part of the gallery too!
Ooh—You're part of the gallery too!
Ooh—You're part of the gallery too!

Hey, hey, hey, now —God's big picture! (three times)

Words and music: Marc and Judy Roth. © 1998 Gospel Light.
Permission to photocopy granted. • *God's Big Picture Leader's Guide*

Picture This!

Lead-in, lead out:

G   F G   G   F G

Hey, hey, hey, now—God's big picture! *(three times)*

Chorus:

G   C   G   F G G   C   G   F G

Welcome to the gallery of God's creation; all through time it's caused a big sensation.

C   F   C   D   D7

Unpack your sketchbook, pull out your pen, get water and paints and we're ready to begin—

            C   C7

Picture this—God creates a world that's good;

            G   C   G

Picture this—People don't do what they should.

            D   D7

Picture this—God calls people for His own;

            G   C   G

Picture this—God's way to live made known.

            C   C7

Picture this—A gallery of judges and kings;

            G   C   G

Picture this—The promises the prophets bring.

            D   D7

Picture this—God's people leave their land;

            G   C   G

Picture this—They return to build again.

Chorus

            C   C7

Picture this—God sends His only Son;

            G   C   G

Picture this—Jesus loving everyone.

            D   D7

Picture this—Jesus died and now He lives;

            G   C   G

Picture this—Eternal life He gives!

            C   C7

Picture this—People learn why Jesus died;

            G   C   G

Picture this—God's family grows world-wide!

            D   D7

Picture this—Jesus' friends do what they should;

            G   C   G

Picture this—The world is changed for good!

G   C   G   F G G   C   G   F G

Welcome to the gallery of God's creation; all through time it's been a big sensation.

            C   F   C7 D   C

The gallery is growing; where are you? Ooh—You're part of the gallery too!

D   C   D   C   G

Ooh—You're part of the gallery too! Ooh—You're part of the gallery too!

Words and music: Marc and Judy Roth. © 1999 Gospel Light.
Permission to photocopy granted. • *God's Big Picture Leader's Guide*

Promises

promise

Chorus:
Promises, You keep Your promises.
Promises, O God, Your word is like rock.

1. Adam and Eve, there in the garden;
   You loved them though they disobeyed.
   You promised someday You would send them a Savior;
   You always do what You say.

Savior

   Chorus

2. Never again, You promised Noah,
   Would You destroy the world by flood.
   You sealed Your promise with a beautiful rainbow;
   Oh God, You always keep Your word.

rainbow
("color" + "sky")

   Chorus

3. Old Abe and Sarah could have no children
   But You still promised them a son.
   Their children's children like the stars in the heavens—
   When You say it, it is done.

stars

heavens, sky

   Chorus

4. Sometimes I'm scared of nighttime noises
   And I don't like to be alone,
   But You have said You will be with me always;
   Oh God, Your Word's strong as stone.

with

me

rock, stone

   Chorus

Words and Music: Judy and Marc Roth. ©1994 Gospel Light.
Permission to photocopy granted. • *God's Big Picture Leader's Guide*

Promises

Chorus:

G   D C   D
Promises,   You keep Your promises;
G   D   C   D
Promises, O God, Your word is like rock.

G   D   C   D
1.   Adam and Eve,   there in the garden;
G   D   C   D
You loved them though they disobeyed.
C   D   G   Em   C
You promised someday You would send them a Savior;
C   D   C   D
You always do what You say.

Chorus

G   D   C   D
2.   Never again,   You promised Noah,
G   D   C   D
Would You destroy the world by flood.
C   D   G   Em   C
You sealed Your promise with a beautiful rainbow;
C   D   C   D
Oh God, You always keep Your word.

Chorus

G   D   C   D
3.   Old Abe and Sarah could have no children
G   D   C   D
But You still promised them a son.
C   D   G   Em   C
Their children's children like the stars in the heavens—
C   D   C   D
When You say it, it is done.

Chorus

G   D   C   D
4.   Sometimes I'm scared of nighttime noises
G   D   C D
And I don't like to be alone,
C   D   G   Em   C
But You have said You will be with me always;
C   D   C   D
Oh God, Your Word's strong as stone.

Chorus

Note: The recorded arrangement contains modulations which are not added here.

Words and Music: Judy and Marc Roth. ©1994 Gospel Light.
Permission to photocopy granted. • *God's Big Picture Leader's Guide*

Psalm 9:1,2,10

I will praise You, O Lord, with all my heart; (I will, I will.)
I will praise You, O Lord, with all my heart; (I will, I will.)

"I will"
(nod head, yes)

I will tell of all Your wonders,
All Your wonders; (I will, I will.)
I will tell of all Your wonders,
All Your wonders. (I will, I will.)

praise (ASL)

Lord (ASL)
(as a royal sash)

heart (ASL)

I will be glad and rejoice in You; (I will, I will.)
I will be glad and rejoice in You; (I will, I will.)

I will sing praise to Your name, O Most High. (I will, I will.)
I will sing praise to Your name, O Most High. (I will, I will.)∗

Those who know Your name will trust in You,
For You, Lord, have never forsaken those who seek You.

tell (ASL)

Repeat to ∗

wonders (ASL)

glad, rejoice (ASL)
(pat several times)

trust (ASL)

never (ASL)

Music: Darla Plice. © 1998 Gospel Light.
Permission to photocopy granted. • *God's Big Picture Leader's Guide*

Psalm 9:1,2,10

```
C                              F      C      G     C
I will praise You, O Lord, with all my heart; (I will, I will.)
C                              F      C      G     C
I will praise You, O Lord, with all my heart; (I will, I will.)
C                              F      C         G     C
I will tell of all Your wonders, all your wonders; (I will, I will.)
C                              F      C         G     C
I will tell of all Your wonders, all your wonders; (I will, I will.)
  F            C          G    C
I will be glad and rejoice in You; (I will, I will.)
  F            C          G  D  G
I will be glad and rejoice in You; (I will,   I will.)
    C              F          C      G     C
I will sing praise to Your name, O Most High; (I will, I will.)
    C              F          C      G   C
I will sing praise to Your name, O Most High; (I will, I will.)*
```

```
Ab                            Eb
Those who know Your name will trust in You;
Fm                 F/A          G          Fm    G
For You, Lord, have never forsaken those who seek You.
```

Repeat song up to *

Ending:

```
   G     C    G     C
(I will, I will. Yes, I will.)
```

Music: Darla Plice. © 1998 Gospel Light.

Psalm 86:8-10

1. Among the gods there is none like You,
   None like You, O Lord;
   Among the gods there is none like You,
   None like You, O Lord;
   No deeds can compare with Yours.
   No deeds can compare with Yours.

Chorus:

All the nations You have made
Will come and worship before You, O Lord;
All the nations You have made
Will come and worship before You, O Lord;
They will bring glory to Your name.
They will bring glory to Your name.

2. For You are great and do marvelous deeds;
   You alone are God.
   For You are great and do marvelous deeds;
   You alone are God.
   No deeds can compare with Yours.
   No deeds can compare with Yours.

Chorus

No deeds can compare with Yours.
No deeds can compare with Yours.
No deeds can compare with Yours.

Music: Mary Gross. © 1998 Gospel Light.
Permission to photocopy granted. • *God's Big Picture Leader's Guide*

Psalm 86:8-10

C   F   C   F   C   G
Among the gods there is none like You, none like You, O Lord;

C   F   C   F   C   G
Among the gods there is none like You, none like You, O Lord;

Am   F   G   Am   F   G
No deeds can compare with Yours; no deeds can compare with Yours.

Am   G   F   C
All the nations You have made

                          F   G   C
Will come and worship before You, O Lord; (Repeat)

C   F C F   C   G   C
They will bring glory to Your name;They will bring glory to Your name.

C   F   C   F   C   G
For You are great and do marvelous deeds; You alone are God.

C   F   C   F   C   G
For You are great and do marvelous deeds; You alone are God.

Am   F   G   Am   F   G
No deeds can compare with Yours; no deeds can compare with Yours.

Am   G   F   C
All the nations You have made

                          F   G   C
Will come and worship before You, O Lord; (Repeat)

C   F   C   F   C   G   C
They will bring glory to Your name; they will bring glory to Your name.

Am   F   G   Am   F   G
No deeds can compare with Yours; no deeds can compare with Yours;

    F   G   C
No deeds can compare with Yours.

Note: The recorded arrangement is in a different key; key is changed here for ease of guitar use.

Music: Mary Gross. © 1998 Gospel Light.
Permission to photocopy granted. • *God's Big Picture Leader's Guide*

Who Is Like You, Lord?

1. I have read the words, I have heard the stories,
   How You rescued baby Moses, how You set Your people free.
   I have read the words, I have heard the stories,
   How You led them through the desert,
   How You rolled back the Red Sea.

read

heard

   First Chorus:
   (Sing it! Sing it!)
   Who is like You, Lord?
   (Sing it! Sing it!)
   Who is pure and holy?
   (Sing it! Sing it!)
   Who is awesome in power?
   Who can do the things that You do?

2. I have read the words, I have heard the stories,
   How You healed the lame and blind, how You quieted the sea.
   I have read the words, I have heard the stories,
   How You died and rose again,
   How You saved my life for me.

   Second Chorus:
   (Sing it! Sing it!)
   No one's like You, Lord!
   (Sing it! Sing it!)
   No one's so pure and holy!
   (Sing it! Sing it!)
   No one is awesome in power!
   No one does the things that You do!

Words and Music: Judy and Marc Roth. Chorus based on Exodus 15:11 from the Song of Moses. ©1994 Gospel Light.
Permission to photocopy granted. • *God's Big Picture Leader's Guide*

Who Is Like You, Lord?

Introduction: D   A   G   A

     D   A   G   A
1. I have read the words, I have heard the stories,
           D   A   G   A
   How You rescued baby Moses, how You set Your people free.
     D   A   G   A
   I have read the words, I have heard the stories,
           D   A   G   A
   How You led them through the desert, how You rolled back the Red Sea.

Chorus:
     D   G   D   A   D
   (Sing it! Sing it!) Who is like You, Lord?
                        G   D   A   D
   (Sing it! Sing it!) Who is pure and holy?
                        G   D
   (Sing it! Sing it!) Who is awesome in power?
             G   A   D   A   G   A
   Who can do the things that You do?

     D   A   G   A
2. I have read the words, I have heard the stories,
           D   A   G   A
   How You healed the lame and blind, how You quieted the sea.
     D   A   G   A
   I have read the words, I have heard the stories,
           D   A   G   A
   How You died and rose again, how You saved my life for me.

Chorus:
     D   G   D   A   D
   (Sing it! Sing it!) No one's like You, Lord!
                        G   D   A   D
   (Sing it! Sing it!) No one's so pure and holy!
                      G   D
   (Sing it! Sing it!) No one is awesome in power!
            G   A   D   A   G   A
   No one does the things that You do!

Words and Music: Judy and Marc Roth. ©1994 Gospel Light.
Permission to photocopy granted. • *God's Big Picture Leader's Guide*

Turn Good Volunteers into Great Teachers

Smart Teacher Training Videos are the smart, easy way to recruit, train and motivate teachers! Developed by Sunday School authorities Wes and Sheryl Haystead, each video includes expert advice, live classroom demonstrations and answers to the most common questions asked by teachers.

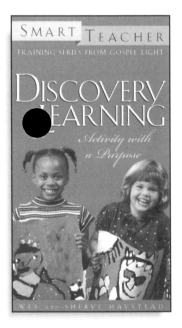

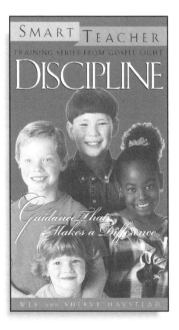

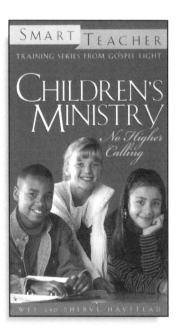

Discovery Learning: Activity with a Purpose
Guide children in the joy of discovering foundational truths for a lifetime of learning.
Video • UPC 607135.003601

Bible Skills for Better Teaching: Helping Kids Make the Connection
Practical ways to build interest, develop Bible skills and make the Bible relevant to kids.
Video • UPC 607135.003588

Discipline: Guidance that Makes a Difference
Behavior challenges give teachers opportunities to demonstrate God's love and forgiveness, and help kids learn to do what's right.
Video • UPC 607135.003618

Children's Ministry: No Higher Calling
Challenge your teachers to consider the value Christ places on children and the astounding benefits ministry to children brings.
Video • UPC 607135.003595

Smart Resources for Your Children's Ministry

Sunday School Smart Pages
Edited by Wes and Sheryl Haystead
Teaching, inspiration, materials, quick solutions and more for teaching ages 2 through 12.
Reproducible.
Manual • ISBN 08307.15215

Sunday School Promo Pages
Wes and Sheryl Haystead
Resources and advice to recruit teachers, gain church support, increase attendance and more.
Reproducible.
Manual • ISBN 08307.15894

5th & 6th Grade Smart Pages
Wes Haystead and Tom Prinz
The most current information, tips and quick solutions for teaching 5th and 6th grades, plus parent education articles.
Reproducible.
Manual • ISBN 08307.18052

Nursery Smart Pages
Legal and safety guidelines, teacher's pages, parent pages, classroom activities, clip art, and much more!
Reproducible.
Manual • ISBN 08307.19067

VBS Smart Pages
Advice, answers and articles for a successful Vacation Bible School. Includes forms, records and clip art.
Reproducible.
Manual • ISBN 08307.16718

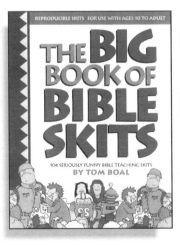

The Big Book of Bible Skits
Tom Boal
104 seriously funny Bible teaching skits. Includes discussion questions.
Reproducible.
Manual • ISBN 08307.19164

The Big Book of Theme Parties, Snacks & Games
Decorating ideas, snack recipes, wacky activities, games, clip art, and more for eight complete themes.
Reproducible.
Manual • ISBN 08307.18206

The Big Book of Bible Games
200 fun games that teach Bible concepts and life application.
Reproducible.
ISBN 08307.18214

Available from your Gospel Light supplier or call 1-800-4-GOSPEL.